CAMPAIGNS AND ELECTIONS
Rules, Reality, Strategy, Choice

THIRD EDITION

John Sides
GEORGE WASHINGTON UNIVERSITY

Daron Shaw
UNIVERSITY OF TEXAS, AUSTIN

Matt Grossmann
MICHIGAN STATE UNIVERSITY

Keena Lipsitz
QUEENS COLLEGE, CITY UNIVERSITY OF NEW YORK

W. W. Norton and Company
New York • London

W. W. Norton & Company has been independent since its founding in 1923, when William Warder Norton and Mary D. Herter Norton first published lectures delivered at the People's Institute, the adult education division of New York City's Cooper Union. The firm soon expanded its program beyond the Institute, publishing books by celebrated academics from America and abroad. By midcentury, the two major pillars of Norton's publishing program—trade books and college texts— were firmly established. In the 1950s, the Norton family transferred control of the company to its employees, and today—with a staff of four hundred and a comparable number of trade, college, and professional titles published each year—W. W. Norton & Company stands as the largest and oldest publishing house owned wholly by its employees.

Editor: Peter Lesser
Project Editor: Linda Feldman
Associate Editor: Samantha Held
Editorial Assistant: Anna Olcott
Managing Editor, College: Marian Johnson
Managing Editor, College Digital Media: Kim Yi
Production Manager, College: Sean Mintus
Media Editor: Spencer Richardson-Jones
Media Associate Editor: Michael Jaoui
Media Assistant Editor: Ariel Eaton
Marketing Manager, Political Science: Erin Brown
Design Director: Rubina Yeh
Designer: Lissi Sigillo
Photo Editor: Cat Abelman
Permissions Manager: Megan Schindel
Composition: Westchester Book Composition
Manufacturing: LSC: Crawfordsville

Permission to use copyrighted material is included on page C-1.

Library of Congress Cataloging-in-Publication Data

ISBN 978-0-393-64053-3 (pbk.)

W. W. Norton & Company, Inc., 500 Fifth Avenue, New York, NY 10110
wwnorton.com
W. W. Norton & Company, Ltd., Castle House, 15 Carlisle Street, London W1D 3BS

1 2 3 4 5 6 7 8 9 0

CONTENTS

4
Financing Campaigns   84

5
Modern Campaign Strategies   124

6
Political Parties   158

7

Interest Groups   186

8

Media   212

9

Presidential Campaigns   248

10
Congressional Campaigns 286

11
State and Local Campaigns 312

12
Voter Participation 342

13

Voter Choice

14

Democracy in Action or a Broken System?

This book aims to present a comprehensive treatment of political campaigns in the United States. It is structured around four key components that shape American campaigns: the *rules* that govern the electoral process; the *reality* that candidates confront when a campaign begins; the *strategies* employed by important campaign actors, including candidates, parties, interest groups, consultants, and the media; and the *choices* made by voters, which are themselves a response to the rules, reality, and strategies.

The rules that govern the electoral process include institutions such as the Electoral College, as well as the laws that govern campaign finance. The reality that parties and candidates confront consists, in part, of current events, the state of the economy, the presence of an incumbent in the race, and the partisan leaning of their constituents. The importance of rules and reality is augmented by the fact that candidates cannot easily change them. Instead, they structure candidate strategy in important ways. The strategic choices made by candidates comprise the familiar elements of modern campaigns, including message development, television advertising, fund-raising, and voter mobilization. These choices mesh with rules and reality to create the "outputs" of campaigns that are manifest to voters. The response of voters to these outputs goes a long way toward answering the question, "Do campaigns affect voters?" We contend that any good answer to that question is a version of "it depends," and we devote significant attention to what magnifies or diminishes the effects of campaigns.

Throughout the book, we also draw attention to the *democratic functions* of campaigns. We discuss debates about the roles campaigns should play in our democracy and how well contemporary campaigns achieve those goals. We focus on four standards. The first, free choice, means that citizens can participate free of coercion or manipulation. The second, political equality, means that laws cannot disadvantage certain groups of citizens—as, for example, Jim Crow laws disadvantaged southern blacks before the civil rights era. The third, deliberation, refers to the quality of the information that citizens receive from the candidates, the media, and other political actors. Is it sufficient to ensure that citizens can make an informed choice? Of course, deliberation also requires that citizens have the time and motivation to think about electoral choices. The fourth standard, free speech, refers to the constitutional protections that affect whether and how the government might regulate political campaigns. Could, for example, the government require that opposing candidates spend identical amounts of money, so that neither candidate will dominate the airwaves? In discussing such debates, we do not promote any one viewpoint, but instead seek to describe how these values can inform both why campaigns are the way they are, and whether we should attempt to reform them. We emphasize the difficulty of meeting all of these standards simultaneously. It is more likely that making campaigns "better" by one standard will make them "worse" by another. For example, ensuring that citizens receive certain kinds of information may violate the candidates' right to free speech.

This book aims to be comprehensive. We discuss electoral rules and realities not only at the national level but also in the fifty states. We focus on campaigns at all levels of office, including presidential, congressional, state, and local. Doing so illuminates both similarities and differences. For example, although state elections and local elections mimic national elections in key respects—such as by having election dates fixed on the calendar, rather than occurring at the discretion of elected officials themselves—any individual state's elections may differ in the specifics, such as the precise date that elections are held. Similarly, although candidates at all levels of office have the same basic goal—to craft a compelling message and thereby win elections—they do so with vastly different levels of resources and thus with different kinds of campaign strategies. A presidential campaign spends more on catering in a week than many local campaigns spend in total.

We also seek to be comprehensive in another respect: by including the perspectives of both campaign professionals and academics. We take into account the views of professionals who work "on the ground" during campaigns and who usually believe that their efforts are consequential. The instructor resources that accompany this book—available at wwnorton.com /nrl—include exercises that simulate some of the decisions that campaign professionals must make.

We also take into account the views of political scientists, who have traditionally been more skeptical about the effects of campaigns, and the views of political theorists, who debate the democratic functions of political campaigns. Ultimately, we hope to provide an insider's perspective on the choices that political actors face in campaigns while simultaneously offering a judicious account of the impact of campaigns on voter attitudes and electoral outcomes.

Perhaps above all, we hope that the book engages readers as citizens. Most Americans experience political campaigns primarily as spectators and profess to dislike what they see. Thus, we want to help readers think critically about two things: what campaigns actually do and what campaigns should do. The former entails identifying when, how, and for whom campaigns matter. With this knowledge, readers will have a more sophisticated view of campaign effects—one that does not attribute great significance to every twist and turn but does not rule out influence entirely. The question of what campaigns should do is meant to engage readers in a broader conversation about the ideals that underpin the electoral process, and whether the process can be reformed to better approximate those ideals.

Revisions to the Third Edition

Highlights of the new edition:

- All chapters cover and contextualize the 2016 campaigns and election results, particularly Chapters 5 (Modern Campaign Strategies), 6 (Political Parties), 8 (Media), and 9 (Presidential Campaigns).

- Revisions to Chapters 4 (Financing Campaigns), 5 (Modern Campaign Strategies), and 7 (Interest Groups) demonstrate how political campaigns, super PACs, and interest groups function in a connected and well-funded network to target their opponents negatively, reach specific voters, and sway public opinion.

- Chapters 5 (Modern Campaign Strategies), 8 (Media), and 12 (Voter Participation) analyze how technology and news media—particularly social media—affect voters' consumption of information about candidates and their eventual decisions at the ballot box.

- There are several new "In Practice" boxes, including a feature on the impacts of technology on modern campaigns in Chapter 3 (The Transformation of American Campaigns), a feature on how candidates control their image on the Internet in Chapter 5 (Modern Campaign Strategies), and a feature on the underrepresentation of women in Congress in Chapter 10 (Congressional Campaigns).

- New and timely anecdotes, including the negative campaign strategies used by both candidates in 2016 (Chapter 3: The Transformation of American Campaigns), the *Access Hollywood* tape and its effects on the Trump campaign (Chapter 8: Media), and the surprising results of local elections in 2016 (Chapter 11: State and Local Campaigns), introduce chapters throughout the book.

Resources to accompany this book

The following resources, developed specifically to accompany this book, are available to students and instructors:

Norton Coursepacks. Easily add high-quality Norton digital media to your online, hybrid, or lecture course—all at no cost. Norton Coursepacks work with and leverage your existing learning management system, so there's no new system to learn, and access is free and easy.

- **Practice quizzes** let students test your knowledge of the chapter.
- **Chapter outlines** provide an overview of the chapter.
- **Flashcards** help students review the key terms from each chapter.

Instructor Resource Website (wwnorton.com/nrl). Accessible to confirmed instructors only, this site includes:

- **PowerPoint slides** of all figures and tables from the text. These are also provided in JPEG format.
- **Test questions** for every chapter.
- **Activity modules**, with detailed instructions for in-class and outside assignments, as well as materials for these activities. These modules allow students to apply what they have learned in the text as they work through hands-on simulations of several aspects of campaigns.

Acknowledgments

We are grateful to those who have assisted us in writing this book. Many scholars read portions of the book at various stages: Scott Adler, Brian Arbour, Suzanne Chod, David Dulio, Philip Habel, Danny Hayes, Valerie Hyman, Phil Jones, Ray LaRaja, Mingus Mapps, Seth Masket, Nate Persily, Andrew Reeves, Travis Ridout, Joe Romance, Wayne Steger, Jessica Trounstine, and Jonathan Winburn.

For their thoughtful feedback, we thank:

Jamie L. Carson, University of Georgia
Anthony Corrado, Colby College
Bernard Fraga, Indiana University
Peter L. Francia, East Carolina University
Michael Franz, Bowdoin College

John Gastil, Pennsylvania State University
Susan Grogan, St. Mary's College of Maryland
Matt Guardino, Providence College
Michael G. Hagen, Temple University
Eitan Hersh, Yale University
Marc Hetherington, Vanderbilt University
Benjamin Highton, University of California, Davis
Sunshine Hillygus, Duke University
Jack Johannes, Villanova University
Tyler Johnson, University of Oklahoma
Cindy D. Kam, Vanderbilt University
Yanna Krupnikov, Stony Brook University
Seth Masket, University of Denver
Hans Noel, Georgetown University
Kathryn Pearson, University of Minnesota
Markus Prior, Princeton University
Priscilla Southwell, University of Oregon
Michael Tesler, University of California, Irvine
Emily Thorson, George Washington University
Nicholas Valentino, University of Michigan
Kenneth F. Warren, Saint Louis University
Jennifer Wolak, University of Colorado

We thank Jake Haselswerdt for providing research assistance. We also thank W. W. Norton for supporting and nurturing this project—including our editor, Pete Lesser, for his expert guidance and feedback; associate editor Samantha Held; editorial assistant Anna Olcott; media editors Spencer Richardson-Jones and Michael Jaoui; assistant media editor Ariel Eaton; project editor Linda Feldman; copy editor Susan McColl; and production manager Sean Mintus.

John Sides
Daron Shaw
Matt Grossmann
Keena Lipsitz

CAMPAIGNS AND ELECTIONS

THIRD EDITION

CHAPTER 1

Introduction

Around 7:22 P.M. on the night of the 2016 presidential election, a member of businessman Donald Trump's campaign team told CNN's Jim Acosta "It will take a miracle for us to win." The Trump campaign wasn't alone in this view—most political observers also thought his opponent, former senator and secretary of state, Hillary Clinton would win. Prominent forecasts put her odds at over 90 percent. She had a solid lead in national polls and, significantly, in polls in the key battleground states. The Clinton campaign was "just so happy," with "the biggest smiles," according to a reporter who arrived at their anticipated victory party at 5 P.M.[1]

All of this changed quickly. As the votes came in throughout the night, one key state after another went to Trump—Florida, Pennsylvania, North Carolina, Michigan, Ohio, Wisconsin—although Clinton had an early lead in the popular vote. Despite the fact her lead would eventually grow to 2 percentage points after all the votes were counted, Trump's solid victory in the Electoral College gave him the presidency. Clinton conceded the election the next morning. It was a surprising end to an unforgettable election.

But, as the saying goes, even if history does not repeat itself, it often rhymes. And the 2016 election was reminiscent of recent elections in at least one sense: a dramatic shift in party power once again upended the ambitions of the incumbent party. This has happened time and again in American politics, including several times within just the last 12 years alone. In 2004, for example, George W. Bush had just been elected to a second term and the Republican Party retained control of both the U.S. Senate and House of Representatives. At a press conference two days after the election, Bush seemed as confident as Clinton's team had been going into the 2016 election. He said, "I earned capital in the campaign, political capital, and now I intend to spend it." A week after Bush's election, his chief political strategist, Karl Rove, called it an "extraordinary

---

[1] Brian Stelter. 2017. "In Their Own Words: The Story of Covering Election Night 2016." *CNN Media*, January 5. http://money.cnn.com/2017/01/05/media/election-night-news -coverage-oral-history/index.html (accessed 9/21/2017).

election" and bragged that the campaign had won "81 percent of all the counties in America."[2] Some commentators, even liberal ones, believed that Republican dominance would continue.[3]

However, the postelection euphoria of Bush and Rove proved short-lived. The war in Iraq, which had begun in March 2003, dragged on and on. The combination of a recession and financial crisis produced the deepest economic downturn that the United States had experienced since the Great Depression. In the last month of his presidency, Bush's approval rating dropped to 30 percent. The capital he thought he'd earned in 2004 was long gone.

In the 2006 midterm election, the Democratic Party struck its first blow, taking back control of the House and Senate. This was the first time since 1994 that the Democrats controlled both chambers. Then, on November 4, 2008, the Democratic nominee, Barack Obama, won the presidency—a victory all the more noteworthy because he became the first African American to hold the office. In his victory speech, Obama was no less ambitious than Bush: "This is our time—to put our people back to work and open doors of opportunity for our

Core of the Analysis

Focusing on four aspects of campaigns—rules, reality, strategy, and citizens' choices—helps us understand the outcomes of American elections:

- The *rules* refer to laws and constitutional doctrines that govern the electoral system and affect how campaigns are carried out and ultimately who wins elections.

- Broader economic and political *realities* shape the tenor of public opinion and often place limits on how much campaigns can affect opinion.

- The *strategies* employed by candidates, political parties, interest groups, and the media reflect their unique interests and agendas and can, when circumstances are right, affect public opinion as well.

- The *choices made by citizens*—whether and how to vote—depend on a mix of long-standing habits, current realities, and new information from the campaign itself.

- The democratic values of free choice, political equality, deliberation, and free speech help us evaluate campaigns.

---

[2] Joshua Green. 2007. "The Rove Presidency." *The Atlantic,* September. www.theatlantic.com/magazine/archive/2007/09/the-rove-presidency/6132 (accessed 9/20/2015).

[3] One example was Michael Lind, writing at the blog *Talking Points Memo.* See: http://themonkeycage.org/2012/11/12/the-perils-of-democrats-euphoria-or-why-the-2012-election-is-not-a-realignment (accessed 9/21/2017).

kids; to restore prosperity and promote the cause of peace; to reclaim the American Dream and reaffirm that fundamental truth—that out of many, we are one." Obama and congressional Democrats moved swiftly despite nearly unanimous Republican opposition to pass a stimulus package intended to help the economy, a climate change bill in the House, and, most notably, health care reform in March 2010.

By the next midterm election in November 2010, however, the economy was only limping toward recovery and Obama's approval rating was about 45 percent—20 points lower than it had been when he was inaugurated. This spelled trouble for the Democrats in Congress, and the party lost six seats in the Senate and a whopping 63 seats in the House of Representatives—the largest loss in the House for the president's party since 1938. In a postelection press conference, Obama acknowledged that the Democrats had taken a "shellacking."

By the 2012 presidential election, Obama and the Democrats bounced back. Obama beat Republican Mitt Romney by a comfortable margin of nearly four points and the Democrats gained seats in both the House and Senate. But Republicans retained control of the House of Representatives, thereby complicating Obama's ability to pursue an ambitious second-term agenda.

In 2014, Republicans once again dominated the midterm election. They expanded their House majority and won a Senate majority as well. For the last two years of his presidency, Obama confronted an even more powerful Republican congressional majority that stymied many of his goals.

In 2016, however, Hillary Clinton seemed destined to become Obama's successor and carry on his legacy. Indeed, many Democrats thought that demographic changes in the country—a liberal generation of young people, increasing ethnic and racial diversity—gave their party an edge in presidential elections that could last for years. But ultimately, Democrats experienced the same disappointment that Republicans did after 2004. Building permanent majorities in American politics is no easy feat.

The years from 2004 to 2016 therefore brought important changes in party power and tempered the ambitions of many political leaders. Frequent shifts between the Democratic and Republican parties have been the norm in presidential elections for the past 150 years. These shifts point toward one of the central questions of this book: *What explains the outcomes of American elections—presidential, congressional, and state and local?* Addressing this question entails attention to others. Why do some candidates choose to run and others do not? Why do some candidates win and others lose? There are many interpretations of elections, but far fewer solid answers to these questions.

An obvious answer to our first question might be campaigns themselves. A political campaign combines elements of two other, nonpolitical types of campaigns. In some ways, it is like a military campaign, with the goal of winning a contest and vanquishing an opponent. It is also like an advertising campaign, with the goal of persuading citizens to buy a product. One might think that political campaigns are always consequential, with millions of dollars being spent, professional strategists scheming, advertisements blanketing the airwaves, and armies of volunteers pounding the pavement. But this is not necessarily so. Elections depend in large part on the overall state of the country, which even brilliant campaigning cannot change. Hence the second central question of this book: *How much does the campaign itself matter?*

It is easy to imagine how campaigns might matter. Campaigns could convince citizens to support one candidate or oppose another, or motivate them to go to the polls on Election Day. Professional campaign operatives frequently argue that campaign strategies accomplish these things. Indeed, it is hard to see how they could believe otherwise: their livelihoods depend on it! Political scientists, however, approach the question differently: rather than relying on personal experience, they use different kinds of evidence to determine how much campaigns actually matter. This entails acknowledging that any campaign's impact, however meaningful, could prove secondary to that of other events. For example, what was more important for Obama's victory in 2008: the $730 million that he spent campaigning or an unpopular George W. Bush and a tanking economy? And what was more important for him in 2012: the $1.1 billion that he and his allies spent or the fact that the tanking economy had actually turned around on his watch?

The fact that presidential campaigns can now cost in the billions of dollars raises the third central question of this book: *How should we evaluate the American electoral process?* One complaint is that American campaigns are just too expensive, and that incessant fund-raising distracts and possibly corrupts politicians. People wonder whether the system allows the best candidates to emerge. They question whether campaigns are fair, informative, truthful, and engaging. They worry that citizens fail to learn what they need to know in order to make political decisions, or that constant mudslinging alienates citizens and leads them to stay home on Election Day. It is important to think through these complaints analytically—to ask, for example, whether negative campaigning really turns citizens off. But it is also important to think critically about what elections and campaigns *should* be like. Evaluating this question will help us understand not only how much campaigns affect citizens but also how much they help or hurt our democracy.

A Framework for Understanding Campaigns and Elections

In this book, we use a simple framework to understand **campaigns** and **elections** in American politics. This framework emphasizes four aspects of campaigns and elections:

- The *rules* that govern elections influence who runs, how campaigns operate, and who wins.
- The broader *reality*—economic, political, and historical—that parties and candidates confront profoundly affects whether they decide to run and how they campaign.
- The *strategic choices* that various actors—including candidates, the media, political parties, and interest groups—make can affect who wins and who loses.
- The *choices of citizens* ultimately decide the outcome.

The goal of this framework is to identify the major features of the American electoral system that influence the actual outcomes of elections—who wins and who loses. We will also see how the elements of the framework depend on each other. For example, the strategic choices of candidates depend on both the electoral rules and the broader reality that candidates confront. Similarly, the choices of citizens, especially in the voting booth, may depend on rules and reality but also on the strategies of candidates, parties, the media, and others, all of whom broadcast information that may influence citizens' feelings about the candidates.

Rules

Any sports fan can see that the rules of the game matter. When college and professional basketball created a longer-distance shot worth three points, it changed the game, making sharpshooting players more valuable and helping teams who had more such players. Although we cannot replay history, it seems likely that over the years teams have won numerous games that they otherwise would have lost if not for three-point shooting.

Elections are no different. Rules affect their every aspect: who is qualified to run for office, when elections are held and thus when campaigns begin, the size and characteristics of constituencies, how much money can be donated and spent, who is eligible to vote, and, ultimately, who wins the election. All of the actors involved in elections—citizens, candidates, parties, interest groups, the media—find themselves subject to rules. For example,

Why were the Republicans, now led by Senate Majority Leader Mitch McConnell, President Donald Trump, and Speaker of the House Paul Ryan, so successful in 2016? Did smart campaigning enable them to win unified control of the presidency and Congress? Or were other factors more important than campaign strategy?

16-year-olds cannot vote. Thirty-year-olds cannot be president. Candidates and parties cannot accept unlimited amounts of money from a wealthy donor. Interest groups cannot coordinate their campaign spending with the candidates it would benefit. Television stations cannot sell advertising time to one candidate but refuse to sell it to that candidate's opponent.

The rules of elections are important because, in many cases, they cannot be changed easily. Changing a rule may require legislation, a Supreme Court decision, or even a constitutional amendment. Moreover, rule changes typically do not happen during the campaign itself. Thus, as the campaign gets under way, the rules constitute a hand that all the candidates are dealt and thereby constrain candidate strategy in important ways. Consider some of the basic rules about campaign finance. Existing laws limit the amount of money that any individual can donate but do not limit the amount of money that any candidate can spend. The former means that candidates must devote a lot of time to fund-raising as they try to amass campaign funds from many individual donors. The latter means that some wealthy people will be tempted to run for office and spend their own money to finance their campaigns. About 20 percent of the money spent by Donald Trump's campaign came from Trump himself. The challenges of financing a campaign under the existing rules also seem to discourage potential female candidates. In a survey of women and men in professions, such as law and business, that frequently lead to political careers, women were less likely than men to say that they had contemplated running for office, and many women cited the challenges of raising money as a dissuading factor.[4]

Reality

The context in which an election occurs—what we call "reality"—also strongly affects a candidate's success or failure. For example, in 2008, when Obama was seeking to become the first African American president, voters had a number of unpleasant issues on their minds: the unpopular war in Iraq, the recession, and the financial crisis, which necessitated emergency measures to shore up large banks in the weeks leading up to the election. All of this helped Obama beat his opponent, Senator John McCain of Arizona, by a decisive margin because voters tend to blame the incumbent party—in this case, the Republicans—when things in the country are not going well.

Obama's experience illustrates the importance of the broader reality candidates face. Here, "reality" refers to several factors in particular: the candidates' biographies, the records of the political parties, and recent and current political and economic events, such as a war or recession. These elements of the broader context are similar in one crucial respect: they are rarely under the control of the candidates themselves. Obama didn't make the war in Iraq or the economic recession happen. Ultimately, the things that candidates can control, such as their campaign strategy, may not overcome the effects of events that conspire against them.

A first important component of reality is the background of the candidates themselves. This may involve their personal lives or their professional lives, including prior service in elected office. Candidates cannot rewrite their biographies from scratch. What they have done or said in the past, both the good and the bad, will follow them. Candidates try to capitalize on the best aspects of their biography, such as a happy family, service to the community or country, and support of popular policies. Opponents will emphasize the worst aspects, such as lies, unpopular actions, and scandals.

A second component of reality involves the legacies that political parties bequeath to candidates. The major parties have each developed reputations for giving attention to specific key issues as well as for holding particular

---

[4] Jennifer L. Lawless and Richard L. Fox. 2008. "Why Are Women Still Not Running for Public Office?" *Brookings Institution Issues in Governance Studies*, May.

positions on those issues.[5] The Democratic Party has traditionally favored government action to help people. The Republican Party has favored lowering taxes, partly in an effort to shrink the size of government. An anti-tax Democrat or a pro-welfare Republican is at odds with these legacies and can have difficulty convincing citizens that their positions are sincere. The parties have also developed coalitions of supporters from different groups in society. The Democratic Party's early commitment to civil rights, despite the resistance of Southern Democrats, earned it the lasting loyalty of African Americans. The Republican Party's conservative positions on social issues, such as abortion and gay rights, have garnered it the support of most evangelical Christians. Candidates find it difficult to make inroads with groups that have not traditionally supported their party.

Another component of reality is current or recent events that are directly connected to government policies and the formal powers of political office. For example, foreign policy crises and wars are particularly important for the electoral prospects of presidents and presidential candidates. The terrorist attacks of September 11, 2001, led the public and Congress to rally behind President Bush. The Republican Party even picked up seats in the 2002 midterms, despite the fact that the president's party typically loses seats in midterm elections. By the 2004 election, when Bush ran as an **incumbent** (the candidate currently holding office), he had lost the goodwill of many Democrats. However, September 11, as well as the Iraq War, still loomed large over the campaign. War and national security issues were central to Bush's message and that of his opponent, Senator John Kerry. Ongoing wars can also help or hurt the incumbent president. Consider Lyndon Johnson, who decided not to run for reelection in 1968 because of the long, costly Vietnam War. Foreign affairs and war may not be completely outside politicians' control, in that presidents help decide how to conduct foreign relations and whether and how to wage war. But presidents cannot control other countries and their armies, and they often confront the unexpected. The same is true for other elected officials and in other policy areas.

A final and especially important component of reality is the economy. Just as the public tends to prefer peace over war, it prefers prosperity to poverty. The public holds incumbent officeholders, particularly the president, responsible for economic conditions, and, as we will discuss in more detail in later chapters, incumbents presiding over a robust economy will typically win a larger share of the vote than those presiding over a weak economy. As with

---

[5] John Petrocik. 1996. "Issue Ownership in Presidential Elections, with a 1980 Case Study." *American Journal of Political Science* 40, 3: 825–50.

foreign affairs and war, elected officials often have some influence on the economy. For example, as we saw soon after Barack Obama took office in 2009, the president and Congress can pass bills that attempt to stimulate the economy or that provide government support to unemployed Americans. These types of measures can be important, but they are often less effective than politicians and the public would like. The ups and downs of the economy depend on many factors outside any politician's control.

Taken together, these elements of reality affect candidate strategies, the decisions of citizens, and, ultimately, election outcomes. Their impact on election outcomes makes it difficult to credit campaign strategy for every victory and blame it for every defeat. Incumbent candidates running during a time of peace and prosperity may win easily, even if their campaigns were full of strategic miscalculations. These same candidates running during an unpopular war and a weak economy may lose, no matter the brilliance of their campaign strategy.

Strategy

The impact of rules and reality can lead to doubts about the effects of campaign strategy. But campaign strategies do matter. One need look no further than fluctuations in the candidates' poll numbers during a campaign. The 2016 campaign provides a recent, dramatic example. Early in 2015, former Florida governor Jeb Bush and Wisconsin governor Scott Walker led the Republican presidential primary polls. But before 2015 was over, both Bush and Walker saw their poll numbers drop precipitously, while candidates who had never held any elective office—like Trump as well as the neurosurgeon Ben Carson—surged. Walker would drop out before the primaries even began. What helps explain these sharp changes in the fortunes of candidates? This question draws our attention to the potential impact of campaign strategy.

Campaigns involve a variety of actors. Most visible are the candidates themselves. Their strategic choices involve every facet of a campaign: whether to run in the first place, what issues to emphasize, what specific messages or themes to discuss, which kinds of media to use, and which citizens to target. Candidates' personal campaign organizations, sometimes with paid professionals on board, create much of the visible campaign activity, from yard signs and bumper stickers to television advertising and YouTube videos. Political parties also make decisions about messages and targeting as they deploy resources on behalf of their candidates, including ads, voter registration drives, and get-out-the-vote operations on Election Day. The same is true of interest groups, which raise and spend money in support of favored candidates. And, throughout the campaign, the news media are crucial. Although

These protesters echo a frequent refrain of presidential candidate Donald Trump in 2016, who promised to "drain the swamp" in Washington by reducing political corruption. Trump's campaign frequently touted his "outsider" status and antipathy for the political "establishment."

candidates can communicate directly with citizens through advertising, many citizens receive information from news media outlets. Thus, the news media's coverage of the campaign may also matter.

All of these actors are in part following their own strategies and in part responding to the strategies of others. Candidates routinely try to "stay on message" but are often sidetracked by responding to their opponents' claims. Parties and interest groups often structure their campaign activity to complement that of their favored candidates, but at times the strategies of the candidates, parties, and interest groups diverge. Interest groups, for example, are far more likely than candidates to air negative advertisements. The media depend on political parties, interest groups, and, especially, candidates for news but often impose their own definition of newsworthiness. The media's agenda frequently diverges from those of the campaigns, and they are often talking about something different from the candidates.[6] This is one reason candidates frequently criticize the coverage they receive.

---

[6] Danny Hayes. 2010. "The Dynamics of Agenda Convergence and the Paradox of Competitiveness in Presidential Campaigns." *Political Research Quarterly* 63, 3: 594–611.

Campaign strategy is the element of elections that candidates and other actors can control. They may not be able to end a war or make the economy grow, but they can craft a slogan, produce a television advertisement, give a speech, and kiss a lot of babies at campaign rallies. Much money is spent doing all of these things. The ultimate question is how much difference it makes.

Citizens' Choices

In any democratic political system, an election's outcome depends on the people. Eligible American citizens have two choices to make in an election: *whether* to vote and *how* to vote. Rules and reality affect these choices. Campaign strategists aim to influence these choices as well, by convincing people to support a particular candidate and encouraging supporters to vote on Election Day. The central question is: How susceptible are citizens to campaign influence? Answering this question also means determining how much citizens are affected by broader realities such as the state of the economy, which might matter more than the campaign itself.

Citizens are not blank slates. They have preexisting political habits and opinions. Some vote in every election. Others never vote. Some tend to vote for Democrats, and some for Republicans. Habits put limits on what a campaign can accomplish. No matter how much money candidates spend, or how catchy and engaging their advertisements are, they will not be able to persuade some citizens to support them or to vote. Moreover, at times campaigns struggle simply to command the public's attention. Some people do not follow politics closely and are not interested in watching the news, candidate debates, or political advertisements. Simply put, many votes are not up for grabs, and those that are may not easily be won with the tools of modern campaigns. Indeed, undecided citizens may respond more to "reality" than to campaign messages.

Journalists often describe campaigns as important, as do campaign consultants, naturally enough. Victorious candidates are presumed to have run skillful campaigns, and losing candidates are presumed to have run poor ones. Hillary Clinton's surprising loss in 2016 provoked many articles about how flawed she was as a candidate, how she never developed a compelling message, how she had not campaigned sufficiently in certain states, and so on. But neither blame for the losing candidate nor credit to the winning candidate is warranted, absent scientific evidence of how much the campaign mattered. Gathering this evidence and demonstrating its persuasiveness are difficult tasks.

Evaluating Campaigns and Elections

Thinking about rules, reality, strategy, and citizen choice helps illuminate what actually happens in campaigns. The next question is: What should happen? Here, "should happen" does not mean "my candidate should win." Rather, we mean: What is good for the democratic political system in which we live?

In democratic systems, campaigns are crucial processes. They are a time during which citizens typically pay the most attention to politics. They also provide a level of interaction between leaders and citizens that is rarely attained at other times. Thus, a lot is at stake in getting this process "right." However, a large majority of the public professes not to like campaigns very much. In a poll conducted immediately after the 2016 election, respondents were asked to grade various people's performances during the campaign, including Clinton, Trump, the press, and pollsters. Majorities gave all of these actors a C or lower. Most (60 percent) even gave voters a C or lower.[7] In general, the public routinely complains that campaigns are too long, too costly, and too negative. In the public's eyes, much can and should be done to reform campaigns.

But campaign reform is not a simple matter. There may be good reasons for the status quo, however objectionable it is to some Americans. Moreover, any reform is likely to involve trade-offs, improving things by one measure but worsening them by another. It is helpful, then, to establish a set of standards by which we can evaluate campaigns. Each of these standards represents a potential goal of a democratic political system. Together they may not capture every conceivable goal, but they do represent a starting point. We will refer to them in many subsequent chapters, as we seek to understand not only how campaigns and elections operate but also whether they can or should be improved.

The first standard is *free choice*. For elections to be truly democratic, citizens must be free from coercion or manipulation. To facilitate their choice, they must also have adequate information about the contending candidates and parties. Campaigns that involve violent intimidation of opposition party supporters do not meet this standard, nor do campaigns in which the incumbent regime controls all major news outlets. In the United States, such behavior is rare but is known to occur. For example, during the 2006 election, a letter written in Spanish was sent to approximately 14,000 residents

---

[7] See www.people-press.org/2016/11/21/voters-evaluations-of-the-campaign (accessed 6/20/2017).

of Orange County, California, all of whom had Latino surnames or foreign birthplaces. The letter suggested that immigrants might go to jail for voting. It was intended to discourage Latino citizens from voting and thereby hurting the reelection prospects of the Latina incumbent, Representative Loretta Sanchez. Sanchez's Republican opponent, Tan Nguyen, was convicted in 2010 for lying to federal investigators about whether he played any role in sending the letter.

Even if such dramatic attempts at coercion are rare, we may ask whether the information that citizens receive in American campaigns is sufficient to ensure free choice. What if, for example, a well-funded incumbent is competing against a poorly funded challenger? Chances are, citizens will hear much more from the incumbent than the challenger. Is this a problem? What if the situation is even more lopsided, and there is no challenger for this incumbent? For example, in the 2016 election, only about 45 percent of U.S. House primary elections featured at least two candidates.[8] Does it violate the standard of free choice when there is only one choice?

A second standard is *political equality*. Citizens must, by this standard, be equal in the eyes of the law. Laws that disadvantage certain citizens violate this standard. One example is Jim Crow laws, which were in effect in many southern states from 1876 until 1965. These laws effectively disenfranchised blacks by a variety of means, such as literacy tests and poll taxes. Blacks, who were often less educated and less affluent than whites, were more likely to fail these tests and be unable to afford the taxes. Although Jim Crow laws were eventually abolished, voter eligibility requirements continue to have implications for political equality. For example, requiring potential voters to supply identification, such as a driver's license, will disproportionately affect those without such identification, who tend to be elderly or members of racial minorities. Thirty-four states have passed laws that request or require identification in order to vote.[9]

The standard of political equality could be applied to candidates as well. The example of the rich incumbent and the poor challenger may violate this standard. But this standard also raises some challenging questions. Must every pair of opposing candidates have identical amounts of money to spend campaigning? What if a challenger has raised little money because he or she seems to lack important qualities or qualifications, leaving potential donors reluctant to give?

---

[8] See http://ballotpedia.org/U.S._House_primaries,_2016#Primary_competitiveness (accessed 11/17/2017).

[9] See www.ncsl.org/research/elections-and-campaigns/voter-id.aspx (accessed 6/20/2017).

A third standard is *deliberation*. Deliberation speaks not just to the quantity but also to the quality of information available to citizens. Interaction between opposing candidates can be evaluated by this standard. For example, in a truly deliberative interaction, the candidates highlight points of similarity and difference between them. This helps citizens decide whom they prefer. Media coverage of campaigns can be evaluated by this same standard. Does the news give citizens information on the similarities and differences between the candidates? Critics often complain that it does not, because campaign reporting is more focused on the latest polls than on the policy proposals of the candidates. The 2016 election provides but one of many examples. A study by the Shorenstein Center on Media, Politics, and Public Policy found that almost half of campaign news stories in 2016 focused on strategy, tactics, and polling. Seventeen percent focused on various campaign controversies and only 10 percent focused on political issues or public policy.[10] Is the public learning enough about the real differences between the candidates when their views on issues are so rarely discussed? Before we are too quick to criticize the media, we must also ask: Does this focus on strategy rather than policy merely reflect the desires of news consumers, who are happy to read about polls but not so interested in long articles about the candidates' views on complicated aspects of policy?

A fourth standard is *free speech*. This is a linchpin of the American political system, one enshrined in the Bill of Rights. Upholding free speech may in fact complicate attempts to promote equality or deliberation. Eliminating disparities between incumbents and challengers in the interest of equality entails limiting the amount of "speech" that incumbents have—for instance, by restricting how and how much they campaign. One way to do this is with campaign finance laws, which affect how much candidates can raise and spend. Ensuring deliberation would mean placing restrictions on what the candidates and news media could talk about, perhaps by forcing candidates to engage each other on specific issues, even if they would rather not discuss those issues. Either could be said to violate the standard of free speech.

Designing the ideal campaign or election is a difficult task, especially because the four standards discussed here are not always compatible. But these standards are still useful for evaluating the rules and institutions that

---

[10] Thomas E. Patterson. 2016. "News Coverage of the 2016 General Election: How the Press Failed the Voters." Shorenstein Center on Media, Politics, and Public Policy. https://shorensteincenter.org/news-coverage-2016-general-election (accessed 6/20/2017).

govern the electoral process—such as the Electoral College and campaign finance laws—as well as the strategies pursued by candidates. For example, Americans commonly complain when candidates attack their opponents. Is this always a bad thing? These standards can help us address that question. They also help us evaluate the behavior of citizens. Does the attention Americans pay to campaigns and their knowledge of the candidates live up to democratic ideals?

Conclusion

To understand and evaluate campaigns, we take into account the perspectives of both political professionals and political scientists—who, as we noted at the beginning of this chapter, often have quite different perspectives on how much campaigns affect elections. Professional campaign operatives and consultants are focused on the nuts and bolts of campaigning—the how-to's—and tend to believe that campaigns have important effects on citizens. Political scientists formulate broader theories of campaigns and elections and then test those theories with empirical research on public opinion, media coverage, and campaign activity. They tend to be more cautious in attributing significance to campaign strategy. However, campaign consultants are increasingly drawing on ideas and tools from political and social science to test the effects of campaign tactics. Our goal is to provide a sense of what happens on the ground in campaigns, and also whether it ultimately matters—both to individual voters and to election outcomes.

The next chapter outlines the basic rules of the electoral process in the United States. Chapter 3 describes how American political campaigns have evolved throughout history. Chapter 4 describes how contemporary campaigns are financed—another aspect of the rules that has important consequences for strategy. Chapter 5 discusses the major elements of modern campaign strategy, drawing on political science theories and evidence as well as the thinking of political consultants; much of this chapter focuses on the behavior of candidates. Chapters 6 to 8 consider the specific roles played by other actors: political parties, interest groups, and the media.

Chapters 9 to 11 delve into three specific categories of campaigns: presidential, congressional, and state and local. An important theme throughout the book is that the rules, realities, and strategies inherent to campaigns may differ across levels of office. Thus, it is important to examine how each type of campaign typically unfolds. Chapters 12 and 13 turn the focus to citizens, including their decision on whether to participate in elections and their decision to support a particular candidate. These two chapters devote particular attention to how much campaigns affect each decision. Finally, Chapter 14 evaluates contemporary American campaigns by the standards presented. Discussion of these standards also appears elsewhere in this chapter, but this final chapter provides a broader perspective on whether American campaigns and elections reflect a "broken system" or effective "democracy in action."

KEY TERMS

campaigns (p. 6)
elections (p. 6)
incumbent (p. 9)

FOR DISCUSSION

1. What are the central differences in how political consultants and political scientists tend to think about the impact of campaigns?

2. Why do the rules constrain candidates when they are campaigning? Why don't candidates simply change the rules to their benefit?

3. What are several dimensions of "reality" that might affect campaign strategies and election outcomes?

4. Why would the standards of deliberation and equality potentially come into conflict with the standard of free speech?

CHAPTER 2

The American Electoral Process

In the spring of 2001, Barack Obama, a state senator in Illinois, was a year removed from his most stunning political defeat. In the 2000 Democratic primary for a U.S. House seat, he had challenged another black Democrat, the incumbent congressman Bobby Rush, and lost by 31 points. Obama struggled to win votes in some parts of Rush's district, particularly black neighborhoods where professors at the University of Chicago—even African American professors like Obama—were viewed with suspicion. Obama had more appeal in South Side neighborhoods around the university, and also North Side neighborhoods closer to downtown, including the so-called Gold Coast along Lake Michigan. The Gold Coast is home to many wealthy (and mostly white) Chicagoans, an ideal group from which to raise money for a political campaign. The problem was that as a state senator, Obama did not represent the North Side and its Gold Coast; his district was on the South Side.

One day that spring, Obama went to a room in a downtown building in Springfield, a room guarded with fingerprint scanners and coded keypads. Inside the room were computers on which a select few employees of the Illinois Democratic Party worked. Their job was to draw legislative districts. The Democrats had won control of the Illinois House and now, the year after the 2000 census, were drawing up a new set of state legislative districts—as was the Republican majority in the Illinois Senate. Obama sat with a Democratic consultant, John Corrigan, and drew himself a new state senate district, one that started in the South Side and then stretched north to the Gold Coast. It was a "radical change," said Corrigan.

After a protracted battle, the Democrats succeeded in implementing their districts. This gave Obama a new district well suited to funding his political ambitions, and it also helped the Democrats win a majority in the Illinois Senate in the 2002 elections. This majority helped Obama by allowing him to more easily establish a record of legislative accomplishments. With this newfound potential for raising money and promoting legislation, Obama was poised to run for the U.S. Senate in 2004.[1]

This chapter is about the rules of campaigns and elections, the first part of the framework introduced in Chapter 1. All democracies depend on rules to govern political life. The anecdote from early in Obama's political career illustrates their importance. Obama was lucky: he had some influence over redistricting, which determined who his constituents would be. Most of the time, political leaders, candidates, and parties do not have this luxury. Rules are often fixed by law, sometimes even by the Constitution itself, and cannot be changed quickly or easily to benefit a party or candidate.

The rules of the American electoral process help us to answer many crucial questions pertaining to campaigns. This chapter explores five of them: who can run for office, when elections are held, where to run, who can vote, and who wins. For each, we first explore what the rules are. The answers are not always straightforward, due in part to a second consideration: who makes the rules. The Constitution, Congress, state legislatures, and political parties all have some say. The rules are not the same for every level of office or in every state. But even general answers are informative.

Knowing what the rules are and who makes them leads to the "why" questions: Why these rules and not others? Rules reflect ideals or values—that is, conceptions of what makes a good or fair electoral process. For example, a good

Core of the Analysis

- Elections are conducted according to rules that determine who runs, when elections are held, where candidates run, who can vote, and who wins.
- The rules often vary across states and levels of office because they are designed by multiple decision makers, including the framers of the Constitution, Congress, state legislatures, local officials, and political parties.
- The rules reflect values about what constitutes a "good" election, but they often further certain values at the expense of others.
- Many rules are largely outside of the control of candidates, political parties, and voters, especially once the campaign has begun.
- The rules strongly affect the decisions of every relevant actor during a campaign, including candidates, parties, interest groups, the media, and voters.

---

[1] This anecdote comes from Ryan Lizza. 2008. "Making It: How Chicago Shaped Obama." *New Yorker*, July 21.

electoral process might feature a vigorous competition between two candidates—one that provides information to citizens and motivates them to vote. But competitive elections are also more expensive, as candidates have an incentive to raise more money so that they can effectively communicate with citizens. Many people wish that elections were not so expensive and fear that soliciting campaign contributions corrupts candidates. So whether one favors increased competition might depend on what one considers more important: informing voters or mitigating the potential for corruption. Inevitably, electoral rules reflect compromises and trade-offs among competing values, and almost never fully codify any particular value. Small wonder, then, that electoral rules are often so controversial.

In this chapter, we will see that perhaps the most important aspect of electoral rules, especially from a candidate's or party's point of view, is their consequences for campaign strategy and for whether candidates are likely to win or lose. Perhaps Barack Obama had philosophical objections to a system in which his party got to redraw the Illinois political map to help both him and his party. But ultimately he did not try to change the rule; he merely tried to make it work in his favor.

When Barack Obama was a member of the Illinois legislature, the rules for redistricting determined who his constituents were. New district boundaries gave him a set of wealthier constituents, and their support helped Obama run a successful U.S. Senate campaign in 2004.

Who Can Run

Who is eligible to run for office? In the American political system, the qualifications usually involve a minimum age, American citizenship, and a minimum time living in the community one seeks to represent. For federal office, the Constitution spells out these requirements. A candidate for the House of Representatives must be at least 25 years old, a citizen for seven years, and an "inhabitant" of the state the district is in. The qualifications for senator are similar, except that the candidate must be at least 30 years old and a citizen for nine years. These more restrictive qualifications are because the framers of the Constitution believed that the Senate demanded more from its members than did the House. James Madison wrote, "The propriety of these distinctions is explained by the nature of the senatorial trust, which, requiring greater extent of information and stability of character, requires at the same time that the senator should have reached a period of life most likely to supply these advantages."[2]

The requirements for president are even more restrictive. Candidates must be at least 35 years old and U.S. residents for at least 14 years (although the Constitution does not specify when that period of residency must have occurred). Moreover, they must be native-born citizens of the United States. Naturalized citizens may run for the House and Senate.

Candidates for state and local offices typically must meet requirements for minimum age and residency, although different localities have different rules. For example, in Louisiana, candidates for governor need to be at least 25 years old, and citizens of the United States and residents of Louisiana for at least the five years before the election. In Minnesota, candidates for governor must also be at least 25, but need only have lived in the state for the year before the election. Candidates for the Louisiana state legislature must be at least 18 years old, state residents for the preceding two years, and residents of their legislative district for at least the preceding year. Candidates for the Minnesota state legislature must be at least 21 years old and must be residents of the state for one year and of the district for at least six months immediately preceding the election. Other states have their own stipulations about age and residency.

Despite specific differences, federal, state, and local qualifications for office reflect a common set of values. One is competence. Age requirements help ensure that candidates have the intellectual and emotional maturity to handle the job. To be sure, age is an imperfect measure of competence. There

---

[2] *Federalist Papers*, no. 62.

have been cases where older politicians, due to age or infirmity, lost a significant degree of competence but still held office. In 1919, President Woodrow Wilson suffered a debilitating stroke. His wife, Edith, took over and saw to it that important tasks were delegated to the proper cabinet secretaries—all of whom were kept in the dark about the president's condition.[3] But although any age threshold is somewhat arbitrary, it would be foolish to have no thresholds whatsoever. Whatever the talents of 13-year-olds, they are probably not ready to be leaders of the free world.

A second value reflected in these qualifications is loyalty. Requiring candidates to be citizens of the United States helps to ensure that they will work for its interests and not those of another country. Residency requirements for state offices reflect a similar concern—the desire to have representatives who will work for their constituents' interests and not the interests of people in some other district or state. Residency requirements also imply a third value: familiarity with the people a candidate seeks to represent. Having lived among his or her constituents could help a candidate better understand their needs. Of course, citizenship does not ensure loyalty and residency does not ensure good representation, but both kinds of requirements may foster a candidate's commitment to these ideals.

Outside of age, citizenship, and residency, there are relatively few requirements in widespread use. Two more deserve brief mention, however. First, although it is not codified in the U.S. Constitution or state constitutions, the dominance of political parties in American elections virtually requires candidates to be party members in order to seek office. Party membership does not necessarily imply years of loyal service, and often parties will accept defectors from a competing party with open arms. That said, candidates cannot credibly hopscotch back and forth among parties, and this leads most of them to commit to a single party. This commitment is valuable to parties, who want to ensure that candidates represent the views of party members. A major-party affiliation is helpful for a prospective candidate because of rules that can make it difficult for **independent candidates**—those unaffiliated with a party—and candidates from smaller political parties simply to get on the ballot. States typically require candidates to collect a certain number of signatures from voters to get on the ballot. In some cases, this requirement is not too onerous; for a potential candidate for the U.S. House of Representatives, Tennessee requires only 25 signatures from registered voters who reside in that House district—a tiny fraction of the 700,000 or so residents in a district. But in Texas, a potential candidate for governor who

---

[3] August Heckscher. 1991. *Woodrow Wilson*. New York: Scribner.

seeks to run in a party that does not already have ballot access must get a number of signatures equal to a larger fraction (1 percent) of all voters in the previous gubernatorial election. One percent may not sound like a lot, but for a candidate in the 2018 gubernatorial election, that entails over 47,000 signatures.[4] This requirement, which does not apply to candidates in established political parties, is one way that ballot access laws can make it harder for new or smaller parties to field candidates.

Second, politicians can sometimes be disqualified from seeking reelection if they have already served in an office for a specified length of time. The shorthand for such a rule is **term limits**: limits on the number of terms politicians can serve in a particular elected office. For example, because of the Twenty-second Amendment (1951), the president can serve only two terms. Members of Congress have no term limits; laws passed by some state legislatures to impose term limits on members of Congress were overturned by the Supreme Court in 1995.[5] However, term limits on governors and state legislators are not prohibited. Thirty-six states limit the number of terms a governor may serve, typically to two.[6] Fifteen states limit the number of terms a state legislator may serve.[7] Term limits imply a certain vision of representation: good representatives are closer to the people, and this can best be achieved with frequent turnover. Otherwise, representatives may go to their respective capitals, spend years in office, and lose perspective on what their constituents want. Critics of term limits tend to emphasize a different ideal: good representatives are more experienced and more knowledgeable about public policy. Under term limits, the argument goes, legislators have little incentive to develop expertise because they will soon be out of a job. Note the tension between the values underlying minimum age and residency requirements on the one hand, and term limits on the other. Minimum age requirements are intended to ensure basic competence, and residency requirements to ensure a better connection with constituents. But to the extent that a longer tenure in office builds representatives' competence and their connection to their constituents, term limits will harm both.

In some respects, the rules regarding age, citizenship, and residency are rarely a constraint on candidates. Most potential candidates are not motivated

---

[4] See www.sos.state.tx.us/elections/candidates/guide/newparty2018.shtml (accessed 8/3/2017).

[5] *U.S. Term Limits, Inc. v. Thornton*, 514 U.S. 779 (1995).

[6] For more information, see http://knowledgecenter.csg.org/kc/system/files/4.9_2013.pdf and http://ballotpedia.org/States_with_gubernatorial_term_limits (accessed 8/3/2017).

[7] National Conference of State Legislatures. "The Term Limited States." www.ncsl.org /research/about-state-legislatures/chart-of-term-limits-states.aspx (accessed 8/3/2017).

to run for office until they are older. Nearly all meet the necessary requirement for U.S. citizenship, with the exception of naturalized citizens, who are not eligible to run for president. (One example is former California governor Arnold Schwarzenegger, who was born in Austria.) Residency is only occasionally an issue, and this is usually not because candidates fail to meet the letter of the law but because opponents claim that although they maintain a home in the state or district, they really live elsewhere (e.g., in Washington, D.C.), or that they arrived too recently in a state to represent it well (as some said when Hillary Clinton moved to New York the year before she mounted a Senate campaign in 2002). In fact, party membership and term limits probably have a larger impact on who can run. The advantages that come with party membership discourage candidates who do not identify with either major party. Term limits regularly force elected leaders to leave office or run for a different office, even when they would prefer to run for reelection to the same office.

The natural criticism of eligibility requirements hinges on the standard of free choice that we discussed in Chapter 1. One might argue that such requirements restrict the choices that citizens have by eliminating candidates who might otherwise be qualified but for one characteristic. Some critics of term limits make precisely this argument: it should not be a law that requires politicians to leave office but the will of the voters as demonstrated by the election of another candidate. The same might be said of other requirements. For example, citizens might also be able to evaluate whether a candidate is mature enough to hold office even without a law that sets a minimum age. The implication is not that eligibility requirements are inherently unnecessary, but that imposing them tends to prioritize other values (such as competence or loyalty) over free choice.

The standard of deliberation is relevant here as well: any requirement that restricts the candidates who can run for office might degrade the quality of deliberation. With fewer candidates running, there is less information available to voters, especially information that might come from perspectives different from those offered by the two major parties. This is easiest to see when considering the plight of many independent candidates, particularly those not affiliated with the Democratic or Republican Party, who can face an uphill battle even to be listed on the ballot. Critics argue that ballot access laws deny voters the ability to consider these alternative candidates. Of course, some hurdle for ballot access may be necessary to prevent unserious candidates from appearing on the ballot. The question is how high that hurdle should be.

When Elections Are Held

At the federal level, the timing of elections is set by the Constitution. Elections for the House of Representatives are held every two years; for the Senate, every six years; for president, every four years. These terms in office vary in part because the framers of the Constitution envisioned a different kind of representation from each type of office. House members were meant to be in closer contact with the people, and shorter terms were meant to help ensure more frequent interaction. By contrast, senators were expected to be more insulated from public opinion and thus better able to deliberate about public policy. George Washington said that "we pour legislation into the senatorial saucer to cool it."[8] For all federal offices, the date of the general election is, by law, the first Tuesday after the first Monday in November.

States typically follow the same practices, with similar terms in office for legislators (typically two or four years) and governors (typically four years). They use the same November election date that was established by federal law in 1845. States vary in what year they elect governors—some hold gubernatorial elections during years with a presidential election, others during even-numbered years (without a presidential election), or, in Virginia and New Jersey, in every other odd-numbered year. Many local elections are not held concurrently with federal elections.

General elections are actually the second stage of the electoral process. Most candidates must first secure the support of their party. This is typically determined in a **primary election**, where candidates compete with others for their party's nomination for a particular office. States have a great deal of leeway in setting the date of their primary, although for the presidential nominations process (discussed further in Chapter 9), the parties pressure states to adhere to a particular calendar. Candidates in some states thus face an earlier primary than candidates in other states. Only after a primary election victory do candidates then compete in the general election.

Not every country has fixed election dates. In many parliamentary systems, there are only minimum requirements for when elections are held. For example, in Israel, they must be held at least every four years, but a majority of the legislature or the president can call for an election at any point. Once an election has been called, the candidates have roughly four weeks to campaign before Election Day. The incentive this creates is obvious: whenever possible, prime ministers prefer to call elections when their party is likely to win.

---

[8] U.S. Senate. "Senate Legislative Process." www.senate.gov/legislative/common/briefing/Senate_legislative_process.htm (accessed 9/20/2017).

The timing of American elections creates different incentives and powerfully affects candidate strategy, including when candidates can start campaigning for office. Because politicians and potential candidates at every level of office know when the next election is scheduled, they can begin preparing for it well in advance. This creates a campaign that is longer than campaigns in many other countries and that requires extraordinary effort from candidates. Presidential candidates often begin campaigning for the nomination years before the November general election. In preparation for the 2016 election, former Florida governor Jeb Bush announced on December 16, 2014, that he was exploring the possibility of running—more than a year before the first primary election and nearly two years before the November 2016 general election.

Politicians routinely express their dislike for this life. In 2016, then-Representative David Jolly (R-Fla.) told *CBS News* that the emphasis placed on fundraising is "beneath the dignity of the office that our voters in our communities entrust us to serve."[9] But most politicians appear unwilling to take chances on letting opponents get a jump on them. They raise money constantly. They travel to their states or districts nearly every week to interact with constituents. They conjure up creative ways to appear in the news media whenever possible.

What is good and bad about this **permanent campaign**? On the one hand, a permanent campaign may help improve the quality of deliberation in the campaign. The longer the candidates campaign, the more information citizens receive, because news coverage and advertising persists for weeks if not months before an election.[10] A permanent campaign can also improve the quality of representation, because such a campaign keeps politicians in constant contact with citizens and perhaps better aware of their needs and interests. Critics respond, however, that much of this effort is for naught. Citizens often do not pay much attention until the election is close at hand, and thus all of the early campaigning may be a waste of time and money. Candidates seem to agree: they intensify their campaigning as the election approaches.

A permanent campaign may also hurt the ideal of free choice by dissuading good candidates from running. Some talented people, faced with the

[9] Cyra Master. 2016. "*60 Minutes*: Fundraising Demands Turning Lawmakers into Telemarketers." *The Hill*, April 24. http://thehill.com/blogs/blog-briefing-room/news/277462 -60-minutes-fundraising-demands-turning-lawmakers-into (accessed 9/20/2017).

[10] Randolph T. Stevenson and Lynn Vavreck. 2000. "Does Campaign Length Matter? Testing for Cross-National Effects." *British Journal of Political Science* 30, 2: 217–35.

Jeb Bush announced that he was exploring the possibility of running for president in December 2014—nearly two years before the 2016 election.

prospect of endless fund-raising and nights away from home, will simply opt out. And for those who do run, campaigning takes time away from learning about policy or writing legislation. The permanent campaign may therefore detract from good governance. This is all the more true if the permanent campaign keeps politicians focused only on short-term electoral benefits even though the country's problems demand long-term solutions.

Where to Run

Where do candidates run for office? For some offices, such as president, senator, and governor, the boundaries of the constituency are easily determined and do not change. The president represents the country as a whole—although, as discussed in Chapter 9, candidates focus their campaigns on "battleground states." Senators, governors, and any other statewide office-holders represent their states. But for others, notably members of the House of Representatives and state legislatures, the answer to this question is more complicated.

Single-Member Districts

With a few exceptions, federal and state legislators are elected in **single-member districts**. That is, each state is subdivided into districts and each district is represented by one legislator. In a handful of states with small populations, such as Alaska and Wyoming, there are no subdivisions and the state is represented by one member of the U.S. House of Representatives. A system of single-member districts contrasts with a system in which each district is represented by multiple representatives. This is the case in **at-large elections**. For example, for elections to Maryland's House of Delegates, many of its 47 districts elect three representatives. Vermont's House of Representatives is composed of some districts represented by one state legislator and some represented by two legislators. Nevertheless, single-member districts are the norm.

Reapportionment

The number of U.S. House districts in each state is proportional to the state's population. The actual number of districts is determined by the process of **reapportionment**. After the decennial census, the total number of House seats stays the same, but the number of representatives in each state may be adjusted depending on changes in state populations.[11] For example, after the 2010 census, Georgia, South Carolina, Utah, Arizona, Nevada, and Washington each gained a seat in the House, Florida gained two seats, and Texas gained four seats. A number of states lost a seat—mainly Midwestern states such as Michigan, Illinois, Iowa, and Missouri—while New York and Ohio each lost two seats. Occasionally, reapportionment generates controversy. After the 1920 census, representatives from rural areas blocked reapportionment because they feared that it would shift power to rapidly expanding urban districts, with potential policy consequences such as the repeal of Prohibition.[12] In 2000, Utah came up 857 residents short of earning an additional seat, which went to North Carolina instead. Utah representatives were upset because the census did not count Utah residents who were traveling abroad as Mormon missionaries—even as the census counted military personnel living overseas, which advantaged states like North Carolina that are home to large military bases. In 2009, two Utah representatives introduced

---

[11] For additional detail on how this is done, see Brian J. Gaines and Jeffery A. Jenkins. 2009. "Apportionment Matters: Fair Representation in the U.S. House and Electoral College." *Perspectives on Politics* 7, 4: 849–57.

[12] Daniel Okrent. 2010. *Last Call: The Rise and Fall of Prohibition*. New York: Scribner.

legislation to require the census to count all Americans living overseas; as yet, no such requirement has been passed.

Redistricting

Far more controversial than deciding the number of seats is the process of drawing district boundaries, known as **redistricting**. Redistricting affects both state legislative and U.S. House district boundaries. As a state senator, Obama was involved in redistricting his state legislative seat. The fights over U.S. House district boundaries are usually more visible in the news media. In most states, both state and congressional district boundaries are drawn by the state legislature, often with the governor's approval required. Less frequently, states use independent commissions, although in some states the legislature picks the members of the commission, making it something less than independent and neutral between the parties.

Malapportionment and "One Person, One Vote" There are two major requirements that U.S. House and state legislative districts must fulfill. First, districts must have nearly equal numbers of residents. This prevents **malapportionment** and ensures that representatives each have essentially the same number of constituents. It was not always this way. Prior to a series of Supreme Court decisions in the 1960s, malapportionment was widespread in both congressional and state legislative districts. While urban areas had typically grown in population relative to rural areas, influential rural legislators had prevented the districts from being redrawn, leaving rural districts with far fewer constituents per representative. In the mid-twentieth century, rural areas held the majority of seats in state legislatures even though more than two-thirds of Americans lived in urban areas.[13]

The Court's dismantling of this system began in 1962 with the case *Baker v. Carr*.[14] In this case, the Court established that issues regarding reapportionment and redistricting were justiciable—meaning that the courts could intervene even though these issues had historically been the domain of legislatures. Without *Baker v. Carr*, subsequent decisions on questions of legislative districts would not have been possible.

The next important case was *Gray v. Sanders* (1963).[15] The case involved Georgia's "county unit" system of deciding the winner of primary elections.

---

[13] Stephen Ansolabehere and James M. Snyder, Jr. 2008. *The End of Inequality: One Person, One Vote and the Transformation of American Politics.* New York: W. W. Norton.

[14] 369 U.S. 186 (1962).

[15] 372 U.S. 368 (1963).

The candidate who won the majority of votes in each county unit was awarded that unit, and the candidate who won the most units was declared the victor. The problem was that the units were not equal in size, which sometimes led to bizarre outcomes. In 1946, for example, one winning candidate actually received 16,000 fewer votes than the loser, but won the vast majority of county units. In rejecting this system, the Court established the important principle of "**one person, one vote**." Because the Fourteenth Amendment (1868) guarantees equal protection under the law, states must have electoral systems in which each person's vote counts equally. Under the county unit system, the vote of a person in a sparsely populated county unit counted more than the vote of someone in a more populous unit.

The Court noted, however, that the Constitution allows deviations from this principle in two important cases. One is the U.S. Senate, which is famously malapportioned. As of 2016, California was estimated to have 39.2 million residents, or about 19.6 million for each of its two senators, while Wyoming had about 585,000 residents, or only about 292,500 residents for each senator. The other involves the Electoral College, which is the institution that formally elects the president. Each state is assigned a number of electors equal to its number of representatives and senators combined. The inclusion of senators in this tabulation makes the votes of the residents of less populous states count a bit more.

The establishment of the "one person, one vote" rule had implications for drawing district boundaries. First, these Court decisions made redistricting actually happen. Previously, many state legislatures simply failed to redistrict after the census even when their state constitution required it. As long as redistricting was left entirely up to the state legislatures, there was no means of forcing them to do it, and naturally the parties in power that were advantaged by existing arrangements were reluctant to do so. Second, the Court's decisions mandated that districts had to be roughly equivalent in population. In two 1964 cases, *Wesberry v. Sanders* and *Reynolds v. Sims*, the Court invalidated Georgia's congressional districts and Alabama's state legislative districts, respectively, because both states' districts were drawn so that they had dramatically different populations.[16] Subsequent Court decisions have established a strict standard of equivalence: today, even small deviations among U.S. House districts might be held unconstitutional, while greater leeway is given to deviations among state legislative districts.[17] A 2016 Court decision held that states could use total population, not just the total

---

[16] *Wesberry v. Sanders*, 376 U.S. 1 (1964); *Reynolds v. Sims*, 377 U.S. 533 (1964).

[17] See *Cox v. Larios*, 542 U.S. 947 (2004).

number of eligible voters, to calculate population sizes.[18] Using only eligible voters would tend to disadvantage districts with larger ineligible populations, such as immigrants who are not naturalized citizens. This would weaken the voting power of Latinos, for example.[19]

The "one person, one vote" rule transformed American elections, legislatures, and public policy. As Stephen Ansolabehere and James Snyder write in their history of this rule, "The American states began in the 1960s as the most unequal representative bodies in the world, and they finished the decade adhering to one of the strictest standards of equal representation."[20] Although it did not eliminate the ability of self-interested politicians to influence legislative district boundaries—see the discussion of gerrymandering later in this chapter—the application of the rule did produce state legislatures that were much more representative of state populations in their partisan and ideological complexion. It also led to a more equitable distribution of government spending within states. Equal votes really did result in more equal power.

Racial Minorities and Voting Rights The second requirement for congressional districts involves racial minorities. After Reconstruction, southern states took various steps to weaken the voting power of African Americans. One way was to draw political boundaries to exclude black voters. In 1960, the Supreme Court took a step toward prohibiting this practice, arguing that a redrawing of the Tuskegee, Alabama, city boundaries to exclude most black voters violated the Fifteenth Amendment (which gave the right to vote to citizens regardless of race).[21] Another strategy was to dilute the voting power of blacks by placing a small number of blacks into each legislative district, thereby limiting their ability to elect a candidate reflecting their background and preferences.

Five years later Congress passed the **Voting Rights Act of 1965 (VRA)**, which sought to address voting laws that discriminated against African Americans. The VRA singled out "covered" jurisdictions, that is, specific states and counties with a history of persistent discrimination, including virtually every county in several southern states. The law forbade these counties from

---

[18] *Evenwel v. Abbott*, 136 S. Ct. 1120 (2016).

[19] Drew DeSilver. 2015. "Supreme Court Could Reshape Voting Districts, with Big Impact on Hispanics." Pew Research Center. http://www.pewresearch.org/fact-tank/2015/12/10/supreme-court-could-reshape-voting-districts-with-big-impact-on-hispanics/ (accessed 9/20/2017).

[20] Ansolabehere and Snyder, *The End of Inequality*, pp. 187–88.

[21] *Gomillion v. Lightfoot*, 364 U.S. 339 (1960).

instituting changes that made African American voters worse off and, to ensure that these counties adhered to the law, they had to submit any change in voting procedures or electoral laws to the Department of Justice for "preclearance." Only after the Department of Justice signed off on the change could it be implemented. After 1965, the VRA was expanded in several ways. In 1975, it was expanded to protect not only blacks but also Native Americans, Asian Americans, and Hispanics. In 1982, amendments to the VRA established an even stricter standard: the voting power of minorities could not be weakened even as an unintentional by-product of some other action. It was no longer necessary to prove that discrimination was the intentional goal.

Over time, the VRA has been interpreted to apply to the redistricting process. How would we know if district boundaries dilute the voting power of minorities, based on the standards in the amended VRA? The Supreme Court took up this question in *Thornburg v. Gingles* (1986).[22] A group of African Americans claimed that the redistricting plan passed by the North Carolina General Assembly would have prevented blacks from electing representatives of their choosing. The Court ruled in favor of the plaintiffs, and in so doing established three criteria for demonstrating that district boundaries dilute minority voting power. First, the minority must be both sufficiently large and geographically concentrated to comprise a majority in a single district. Second, the minority must be politically cohesive, meaning that members tend to have similar political preferences. Third, racially polarized voting, wherein the majority typically votes as a bloc for a candidate other than the one the minority prefers, must be present. Plaintiffs must prove that these three conditions are met and then show that a proposed redistricting scheme would diminish the ability of minorities to elect a candidate of their choosing. The decision has been interpreted as a broad endorsement of the VRA as amended in 1982.[23]

In 2013, however, the Supreme Court struck down the part of the VRA that defined which states and counties were "covered."[24] A narrow majority of the Court argued that the definition according to the law, which was based on data from the 1960s and early 1970s, was no longer valid. The majority argued that the formula was "based on 40-year-old facts having no logical relation to the present day." Although the Court left intact the provision that

---

[22] 478 U.S. 30 (1986).

[23] See T. Alexander Aleinikoff and Samuel Issacharoff. 1993. "Race and Redistricting: Drawing Constitutional Lines after *Shaw v. Reno*." *Michigan Law Review* 92, 3: 588–651.

[24] *Shelby County v. Holder*, 570 U.S. ___ (2013).

states and counties must seek preclearance, there is currently no way to enforce preclearance if there is no formula to define which states and counties must seek it. Congress would have to pass legislation that establishes a new formula and, to date, it has not done so.

But there are other ways that the federal government can use the VRA to ensure that redistricting does not dilute the voting power of minorities. Because the VRA prohibits discriminatory voting laws, the Department of Justice, among others, could bring suit against a state if it believed the state's redistricting plan would hurt minorities. In 2017, for example, one such suit led federal judges to rule that the Texas congressional map, drawn in 2011, discriminated against minorities.[25]

Besides "one person, one vote" and the constraints on diluting minority voting power, there is little else in federal law that formally constrains the drawing of district boundaries. Districts are often drawn to be relatively compact and also contiguous. *Contiguity* means that a district is not composed of "islands" of territory within a state, as would be the case for a district that was made up of a couple neighborhoods in San Francisco, a couple in Los Angeles, and nothing in between. Districts are also often drawn to correspond to **communities of interest**, such as existing towns or cities. These guidelines are not codified as formal rules at the federal level, but some states require that districts respect community boundaries.

Gerrymandering Without more explicit rules, the people in charge of drawing district boundaries can engage in **gerrymandering** (with the resulting set of districts constituting a "gerrymander"). Gerrymandering is the deliberate manipulation of district boundaries for some political purpose, and often results in oddly shaped districts. The term was coined in response to a redistricting plan implemented under Massachusetts governor Elbridge Gerry in 1812 that included a district thought by some to resemble a salamander. "Elbridge Gerry's salamander" begat "gerrymander."

Gerrymandering can serve multiple aims. It can protect incumbents by ensuring that their districts are populated with voters likely to support them. Alternatively, the party in control of the redistricting can try to maximize the number of seats it can win. To do so, it may "pack" voters from the opposite party into as few districts as possible. It may "crack" apart an existing district where the opposite party has been dominant, forcing that district's

---

[25] Alexa Ura and Jim Malewitz. 2017. "Federal Court Invalidates Part of Texas Congressional Map." *Texas Tribune*, August 15. https://www.texastribune.org/2017/08/15/federal-court-invalidates-part-texas-congressional-map (accessed 8/24/2017).

incumbent into a new district with many constituents who do not know him or her. "Hijacking" forces two incumbents from the opposite party to compete against each other. Much about gerrymandering seems objectionable on its face, but the Supreme Court has let many gerrymanders stand.

Gerrymandering can also create districts that maximize the number of voters who are racial minorities, thereby helping to ensure the election of representatives who are racial minorities themselves. Districts in which racial minority voters make up the majority of voters are sometimes called **majority-minority districts**, and the VRA has been read to require these districts in some cases, to ensure that the voting power of minorities is adequately protected. However, the Court has raised objections to some redistricting plans geared toward empowering African Americans under the auspices of the VRA. The most famous case was a North Carolina plan that included a district (the 12th District) some 160 miles long, which was drawn to include black communities in several different cities and was sometimes scarcely any wider than the interstate highway that connected these cities (see Figure 2.1). In *Shaw v. Reno* (1993),[26] the Court's majority described this district as "highly irregular," expressed considerable discomfort with racial gerrymanders in general, and argued that they were subject to the Court's highest standard of review, known as "strict scrutiny," because they could in theory violate the Fourteenth Amendment's equal protection clause. This district was then subject to years of court battles, including three further Supreme Court cases, as well as much tinkering with its boundaries.[27] Ultimately, the Supreme Court upheld the district only after North Carolina successfully argued that its boundaries reflected a political goal—to create a safe Democratic seat—rather than a racial goal.

More recently, Court majorities have raised a similar concern about some state legislative and congressional district maps, including, once again, in North Carolina as well as in Alabama and Virginia.[28] These cases involved maps drawn by Republicans, and plaintiffs in these cases argued that Republicans had diluted the voting power of minorities—not by spreading them out across districts, but by packing minority voters into a small number of districts. These cases do not mean that states cannot take race into account when

---

[26] 509 U.S. 630 (1993).

[27] Those decisions were *Shaw v. Hunt*, 517 U.S. 899 (1996), *Hunt v. Cromartie*, 526 U.S. 541 (1999), and *Easley v. Cromartie*, 532 U.S. 234 (2001); the latter is sometimes also called *Hunt v. Cromartie* (2001).

[28] The North Carolina case is *Cooper v. Harris*, 581 U.S. ___ (2017). The Alabama case is *Alabama Black Legislative Caucus v. Alabama*, 575 U.S. ___ (2015). The Virginia case is *Bethune-Hill v. Virginia State Board of Elections*, 580 U.S. ___ (2017).

FIGURE 2.1 North Carolina's 12th Congressional District, 1992–98

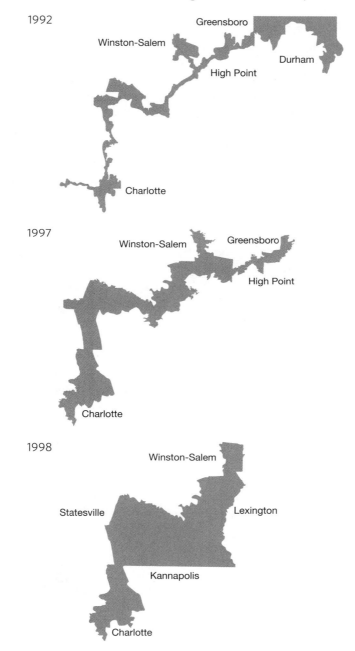

Source: National Conference of State Legislatures. "North Carolina Redistricting Cases: The 1990s." www.senate.leg.state.mn.us/departments/scr/redist/redsum/NCSUM.HTM (accessed 9/20/2017).

drawing districts, but they have forced states that draw such districts to justify them on different, and more demanding, terms. It is also worth noting that in many of these cases, the Court was narrowly divided, signaling that there were sharp disagreements among the justices on racial gerrymandering.

The Court's concern about racial gerrymandering has not extended to other forms of gerrymandering. In 1973, the Court upheld a Connecticut plan that created separate Democratic and Republican strongholds and thereby provided considerable protection for incumbents.[29] The Court saw benefits in the plan because it provided a legislative body that mirrored the partisan composition of Connecticut voters. Subsequent decisions confirmed that incumbent protection was not necessarily problematic in the view of the Court.[30]

The Court has also yet to declare partisan gerrymanders unconstitutional. The Court has confirmed that the questions raised by partisan gerrymanders are justifiably the domain of the courts under the Fourteenth Amendment's equal protection clause,[31] but in that case and in later cases, it has not sought to define or apply a standard by which partisan gerrymanders could be evaluated. This was evident in a 2004 case in which the Court considered, but did not invalidate, a Pennsylvania partisan gerrymander.[32] However, in that case several justices indicated the need for such a standard, and a more recent case from Wisconsin that has made its way to the Court argues for it. The case, *Gill v. Whitford*, again involves a Republican-drawn map, which the plaintiffs contend is an unconstitutional gerrymander that violates the Fourteenth Amendment's guarantee of equal protection. Part of the plaintiffs' argument is based on a measure developed by two scholars that attempts to capture how much a redistricting plan advantages one party.[33] The question is whether a majority of the Court will agree that this or some other measure constitutes a defensible standard, and that the Wisconsin plan violates this standard.

Reapportionment and especially redistricting constrain political candidates in an important way: candidates have only limited control over who their constituents are. Their input is limited by the timing of redistricting,

---

[29] *Gaffney v. Cummings*, 412 U.S. 735 (1973).

[30] See Nathaniel Persily. 2006. "The Place of Competition in American Election Law," in *The Marketplace of Democracy: Electoral Competition and American Politics*, eds. Michael P. McDonald and John Samples. Washington, DC: Brookings Institution Press, pp. 171–95.

[31] *Davis v. Bandemer*, 478 U.S. 109 (1986).

[32] *Vieth v. Jubelirer*, 541 U.S. 267 (2004).

[33] Nicholas O. Stephanopoulos and Eric M. McGhee. 2015. "Partisan Gerrymandering and the Efficiency Gap." *University of Chicago Law Review* 82, 2: 831–900.

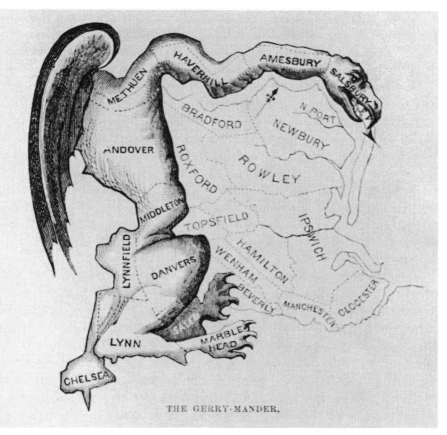

THE GERRY-MANDER.

The term *gerrymander* comes from a strangely shaped district designed under Governor Elbridge Gerry in Massachusetts in 1812. Gerry's goal—and the goal of many gerrymanders since—was to give an electoral advantage to partisan allies. However, gerrymanders may also have other purposes.

which occurs only every 10 years following the census. The 10-year cycle is not set by law. In 2003, the Republicans in the Texas state legislature initiated a new round of redistricting for Texas's U.S. House districts, taking advantage of the fact that Republicans had won control of the legislature in 2002. The resulting plan shifted the Texas congressional delegation from 17 Democrats and 15 Republicans in 2002 to 11 Democrats and 21 Republicans after the 2004 elections. But this example is the exception rather than the rule, and most states adhere to the norm of redistricting after the decennial census. Moreover, candidates may be constrained by the process by which district boundaries are drawn. In those states where the state legislature decides on the district boundaries, politicians in the minority party may have little if any input. Constituencies are thus somewhat fixed and constitute part of the reality that candidates must face.

How does limited control over their constituency affect candidate strategy? In some cases it may forestall a candidate's political career: in a district strongly skewed toward one party, a candidate of the opposite party is unlikely to win and, perhaps, to run for office in the first place. At the same time, a particular redistricting cycle may endanger or even end the career of someone already in office, particularly if district boundaries change dramatically and the incumbent must confront large numbers of new constituents who are not supporters. Campaign messages also reflect the realities of district boundaries and constituent demographics. The issues that candidates emphasize, the groups they target, and actions they take if elected to office all reflect the nature of their constituency.

The redistricting process and the prevalence of gerrymandering raise philosophical questions as well. Gerrymandering can limit the competitiveness of legislative elections and instead favor an incumbent legislator or a particular party, leaving opposing candidates or parties on very unequal footing. Their underdog status makes it difficult for opposing candidates to raise money and effectively advertise their candidacy. The resulting election may fall short of the ideals of both free choice and deliberation. Although voters are not being coerced into making a choice, their choices may be limited because gerrymandering makes it difficult for certain candidates to run. In such cases, citizens receive less information than they would if the election were competitive, and thus find it harder to deliberate about the candidates' relative merits. Critics also argue that, in noncompetitive gerrymandered districts where one party dominates, the favored party's candidates will cater only to that party's base once elected, becoming more ideologically extreme and further polarizing the parties in the state legislature or Congress.

At the same time, gerrymandered districts may actually make elections more representative. Districts drawn to guarantee that a particular party wins usually have a large majority of voters from that party. Most voters in that large majority will typically feel well represented by their representative. Compare that with a district where voters are divided 51 to 49 percent between the two major parties. If the majority always wins with 51 percent of the vote, a much larger fraction of voters than in the gerrymandered district—possibly even 49 percent—will feel poorly represented. Partisan loyalties are not the only relevant loyalties either. Gerrymandered districts can also give racial minorities a chance to elect the representative of their

The Technology behind Redistricting

The process of redistricting involves precise decisions about where to draw district boundaries. No matter whether the goal is to promote competition, protect incumbents, or favor a political party's candidates, the architects of the new map scrutinize neighborhoods down to the city block and street—looking for any potentially favorable adjustment. How do they do this?

Years ago, the process of redistricting could be extraordinarily labor-intensive. It involved teams of people poring over paper maps, often with calculators in hand to tabulate past voting results and figure out the partisan complexion of particular areas. District boundaries would be sketched in different-colored markers. Contemporary redistricting, however, draws heavily on electronic geographic information systems (or GIS). GIS programs can store data about geographical units, allowing users to draw new boundaries with clicks of the mouse. These systems first became prominent in the 1991 redistricting, when all but four states used GIS in their congressional or state legislative redistricting.[1] Some states also relied on consulting firms that could provide specialized expertise in GIS.

By the next round of redistricting, in 2001, there had been further innovations. Computers were more powerful and redistricting software was widely available. Essentially, anyone with a laptop could purchase this software, download geographical data from the U.S. Census Bureau or a state government agency, and draw their own district boundaries. Some software packages will automatically draw district boundaries based on a particular criterion—making the process even easier. It is more difficult, however, for software to take account of all relevant criteria—such as the need to make districts that have equal populations, are somewhat compact, abide by the Voting Rights Act, and so on. Thus, participants in the redistricting process—such as state legislators—must do more than simply approve the district boundaries the software has produced.

Computer software remains an imperfect tool, and its increasing prominence has troubled some observers. They fear that because politicians can rely on more precise data and more powerful computing, they can draw even better gerrymanders. For example, in his dissenting opinion in the *Vieth v. Jubelirer* (2004) decision, Supreme Court justice David Souter cited concerns about the use of technology in redistricting and wrote, "[T]he increasing efficiency of partisan redistricting has damaged the democratic process to a degree that our predecessors only began to imagine."

At the same time, there are limitations on what computers can do. Moreover, many controversial gerrymanders—including Elbridge Gerry's original in 1812—preceded the development of computers. If politicians want to create oddly shaped districts, they probably do not need a computer to do so. In fact, the widespread availability of redistricting software actually allows people besides politicians—including interest groups and citizens—to try their hand at redistricting. If you are interested, see the Public Mapping Project at publicmapping.org.

---

[1] Micah Altman, Karin Mac Donald, and Michael McDonald. 2005. "From Crayons to Computers: The Evolution of Computer Use in Redistricting." *Social Science Computer Review* 23, 3: 334–46.

choice. None of this means that competitiveness is unimportant or undesirable, simply that it must be balanced against alternative considerations.

Concerns about redistricting's effects on competition and polarization have led a number of states to reform their redistricting process—for example, by placing responsibility with an independent commission rather than the state legislature and by instituting more detailed rules about how districts can be drawn. Washington State, for instance, requires that its commission exercise its powers "to provide fair and effective representation and to encourage electoral competition." In 2015, the Supreme Court strengthened the institution of independent redistricting commissions by ruling that citizens could take away redistricting power from legislators and give it to a commission (as had happened in Arizona via initiative).[34] There is evidence that redistricting processes that involve courts and commissions produce a larger number of competitive districts than processes involving only the state legislature.[35]

At the same time, even as redistricting often advantages the party that controls the process, political science research suggests that its effects are not always as large as critics suggest. It does not necessarily advantage incumbents, reduce competitiveness, or exacerbate political polarization.[36] Furthermore, there are limits to how much redistricting reforms can increase competition. In some areas of the country, preexisting residential segregation naturally produces politically homogeneous communities. It would be difficult, for example, to carve out a Republican congressional district in Berkeley, California—unless one were willing to draw some pretty contorted salamanders.

---

[34] *Arizona State Legislature v. Arizona Independent Redistricting Commission*, 576 U.S. ___ (2015).

[35] Jamie L. Carson, Michael H. Crespin, and Ryan D. Williamson. 2014. "Reevaluating the Effects of Redistricting on Electoral Competition, 1972–2012." *State Politics and Policy Quarterly* 14, 2: 165–77.

[36] The evidence regarding the incumbency advantage and polarization is fairly clear. There is more debate about the effects of redistricting on competitiveness. See Alan I. Abramowitz, Brad Alexander, and Matthew Gunning. 2006. "Incumbency, Redistricting, and the Decline of Competition in U.S. House Elections." *Journal of Politics* 68, 1: 75–88; John N. Friedman and Richard T. Holden. 2009. "The Rising Incumbent Reelection Rate: What's Gerrymandering Got to Do with It?" *Journal of Politics* 71, 2: 593–611; Andrew Gelman and Gary King. 1994. "Enhancing Democracy through Legislative Redistricting." *American Political Science Review* 88, 3: 541–59; Michael P. McDonald. 2006. "Drawing the Line on District Competition." *PS: Political Science and Politics* 39, 1: 91–4; Nolan McCarty, Keith T. Poole, and Howard Rosenthal. 2009. "Does Gerrymandering Cause Polarization?" *American Journal of Political Science* 53, 3: 666–80.

Who Can Vote

Electoral rules affect not only candidates but also citizens, particularly their eligibility to vote. The qualifications for voting have changed a great deal throughout American history. Early restrictions based on race were invalidated by the Fifteenth Amendment (1870) and, perhaps more consequentially, by the Voting Rights Act of 1965. Restrictions based on sex were invalidated by the Nineteenth Amendment (1920). Restrictions based on wealth were invalidated by the Twenty-fourth Amendment (1964), which banned **poll taxes**—fees that one had to pay in order to vote—that were used to disenfranchise black voters in the South. Restrictions based on level of education were invalidated by the VRA, which banned the use of **literacy tests**—another way by which southern blacks were disenfranchised. Restrictions based on age were relaxed by the Twenty-sixth Amendment (1971), which lowered the voting age from 21 to 18. These reforms dramatically expanded the size of the American electorate.

Two remaining restrictions are in place nationwide: the minimum voting age of 18 and the requirement that eligible voters be native or naturalized citizens. Other restrictions vary across states. States differ in how they treat criminals and the mentally ill. Although nearly every state bans convicted

Poll taxes, like this one required in Texas in 1939, limit who can vote. Laws that require the payment of poll taxes were invalidated by the Voting Rights Act of 1965.

felons from voting while in prison—only Maine and Vermont permit inmates to vote—states differ in whether they allow convicted felons to vote while on parole or probation. They also differ in whether they deny convicted felons the right to vote after their sentence is served and in the process by which felons can regain the right to vote.[37] These laws have become increasingly consequential as the number of convicted felons has grown over time. State laws about the mentally ill are similarly wide-ranging, although it is not clear how often any restrictions related to voting by the mentally ill are actually enforced.

States also differ in whether they require citizens to register as a member of a political party in order to participate in primary elections. In a **closed primary**, only citizens registered with the party can vote in that party's primary. For example, New York's presidential primary is closed. This meant that two of Donald Trump's children, Eric and Ivanka, were unable to vote in the 2016 primary because they were registered as unaffiliated with a party and did not change their party registration by the state's deadline for doing so before the election. In a **semi-closed primary**, both unaffiliated voters and those registered as members of the party can vote in that party's primary. In an **open primary**, all voters can vote in either party's primary, but not both. In a **blanket (or jungle) primary**, there is a single ballot with the candidates for each party listed, and citizens can mix and match, voting for a Democratic nominee for senator, a Republican candidate for governor, and so on. This form of primary was invalidated by the Supreme Court in 2000[38] on the grounds that it violated the parties' First Amendment right of association: a party's nominee could be chosen in part by people who do not affiliate with that party and who even actively oppose it. The blanket primary survives only in a nonpartisan form. For example, in Louisiana, all candidates are listed on the ballot, and if a candidate wins 50 percent of the vote, he or she is elected to that office after the first round of balloting. If no candidate wins 50 percent of the vote, the top two vote-getters for any office go on to the general election, regardless of their party affiliation. In Washington and California, the same ballot structure is used, but there is no possibility of winning the election outright at the primary stage. The top two vote-getters go on to the general election no matter how much of the vote the front-runner received.

---

[37] The Sentencing Project. 2010. "State-Level Estimates of Felon Disenfranchisement in the United States, 2010." http://sentencingproject.org/doc/publications/fd_Felony%20Disenfranchisement%20Laws%20in%20the%20US.pdf (accessed 9/20/2017).

[38] *California Democratic Party v. Jones*, 530 U.S. 567 (2000).

Restrictions on who may vote are enforced via a system of voter registration. In every state except North Dakota, citizens must register to vote and provide evidence that they meet certain criteria. Among the states that require registration, laws differ about when citizens must register in order to be eligible to vote—ranging from 30 days prior to the election to the day of the election itself. Fourteen states as well as the District of Columbia have implemented **same-day (or Election Day) registration**.[39] Thirty-four states have passed voter identification laws that require citizens to present some form of identification before voting.[40] These laws differ in what forms of identification are acceptable and in the procedures that voters must follow if they show up to vote but do not have one of the required forms of identification.

All of these requirements have an impact on campaign strategy by affecting the number of citizens who actually vote. The more onerous the requirements, the more likely it is that some eligible citizens cannot or will not register to vote or turn out on Election Day.[41] For example, in 2012, voter turnout in states that did not have Election Day registration was, on average, 10 points lower than in states with Election Day registration, although there is some debate about how much of that gap was actually caused by other factors.[42] Less clear, however, is whether voter identification laws actually reduce turnout. There is no solid evidence, as yet, that this is the case.[43]

Some countries, such as Brazil and Australia, make voting compulsory. The American system instead leaves the responsibility up to citizens, and many eligible citizens choose not to vote. This leads to a second consequence for campaign strategy, one that reflects both an opportunity for and a burden on

---

[39] National Conference of State Legislatures. 2015. "Same Day Voter Registration." www.ncsl.org/research/elections-and-campaigns/same-day-registration.aspx (accessed 8/7/2017). This does not include Maryland or North Carolina, who allow same-day registration only during the early voting period, not on Election Day itself.

[40] National Conference of State Legislatures. 2014. "Voter Identification Requirements." www.ncsl.org/research/elections-and-campaigns/voter-id.aspx (accessed 9/20/2017).

[41] See Raymond E. Wolfinger and Steven J. Rosenstone. 1980. *Who Votes?* New Haven, CT: Yale University Press.

[42] Demos. "What Is Same Day Registration? Where Is It Available?" www.demos.org/publication/what-same-day-registration-where-it-available (accessed 10/5/2017). See also Craig Leonard Brians and Bernard Grofman. 2001. "Election Day Registration's Effect on U.S. Voter Turnout." *Social Science Quarterly* 82, 1: 170–83; Michael Hanmer. 2009. *Discount Voting.* Cambridge: Cambridge University Press.

[43] See, for example, Robert S. Erikson and Lorraine C. Minnite. 2009. "Modeling Problems in the Voter Identification–Voter Turnout Debate." *Election Law Journal* 8, 2: 85–101; Justin Grimmer, Eitan Hersh, Marc Meredith, Jonathan Mummolo, and Clayton Nall. 2017. "Comment on 'Voter Identification Laws and the Suppression of Minority Voters.'" Working Paper. http://stanford.edu/~jgrimmer/comment_final.pdf (accessed 8/7/2017).

candidates and parties. They have the opportunity to mobilize citizens to vote, including some who perhaps otherwise would not have participated. Successful mobilization can help a candidate win, but mobilization efforts demand time, energy, and money that may also burden a campaign.

Rules about voter registration affect campaign strategy in a third way: by affecting the types of citizens who are eligible or likely to vote. For example, some research suggests that making it easier for felons to vote helps Democratic candidates—in part, because felons and ex-felons are disproportionately African American, they are more likely to vote Democratic than the population as a whole.[44] Election Day registration, too, seems to encourage the participation of two groups, young people and nonwhites, who are more likely to vote Democratic than Republican.[45]

Candidates and parties naturally tend to resist reforms that they fear will increase voter turnout among members of the opposite party. That said, most such reforms would not necessarily lead to a vastly different political landscape. The predicted changes in turnout among particular demographic groups due to proposed reforms are not always large. Moreover, many elections are won by such large margins that changes in turnout would probably not affect the outcome.[46] Predicting the effects of election reforms is fraught with uncertainty, and this uncertainty, along with concerns about adverse effects on their own and their party's electoral prospects, makes politicians wary of reform.

Perhaps the primary value considered throughout the history of voting rights has been political equality. Much of the battle for voting rights, particularly for women and African Americans, was about changing laws that denied these rights to a particular group. As noted in Chapter 1, ongoing

---

[44] Jeff Manza and Christopher Uggen. 2004. "Punishment and Democracy: Disenfranchisement of Nonincarcerated Felons in the United States." *Perspectives on Politics* 2, 3: 491–505.

[45] R. Michael Alvarez, Stephen Ansolabehere, and Catherine H. Wilson. 2008. "Election Day Registration in the United States: How One-Step Voting Can Change the Composition of the American Electorate." Caltech/MIT Voting Technology Project Working Paper. http://vote.caltech.edu/working-papers/5 (accessed 9/20/2017); Stephen Knack and James White. 2000. "Election-Day Registration and Turnout Inequality." *Political Behavior* 22, 1: 29–44. However, the introduction of Election Day registration in Wisconsin appeared to help Republicans more than Democrats: Jacob R. Neiheisel and Barry C. Burden. 2012. "The Impact of Election Day Registration on Voter Turnout and Election Outcomes." *American Politics Research* 40, 4: 636–64.

[46] Jack Citrin, Eric Schickler, and John Sides. 2003. "What If Everyone Voted? Simulating the Impact of Increased Turnout in Senate Elections." *American Journal of Political Science* 47, 1: 75–90.

debates about voting rights still concern political equality. Conflicts over voter identification laws are a good example, because certain groups—particularly racial and ethnic minorities as well as the youngest and oldest eligible voters—are less likely to have the forms of identification that these laws typically require.[47] Recently, federal courts have thrown out voter identification laws in Texas and North Carolina, arguing that these laws were written intentionally to discriminate against racial minorities—a direct violation of the VRA.

A second relevant value is the level of participation. For many people, "good" elections are ones in which large percentages of eligible citizens vote—and, in their view, turnout in the United States is too low. If so, then rules about voter qualifications should be structured to ensure that as many people as possible can and will participate. Compulsory voting would even be a reasonable step, from this perspective.

But maximizing equality and participation may not be the only relevant goals. It may be justifiable to limit participation, even if those limits fall disproportionately on certain groups. Restrictions with regard to age and mental illness imply a concern about competence; very young people or people who are mentally ill are assumed, correctly or incorrectly, unable or unready to vote. Requiring citizenship implies a concern about loyalty; the people choosing a country's leaders should be "members" of that country themselves. Disenfranchising felons reflects the belief that the right to vote depends on a willingness to obey the law. Requiring party registration for a primary election reflects a belief that a party's candidates should be chosen by voters loyal to that party. Requiring voters to register ahead of the election, or to provide identification on Election Day, is intended to prevent such fraud as impersonating another voter or attempting to vote more than once. All of these rationales can be critiqued. For example, cases of voter fraud are exceedingly rare.[48] The broader point is that electoral rules are geared not simply toward promoting strict equality before the law or encouraging citizens to participate; they are intended to further other goals as well.

---

[47] See Matt A. Barreto, Stephen A. Nuño, and Gabriel R. Sanchez. 2009. "The Disproportionate Impact of Voter-ID Requirements on the Electorate—New Evidence from Indiana." *PS: Political Science and Politics* 42, 1: 111–16.

[48] Justin Levitt. 2007. "The Truth about Voter Fraud." Brennan Center for Justice at New York University School of Law. www.brennancenter.org/publication/truth-about-voter-fraud (accessed 9/20/2017).

Who Wins

Once candidates have campaigned and citizens have voted, a crucial question arises: How are votes counted to determine a winner (or winners)? In the United States, most elections adhere to a simple winner-take-all or "first past the post" principle. Typically, the person with the most votes (a plurality of votes) wins the election. For example, in order for a presidential candidate to win a state and therefore receive all of that state's Electoral College votes, the candidate need only win more votes than any other candidate in that state. (We'll discuss the implications and consequences of the Electoral College, in particular, in Chapter 9.) A plurality is not necessarily a majority, or more than half of the votes. **Plurality rule** is more common than majority rule in American elections, although some states do have rules in place for certain offices to ensure that the winning candidate is elected by a majority. This often entails a runoff election between the top two vote-getters, as in the Louisiana system discussed earlier.

The American system of plurality rule in single-member districts differs from that of many other democracies. A helpful contrast involves those countries whose legislatures are chosen by **proportional representation**, such as Israel (see Box 2.1). In these systems, seats are allocated to parties in proportion to the percentage of the vote they received overall. A party that wins 20 percent of the vote can expect to receive 20 percent of the seats, although many countries have a threshold such that a party must win at least some minimum percentage of the vote to gain any seats. To achieve proportionality, these systems often do not have single-member districts but either nationwide elections or districts with multiple winners. Voters vote for a slate of candidates chosen by the party, rather than for an individual candidate nominated via a primary election. To be sure, proportional systems differ from each other in their specific rules, and some countries combine features of both kinds of systems. But this general description highlights the major points of contrast between these systems and the American system.

A candidate competing in a plurality election must get the most votes; second place, even by a margin of only one vote, gives the loser nothing. One implication of this was spelled out by the French political scientist Maurice Duverger, in what became known as **Duverger's Law**: in a system with single-member districts and plurality voting, there is a strong tendency for only two parties to emerge, and candidates not affiliated with either of those parties face serious obstacles. This is because in an election with more than two candidates, voters in a plurality system often engage in **strategic voting**—voting for a candidate who is not their first choice but has a better chance of winning. Some supporters of independent candidates or candidates from minor parties do not want to "waste" their vote on a candidate who has little chance of winning a seat, so they end up defecting to whichever of two major-party candidates they like better (or dislike less). Third-party or independent candidates typically fare poorly. Duverger's Law helps explain why the American party system is characterized by long periods of two-party dominance. By contrast, in a system that uses proportional representation, candidates from smaller parties may still win some seats, even if they have no chance of winning the most votes, so their supporters are less likely to defect.

The use of plurality rather than proportional rules in the United States gives candidates a strong incentive to affiliate with a major party. It also gives parties and candidates the incentive to invest significant effort only in competitive races. For example, political parties raise money that they can then spend on behalf of any of their candidates. Where is that money best spent?

BOX 2.1

Proportional Representation in Israel

Unlike election to the U.S. Congress, election to the federal legislature in Israel, called the *Knesset*, relies on a system of proportional representation. A brief overview of this system provides some useful contrasts with the American system.

First, the Israeli system does not have districts. Representatives to the Knesset are elected in nationwide elections and do not represent any specific districts.

Second, voters in Israel vote for party lists, not for individual candidates. Party leaders compose these lists, as opposed to having voters nominate candidates via primary elections. The order of candidates on the party list determines who ultimately gets a seat. If a party wins only one seat, then the first person on that party's list joins the Knesset.

Third, parties are given seats in the Knesset in proportion to the number of votes they receive, with one stipulation: to be given any seats, the party must receive at least 2 percent of the vote. This relatively low threshold is quite favorable to small parties. In the Israeli election in 2015, 10 different parties won seats in the legislature. As an example of how proportional the allocations of seats are, consider the top vote-getter, the Likud Party: it received 23.4 percent of the votes and 25 percent of the seats (30 out of 120). In the 2016 U.S. House elections, Republican candidates received 50.6 percent of the major-party vote nationwide, but controlled 55.4 percent of seats (241 out of 435).

In an uncompetitive district where it might help the party's candidate win, say, 30 percent of the vote instead of 15 percent? Probably not. In a winner-take-all election, 30 percent of the vote earns nothing more than 15 percent. Instead, parties will target more competitive districts where this money might make the difference between winning and losing. The same logic applies to presidential candidates, given the winner-take-all nature of the Electoral College. It makes little sense for candidates to campaign in states where they are virtually guaranteed to win or to lose. They go instead to the "battleground" states where the outcome is in doubt and additional campaign dollars may make the difference.

The dominance of the two major parties is one criticism of the American system and is frequently cited by reformers as a reason for favoring a system of proportional representation instead. Proportional representation, the argument goes, enhances free choice by providing more options for voters. These increased options may also enhance the deliberative potential of elections, as a wider range of issues and policy proposals is likely to be discussed by candidates from different parties. Fewer votes are "wasted" because more citizens are encouraged to select their first choice. In particular, minorities—whether political, racial, or otherwise—may find it easier to elect representatives of their choice under a proportional system. Some supporters also argue that citizens may be more likely to vote if more options are available that truly represent their preferences, although there is not much evidence that turnout is higher in proportional systems.[49]

On the other hand, proportional representation is sometimes criticized for promoting a multiparty system that often results in elections lacking a clear winner. In a proportional system, it is common for no one party to win a majority of seats in the legislature. Then two or more parties must form a coalition to achieve a majority and govern the country. Critics argue that negotiations among parties may produce coalitions that voters did not anticipate or intend. To take a hypothetical example, imagine that a country had three parties, Left, Right, and Center, and none got the majority of the vote. It turns out that most voters of the Center Party prefer the Left Party to the Right Party. But after the election, Center and Right form a coalition. Is this what Center Party voters want? If they had known that this coalition would result, might they have voted for the Left Party instead?

---

[49] André Blais. 2007. "Turnout in Elections," in *The Oxford Handbook of Political Behavior*, eds. Russell J. Dalton and Hans-Dieter Klingemann. Oxford: Oxford University Press, pp. 621–35.

A second criticism is that proportional representation produces less stable government. Coalitions can be fragile. If one party leaves the coalition, the coalition may fall apart, necessitating a new election. Finally, proportional systems often lack the personal form of representation that can be provided in single-member districts, where representatives have long histories in their communities and know their constituents well.

Supporters of proportional representation have answers for all of these criticisms, noting that instability is far from inevitable and that personal representation may provide little consolation to constituents who sharply disagree with their homegrown representative. The larger point remains: any set of rules will promote certain values over other values.

Conclusion

This chapter has discussed the basic rules of the American electoral system—rules that govern nearly every aspect of the electoral process. Even in this brief overview, it is clear that the American system reflects no grand logic. It is the result of many compromises that are guided by multiple decision makers, including the framers of the Constitution, the Supreme Court, and federal, state, and local lawmakers. As such, the rules can change over time and vary across states and localities. The rules are also products of contending values about what a "good" election looks like. Whether rules strike observers as fair or unfair will depend in part on which values they hold dear. Moreover, it is challenging to construct electoral rules that uphold all these values simultaneously. Trade-offs are inevitable.

The rules that govern elections affect all of the actors whose roles we describe in later chapters. The rules provide the framework for the decisions of candidates, parties, and citizens alike. They are rarely as newsworthy as a candidate's gaffe or a hard-hitting campaign advertisement, but they are important nonetheless. Electoral rules are all the more important because they are not easy to change and remain largely outside of the control of candidates, parties, and citizens. Passing new laws and amending the Constitution are difficult. Candidates instead adapt. The rules then become part of the hand that candidates are dealt, at least once the campaign is under way.

Even seemingly arcane rules can be consequential. The adoption of the new district that Obama helped draw as a state senator literally came down to a piece of paper that was picked out of a hat. The Democrats, who controlled the Illinois House, had drawn up one set of districts. The Republicans, who controlled the Illinois Senate, had drawn up another. The two parties could not agree, and a redistricting commission composed of four Democrats and four Republicans was convened to select the new map. When it, too, failed to reach agreement, the Illinois Supreme Court submitted the names of one Democrat and one Republican to break the deadlock. One of those names was to be drawn from a hat—a hat made to resemble Abraham Lincoln's stovepipe hat, no less—and that person would then be the tie-breaking vote on the commission. The Democrat's name was drawn and his vote enacted the Democrats' map and thus Obama's new district. The rest, as they say, is history.

KEY TERMS

independent candidates (p. 22)

term limits (p. 23)

primary election (p. 25)

permanent campaign (p. 26)

single-member districts (p. 28)

at-large elections (p. 28)

reapportionment (p. 28)

redistricting (p. 29)

malapportionment (p. 29)

one person, one vote (p. 30)

Voting Rights Act of 1965 (VRA) (p. 31)

communities of interest (p. 33)

gerrymandering (p. 33)

majority-minority districts (p. 34)

poll taxes (p. 41)

literacy tests (p. 41)

closed primary (p. 42)

semi-closed primary (p. 42)

open primary (p. 42)

blanket (or jungle) primary (p. 42)

same-day (or Election Day) registration (p. 43)

plurality rule (p. 46)

proportional representation (p. 46)

Duverger's Law (p. 46)

strategic voting (p. 46)

FOR DISCUSSION

1. What are arguments for and against term limits?

2. What formal rules and informal norms govern the drawing of U.S. House districts during redistricting?

3. How might different rules about who can vote affect how candidates campaign?

4. How does the American system's combination of single-member districts and plurality rule disadvantage minor political parties and independent candidates?

CHAPTER 3

The Transformation of American Campaigns

On May 23, 2016, the online political newsletter *Morning Consult* published an article titled "Why 2016 Will Be the Most Negative Campaign in History."[1] Relying on an analysis of public opinion polls and television advertisements, the article painted a bleak picture of what to expect from a presidential campaign between Donald Trump and Hillary Clinton:

> The 2012 campaign between President Obama and former Massachusetts Gov. Mitt Romney devolved into the most negative presidential contest in modern American history. The 2016 race could make that battle look tame by comparison.
>
> If the key to winning a presidential election once [laid] in appealing to the broadest swath of voters, America's political parties have failed. The two likely nominees, Republican Donald Trump and Democrat Hillary Clinton, will begin a general-election campaign later this summer with lower popularity ratings than any presidential candidate in the modern political era.
>
> And while voters maintain they don't like seeing negative advertising, both Democrats and Republicans have signaled that the tone of the general election battle is likely to spiral into a morass of attacks that will use fear to motivate voters who are unenthusiastic about either candidate. Campaigning to persuade undecideds is out; campaigning to motivate the partisan base is in. . . . The lack of persuadable voters in recent election cycles has put a premium on mobilizing every possible partisan voter. And with such a paucity of public support for either Clinton or Trump, those partisans are most likely to be motivated by fear, rather than hope or optimism. The logical step for either campaign, then, is to drive up negative impressions of the rival.

---

[1] Reid Wilson. 2016. "Why 2016 Will Be the Most Negative Campaign in History." *Morning Consult*, May 23. https://morningconsult.com/2016/05/23/2016-will-negative-campaign-history (accessed 6/5/2017). Reprinted with permission.

There is some truth to *Morning Consult*'s characterization of 2016, especially the idea that the polarized politics of today provides incentives for mobilizing the base rather than competing for persuadable voters. During the 2016 campaign, Donald Trump repeatedly referred to Hillary Clinton as "crooked Hillary,"[2] said she was a "dangerous" and "pathological" liar who was "unbalanced" and "unstable," and warned voters that a Clinton presidency would lead to the "destruction of this country from within."[3] Hillary Clinton referred to Trump's supporters as a "basket of deplorables,"[4] and went on to say that Trump was "not just unprepared, he's temperamentally unfit to hold an office." She criticized his ideas as "dangerously incoherent. They're not even really ideas, just a series of bizarre rants, personal feuds, and outright lies."[5] In a polarized era, these attacks played particularly well to hard-core Republican and Democratic voters, respectively. If nothing else, the 2016 campaign showed that Republicans loved to hate Hillary Clinton and Democrats loved to hate Donald Trump.

But was 2016 "the most negative presidential campaign in history"? Negativity has always been a central feature of American political campaigns. In fact, the negativity that occurred in 2016 and 2012 pales in comparison with that seen in some previous campaigns. For example, in the election of 1828, a local newspaper printed this attack against Democratic candidate Andrew Jackson: "Gen. Jackson's mother was a common prostitute brought to this country by the British soldiers. She afterwards married a mulatto man, with whom she had several children, of whom Gen. Jackson was one." In 1860, Abraham Lincoln was attacked as "a fourth-rate lecturer, who cannot speak good grammar and who, to raise the wind, delivers his hackneyed, illiterate compositions at $200 a piece." As if that were not enough, Lincoln was also characterized as "a horrid looking wretch. . . . Sooty and scoundrelly in aspect, a cross between the nutmeg dealer, the horse swapper, and the night man, a creature fit evidently for petty treason, small stratagems, and all sorts of spoils."[6]

---

[2] Alan Rappeport. 2016. "Donald Trump's Latest Jab at Hillary Clinton: 'No Stamina.'" *New York Times*, August 16. www.nytimes.com/2016/08/17/us/politics/donald-trump-hillary -clinton-stamina.html (accessed 9/26/2017).

[3] Jeremy Diamond. 2016. "Trump Escalates Attacks on Clinton's Character." *CNN*, August 5. www.cnn.com/2016/08/05/politics/donald-trump-hillary-clinton-unhinged-lock -her-up/index.html (accessed 9/26/2017).

[4] Amy Chozick. 2016. "Hillary Clinton Calls Many Trump Backers 'Deplorables,' and G.O.P. Pounces." *New York Times*, September 10. www.nytimes.com/2016/09/11/us/politics /hillary-clinton-basket-of-deplorables.html (accessed 9/26/2017).

[5] Philip Elliott. 2016. "Hillary Clinton Tears into Donald Trump on Foreign Policy, Temperament." *Time*, June 2. http://time.com/4355791/hillary-clinton-donald-trump-temperament (accessed 9/26/2017).

[6] These examples come from Paul F. Boller, Jr. 1984. *Presidential Campaigns.* New York: Oxford University Press.

This chapter focuses on the lessons that past campaigns can teach us about contemporary American campaigns. Are there certain patterns and characteristics that appear time and time again? Or is the essential nature of campaigns dynamic, shifting as the American electorate and its candidates evolve? In this chapter, we argue that the rules and the reality that drive election campaigns change infrequently, producing continuity in most aspects of American campaigns. But when these factors do change, they tend to do so abruptly, producing periods in which campaigns innovate and campaign strategies adapt. There have been at least four major eras of American political campaigns: 1788–1824 ("Pre-Democratic Campaigns"), 1828–92 ("Mass Mobilization Campaigns"), 1896–1948 ("Progressive Era Campaigns"), and 1952 to the present ("Candidate Campaigns"). Each is distinct enough from the others to warrant its own category, but each also contains elements common to the other eras (see Figure 3.1).

We will also see that the American campaign as we know it today has roots in the 1950s but really took on its current characteristics around 1972. This was due to four central factors: (1) changes in campaign finance and party nomination rules, (2) a new political reality driven by social upheaval and the Vietnam War, (3) changes in strategy driven by the rise of the survey and marketing industries and the expansion of television, and (4) the expansion of the electorate to include previously disenfranchised blacks and 18- to 20-year-olds. Some observers have argued that in more recent years the increased competitiveness of elections, the polarization of the two major parties, and new technological advances—most notably, the development of the Internet and social media—have ushered in a new era. As we will see, it is unclear whether we are currently in a new period of campaigning that differs significantly from previous eras. We will explore this question toward the end of the chapter.

Core of the Analysis

- Many aspects of modern campaigns can be seen in campaigns throughout American history.
- Changes in the conduct and content of campaigns have been produced by changes in rules, reality, strategy, and the electorate.
- Campaigns can be sorted into roughly four eras, each of which is distinguished by distinct forms of campaigning.
- There are also commonalities across these eras, particularly in the length, expense, and content of American campaigns.
- The increasingly competitive and polarized party system and the penetration of the Internet may or may not signify a new era for campaigns.

The First Campaign Era: Pre-Democratic Campaigns, 1788–1824

In some ways, the earliest era of campaigning, which we refer to as the **era of pre-democratic campaigns**, is unique. The first two presidential contests, which resulted in unanimous elections of George Washington, were like no others in American history. Washington was considered the logical choice for the job—indeed, there are some who believe the Constitution would not have been ratified had lawmakers not assumed Washington would serve as the first president—and there was no serious campaign against him. Unsurprisingly, the sum total of Washington's campaign expenditures in 1788 was two casks of Virginia spirits provided for electors.[7] Similarly, the election of John Adams as Washington's successor in 1796, though contested, involved only trace elements of the partisan effort, conflict, and machinations that emerged a scant four years later.

The 1800 election between John Adams and Thomas Jefferson marked a turning point within the first era in American election campaigns. Adams's first term as president was distinguished by the unraveling of the uneasy truce that had held during Washington's tenure. In its place, two camps emerged. On one side was the **Federalist Party**. The Federalists believed in a strong federal government, preferred to ally with Great Britain, and were suspicious of the radicalization of the French Revolution. The Federalists, who were especially numerous in New England and the mid-Atlantic states, were led by many of the architects of the Constitution, including John Adams and Alexander Hamilton. On the other side was the **Democratic-Republican Party**. The Democratic-Republicans distrusted the expanding federal government and suspected that it only served the commercial interests of the northeastern states. They preferred an alliance with France, even in the face of the French Revolution, to an alliance with Great Britain and its monarchy. Democratic-Republicans, who were numerous in the southern states, were led by Thomas Jefferson and his trusted ally James Madison.

The actions of these two camps as the presidential election of 1800 approached illustrate one of our major themes: the importance of the rules that govern campaigns and elections. At that point in time, presidential electors were chosen by state legislators and not by ordinary citizens. In fact, citizens did not come to dominate the presidential election process until the 1820s, which is why we characterize this era as one of "pre-democratic campaigns." Because state legislators were so consequential, presidential

---

[7] Boller, *Presidential Campaigns.*

FIGURE 3.1 The Four Major Eras of Political Campaigns

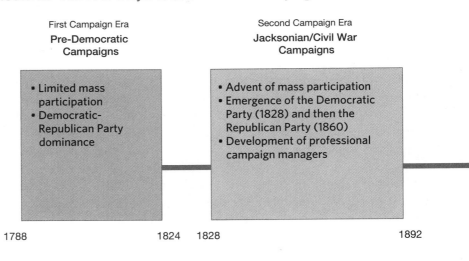

candidates sought their support and attempted to influence the composition of state legislatures. Candidates also tried to get legislatures to adopt rules that would give them more votes in the Electoral College. In early 1800, for example, Jefferson's Democratic-Republicans worked hard to win a majority of seats in Pennsylvania's lower house and then attempted to change Pennsylvania's rules so that all of the state's electors would go to the candidate whose party commanded a legislative majority. The Pennsylvania Senate, where Adams's Federalists had a majority, blocked the move. This state-by-state effort to craft favorable electoral rules offers the earliest glimpse of the strategic emphasis on "battleground states" that dominates contemporary presidential campaigns.

The importance of state legislators also led to another innovation in strategy: the first organized attempts to get eligible citizens to the polls, what we would refer to today as "Get Out the Vote" efforts. In New York, Aaron Burr built a political network that helped the Democratic-Republicans win crucial seats in the state legislative elections of 1798—seats that would prove important in 1800, when Burr became Jefferson's running mate. In building this network, Burr employed several strategies that later became staples of political campaigns, including identifying sympathetic citizens and turning them out to vote on Election Day.

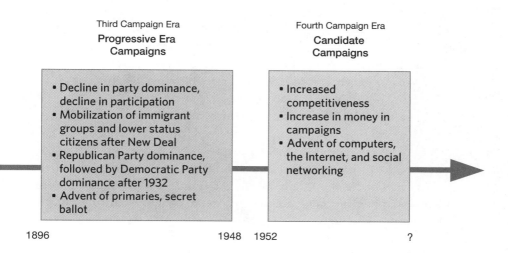

The 1800 election also featured the kind of negative campaigning that pundits today sometimes bemoan. There were attack ads, many of which centered on Jefferson's sympathies with the French Revolution as well as his religious faith (or lack thereof). One such passage from a Federalist newspaper attacks Jefferson and other members of the "anti-federal junto":

> Citizens choose your sides. You who are for French notions of government; for the tempestuous sea of anarchy and misrule; for arming the poor against the rich; for fraternizing with the foes of God and man; go to the left and support the leaders, or the dupes, of the anti-federal junto. But you that are sober, industrious, thriving, and happy, give your votes for those men who mean to *preserve the union* of the states, the purity and vigor of our excellent Constitution, the sacred majesty of the laws, and the holy ordinances of religion.[8]

The central difference between the 1800 election and contemporary presidential elections is how little campaigning the candidates themselves actually did in the earliest presidential contests. For the most part, the organizational activity and the negative campaigning were carried out by

---

[8] Edward J. Larson. 2007. *A Magnificent Catastrophe*. New York: Free Press, p. 93.

surrogates. Although Adams did some campaigning during a trip from Massachusetts to Washington, D.C., in the spring of 1800, it was mainly Hamilton and other Federalists who worked on his behalf to influence legislative elections and wrote letters and articles excoriating Jefferson and his Democratic-Republican allies on every issue of the day. Jefferson stayed mainly in his Virginia home, Monticello, communicating by letter with Madison, Burr, and other Democratic-Republican leaders.

The election of 1800 culminated in Jefferson's victory. Popular discontent over the prospect of higher taxes and more intrusive government worked against Federalist arguments. Moreover, the Federalists made several key mistakes, such as supporting the Alien and Sedition Acts, which had been passed in 1798 under the Adams administration and which made it illegal for the press to publish "false, scandalous, and malicious writing" about the government or its officials.

The next 25 years brought relative stasis to American political parties and campaigns. Federalist presidential candidates attempted to hold electors in their New England base while winning over electors in the mid-Atlantic and southern states by emphasizing the need for greater national government support of commercial development and infrastructure. Meanwhile, Madison and James Monroe maintained—and in ways expanded on—the coalition established by Jefferson. Candidates and their surrogates continued to campaign behind the scenes, writing letters, encouraging supporters, dictating strategy, and suggesting lines of argument and attack. The brutality of 1800 abated somewhat, but campaigns were marked by differences over policy as well as personal attacks.

However, conditions were changing even as Jefferson assumed the presidency in the spring of 1801. Most notably, states began changing their rules so that presidential electors would be chosen by a statewide popular vote. Moreover, they also began changing their standards for citizenship in ways that significantly expanded the eligible electorate. This set the stage for a more democratic mode of campaigning.

The Second Campaign Era: Mass Mobilization Campaigns, 1828–92

The two decades between 1820 and 1840 saw the development of the first mass democratic electorate. Politicians began to campaign with the goal of winning over this electorate rather than state legislatures, thus changing the nature and meaning of campaigning. The 1828 presidential campaign was particularly important in setting the tone for all subsequent American campaigns. Although the level and sophistication of campaigning varied over time and from place to place after the 1828 election, its innovations became increasingly widespread.

The 1828 campaign arguably began four years earlier, when a political slight against Andrew Jackson produced a personal vendetta. In the presidential election of 1824, Jackson was the most popular candidate running. He received 41 percent of the national vote, winning 7 states worth 99 electoral votes. Unfortunately for Jackson, there were 261 total electoral votes, and 131 votes were needed to win the presidency. His competitors, John Quincy Adams (84 electoral votes), William Harris Crawford (41 electoral votes), and Henry Clay (37 electoral votes), had more than enough electoral votes among them to prevent the race from being decided in the Electoral College. Because no candidate won an Electoral College majority, the election was decided in the U.S. House of Representatives, where, as stipulated in the Constitution, each statewide congressional delegation was to cast a single vote. In this case, a reputed deal between the Speaker of the House, Henry Clay, and supporters of John Quincy Adams resulted in the election of Adams. Jackson was outraged. Perhaps more significant, so were his supporters.

Jackson and a handful of confidants, stung by the "stolen" election of 1824, began to lay plans to avoid what they felt would be another "theft" in 1828. As in modern presidential campaigns, all of this began well in advance of the election itself. Jackson's message centered in part on his status as a war hero. (Jackson had won fame by defeating the British army at the Battle of New Orleans in 1815.) It also centered on his promise to "clean house" and fight northeastern commercial interests that had become entrenched in Washington and who, Jackson argued, enriched themselves at the expense of the country's "common folk."

Jackson's campaign operation provided the template for all subsequent American campaigns, especially presidential campaigns. The first element of that template was its structure. The campaign was led by a small group of friends and supporters who were motivated by their personal loyalty to Jackson. These individuals recruited political operatives in important counties. The operatives were not paid, but Jackson's promise to "clean house" led them to (reasonably) expect that they would receive jobs in a Jackson administration. This expectation—that working on the campaign could lead to a government job—remains to this day.

The second element of the template was the emphasis on organizing voters. This may seem like an obvious strategy, but in fact it was an important innovation. It was made possible by changes in state voting laws—such as abolishing the requirement that citizens own property in order to vote—which enfranchised a larger segment of the electorate and thus created more eligible citizens to target. Jackson's operatives were in charge of mobilizing eligible voters in their counties.

The third element of the template concerns how these voters were organized. As in previous campaigns, Jackson's followers promoted his candidacy with a sustained public relations campaign in local newspapers, writing letters and enlisting the aid of sympathetic editors. But the need to appeal to a mass electorate necessitated a new tactic: entertainment. Jackson's and subsequent campaigns featured rallies, public speeches, picnics, torchlit parades, songs, slogans, and bombastic rhetoric. Policy issues took a backseat to partisan allegiances and personalities. Thus, even though many criticize modern campaigns for their superficiality, the 1828 election shows that American campaigns have long emphasized style over substance.

This emphasis on reaching out to the masses gave rise to a further innovation: candidates themselves increasingly campaigned for office. To be sure, many candidates were still reticent about campaigning, but as early as the 1840s it was no longer an entirely unheard-of concept. For example, when Stephen Douglas ran for the U.S Senate in 1858, he campaigned tirelessly on his own behalf, making dozens of speeches across the state of Illinois. During the course of this campaign, Douglas participated in seven public debates with his opponent, a state legislator named Abraham Lincoln. As was often the case for candidates in this era, Douglas's actions were influenced by his expectation that the election would be close. Candidates appeared more likely to embrace electioneering when facing tough competition.

Many subsequent campaigns during this era adopted the strategies pioneered in 1828. After Jackson's victory, his supporters formed the core of what was to become the **Democratic Party**. Beginning in 1832, the Democrats faced stiff competition from the newly formed **Whig Party**, which favored congressional authority over presidential authority and supported a program of modernization and economic protectionism. This competition came to a head in 1840, when Whig candidate William Henry Harrison attempted to unseat Jackson's successor, incumbent Democratic president Martin Van Buren.

Just as Jackson's campaign did in 1828, Harrison's campaign emphasized his war record, particularly his role in the battle of Tippecanoe, a famous victory for U.S. forces against an American Indian confederation in the Indiana Territory in 1811. The Democrats charged that Harrison was the sort of fellow who would just as soon live off his pension, sipping hard cider on the

THE UNDECIDED POLITICAL PRIZE FIGHT.

In the nineteenth century, candidates were more likely to engage personally in campaigning when the election was expected to be close. When Stephen Douglas ran for the U.S. Senate in 1858, he campaigned vigorously against Abraham Lincoln in a closely fought race, as this cartoon depicts.

porch of his log cabin. Harrison's campaign countered by turning this into a virtue, presenting Harrison as a man of the people—a strategy that Jackson had used 12 years earlier. Meanwhile, the emphasis on mobilizing eligible voters continued apace. More citizens—80 percent of those eligible—voted in 1840 than in any previous presidential contest, thanks in part to campaign rallies, parades, and other hoopla. The strategies of 1828 proved successful again, and Harrison won relatively easily.

Even growing disagreements over slavery and the Civil War itself did not create significant changes in political campaigns. As the Whig Party split up over the issue of slavery, a series of antislavery parties emerged: the Free Soil Party, the Liberty Party, and (finally) the **Republican Party**. Although the Republicans were a party dedicated to the preservation of the Union and hostile to slavery, they adopted the campaign tactics and strategies of the Whigs. In the 1860 election, fought on the eve of the Civil War, the Republicans chose not to emphasize the policies of their nominee, Abraham Lincoln. Instead, in almost every broadside and campaign missive they spoke of Lincoln's honesty and his connection with the common man. After the end

When the Democrats claimed that William Henry Harrison was the type of man who would live off his pension, sitting on his porch drinking hard cider, Harrison's supporters turned the charge around to portray Harrison as a man of the people. In this 1840 engraving, Harrison is depicted welcoming a veteran with his "hard cider hospitality."

of the Civil War, campaigns continued to focus on pageantry, personality, and symbolic (rather than substantive) issues. In the presidential elections of 1868 and 1872, for example, the newly dominant Republicans nominated General Ulysses S. Grant, and focused their campaigns on reminding Americans who had been on the winning side in the war.

The 1876 presidential election provides a striking example of campaigning from this period. By then, the Republicans were faltering after the scandal-plagued second term of President Grant. In the election for his successor, Rutherford Hayes, a Republican, faced off against Samuel Tilden, a Democrat. Hayes and Tilden agreed on almost all of the major issues of the day, but, once again, the campaign was rancorous. Republicans continued to link the Democrats with the South's secession during the Civil War. One supporter of Hayes claimed: "Every man that endeavored to tear the old flag from the heavens that it enriches was a Democrat. Every man that tried to destroy this nation was a Democrat. . . . The man that assassinated Abraham

The 1876 presidential race, between Republican Rutherford Hayes and Democrat Samuel Tilden, brought up bitter rivalries from the Civil War. The election was so close that it was decided (controversially) by an election commission. This 1877 cartoon calls for an end to the rancor surrounding the election.

Lincoln was a Democrat. . . . Soldiers, every scar you have on your heroic bodies was given you by a Democrat!"[9] For their part, Democrats thought up some bold lies, too. Hayes was said to have stolen the pay of dead Civil War soldiers in his regiment, cheated Ohio out of vast sums of money as governor, and shot his own mother.

Perhaps more important, the resolution to the 1876 presidential election brought about one of the major changes that would contribute to a new era of political campaigns. Four states—Oregon, South Carolina, Louisiana, and Florida—had disputed election results, and Hayes needed all four of them to win, while Tilden needed only one. An election commission was appointed, with five senators, five representatives, and five Supreme Court justices. Seven of the members were Republicans, seven were Democrats, and one was independent. But the independent—Justice David Davis—was elected to the Senate by the Illinois legislature before the commission completed its work and had to be replaced by Justice Joseph Bradley, a Republican.

---

[9] Boller, *Presidential Campaigns*, p. 134.

Bradley voted with the Republicans on all disputes, and Hayes ended up winning the election. As part of their efforts to appease outraged Democrats, Hayes and the Republicans agreed to pull federal troops out of Louisiana and South Carolina, hastening the end of the **Reconstruction** era efforts to enfranchise African Americans in the South. The end of Reconstruction meant an end to widespread black participation in southern politics and essentially delivered the South to the Democrats for the next 100 years.

In a second change that affected campaigning, the latter half of the 1800s saw the gradual weakening of the partisan press. During the American Revolution and in the days after the ratification of the U.S. Constitution, most newspapers were essentially party organs, sometimes created and funded by candidates and parties, writing stories that promoted a particular political agenda. By the 1830s, some East Coast cities—with their burgeoning middle- and working-class populations—began to see the development of the "penny press": for one cent (more traditional newspapers cost six cents) people could get information on crime, gossip, and adventure. By the late 1800s, many newspapers had become more financially independent, thanks in part to sensationalized coverage of people and events that attracted readers. The newspapers of publishing moguls William Randolph Hearst and Joseph Pulitzer were prime examples of this kind of coverage, which was commonly referred to as "yellow journalism" (due to the yellow parchment that Pulitzer's newspapers were printed on). Newspapers no longer needed the funds provided by political parties, and so their connections to those parties began to weaken. At the same time, journalism was becoming increasingly professionalized, with an emphasis on objectivity and impartiality. This was, for example, the approach emphasized in elite metropolitan newspapers such as the *New York Times*. The norm of impartiality began to crowd out the openly partisan journalism of earlier periods.

A third and final change was that political party organizations, which had grown stronger throughout the nineteenth century, were about to face challenges. Their growth was particularly notable in such cities as New York and Boston, where waves of immigrants became the loyal foot soldiers of local party organizations and were often rewarded with government jobs and services. The parties functioned as **political machines**—a uniquely American combination of mass politics and government programs, with more than a whiff of money and corruption. In the local urban campaigns of the 1800s, issues were almost incidental, particularly when compared with party performance and loyalty. Similarly, candidates were often irrelevant; their personal background and qualifications were less important than their party membership. Political power was wielded by party bosses, who never stood for election.

Although political machines politics were never as pervasive as is sometimes assumed, they were still controversial. The crushing economic depression of the 1890s helped usher in a new era, one that would hamstring the parties, elevate the importance of individual candidates, and demobilize segments of the American electorate.

The Third Campaign Era: Progressive Era Campaigns, 1896–1948

The third era of campaigns, which began with the 1896 presidential election, had two important features: the continued trend toward more personal campaigning, with candidates increasingly involved in day-to-day electioneering, and reforms that weakened political parties and their ability to mobilize potential voters, resulting in a dramatic decline in voter participation.

Candidates for the House of Representatives and Senate had routinely campaigned on their own behalf throughout the 1800s, giving speeches, writing letters, and frequently meeting their opponents in debates. Even a few presidential candidates took their turns on the campaign trail, openly seeking the support of American voters.

But the 1896 election was different. The Democratic nominee for president, William Jennings Bryan, ran a campaign that was especially aggressive in its appeal to Americans. He traveled over 18,000 miles by train, made more than 600 speeches (sometimes 10 or 20 in a day), and addressed 5 million people over the course of the campaign (Figure 3.2). His campaign speeches were filled with religious imagery, and his entire effort took on the aura of an evangelical crusade.

Bryan's Republican opponent, William McKinley, ran a much quieter but no less energetic campaign. After the Democratic National Convention, in which Bryan delivered his famous "Cross of Gold" speech, appealing to farmers and factory workers by proclaiming support for easing the money supply and rejecting close adherence to the gold standard, Republican strategists were worried. But McKinley refused to mimic Bryan's efforts.

> I cannot take the stump against that man. . . . I can't outdo him and I am not going to try. . . . If I should go now, it would be an acknowledgment of weakness. Moreover, I might just as well put up a trapeze on my front

FIGURE 3.2 Contemporary Map of Bryan's Campaign Travels, 1896

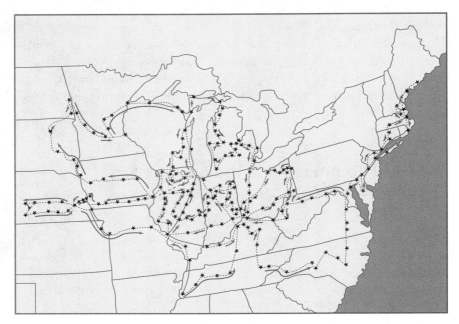

lawn and compete with some professional athlete as go out speaking against Bryan.[10]

Instead, McKinley emulated Benjamin Harrison's 1888 **front-porch campaign**, conducting business from his home in Canton, Ohio. His manager, Mark Hanna, arranged for hundreds of delegations representing various interest groups and demographic groups to visit McKinley, whereupon the candidate would deliver a short speech that was often reprinted in the newspapers. McKinley also raised and spent $7 million (the equivalent of about $194 million today) and enlisted 18,000 speakers across the country on his behalf. Bryan spent only $300,000 (the equivalent of about $8 million today) and, lacking the support of many influential Democrats, largely spoke on his own behalf. These differences between McKinley and Bryan illustrate how reality—in this case, the backgrounds, connections, and abilities of the candidates—influenced their campaign strategies. Despite Bryan's efforts, McKinley beat him by five points.

---

[10] Boller, *Presidential Campaigns*, p. 173.

While the 1896 presidential campaign was distinct from those that came before and immediately after, in several ways it proved to be a harbinger of modern campaigns. It was the first presidential election in which a major party nominee (McKinley) used the primary elections to help win the nomination. It also provided a blueprint for the candidate-centered campaigning that dominated the twentieth century. Beyond campaign strategies and tactics, the 1896 election reshuffled the parties' coalitions to the Republicans' advantage by strengthening their hold on businessmen, professionals, skilled factory workers, and prosperous farmers while crushing the Democrats' dream of a national majority of poorer farmers, unskilled industrial laborers, and white Southerners.

In the 1912 presidential election, the candidates were also quite involved in their campaigns. This election featured an unusual three-way race. The candidates included not only the incumbent president, Republican William Howard Taft, and his Democratic opponent, Woodrow Wilson, but also former president Theodore Roosevelt, who ran as the nominee of the **Progressive (or "Bull Moose") Party** after being denied the Republican nomination by Taft's forces.

Taft mostly sat on the sidelines, giving few speeches and almost no interviews. But for the first time, two major presidential candidates—Wilson and Roosevelt—campaigned vigorously and personally. Roosevelt toured the country by rail, made hundreds of speeches, and worked the press with intensity and candor. Wilson also spent extensive time on the campaign trail. The passion of the campaign was embodied in the events of October 14, when Roosevelt was shot at close range before a speech in Milwaukee. Refusing to be driven to the hospital, Roosevelt insisted on giving his speech, which lasted for well over an hour. Later, doctors found that the bullet had fractured his fourth rib and lodged near his lung. He took two weeks off from the campaign, while Wilson and Taft halted their own activities out of a sense of fairness and respect. But Roosevelt was soon back on the trail, and by Election Day he had utterly exhausted his voice (although Wilson ultimately won). With increasingly few exceptions, this was to be the new style of presidential campaigns: personal, aggressive, and relentless.

The second major development of this era was the reforms that weakened political parties. Up until the turn of the century, the Republican and Democratic parties had been extremely effective at mobilizing citizens to vote. But the Progressive movement—a loose association of activists dedicated to reforming government—believed that strong party organizations were often corrupt and empowered party bosses at the expense of ordinary citizens. The Progressives helped institute or advance three significant strands of reform.

One important reform built on the creation of the federal **civil service** in 1872.[11] The civil service gave federal government jobs to individuals on the basis of their professional qualifications and not party loyalty, which was naturally the most important criterion when party organizations controlled government jobs. At the turn of the century, the number of civil service positions in the federal government expanded considerably. This undermined the parties' abilities to incentivize and compensate campaign workers.

Two other strands of reform concerned elections. One was ballot reform: in particular, the adoption of the **Australian ballot**, which protects the secrecy of voter preferences and prevents parties from monitoring voters and rewarding or punishing them accordingly. Second was the use of primary elections to determine nominees. Primaries, which were adopted in a small number of states during this era, took power out of the hands of party leaders, who had typically been responsible for selecting candidates for office, and gave it to voters.

These reforms once again provide examples of how rules affect campaign strategy and the subsequent behavior of voters themselves. In this case, the reforms reduced the control parties had over candidates and voters. Individual candidates could then tailor messages to fit specific constituencies rather than simply adopting the positions of their party. Voters, now more anonymous because of the secret ballot, were freer to defect from the party line.

Perhaps most important, these reforms had an unintended chilling effect on voter participation and turnout. In major cities such as New York, Boston, and Philadelphia, reforms that limited the benefits that parties could offer to encourage campaign workers crippled the mobilization and outreach efforts of parties. At the same time, in the South, selective enforcement of ballot reforms was used as a means to disenfranchise eligible black voters. For example, the secret ballot served as a *de facto* literacy test: many blacks could not read, and because their vote was now to be secret, no person could assist them in the voting booth (these rules were not so rigorously enforced for Southern white voters who could not read). As a consequence, turnout plummeted. Even in the wild and woolly election of 1912, turnout was 20 points lower than in the 1896 election. Subsequent national events like the

---

[11] The term *civil service* has two distinct meanings: (1) a branch of governmental service in which individuals are employed on the basis of professional merit as proven by competitive examinations, or (2) the body of employees in any government agency other than the military. We are referring to the first of these definitions.

Great Depression and World War II also failed to increase turnout to its previous levels. Turnout in the presidential elections between 1932 and 1948 averaged 58 percent—compared with 74 percent in the second era of campaigns (1828–92).

This third era of campaigning came to a close amid more important transformations in the nature of news media. The continued movement away from the partisan press toward a more professional style of reportage created the need for candidates and parties not only to counter the negative stories in the outlets of the partisan opposition but also to shape how journalists reported on the campaign.

In addition, important technological innovations began to change campaign strategy. The days of torchlit parades and four-hour speeches were passing into history. A more complete continental rail system, soon to be followed by air travel and a national network of interstate highways, gave candidates a greater ability to travel. Campaigns could adjust strategies more quickly as the telephone replaced telegrams and letters. Even something as simple as the microphone allowed candidates and their surrogates to address larger crowds. Finally, the radio emerged as a revolutionary way for people to reach mass audiences, although its campaign potential would not be realized until the 1940s and '50s. But all these changes taken together were not as transformational as the technology that would inaugurate the fourth era of campaigns: television.

The Fourth Campaign Era: Candidate Campaigns, 1952–?

Since the 1950s, American political campaigns have been defined by television. The development of broadcasting technology and the proliferation of television sets across the United States in the 1950s ushered in a new age of political communication. Although campaigns continued to revolve around **retail politics**—door-to-door canvassing, speeches to crowds by the candidates and their supporters, and other in-person interactions—well into the 1960s, presidential and Senate candidates of the 1950s began to focus on **wholesale politics**, which mostly consisted of producing and airing television and radio advertisements to reach mass audiences. Dwight Eisenhower's 1952 and 1956 presidential election campaigns purchased advertising in specific time slots in selected media markets in battleground states. The New York advertising agency Doyle Dane Bernbach devised similar strategies for both John F. Kennedy in 1960 and Lyndon Johnson in 1964.

The rise of television had four important consequences for campaign strategy: it elevated the role of fund-raising, shifted power from parties to individual candidates, altered the content of political messaging, and changed the geographic unit for targeting and measuring the effects of the campaign. First, the allure of reaching millions of potential voters through television ads was something few campaigns could resist. But the cost of television advertising dwarfed the expenses of candidate travel, campaign literature, and wages for staff and workers. As a result, parties and candidates had to spend more time and effort on fund-raising. Indeed, the need to raise money in order to produce and air television ads has become one of the most prominent features of American politics today. As we note in Chapter 4, many House candidates report spending as much as half of their day raising money during election years. These fund-raising demands increased the pressure on officeholders (and candidates) to recruit and train more staffers, and to do so early in the campaign cycle. The demands also meant that accountants and lawyers became commonplace in campaigns.

Second, the rise of television shifted the focus away from political parties and onto individual candidates. We have noted that American campaigns have always tended to focus on personalities rather than policies. But this tendency was magnified with the advent of a medium that put candidates into the living rooms of American voters. Television made politicians stars in a more personal and immediate way than ever before.

Third, television changed the content of political communication, further emphasizing the sloganeering that had dominated American campaigns since the 1830s. The restricted length of television commercials—political ads usually last no more than 30 seconds—makes it imperative to communicate a message quickly and memorably. Moreover, political ads compete not only against other campaign ads but also against expensively produced, and often very entertaining, commercial product ads.

Finally, the rise of television has shifted the strategic focus of consultants away from precincts, cities, and counties and onto media markets. The fundamental unit of analysis in campaigns had long been the county. But television advertisements are bounded by signal reach and are measured at the level of the media market. These media markets have become the fundamental units of political and campaign analysis. Consultants are constantly evaluating media market demographics—the characteristics and loyalties of the voters within them—calibrating and recalibrating the cost per persuadable voter (see Chapter 5) of advertising in certain markets based on TV ad rates and how many swing voters there are in a specific locale.[12]

More generally, the logic and sequencing of a television advertising campaign have come to dominate the strategy of most high-level political campaigns. The itinerary and the talking points of any candidate on a given day often reflect the television advertising strategy, as candidates visit the markets in which their advertisements are running and repeat the messages contained in those advertisements. Campaigns thus look to reinforce their TV advertisements with other sorts of campaign activity.

A separate development of the fourth campaign era rivals the rise of television in its effect on campaigns: the rise of primary elections as the dominant means for selecting candidates. The nominating conventions that marked the 1800s and the first half of the 1900s were still the method of choice for choosing candidates well into the 1960s. But the exclusion of black voters from selection processes throughout the South and dramatic protests at the Democratic National Convention in 1968 by voters who felt excluded from the nomination system resulted in reforms that led states to opt for primary elections. By the mid-1970s, over 40 states were using primary elections of some sort to select candidates.

The move to primary elections reinforced some of the effects of television's rise. Candidates often needed to raise and spend money to compete in both the primary and the general election. This necessitated raising money earlier, which in turn necessitated building an effective campaign organization as much as 18 months before Election Day. Primary elections also changed how candidates thought about their campaign message, as they needed to develop a message that distinguished themselves from other candidates in the same party. Some observers argue that this meant taking more ideologically extreme positions in order to appeal to presumably more partisan and ideological primary voters.[13] Others argue that primary elections make campaigns more focused on biography and personality because candidates have no other way to distinguish themselves from competitors within their party, most of whom share their views on issues. For example, in the

---

[12] The rise of television has affected campaigning in other countries, as well. But in many of these other countries, political advertising is restricted. In some countries, laws limit or even prohibit commercial advertising. Elsewhere, television stations are owned by the government and there is little or no advertising on the public airwaves.

[13] This, in turn, could create difficulties for candidates who take more ideologically extreme positions to win primary elections, but then have to reposition themselves as more centrist for the general election (see Chapter 9).

2008 Democratic presidential primary, Hillary Clinton and Barack Obama differentiated themselves from each other mainly in terms of who had the most experience (Clinton's argument) or who would best bring about change (Obama's argument).

While not as significant as television or primary elections, the proliferation of polling is another noteworthy development of the fourth campaign era. Campaigns have always attempted to craft popular messages and present the most appealing side of their candidate. But the application of probability theory and statistical inference—developed by mathematicians—to the public at large turned guesswork into a science. George Gallup, among others, pioneered the field of **survey research** in the 1930s and '40s, in which representative samples were drawn from the broader population in order to produce more accurate estimates of public opinion. The commercial applications of survey research were obvious, but political practitioners soon discovered its utility for candidates for office.

Widespread polling by campaigns did not occur until the 1960s and especially the 1970s, when telephones became sufficiently widespread to ensure both the representativeness of survey samples and cost-effectiveness. Since that time, polling has become a staple of campaigns, and top pollsters have become famous and sought-after individuals. Polls have also increased our understanding of what citizens think and how they will react to issue positions and messages. Some claim that polls and pollsters have effectively trivialized and cheapened political discourse as candidates simply advocate whatever message appears popular with citizens. Regardless of whether that is true, polling has particular relevance in an era where television advertising is central. Polls help candidates formulate and test messages before spending millions of dollars to broadcast them.

A final change in this fourth era speaks to an important reality that candidates confront: the balance of partisanship in the electorate as a whole. This era began with the Democratic Party somewhat dominant in national politics. Despite Republican success in presidential elections—the GOP has won 10 of 17 presidential elections between 1952 and 2016—the Democrats largely controlled the U.S. Congress until the 1994 election. Their advantage stemmed in part from the simple fact that since President Franklin Delano Roosevelt's New Deal, more people have identified themselves as Democrats than as Republicans. The allegiance of many to the Democratic Party was an apparent result of the perceived success of the Roosevelt administration.

But by the 1990s, the Democrats' advantage began to diminish. The Democratic Party's support of civil rights reform, abortion rights, and gay rights cost them support among several groups, such as white southerners and Catholics, that had been linked with the Democratic Party. Their gains among other groups, especially blacks, were not enough to make up the difference (Figure 3.3). For example, in 1952, much more of the public identified with or leaned toward the Democratic Party (59 percent) than the Republican Party (36 percent). But by the 1990s, the Democrats' 23-point edge had shrunk by half—to an average of 12 points over the period between 1990 and 2008.[14] This slimmer margin, combined with the wholesale transformation of the South from solidly Democratic to largely Republican,

FIGURE 3.3 **Average Percent Democratic Margin in Presidential Elections among Key Social Groups**

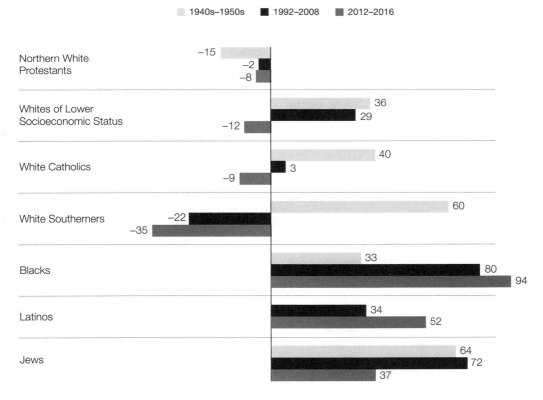

Sources: Gallup Poll, 1940-48 Gallup Year Books; American National Election Studies, 1952-2016.

[14] These data are from American National Election Studies. www.electionstudies.org /nesguide/toptable/tab2a_2.htm (accessed 9/26/2017).

produced a series of very competitive elections and ultimately allowed the Republicans to take control of the House of Representatives in 1994 for the first time in 40 years. (See Chapter 13 for the demography of the 2016 presidential vote.) It is not surprising that a more competitive electoral environment creates even greater incentives for candidates to raise and spend money. Moreover, with the presidency or control of the Congress much more in play, candidates and parties focus even more on a handful of competitive districts and battleground states.

The innovations of technology and polling, combined with the shift to primary elections and increasingly competitive national elections, have made modern campaigns qualitatively different from their forebears. At the same time, there is continuity between the past and modern campaigns. The need to raise money to run a campaign is nothing new; this fourth era simply made it a much more significant task. Similarly, the personalized campaigns of the modern era—where candidates take to the airwaves to present themselves to potential voters—merely magnify a tendency that has always been present in American campaigns. Indeed, despite the many dim opinions of modern campaigns, it is not clear that they are less substantive or any more negative than campaigns were in the past. Table 3.1 provides a review of the main characteristics of campaigns in the four major eras.

What about Today?

The new technologies that have been crucial to this fourth era are beginning to sound anachronistic today. After all, campaigns no longer rely exclusively on television. What about the Internet, including YouTube, Facebook, Twitter, Instagram, and Snapchat? Have we moved into a new era of electioneering—one dominated by electronic communication and social networking? Have these new technologies, and other recent developments, transformed campaigns? Let us consider the ways in which campaigns today both differ from and resemble previous campaigns. Ultimately, it would appear that the factors unique to today's campaigns, however important they may be, do not outweigh the ways in which contemporary campaigns resemble their ancestors.

New Developments

Public Opinion and Data Collection Clearly, technological innovations have influenced campaign strategy. For example, innovations in the measurement of public opinion, such as **focus groups** (in which small groups of people are

TABLE 3.1 Characteristics of the Four Major Eras of Campaigns

Campaign Era	Focus of Campaigns	Campaign Method/Style
First (1788–1824)	Limited electorates for most races; state legislatures choose presidential electors.	Candidates do not campaign themselves, but encourage, cajole, and direct from behind the scenes. Use of friends, surrogates, and a partisan press.
Second (1828–92)	Mass electorates for all races. Campaigns seek to expand the participation of supportive groups, and reach out in attempts to persuade unaffiliated groups.	Some candidates campaign personally and directly, but many still emphasize indirect campaigning that relies on party organizations and personal relations. Campaigns are taken to the people. Many characteristics of contemporary campaigns emerge—for example, slogans, songs, parades, conventions.
Third (1896–1948)	Campaigns tend to be fought over peripheral issues, while personalities and broad appeals dominate. Parties continue to use labor-intensive methods to mobilize eligible voters, but they no longer control the allocation of government jobs or the ballot. Mass communication and transportation technologies begin to change the style and nature of campaigns by the end of the era.	Personal campaigning becomes the norm by the time of FDR. The general election campaign lasts from early October until Election Day.
Fourth (1952–?)	Campaigns focus on raising money in order to pay for television advertisements. They also attempt to position candidates to win the support of their party base (to protect against a primary-election challenge) as well as the general electorate.	Candidates campaign personally for both money and votes. Mass communication efforts dominate and one-on-one outreach fades, at least until the 2000s. Campaign supporters work to "spin" media to present their interpretation of news and events.

asked their detailed impressions of candidates, advertisements, and so on) and dial groups (in which people are asked to use a 0–100 dial to rate their reactions to what they are seeing on a screen) have allowed campaigns to estimate more precisely who they should be talking to and what they should be saying.

Moreover, campaigns no longer have to rely on the information they can collect via polls or other indirect means. Both parties have constructed enormous databases with information on the vast majority of Americans.[15] These databases build on the information in state voter files, which record addresses, whether people actually vote, and, sometimes, party registration. The data are then merged with data from census reports and private marketing firms. A typical profile for any individual might include name, age, address, phone, voting history, political donations, estimated income, race, family structure, mortgage data, magazine subscriptions, and other indicators. This enables campaigns to engage in more sophisticated targeting strategies, using this information to estimate people's political views and the likelihood that they will turn out to vote. Campaigns can even target special interest groups—say, subscribers to *Guns & Ammo* magazine.

Beginning in 2012 and certainly by 2016, practitioners and pundits noted the emergence of "**big data**" and campaign "**analytics**" and pondered their impact on the conduct and quality of campaigns. In the context of American elections, *big data* refers to these large data sets containing extensive information on individual voters. *Analytics* refers to the use of sophisticated statistical models to identify politically meaningful patterns in these voter data. How do big data and analytics affect campaigns? They allow campaigns to identify with great precision specific groups of voters for particular forms of outreach. For example, campaigns might use big data and analytics to identify voters who are particularly open to persuasion if contacted and presented with information about a candidate's views on gun-owner rights. In 2016, some of the more aggressive campaigns—including Hillary Clinton's—used the results of their analytics instead of traditional polling to estimate the vote, especially as Election Day drew near.

In addition to the proliferation of data and statistical modeling, 2012 and 2016 also saw the rise of **field experiments** as an important new way for campaigns to test outreach and persuasion. Field experiments randomize

---

[15] Jon Gertner. 2004. "The Very, Very Personal Is the Political." *New York Times Magazine*, February 15. www.nytimes.com/2004/02/15/magazine/15VOTERS.html (accessed 9/26/2017).

subjects (in this case, voters) into treatment and control groups and then compare outcomes. For example, a campaign might test the effectiveness of different subject headings on a fund-raising e-mail to potential contributors by conducting the following field experiment: identify a group of 1,000 potential donors; randomly assign 333 of them an e-mail with the subject heading "Give now"; randomly assign another 333 an e-mail with the subject heading "We need you"; randomly assign another 333 to a control group that received no mail. Then see whether the number of click-throughs is different across the three groups. Both Democratic and Republican campaigns have conducted field experiments, although the systematic and rigorous commitment of the Obama team in 2012 to scientific testing was unprecedented.

Media New developments in the media have multiplied the ways candidates can disseminate their message and target particular audiences. The rise of cable television and talk radio is one such development. Both have increased opportunities to target advertisements at relatively small but demographically distinct audiences. For example, conservative candidates can reach a large and like-minded audience through the talk radio shows of hosts like Rush Limbaugh and Sean Hannity. Cable news networks such as CNN, Fox News, MSNBC, and HLN (formerly Headline News) also present new opportunities (or possibly burdens) for candidates. Because these networks broadcast news virtually 24 hours a day, it means that candidates can put out a new message and see it picked up and rebroadcast almost instantly. At the same time, continuous news can create distractions for candidates, who may also feel compelled to respond to stories that quickly circulate on these networks even though they would prefer to talk about other issues entirely.

Then there is the computer and Internet revolution, accompanied by the emergence of political, candidate, and social networking websites, and the rise of e-mail and text-messaging technologies, all of which facilitate the widespread and instantaneous transmission of information. Although larger proportions of people still consume traditional media like television and newspapers, consumption of information online is growing quickly—a trend we discuss in Chapter 8.

So rather than simply air television advertisements and send out generic mail pieces, campaigns today engage in a variety of more targeted, personal campaign activities. They develop and provide apps where supporters can volunteer and connect with others; where they can access information and

Five Ways Technology Has Changed Campaigns

Although there has been a great deal of continuity in political campaigns across time, it is unquestionable that technology has changed the conduct and content of elections in the past 15 years.

Social Media. Twitter, Instagram, Snapchat, and Facebook have transformed the way candidates interact with their constituencies. As recently as 2004, social media were hardly a factor. The candidates didn't speak directly to the public through social network channels, and regular people didn't have nearly as many outlets from which to gather information and debate about politics. Facebook had launched about nine months before the election and was not widely available. Twitter did not exist until 2006, and didn't catch on until several years after its launch. In 2008 and 2012, we saw progressively greater use of social media by candidates and campaigns; Barack Obama's innovative use of these platforms is well known. By 2016, social media were ascendant. Donald Trump's pervasive use of Twitter during the 2016 campaign not only serves as the exemplar for using social media to get the message out, but it may also herald the end of television's dominance of presidential campaign communication.

The Threat of "Going Viral." Candidates—presidential candidates in particular—are always under scrutiny during a campaign. But new technology allows the news media, opposing campaigns, and ordinary citizens to examine everything a candidate does and to share embarrassing moments with the world. Candidates have to assume that there is always someone around with a smartphone or other recording device capturing their actions and words. While this has brought transparency to elections, it has also increased the significance of arguably trivial missteps. For example, when Republican presidential candidate Marco Rubio paused during a televised speech in early 2016 to take a drink of water, a meme was created that sparked an outpouring of commentary.

New Issues. The rise of new technology and information platforms has itself sparked important new issues about which candidates are expected to be knowledgeable. Cybersecurity and net neutrality, for example, are among the cutting-edge issues that all candidates need to address or risk being seen as clueless and out-of-date.

Connecting with Young Voters. Candidates who do not use Twitter, Snapchat, or other social media platforms will almost certainly have difficulty connecting with young voters. A popular Vine circulated in July 2015 that highlighted Hillary Clinton's stiff and awkward use of Snapchat. Clinton held the phone too close to her face to let her audience know she was "just chillin' . . . in Cedar Rapids." The Vine was looped more than 17 million times, got over 131,000 likes and 10,000 comments, and was reposted on Vine more than 76,000 times.

Smarter Campaigns. Campaigns have always relied on empirical information to guide their understanding of the electorate and their resource targeting. Since the 1960s, polls and historical data have been the dominant source of that information. Enhanced voter file information (big data) and complex modeling (analytics) have emerged as another way for candidates to discern what they need to talk about, how they should position themselves on issues, and toward whom they should tailor their appeals.

goals provided by the campaign; and where they can find "talking points" for their conversations with bloggers, reporters, and journalists. They post videos for subscribers to their YouTube pages. They send out blast e-mails to raise funds from small groups with similar issue interests. They direct volunteers from a community to visit specific households, where they will talk to potential voters and make specific appeals driven by polling information, and send their responses back to the campaign using smartphones.

Partisan Polarization and Demographic Change The narrowing gap between numbers of self-identified Democratic and Republican voters has been accompanied by another trend: the ideological sorting and polarization of the parties. **Sorting** means that people's partisan preferences have become more closely aligned with their political views. Liberals have moved to the Democratic Party, while conservatives have moved to the Republican Party. In the past, parties were not so ideologically homogeneous. This trend has the potential to reshape campaign strategy. It may become harder for candidates to find ways to persuade voters who identify with the opposing party to support them; after all, it is unlikely that they will have enough common political ground. Instead, candidates may focus even more on mobilizing their own party's faithful, "the base," as we saw in the example offered at the beginning of the chapter. The expansive databases of information about individual citizens help make this possible, as candidates can more accurately locate, and subsequently communicate with, those people who are already likely to support them.

Other demographic changes are afoot in the American electorate. As noted earlier, the electorate expanded in the mid-twentieth century in key ways as a result of the enfranchising of 18- to 20-year-olds and the removal of impediments that had made it difficult for some blacks to vote. But an even more important transformation may be at work thanks to the nation's growing ethnic diversity. Immigration and high fertility rates have greatly increased the share of the American population that identifies as Asian or Latino. For example, the Census Bureau projects that by 2060, whites will make up less than 50 percent of the population (44 percent); Latinos will make up 29 percent, compared with 17 percent in 2014.[16] Campaign strategists are already seeking ways to reach these potential voters. Spanish-language political advertisements have become commonplace. In 2016,

---

[16] The projections are available at www.census.gov/content/dam/Census/library/publications /2015/demo/p25-1143.pdf (accessed 10/05/2017).

Democratic vice-presidential candidate Tim Kaine delivered an entire speech in Spanish. In 2010, the California gubernatorial candidate Meg Whitman produced an advertisement in Chinese. It will be even more interesting to see whether the agendas and opinions of these populations lead candidates to develop different messages. For example, a candidate who seeks to appeal to Latinos may need to talk about immigration differently than a candidate who seeks to appeal to whites. The fact that Latinos and Asian Americans have tended to vote Democratic has raised concerns among some Republicans, who believe that their party needs to broaden its appeal in this diversifying electorate.

The Case for Continuity

These changes in technology, the media, and demographics are no doubt important, but they do not necessarily make campaigns today significantly different from the campaigns of the fourth era. In fact, some apparent innovations are modern-day versions of campaign strategies from centuries past. For example, the rebirth of partisan or ideological media on talk radio and cable news harks back to the partisan press of the 1800s. Similarly, sending volunteers door to door to mobilize potential voters, even if they are carrying smartphones or iPads, is fundamentally similar to the campaigning of old-school party organizations. Indeed, these recent trends in campaigns make them look like updated versions of nineteenth-century campaigns rather than the slick, mass media–obsessed campaigns of the 1980s.

In other respects as well, contemporary campaigns have not changed that much. For example, the proliferation of primary elections in the 1960s and '70s was most responsible for lengthening campaigns—today's campaigns are not significantly longer than campaigns were in the 1980s. Presidential campaigns in 1988 and 1992 began in earnest during the late summer of the year before the election; in 2015, Hillary Clinton declared her candidacy in the late spring (April 12) while none of the Republican candidates declared their candidacy before late March (Ted Cruz was the first in, declaring his candidacy on March 23, 2015).

If campaigns have not gotten significantly longer of late, have they gotten more expensive? As we will show in Chapter 4, the presidential elections of 2008, 2012, and 2016 set all-time records for candidate fund-raising and expenditures. In fact, federal election campaigns in the United States in 2016 cost about $6.8 billion. But it is unclear whether this spike in 2008–16 will be sustained. The overall trend in American campaign spending over the past 150 years is uneven, with ebbs and flows. It is still too early to declare that fund-raising and spending have been transformed.

Other frequent complaints about recent campaigns concern their content: they don't focus enough on policy, they lack substance, they are too negative, and so on. As we have suggested throughout this chapter, American political campaigns have always focused on personality more than policy. Even now, with the political parties taking increasingly distinct positions on the issues, this polarization is not always reflected in how candidates campaign. Candidates—such as Donald Trump—are often reluctant to sacrifice their broader electoral appeal in favor of party loyalty or ideological purity. This behavior derives in part from American electoral institutions and rules. Officeholders represent single districts and are elected through plurality elections. When the "winner takes all," there is less incentive to do anything that might reduce your risk of winning. Candidates do care about policies, of course, but you cannot implement a policy if you do not win the election.

Thus, in American campaigns issue positions are often ambiguous. Candidates say they are for "middle-class tax cuts," or "saving Social Security," or "strengthening American defense." The logic here is straightforward: candidates know that specific issue positions involve costs and trade-offs that may alienate some voters, so they tend to endorse broadly popular goals rather than any specific means of achieving those goals. Of course, present and past campaigns have involved clear and specific policy differences. Nevertheless, there is a venerable tradition of policy ambiguity in American campaigns.

Similarly, negative campaigning is hardly a recent invention. American political campaigns have been negative ever since Federalists were calling Thomas Jefferson an infidel. This does not mean that negative campaigning is necessarily more common or more important to vote choice than positive campaigning, now or then. It means that American campaigns have always involved contrasting the relative merits of the candidates, which typically necessitates providing unflattering information about one's opponent. But are contemporary campaigns any more negative than those of earlier campaign eras? It is difficult to say. No one has conducted a study comparing the information received by typical Americans in 1840 and in 2016, for example. If such a study were done, it seems likely it would reveal that today's voter would get substantially more information and a similar ratio of positive to negative information.

Conclusion

In this chapter, we have made the case that the United States has seen substantively different campaign eras. These differences have arisen for a variety of reasons, but chief among them is the transformation in information and communications technology, particularly the development of broadcast media such as television. At the same time, campaigns throughout U.S. history have shared common qualities, including a focus on the candidates' biographies and personalities and a willingness to attack opponents. Thus, although most Americans believe that campaigns have gotten "worse," it is difficult to prove that this is true. As we noted in Chapter 1, the quantity and quality of information provided to citizens are important criteria by which to judge campaigns. We are quite certain that more information is available to Americans today than 200 years ago, and it is far from clear whether that information is less useful or more superficial. This does not make contemporary campaigns "good" in any absolute sense, and there are reasonable arguments about how they might become better. Still, a historical perspective can be important in making such assessments.

KEY TERMS

era of pre-democratic campaigns (p. 55)

Federalist Party (p. 55)

Democratic-Republican Party (p. 55)

Democratic Party (p. 60)

Whig Party (p. 60)

Republican Party (p. 61)

Reconstruction (p. 64)

political machines (p. 64)

front-porch campaign (p. 66)

Progressive (or "Bull Moose") Party (p. 67)

civil service (p. 68)

Australian ballot (p. 68)

retail politics (p. 69)

wholesale politics (p. 69)

survey research (p. 72)

focus groups (p. 74)

big data (p. 76)

analytics (p. 76)

field experiments (p. 76)

sorting (p. 79)

FOR DISCUSSION

1. In what ways are today's campaigns similar to those of the second campaign era (1828–92)?

2. Thinking back to the second and third campaign eras, under what circumstances were candidates more likely to campaign personally for elected office? Why would this have been the case?

3. How did the rise of television and primary elections influence campaigns?

4. Some have argued that the Internet and the computer revolution have reinvigorated the more personal approach to campaigning that characterized earlier campaign eras. Do you agree or disagree with this argument?

CHAPTER 4

Financing Campaigns

Every election year, commentators and citizens bemoan the amount of money spent in American elections. The 2016 presidential election was no different. Together, the Democratic and Republican presidential candidates spent $1.45 billion in the primary and general elections combined.[1] This continued a string of presidential elections in which spending easily topped the $1 billion mark: candidates spent about $1.9 billion in 2008 and $1.4 billion in 2012. Small wonder, then, that even before the 2016 presidential campaign began in earnest, 84 percent of respondents in a May 2015 poll said that money has too much influence in political campaigns.[2]

It can be difficult to compare presidential spending over time, as it varies from year to year depending in part on the competitiveness of the primary elections. Long and competitive presidential primaries in both parties in 2008 and 2016 and in the Republican Party in 2012 contributed to the unprecedented levels of spending. But one major factor has clearly led to additional spending: an increasing number of presidential candidates have shunned **public funding**— funds provided to candidates by the federal government in exchange for their agreeing to restrictions on fund-raising from private donors. Several primary candidates in 2008 and all of the serious ones in 2012 and 2016 refused public funding. In 2008, Barack Obama was the first general election candidate to refuse such funding, which is why he was able to spend more than double what his Republican opponent John McCain spent. In 2012 and 2016, both major-party nominees declined public funds. The difference this makes is obvious: in 2004, for example, both general election candidates, George W. Bush and John Kerry,

---

[1] See the data compiled by the Center for Responsive Politics (OpenSecrets.org): www
.opensecrets.org/overview/index.php?display=T&type=A&cycle=2016 (accessed 9/9/2017).
The figures in this paragraph are in 2016 dollars.

[2] Sarah Dutton, Jennifer De Pinto, Anthony Salvanto, and Fred Backus. 2015. "Poll:
Americans Say Money Has Too Much Influence in Campaigns." *CBS News*, June 2. www
.cbsnews.com/news/poll-americans-say-money-has-too-much-influence-in-campaigns
(accessed 9/9/2017).

accepted just under $100 million in public funding (in today's dollars). This is a paltry sum compared with what candidates can raise and spend without public funding. With so much private money available to presidential candidates, they seem no longer willing to accept the spending limits that come with public funding. It is likely that the public funding system is defunct, and presidential candidates will continue to raise comparable sums of money.

But even in elections in which there has never been public funding, like U.S. congressional elections, spending has increased as well. The average candidate in a general election for the House of Representatives spent about $427,000 in 1980 and $1.3 million in 2016.[3] The trend in Senate races is more variable, in part because it depends on which states have Senate races in any given year, but spending has still increased over time. The average general election candidate for the Senate in 1980 spent about $3 million; the average Senate candidate in 2016 spent $8.3 million (Figure 4.1).

What does all this money buy? More than half of the average campaign's expenditures go to efforts to persuade and mobilize voters. For example, in the 2012 presidential election, more than half (58 percent) of candidates' spending went to produce advertisements and to buy time on television stations and other outlets where those advertisements aired. The next largest category of spending (14 percent) was fund-raising itself—illustrating the old idea that it takes money to make money. Much of the rest was spent on salaries (8 percent) and

Core of the Analysis

- The rules governing campaign finance place caps on donations but not on spending, which has allowed the cost of American campaigns to increase.
- These rules have an important implication for strategy: candidates and parties must raise the money necessary to fund their campaigns. Private donations are more important than public funding provided by the government.
- Campaign finance rules also allow independent groups, corporations, and labor unions to raise and spend money to try to elect or defeat candidates of their choice.
- These rules reflect a fundamental philosophical trade-off between two competing values: the right of donors and candidates to free speech and the need to guard against the potentially corrupting influence of money.

---

[3] These figures are in 2016 dollars.

FIGURE 4.1 Congressional Candidate Spending, 1980–2016

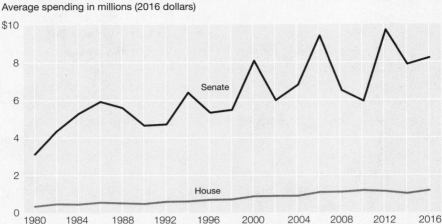

Average spending in millions (2016 dollars)

Source: Campaign Finance Institute. House: www.cfinst.org/pdf/vital/VitalStats_t2.pdf; Senate: www.cfinst .org/pdf/vital/VitalStats_t5.pdf (both accessed 9/9/2017).

administrative expenses (8 percent), such as travel, hotels, and rent for campaign offices.[4]

Candidates are not the only ones raising and spending more money. The political parties are also raising much more money in congressional elections, which they donate to candidates, spend on behalf of candidates, and use to mobilize voters—among other things. In the 1992 electoral cycle, the Republican and Democratic parties raised roughly a combined $630 million. In the 2016 cycle, they raised almost $1.5 billion (Figure 4.2).[5]

The other major actors spending money in elections are outside groups that work independently of the candidates and parties, but can raise and spend money to support candidates. Their spending in presidential elections increased from $13 million in 1992 to $652 million in 2008, then climbed dramatically to $1.3 billion in 2012 and again to $1.6 billion in 2016 (Figure 4.3). Independent group spending in midterm elections has increased sharply as well. Later we discuss the changes to federal election law that have allowed these independent groups to play a larger role.

Despite these increasing costs, it is not obvious whether American political campaigns are "too" expensive. By some metrics, in fact, they are cheap. For

---

[4] See the breakdown at OpenSecrets.org. "Expenditures." www.opensecrets.org/pres12 /expenditures.php (accessed 9/9/2017).

[5] These figures are in 2016 dollars and include all fund-raising by the Democratic and Republican national committees, as well as by their respective campaign committees for the House of Representatives and the Senate.

FIGURE 4.2 Political Party Spending in All Federal Races, 1992–2016

Total spending in millions (2016 dollars)

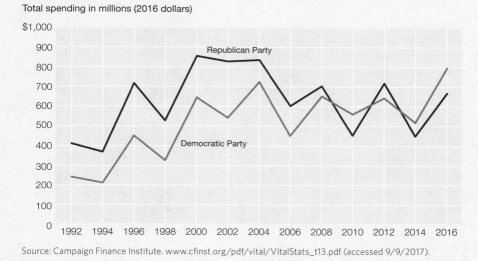

Source: Campaign Finance Institute. www.cfinst.org/pdf/vital/VitalStats_t13.pdf (accessed 9/9/2017).

FIGURE 4.3 Spending by Independent Groups, 1990–2016

Total spending in millions (2016 dollars)

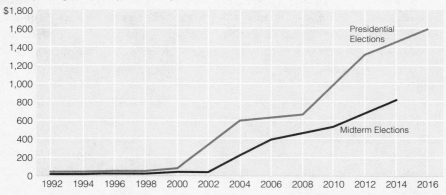

Note: These data are the totals spent by independent groups (not including party committees), in 2016 dollars.
Source: Center for Responsive Politics (OpenSecrets.org).

example, Americans spent more on almonds in 2014 than was spent in that year's midterm election.[6] Some even wonder why American campaigns are not more expensive; given the value of government policies to interest groups and corporations, they contribute remarkably little money to political candidates and parties.[7] Ultimately, it may not be necessary to determine whether American political campaigns are too costly. The more important questions are *why* American elections cost what they do and what consequences this money has for elections and the political system. Much of the answer lies in the rules of American campaign finance.

As we discussed in Chapter 2, electoral rules govern crucial aspects of political campaigns. Campaign finance rules affect both sides of campaign finance: donors, including individuals and interest groups, and spenders, including political candidates, parties, and interest groups. Regarding donors, the rules determine who can give, to whom they can give, and how much they can give. Regarding recipients, the rules determine whether, how much, and when they can spend. As with the electoral rules discussed previously, there is no single set of campaign finance laws. Federal law governs federal elections, but state and local laws govern state and local elections. Any state's campaign finance laws may differ from federal law and from the laws of other states.

Campaign finance rules affect candidate strategies, most notably by allowing (or, perhaps, forcing) candidates to raise money for their campaigns. Although systems of public financing exist, American campaigns largely depend on private donations. Campaign finance rules also empower parties and interest groups, each of which can raise and spend money on behalf of the candidates they favor or against candidates they oppose. The increasing role of these outside groups has raised fears that they will have too powerful an impact on elections.

Campaign finance rules are controversial as, like all rules, they attempt to balance different and sometimes conflicting values. One value is the right of citizens and candidates to express themselves. Without money, certain modes of expression are impossible. Another is the need to insulate candidates from the potentially corrupting influence of money. We want leaders to make decisions based on what is good for the country, or at least their constituents, not simply what is good for donors to their campaign. The trade-offs are evident: limiting

---

[6] Binyamin Appelbaum. 2014. "Who Wants to Buy a Politician?" *New York Times Magazine*, December 9. www.nytimes.com/2014/12/07/magazine/who-wants-to-buy-a-politician.html (accessed 1/4/2015).

[7] Stephen Ansolabehere, John M. de Figueiredo, and James M. Snyder, Jr. 2003. "Why Is There So Little Money in U.S. Politics?" *Journal of Economic Perspectives* 17, 1: 105–30.

the money raised and spent on campaigns might mitigate the potential for corruption, but it might also infringe on the right to free expression.

In this chapter, we begin by explaining the rules central to financing federal campaigns. In the process, we describe the important legislation and Supreme Court decisions that have shaped these rules. We also describe how state campaign finance laws differ from federal law. We will once again see that the central consequence of these laws, from the perspective of candidates, parties, and interest groups, concerns campaign strategy and each candidate's chances of winning. It is usually not possible for candidates to change the rules, but they can make them work to their advantage.

Rules for Donors

The rules for donors involve two basic questions: who is allowed to give and how much they can give. The central feature of this aspect of campaign finance law is the limits placed on donors, particularly on the amount of money that they can give to candidates and parties.

Who Can Give?

There are two main types of donors in American political campaigns: individuals and organized interest groups. Individual Americans are free to donate to any candidate, political party, or interest group, provided that they are either citizens or permanent residents. And while Americans have to be 18 to vote, there are no restrictions on the age of political donors. Minors can give, as long as it is their money and they do so voluntarily.

Organized interest groups can also donate, as long as they are not themselves tax-exempt groups. (Otherwise, the federal government would be indirectly subsidizing political campaigns by allowing groups to keep money they would have paid in taxes and then give it to particular candidates.) Potential donors therefore include corporations and labor unions, but not charities and churches. Neither corporations nor unions, however, can donate simply by giving some of their revenue directly to candidates or parties. Corporate donations were banned in 1907 with the passage of the **Tillman Act**. Labor union donations were banned in 1947 with the passage of the Taft-Hartley Act. Instead, corporations and labor unions must establish separate **political action committees (PACs)**, which are groups that directly work toward the election of candidates, to pass or defeat legislation, or to advance a political agenda on the corporation or union's behalf. Some small amount of corporate revenue can be spent to set up the PAC, but thereafter the PAC must raise money on its own. The PACs that give the largest amounts to political campaigns typically represent labor unions or industry associations (for example, the National Association of Realtors or the National Beer Wholesalers Association).

Membership organizations (groups with members who pay dues) must also establish PACs in order to give to candidates. Thus, there are PACs that represent groups with issue-oriented or ideological agendas, such as the National Rifle Association and Planned Parenthood. Political parties and political leaders can establish their own PACs as well. Political party organizations with PACs include the Democratic Senatorial Campaign Committee and the National Republican Congressional Committee. The PACs of political leaders, sometimes called "leadership PACs," raise money and donate to candidates whom those politicians favor. For example, Representative Nancy Pelosi (D-Calif.), showing affection for terrible puns, has her "PAC to the Future." The Republican Speaker of the House, Paul Ryan, calls his "Prosperity Action."

Campaign donations by PACs have increased sharply over time. PAC donations to congressional candidates grew from $125 million in 1978 to $441 million in 2016 (Figure 4.4). But this increase conceals an important fact: individuals donate more money to campaigns than do PACs. This is somewhat counter to the impression fostered by media coverage, which exaggerates PAC contributions.[8] In 2016, individuals contributed 52 percent of the funds raised by House candidates, while PACs contributed 39 percent.[9] The remainder came from donations from parties, the candidates themselves, and a few other sources.

Campaign finance law also provides for the disclosure of donors. New rules about disclosure were established in 1971 by the **Federal Election Campaign Act (FECA)** and then revised by amendments to the act in 1974. Candidates, parties, and PACs must each maintain a central committee where all donations are received. They are then required to file regular reports with the **Federal Election Commission (FEC)**, identifying anyone who has given them at least $200, with additional reports filed immediately before and after the election. In the final days of the campaign, any donation of $1,000 or more must be reported within 48 hours. In turn, the FEC maintains a searchable database of campaign donors. One can see that, for

---

[8] Stephen Ansolabehere, Erik C. Snowberg, and James M. Snyder, Jr. 2005. "Unrepresentative Information: The Case of Newspaper Reporting on Campaign Finance." *Public Opinion Quarterly* 69, 2: 213–31.

[9] Campaign Finance Institute. 2017. *Campaign Funding Sources: House and Senate Major Party Election Candidates, 1984–2016.* www.cfinst.org/pdf/vital/VitalStats_t8.pdf (accessed 10/25/2017).

FIGURE 4.4 **PAC Contributions to Congressional Candidates, 1978–2016**

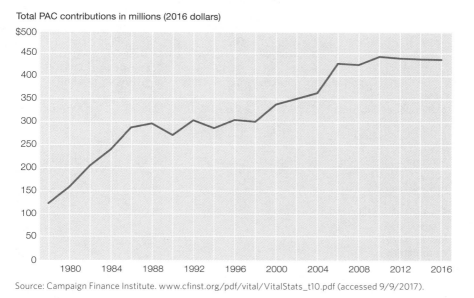

Total PAC contributions in millions (2016 dollars)

Source: Campaign Finance Institute. www.cfinst.org/pdf/vital/VitalStats_t10.pdf (accessed 9/9/2017).

example, Ben Affleck, identified in the database as an actor living in Santa Monica, California, has given money to various Democratic candidates, including Hillary Clinton, Barack Obama, and Massachusetts Senator Elizabeth Warren. Another actor, Chuck Norris of Dallas, Texas, has given money to a wide array of Republican candidates, including Senator John Cornyn of Texas, George W. Bush, and Mike Huckabee (with whom Norris campaigned extensively in 2008).

How Much Can Donors Give, and to Whom?

Under federal campaign finance law, there are limits on campaign donations. These limits were established by the amendments to the FECA in 1974 and remained unchanged until 2002, when new legislation, the **Bipartisan Campaign Reform Act (BCRA)**, adjusted the limits upward and indexed them to inflation, meaning that the limits will continue to increase in the future.[10] Limits are imposed on individuals, political party committees, and PACs, and affect what they can give to candidates, parties, and PACs, and, in some cases,

---

[10] This, and all of the major provisions of the BCRA, were upheld by the Supreme Court in *McConnell v. Federal Election Commission*, 540 U.S. 93 (2003). However, as we discuss later, a 2010 decision, *Citizens United v. Federal Election Commission*, 558 U.S. 310, overturned some provisions.

TABLE 4.1 Contribution Limits in the 2017–18 Election Cycle

	To Candidate	To National Party Committee	To State, District, and Local Party Committees	To Other Committees (e.g., PAC)	Overall Limits
Individual	$2,700 per election	$33,900 per year	$10,000 combined per year	$5,000	No limit
National party committee	$5,000*	No limit	No limit	$5,000	No limit
State, district, and local party committees	$5,000	No limit	No limit	$5,000	No limit
PAC	$5,000	$15,000	$5,000 combined per year	$5,000	No limit

* A national party committee and its senatorial campaign committee may also contribute up to $47,400 combined per campaign to each Senate candidate.
Source: Federal Election Commission. "How Much Can I Contribute?" http://classic.fec.gov/ans/answers _general.shtml#How_much_can_I_contribute (accessed 9/9/2017).

the total amount that they may give to all candidates and parties. Table 4.1 summarizes the limits in effect for the 2017–18 election cycle. As of 2018, individuals can donate $2,700 to any given candidate per election, for a maximum of $5,400 to each candidate for the primary and general elections combined. There was previously an overall limit on how much individuals could give to all federal candidates combined, but this limit was struck down by the Supreme Court in 2014.[11] PACs can give no more than $5,000 per election to any candidate, with no overall limit. (See Table 4.2a for more on contribution limits as they apply to candidate committees and PACs.)

Most states follow federal law in imposing limits on individual and PAC contributions for gubernatorial and other state-level races. Twelve states—Alabama, Indiana, Iowa, Mississippi, Missouri, Nebraska, North Dakota, Oregon, Pennsylvania, Texas, Utah, and Virginia—have no such

---

[11] *McCutcheon v. Federal Election Commission*, 572 U.S. ___ (2014).

TABLE 4.2a A Donor Taxonomy: Groups with Contribution Limits

	Candidate Committee	Political Party (PAC)	Federal PAC
Example	McCaskill for Missouri	Democratic Congressional Campaign Committee	American Meat Institute PAC
Description	Committee formed by the candidate to raise and spend money during the campaign.	PACs formed by the parties that donate money to the candidates or spend it for other purposes, such as get-out-the-vote efforts.	PACs organized by interest groups that collect contributions from members or employees and then donate to candidates, parties, or other PACs.
Limits on contributions to the group	Individuals: $2,700 per election PACs: $5,000 per election Corporations: Cannot give except via a PAC	Individuals: $33,900 per year to a national party committee PACs: $15,000 Corporations: Cannot give except via a PAC	Individuals: $5,000 per year PACs: $5,000 per year Corporations: Cannot give except to their own PAC
Limits on how the group can use its money	A candidate committee cannot contribute more than $2,000 to another candidate committee or $5,000 to a PAC.	A political party PAC can give no more than $5,000 a year to a candidate committee or another PAC.	A federal PAC can give $5,000 per election to a candidate, $5,000 per year to another PAC, and $15,000 per year to a party PAC.
Are donors disclosed?	Yes, to the Federal Election Commission (FEC).	Yes, to the FEC.	Yes, to the FEC.

limits.[12] The actual limits of the other states, however, vary widely. As of the 2017–18 election cycle, individual donors could give a candidate for the Massachusetts state legislature no more than $2,000 over these two years, while in Ohio, donors could give state legislature candidates up to $12,707.79. State restrictions on donations by PACs and parties are similarly diverse.

Political Parties and Soft Money

Current federal restrictions on contributions are now more far-reaching than they were before the BCRA passed in 2002. Before 2002, political party organizations, such as the Democratic National Committee and Republican National Committee, could raise **soft money**. These were donations that were not subject to contribution limits or disclosure provisions. **Hard money** donations, by contrast, are subject to these rules. During the 1990s, the parties became increasingly successful at raising soft money: in 2000, the Democratic and Republican parties raised a combined $637 million.[13]

Soft money contributions could be spent on registering and mobilizing voters and on some kinds of political advertisements, but not on **express advocacy**—that is, directly advocating for a particular candidate. Spending on ads that stopped short of express advocacy was permitted; the key was whether an ad used words like "vote for" or similar **magic words**. Parties found ways to craft ads that conveyed a clear partisan message anyway, often by merging criticisms of a candidate from the opposite party with **issue advocacy**, or arguments for positions on a particular issue. Consider this ad from a 1998 Wisconsin congressional race, in which a party organization, the Democratic Congressional Campaign Committee, targeted Mark Green, the Republican candidate:

> Mark Green has taken over $22,000 from the health care industry's lobbyists. It's no wonder that he voted against keeping our medical records private, allowing HMOs and insurance companies to make our records public. It's no wonder he wanted to let negligent health care providers off the hook, even when they operated under the influence of drugs or alcohol. Tell Mark Green our health care isn't for sale. Support HMO reform.

---

[12] National Conference of State Legislatures. 2017. "State Limits on Contributions to Candidates." www.ncsl.org/Portals/1/Documents/Elections/Contribution_Limits_to _Candidates_2017-2018_16465.pdf (accessed 9/9/2017).

[13] OpenSecrets.org. "Soft Money Backgrounder." www.opensecrets.org/parties/softsource .php (accessed 9/9/2017). In nominal dollars, the amount was $457 million, which is approximately $637 million in 2016 dollars.

The ad avoids the magic words and is ostensibly about an issue—namely, reform of health maintenance organizations (HMOs) and insurance companies. Nevertheless, the partisan intent is clear. Citizens are not fooled, either. In a 2000 study, participants watched several party-sponsored ads that were intended as issue advocacy but which included critical statements about the opposing presidential candidates. The vast majority of participants, about 80 percent, said that the primary objective of the ad was to "persuade you to vote against a candidate," not to "present an issue."[14]

The ability of parties to raise soft money was a big loophole in the rules. A labor union or corporation could not give a million dollars directly to a candidate but could give it to party committees. Critics argued that this created the appearance of, and perhaps the reality of, corruption, and so the BCRA banned soft money. Now, the only money that national parties can raise is hard money that is subject to contribution limits. Although critics of the BCRA feared that it would impoverish the parties, this has not come to pass. In fact, the Democratic and Republican National Committees raised $2.3 billion in 2016, significantly more than they raised before the BCRA was passed.[15]

Independent Groups

The BCRA did not close a second loophole, however. Independent groups, which are unaffiliated with political parties or candidates, are able to raise soft money without contribution limits (see Table 4.2b). As we discuss later, independent groups may not give this money directly to candidates, as traditional PACs do. Rather, they spend it independently of candidates on things such as political advertising, although their goal is still to help elect or defeat candidates. Spending by these groups increased dramatically after passage of the BCRA and then again after the 2010 *Citizens United v. Federal Election Commission* decision, which we will discuss in greater detail later in this chapter (also see Figure 4.3 on p. 87).

There are three main legal categories of independent groups, some identified by a confusing array of numbers and letters that correspond to designations under the federal tax code as administered by the Internal Revenue Service. The crucial differences among them involve federal laws about

---

[14] David B. Magleby. 2000. *Dictum without Data: The Myth of Issue Advocacy and Party Building.* Provo, UT: Center for the Study of Elections and Democracy.

[15] OpenSecrets.org. "Political Parties: Overview." www.opensecrets.org/parties/index.php (accessed 9/10/2017).

TABLE 4.2b A Donor Taxonomy: Independent Groups

	Independent Expenditure-Only Committee	527 Organizations	Nonprofits: 501(c)4, 501(c)5, 501(c)6
Example	American Crossroads	American Solutions Winning the Future	Crossroads Grassroots Policy Strategies, U.S. Chamber of Commerce
Description	A PAC that pays for communications that can support or oppose a candidate by name.	A tax-exempt group that raises money for political activities, including voter mobilization and issue advocacy. These groups haven't typically supported or opposed a candidate by name, but are beginning to do so.	Tax-exempt groups that can engage in political activity, but it cannot be their primary purpose. These groups haven't typically supported or opposed a candidate by name, but are beginning to do so.
Limits on contributions to the group	Unlimited	Unlimited	Unlimited
Limits on how the group can use its money	These groups cannot donate to a candidate or PAC or coordinate their spending with parties or candidates.	These groups cannot donate to a candidate or PAC or coordinate their spending with parties or candidates.	These groups cannot donate to a candidate or PAC or coordinate their spending with parties or candidates.
Are donors disclosed?	Yes, to the FEC.	Yes, to the Internal Revenue Service.	No, unless the contributor gives money for a specific political advertisement.

Source: Adapted from "A Donor Taxonomy." 2010. *New York Times*, September 21. www.nytimes.com /imagepages/2010/09/21/us/politics/21money-graphic.html (accessed 3/16/2015).

whether they must disclose their donors and whether and how they can be involved in campaign activity.

The first category of groups is **independent expenditure committees**— a type of actor that first came into existence during the 2010 campaign. These are PACs that pool donations from various sources and then use the funds to advocate explicitly for or against candidates. Because these PACs are not associated with a specific political party, corporation, or interest group, but gather contributions from multiple sources—individual donors, corporations, unions, and so on—they have been termed **super PACs**. Unlike traditional PACs, they can collect donations of unlimited amounts as a consequence of *Citizens United*. However, like traditional PACs, they are required to disclose their donors. Super PACs were initially created by people seeking to influence national elections, but over time they have become increasingly involved in state elections as well.[16] For example, super PACs may raise money from wealthy donors but then give that money to other organizations working to influence elections for governor or state legislatures.

The second category of independent groups is **527 organizations**. (The number *527* refers to a specific section of the tax code.) 527s are officially designated as political organizations under the tax code and are also required to disclose their contributors to the Internal Revenue Service. These organizations came to the fore in 2004, the first election after the BCRA's ban on soft money for parties. 527s like America Coming Together (ACT), MoveOn .org, and the Swift Boat Veterans for Truth raised and spent a substantial amount of money—over $850 million.[17] Because donations to 527s are not subject to contribution limits, wealthy Americans can give them large amounts of money; the financier George Soros gave $24 million ($33 million in 2016 dollars) to nine different left-leaning 527s in 2004.[18] After 2004, 527s played less of a role. MoveOn.org shut down its 527, partly because the Obama campaign asked it not to use its 527 to support Obama. Nevertheless, 527s still spent about $693 million (in 2016 dollars) in the

---

[16] Derek Willis. 2014. "The Special Powers of Super PACs, and Not Just for Federal Elections." *New York Times*, December 8. www.nytimes.com/2014/12/09/upshot/the -special-powers-of-super-pacs-and-not-just-for-federal-elections.html (accessed 1/4/2015).

[17] OpenSecrets.org. "527s: Advocacy Group Spending." www.opensecrets.org/527s/index .php (accessed 9/10/2017). In 2004 the nominal amount was $612 million, which is approximately $850 million in 2016 dollars.

[18] OpenSecrets.org. "Top Individual Contributors to Federally Focused 527 Organizations, 2004 Election Cycle." www.opensecrets.org/527s/527indivs.php?cycle=2004 (accessed 9/9/2017).

2008 election. In the wake of the *Citizens United* decision, many interests turned to super PACs as their preferred vehicles for raising campaign funds because they can openly support or oppose a candidate by name. As a result, 527s spent much less in the 2016 election ($495 million) than in 2004.

The third category of independent groups is known as **501(c) organizations**. These groups are designated as nonprofit organizations, are not required to pay taxes, and are not required to disclose their donors. There are various kinds of 501(c) organizations that are further designated with an additional number. For example, 501(c)3 organizations include charities, churches, and educational institutions. An example would be the March of Dimes. 501(c)4 organizations, such as the League of Women Voters, are designated as "social welfare" organizations under the tax code, meaning that their goal is to "operate primarily to further the common good and general welfare of the people of the community (such as by bringing about civic betterment and social improvements)."[19] 501(c)5 organizations include agricultural, horticultural, and labor organizations. For the purpose of U.S. campaigns, the most important 501(c)5 organizations are labor unions. 501(c)6 organizations include business leagues and chambers of commerce— the most important among them being the U.S. Chamber of Commerce.

Tax laws place restrictions on the campaign activities of 501(c)3 and 501(c)4 organizations. Organizations with 501(c)3 status are prohibited from participating in political campaigns, although some occasionally attempt to bend or skirt the law. For example, a 501(c)3 organization might post a sign on its property endorsing a candidate. By contrast, 501(c)4 organizations are allowed to participate in campaign activity as long as that activity is not their "primary purpose." Since the 2010 election, 501(c)4 organizations became prominent, particularly those working to support Republican candidates. These organizations, which like many 527s used nondescript names like Crossroads Grassroots Policy Strategies, attracted some donors, particularly corporations, that did not want their identities revealed. Some questioned whether groups like Crossroads were flouting the law by making campaign activity their primary purpose, although it appears unlikely that these groups will be investigated. For one, there is limited staffing and funding at the Internal Revenue Service.[20] Moreover, when the IRS attempted to determine whether groups applying to become 501(c)4 organizations were likely to be primarily political

---

[19] Internal Revenue Service. 2017. "Social Welfare Organizations." www.irs.gov/Charities-& -Non-Profits/Other-Non-Profits/Social-Welfare-Organizations (accessed 10/25/2017).

[20] Michael Luo and Stephanie Strom. 2010. "Donor Names Remain Secret as Rules Shift." *New York Times*, September 20. www.nytimes.com/2010/09/21/us/politics/21money.html (accessed 1/4/2015).

organizations, a scandal arose in 2013 over whether the IRS was targeting conservative groups in particular. The scandal has arguably made it less likely that the IRS will begin to regulate these groups more stringently. And even if the IRS did, this would not address another concern of critics, which is that these groups can legally raise and spend money without disclosing their donors.

Rules for Spenders

The spenders in American political campaigns include candidates, parties, PACs, and independent groups. The rules for spenders involve three basic questions: how much they can spend, and when and how they can campaign. These rules, particularly regarding independent groups, are among the most controversial aspects of campaign finance law.

How Much Can They Spend?

Central to American campaign finance law is this principle: contributions are limited, but spending is not. The federal government cannot limit how much candidate campaign committees, party committees, PACs, or independent groups such as 527s spend on campaign activity. And candidates can spend an unlimited amount of their own money on their campaign—that is, they can "self-finance."

Originally, the FECA contained both spending and contribution limits. But when the FECA provisions were challenged in the Supreme Court in the 1976 case **Buckley v. Valeo**,[21] the Supreme Court upheld only the contribution limits. The Court reasoned that although donating to candidates was an act of speech subject to First Amendment protections, the federal government had a compelling interest in preventing the possibility of corruption, which might arise if a candidate could raise large amounts of money from a few donors. Thus, contribution limits were declared constitutional. However, the Court ruled that there was no compelling interest in limiting spending, and thus the spending limits violated the free speech clause of the First Amendment.

At the federal level, spending can be limited only in presidential races, and then only with the agreement of the candidates. The FECA set up a system of public financing for presidential elections, which was upheld by the Court in *Buckley* and remains in place today. Public financing comes from tax dollars; there is, in fact, a box on federal tax forms that taxpayers

---

[21] 424 U.S. 1 (1976).

can check if they want to give a small amount of money to help finance federal campaigns.

In the nomination phase, public financing comes in the form of matching funds. If candidates have raised a certain amount in a certain number of states, the federal government will give them funds equal to the contributions they received from individuals, up to $250 for any single contribution. Thus, if an eligible candidate received 1,000 donations of $250, or $250,000, she would receive an additional $250,000 in matching funds. To be eligible for public funding, a candidate must first raise at least $5,000 in each of 20 different states. The requirement to raise at least some money helps to ensure that only viable, serious candidates qualify for matching funds. If candidates accept matching funds, however, they must then agree to a spending limit. In 2016, the limit was approximately $48 million overall, with specific limits by state depending on population size.[22] Again, the public-funding system is voluntary, and some candidates refuse matching funds in the primaries because they want to raise and spend more than this limit. In 1980, Republican John Connally was the first primary candidate to take this step. In 1996, Steve Forbes became the next candidate to do so. By 2012, it had become accepted practice, with every Republican candidate as well as Barack Obama refusing matching funds. In 2016, only one candidate in the presidential primary—Democrat Martin O'Malley—accepted public financing.

Presidential general elections also have a public financing option. After each party holds its nominating convention, the nominee for that party can receive a fixed amount of money from the federal government. This amount is indexed for inflation and varies from election to election. In 2016, it was $96.1 million. The candidate must then agree to spend only that amount—although, of course, party committees and independent groups may also be spending money in ways that help the candidate. Until 2008, every major-party presidential candidate accepted public funds for the general election.[23] That year, Obama refused public funding, allowing him to spend more than his opponent, John McCain. In 2012, both Obama and Romney spurned public funds. In 2016, so did both Clinton and Trump.

Public financing systems also exist in some states. As in the presidential system, all are optional and come with strings attached, such as minimum fund-raising requirements, pledges to limit or refuse private donations, and

[22] Federal Election Commission. 1996 (updated 2017). "Public Funding of Presidential Elections." https://transition.fec.gov/pages/brochures/pubfund.shtml (accessed 9/9/2017).

[23] Minor-party and independent candidates are not eligible for federal funds unless they meet the vote threshold from the previous election. If they adhere to FECA regulations, they can retroactively apply for public money.

spending limits. For example, in New Jersey, gubernatorial candidates must, as of 2017, raise $430,000 to be eligible for public financing. The state will then match every $4,300 in private contributions with $8,600 in public money—up to $4 million for the primary election campaign and $9.3 million for the general election campaign. However, participating candidates may not spend more than $6.4 million in the primary campaign and $13.8 million in the general campaign.[24]

Three states have gone further and established full public funding, also known as **clean elections systems**, for statewide or legislative elections, or both.[25] Arizona's system will illustrate. To be eligible, candidates for state offices must gather at least 200 contributions of $5 or more. Once candidates decide to accept public financing, they receive a grant from the state and may not receive any further private donations. For example, gubernatorial candidates in Arizona in 2014 were limited to $1.1 million. These amounts reflect the goal of limiting the amount of money spent on campaigns.

When and How Independent Groups May Campaign

A final set of rules applies to when and how campaigning can take place. In line with the lack of limits on campaign spending, the American system also imposes few restrictions on when and how candidates may campaign. In contrast, some other democratic countries restrict televised political advertising. For example, in Belgium, France, Great Britain, and Spain, candidates and parties cannot buy broadcasting time on either commercial or public television. In lieu of purchased time, these countries provide free air time either on commercial or public television, albeit with substantial restrictions on when and how much advertising can be aired.[26] The lack of such restrictions in the American system is one reason why campaigns are so expensive: the largest category of candidate spending is for television advertising, and that advertising can be aired at any point and in whatever amount. It is not surprising that in competitive races, this makes for long campaigns with seemingly endless advertisements.

---

[24] Jeffrey Brindle. 2017. "Gubernatorial Public Financing Program Brings Better Elections at Minimal Cost." *Insider NJ*, May 15. www.insidernj.com/gubernatorial-public-financing -program-brings-better-elections-minimal-cost/ (accessed 9/9/2017).

[25] National Conference of State Legislatures. 2017. "Overview of State Laws on Public Financing." www.ncsl.org/research/elections-and-campaigns/public-financing-of-campaigns -overview.aspx (accessed 9/9/2017).

[26] Christina Holtz-Bacha and Lynda Lee Kaid. 2006. "Political Advertising in International Comparison," in *The Sage Handbook of Political Advertising*, eds. Lynda Lee Kaid and Christina Holtz-Bacha. Thousand Oaks, CA: Sage, pp. 3–13.

Experiments in Online Fund-Raising

Candidates frequently send dozens if not hundreds of e-mails to their supporters, asking them to contribute money, or more money, to the campaign. These e-mails were a crucial part of the Obama campaign's fund-raising strategy in 2012. More so than Mitt Romney, Obama relied on donations in small amounts to fund his campaign, although he took in plenty of large donations, too.[1] How did the Obama campaign motivate supporters to give and give again? They invested in a little science.

In particular, the Obama fund-raising team conducted experiments with their fund-raising e-mails. Before they sent a blast e-mail to their list of supporters, they selected small groups of supporters at random and sent each group a different version of the e-mail. These groups would see different subject lines, different text, different colors, and so on. Then the Obama team would see which e-mail elicited the most donations. The "winning" e-mail would then be sent to all supporters.

For example, in one experiment, the Obama team determined that the subject line "I will be outspent" raised far more money than "If you believe in what we're doing" or "Do this for Michelle." More generally, the Obama team determined that a casual tone and even occasional profanity ("Hell yeah, I like Obamacare") also increased donations. Most of these findings were not anticipated in advance. The Obama team would routinely bet on which e-mails would be most successful in each experiment. For the most part, they were wrong. Amelia Showalter, Obama's director of digital analytics, said, "We were so bad at predicting." This is why the science was so valuable.[2]

But science goes only so far. The Obama team discovered that new e-mail tactics tended to work for a while, but then they would wear off and new tactics were required. Moreover, what worked best in the Obama campaign did not necessarily work as well in other campaigns. Showalter described how the Obama campaign's e-mails tended to raise more money when they were shorter, but Senator Elizabeth Warren's campaign found that longer e-mails written by Warren herself tended to be most effective for them.[3]

Nevertheless, these experiments have spawned many more by other candidates, party committees, and interest groups. All of this science is likely to increase the efficacy of online fund-raising.

---

[1] See www.cfinst.org/pdf/federal/president/2012/Pres12_30G_Table4.pdf (accessed 1/4/2015).
[2] Joshua Green. 2012. "The Science behind Those Obama E-Mails." *Bloomberg Businessweek*, November 29. www.businessweek.com/articles/2012-11-29/the-science-behind-those-obama-campaign-e-mails (accessed 1/4/2015).
[3] John Sides and Lynn Vavreck. 2014. "Obama's Not-So-Big Data." *Pacific Standard*, January 21. www.psmag.com/navigation/politics-and-law/obamas-big-data-inconclusive-results-political-campaigns-72687/ (accessed 1/4/2015).

The American system places more restrictions on independent groups than on the candidates or parties. A first rule is that if these groups want to spend their resources to support a candidate or the candidates of a party, they cannot consult with, coordinate with, or receive help from the candidates or the party. If a labor union PAC wants to help a Democratic candidate, neither that candidate nor her staff can assist with PAC fund-raising, the production of a television advertisement sponsored by the PAC, or the PAC's decision on when and where to air the ad. However, candidates and their supporting groups have found ways to bend this rule, despite renewed vigilance by the U.S. Department of Justice. In 2016, for example, several politicians established super PACs and began working with them closely before they had officially declared their candidacy for the presidency—in essence, delaying their "official" presidential campaign to allow more time to fundraise for their super PAC. Candidates have done other things that skirt the no-coordination rule, such as independently placing footage of themselves campaigning on YouTube, which super PACs then use in their campaign advertisements.[27]

Second, there are restrictions on the content of advertising by independent groups. When the BCRA was passed in 2002, its proponents were worried that, with a ban on soft money contributions to political parties, even more soft money would flow to independent groups, who would use these contributions to engage in issue advocacy, including the production of ads that lacked the "magic words" but were essentially endorsements of (or attacks on) a candidate. So, the BCRA established new rules. First, it defined a new and expanded category of *electioneering communications*: ads that referred to a clearly identified candidate for federal office (regardless of whether the magic words were mentioned), that occurred up to 60 days before a general election or 30 days before a primary election, that were publicly distributed on radio or television, and that were broadcast to an electorate of at least 50,000 people. The BCRA then stated that electioneering communication could not be funded with corporate or union treasury funds—that is, the revenue that corporations or unions raise as part of their regular operations. In order to engage in electioneering communication, these groups would have to establish PACs and raise hard money subject to contribution limits and disclosure provisions. Of course, the BCRA's rules on electioneering communication

---

[27] Matea Gold and Colby Itkowitz. 2015. "Justice Department Ramps up Scrutiny of Candidates and Independent Groups." *Washington Post*, February 27; Paul Blumenthal. 2015. "2016 Candidates Thumb Their Noses at Campaign Finance Rules." *Huffington Post*, March 18; Matea Gold. 2015. "It's Bold, But Legal: How Campaigns and Their Super PAC Backers Work Together." *Washington Post*, July 6.

contained exceptions. They did not regulate ads that occur outside the 30- or 60-day windows, or other forms of campaigning such as direct mail, online ads, or telephone calls.

Subsequent Supreme Court decisions weakened these BCRA provisions substantially. The most important decision, **Citizens United v. Federal Election Commission**, was handed down in 2010.[28] Citizens United is a nonprofit organization that received corporate funding to produce a documentary film, *Hillary: The Movie*, which was critical of Hillary Clinton. The group wanted to run commercials advertising the film and to air it on cable television during the 2008 presidential primaries. The FEC considered this to be an electioneering communication—essentially, an argument that Clinton should not be elected—that could not be aired 30 days before a presidential primary. Citizens United asserted that the documentary was factual and politically neutral.

During oral arguments, the more conservative justices on the Court took the unusual step of going beyond the narrow questions surrounding the documentary to consider a more fundamental issue: whether corporations and unions could be banned from spending their general treasury funds for electioneering communication. Commentators assumed that this signaled the conservatives' willingness to overturn the ban, and, indeed, that hunch was correct. In a 5–4 decision, the Court ruled that the ban was unconstitutional. While corporations and unions are not literally people, the majority argued that "associations of persons" also have a right to free speech. The Court's decision opened the door to advertising by corporations and labor unions— not simply their PACs—that both targeted specific candidates (express advocacy) and was aired within the 30- and 60-day windows. The decision called into question laws in 24 states that had imposed similar restrictions or bans on independent expenditures by corporations or unions. It also provoked criticism by President Obama in his 2010 State of the Union address, a speech made in front of members of both houses of Congress and the Supreme Court. We discuss the debate over *Citizens United* in more detail later in the chapter.

Some commentators feared that the *Citizens United* decision would lead to a flood of spending and advertising by independent groups. Analyses in the wake of 2010 suggested that these concerns might have been overblown. In the 2010 election, the amount of money spent by independent groups substantially increased relative to the previous midterm election in 2006. However, the spending of other actors, including the candidates and parties, also

---

[28] *Citizens United v. Federal Election Commission*, 558 U.S. 310 (2010).

increased, particularly in Senate races, where the fraction of advertisements that were sponsored by independent groups, as opposed to candidates or political parties, was no greater in 2010 than in 2008. In U.S. House races, this fraction doubled from 6 percent in 2008 to 12 percent in 2010, but even the 12 percent figure was a much smaller fraction than in 2000, when interest group advertisements constituted 17 percent of all advertisements in House races.[29]

In many ways, it was the elections of 2012, 2014, and 2016 that confirmed the worst fears of those who believed the *Citizens United* decision would open the floodgates of spending in campaigns. Outside groups spent far more in 2012 and 2016 than they had in 2008: $1.35 billion in 2012 and $1.6 billion in 2016, compared with $652 million in 2008 (all figures in 2016 dollars; see Figure 4.3 on p. 87). Similarly, in the 2014 midterm election, outside spending was much higher than in 2010.

If party and candidate spending had also increased dramatically in these recent elections then there would be less cause for concern, but that was not the case. As a result, the percentage of all Senate ads sponsored by independent groups has increased in every election since 2010: from 15 percent in 2010 to 30 percent in 2012, 36 percent in 2014, and finally 38 percent in 2016. The percentage of presidential ads sponsored by such groups increased from 19 percent in 2004 to 31 percent in 2012 and 28 percent in 2016. In House races, there was not much increase between 2010 and 2016, but the percentage of ads sponsored by independent groups was still much higher in these elections than in the pre–*Citizens United* era.[30]

Commentators have also speculated about whether independent spending decides elections. That is less clear. Outside groups typically target the most competitive races, where candidates and parties are also campaigning heavily. This means advertisements sponsored by independent groups may be drowned out in the general din of the more numerous advertisements from candidates and parties. Indeed, in 2010, Democratic candidates' disadvantage in terms of independent group spending was largely compensated for by their advantage in spending by candidates and party organizations. Similarly, in 2012, Obama compensated for Romney's 3–1 advantage in outside group

---

[29] Michael M. Franz. 2011. "The *Citizens United* Election: Or Same as It Ever Was?" *Forum* 8, 4: article 11.

[30] Michael M. Franz. 2013. "Interest Groups in Electoral Politics: 2012 in Context." *Forum* 10, 4: 62–79. Erika Franklin Fowler and Travis N. Ridout. 2015. "Political Advertising in 2014: The Year of the Outside Group." *Forum* 12, 4: 663–84. Erika Franklin Fowler, Travis N. Ridout, and Michael M. Franz. 2016. "Political Advertising in 2016: The Presidential Election as Outlier?" *Forum* 14, 4: 445–69.

spending by raising significantly more than his opponent in individual contributions. Moreover, there is simply no guarantee that the balance of outside spending will determine who wins. In 2016, Clinton spent far more than Trump—both in terms of what she raised herself and what outside groups spent on her behalf—and still lost.

Does this mean that outside group spending does not matter? Absolutely not. In 2012, if one excludes ads sponsored by interest groups, for every 53 ads that Romney aired in a media market, Obama aired 100 ads in the same media market. When one includes ads by independent groups, for every 82 ads favoring Romney in a media market, there were 100 Obama ads.[31] In other words, it can be argued that outside group spending kept Romney in the game and enabled him to mount a strong challenge against an incumbent president. Thus, an advantage in independent spending does not guarantee that a candidate will win an election, but it can improve his or her chances.

Campaign Finance Rules and Political Strategy

As we discussed in Chapter 2, understanding electoral rules is important because they profoundly influence the actions of citizens, candidates, parties, and interest groups. This is true regarding campaign finance law as well. Here, we identify some of the implications of the campaign finance system for each category of actors.

Citizens

By making private donations central to campaign fund-raising, the American system allows private citizens another avenue by which to express their political voice, one distinct from voting or writing to a member of Congress, for example. As with other forms of political participation, donating provides citizens another means by which they can establish a tie with candidates and hold elected leaders accountable for their performance in office. Donations are a particularly powerful way to encourage accountability: the central goal of any candidate is to be elected, and it is virtually impossible to do so without the resources provided by donations.

---

[31] Franz, "Interest Groups in Electoral Politics."

How do citizens decide what candidates to support with donations? Most of the time, the decision is straightforward: a donor gives to a candidate who shares her values and goals.[32] But the decision can be strategic as well. Consider, for example, primary elections, in which there are often few differences between the candidates. How might donors decide then? One important factor is whether donors expect a candidate to win. If two candidates have similar platforms, donors often prefer to support the likely winner rather than "waste" their money on a likely loser. Potential donors will thus look to various indicators of candidates' viability, including polls, news coverage, and donations by other individuals and interest groups.[33]

Candidates

Campaign finance rules profoundly affect political candidates. By not limiting spending, the American system gives candidates the incentive to raise and spend as much as possible. By limiting the amount of each donation, the system makes it particularly onerous to raise money because candidates must raise it from a larger number of donors. If there were no limits on the size of donations, a candidate could conceivably fund his campaign with money from a single rich donor. Instead, candidates ask for contributions from thousands of donors, with phone calls, at receptions and dinners, and so on. One study of House candidates in the 1996 and 1998 elections found that a substantial fraction (42 percent) reported spending at least a quarter of their time engaged in fund-raising. Almost a quarter of these candidates (24 percent) reported spending at least half their time fund-raising.[34] The manager of Barack Obama's 2004 Senate campaign described the strategy bluntly: "Put him on the phone and let him beg." He wanted Obama on the phone four hours a day, purely trying to raise money.[35] More recently, an orientation given to newly elected Democratic members of Congress by the

---

[32] Ansolabehere et al., "Why Is There So Little Money in U.S. Politics?"; Michael J. Barber, Brandice Canes-Wrone, and Sharece Thrower. 2017. "Ideologically Sophisticated Donors: Which Candidates Do Individual Contributors Finance?" *American Journal of Political Science* 61, 2: 271–88.

[33] Diana C. Mutz. 1995. "Effects of Horse-Race Coverage on Campaign Coffers: Strategic Contributing in Presidential Primaries." *Journal of Politics* 57, 4: 1015–42.

[34] Paul S. Herrnson and Ronald A. Faucheux. 2001. *The Good Fight: How Political Candidates Struggle to Win Elections without Losing their Souls*. Washington, DC: Campaigns and Elections.

[35] William J. Feltus, Kenneth M. Goldstein, and Matthew Dallek. 2017. *Inside Campaigns: Elections through the Eyes of Political Professionals*. Washington, D.C.: Sage/CQ Press, p. 93.

Democratic Congressional Campaign Committee also recommended that they spend four hours each day making phone calls to raise funds.[36]

Candidates will likely face even greater incentives to raise money in the wake of the *Citizens United* decision. The trend of increasing independent spending may heighten candidates' fear of an advertising blitz sponsored by independent groups, much of which would likely attack them.

Given this reality, candidates must seek out efficient ways to raise money. The Internet is helpful, as fund-raising online does not require receptions or dinners. For example, in 2016, Vermont Senator Bernie Sanders mounted a well-funded campaign in the Democratic presidential primary supported in large part by small donors, many of whom donated online.[37] Another strategy is to recruit "bundlers," relatively wealthy donors who can enlist a set of friends and acquaintances to donate. Bundlers are so valuable that campaigns use catchy names to recognize them. For the 2000 and 2004 Bush presidential campaigns, bundlers were called "Pioneers," "Rangers," and "Super-Rangers" if they supplied $100,000, $200,000, and $300,000, respectively, in donations.

Fund-raising takes considerable time and energy and will continue to do so. But not every candidate faces the same burden. The American system of campaign finance advantages incumbents to a significant degree. As we discuss further in Chapter 10, incumbent members of Congress are typically much more successful than challengers in raising money. They are better known. They already have the status and power that make them valuable to donors and interest groups. They are usually perceived as the likely victor. All of this stacks the deck against challengers.

The campaign finance system may also benefit wealthy candidates. The lack of spending limits means that candidates can fund their own campaigns, potentially giving wealthy individuals a significant advantage over the less wealthy. Thus, American elections often feature candidates who spend large amounts of their personal wealth to get elected. For example, in the 1992 presidential campaign, Ross Perot spent $63 million of his own money running as an independent candidate. Similarly, in 2016 about 20 percent of Donald Trump's campaign funds came from his own bank accounts, while less than

---

[36] Ryan Grim and Sabrina Siddiqui. 2013. "Call Time for Congress Shows How Fundraising Dominates Bleak Work Life." *Huffington Post*, January 8. www.huffingtonpost.com/2013/01/08/call-time-congressional-fundraising_n_2427291.html?1357648217 (accessed 1/4/2015).

[37] Kenneth P. Vogel. 2016. "How Bernie Built a Fundraising Juggernaut." *Politico*, February 10.

The limits on how much individual donors can contribute mean that candidates have to spend much time and effort amassing enough contributions to fund their campaigns by attending fund-raisers, wooing potential donors, and soliciting contributions. Here, Bill Schuette, the Republican candidate for governor of Michigan in 2018, mingles with attendees at a barbecue fund-raiser in Midland, MI.

1 percent of Hillary Clinton's campaign funds came from hers.[38] Self-financing can discourage some potential opponents from running against a wealthy, self-financed candidate.

However, the experiences of self-financed candidates also suggest that personal wealth does not guarantee victory. In 2016, for example, Democrat David Trone ran for a U.S. House seat in Maryland, gave his campaign $14 million while raising only $6,000 from others, and lost in the primary.[39] Why might self-financing candidates lose so handily? First, it is important to remember that many candidates are essentially forced to spend their own money because they are facing strong opposition and could easily be defeated if they only use what they raise from other donors, or because they are languishing in the polls and desperately need to give their campaign a jolt. In

---

[38] See www.opensecrets.org/pres16/candidate?id=N00023864 and www.opensecrets.org /pres16/candidate?id=N00000019 (accessed 9/9/2017).

[39] See www.opensecrets.org/overview/topself.php (accessed 9/9/2017).

the 2004 presidential primaries, Senator John Kerry mortgaged his house so that he could loan $6.4 million to his campaign, which was struggling at that time (although he did go on to win). Second, dollars raised from other donors appear to produce more votes than dollars provided by the candidate. This may reflect the additional benefits of cultivating a network of supportive donors. Private donations signal the strength of the candidate to the media and political elites. It will surprise no one that a candidate would give his or her own campaign $3 million—after all, it is the candidate's money, and the candidate wants to win. But if 3,000 people give the candidate $1,000 each, it may convince others that the candidate is a serious contender. Moreover, the act of fund-raising may generate local media coverage of fund-raising events and may strengthen a candidate's ties to crucial interest groups and blocs of voters. Thus the possibility of self-financing entails a complex series of strategic calculations.[40]

As we discussed earlier, in presidential elections, candidates may accept public funding. But this necessitates another strategic calculation, because the public funding comes with a spending limit. For a lesser-known candidate in the presidential primaries, accepting the money may be an easy decision. Unfamiliar candidates struggle to raise private donations and may be able to spend far more if they accept matching funds, despite the accompanying spending limit. Better-known candidates will be tempted to rely on private donations because they believe that there is more money to be raised from the many private individuals and interest groups that will donate rather than public funds. Many believe that the fact that almost no major-party presidential candidates in the 2012 and 2016 primaries or general elections accepted public funds signaled the death knell of the public financing system for presidential elections. This is very likely true unless the level of public funding is raised enough to make it attractive to candidates once again.

By accepting private donations, candidates face another strategic imperative: keeping donors happy. Donors can withhold their money to ensure accountability, and it is up to the candidate to make sure that donors are not disappointed. The problem, however, is that what donors want may not match up with what voters want. Thus, candidates may find themselves forced to take one position to please donors but another position to please voters—a difficult balancing act and one that often attracts criticism if contradictory positions become public knowledge.

---

[40] See Jennifer A. Steen. 2006. *Self-Financed Candidates in Congressional Elections.* Ann Arbor: University of Michigan Press.

Political Parties and Interest Groups

Under the current rules, political parties and interest groups, including corporations and unions, can raise and spend their own money on campaign activities. The BCRA's ban on soft money has not hindered the parties in this regard, and the Supreme Court's decision in *Citizens United* gave interest groups even freer rein to spend independently. This poses both an opportunity and a challenge for candidates. On the one hand, they may benefit from the campaign activities of their party and of interest groups that support them. On the other hand, they may find that their party and ostensibly supportive interest groups are not interested in helping them. They may also be attacked by the opposing party and its aligned groups. Thus, the presence of parties and interest groups can both facilitate and complicate the efforts of candidates.

A dispute within the Democratic Party during the 2006 election illustrates the complex ways in which the strategies of candidates and parties interact. The chair of the Democratic National Committee (DNC), the former Vermont governor and 2004 presidential candidate Howard Dean, advocated a "50-state strategy"—one that would invest the DNC's money in building up the Democratic party organization in every state, even in states where the party rarely won elections. This was a boon to many Democrats in such states, who typically did not attract much support from the party. At the same time, the chair of the Democratic Congressional Campaign Committee (DCCC), Rahm Emanuel, had a very different strategy: he sought to use DCCC money to bolster Democratic House candidates in competitive races, and thought it was wasteful to spend party money in states where the party had little chance of winning. This was a boon to Democrats in hard-fought campaigns, but not to Democrats in Republican-dominated states. No matter which strategy the party pursued, some Democratic candidates would benefit more than others.

Like political parties, interest groups must make strategic decisions about which candidates to support, through either donations or independent expenditures. This will depend on their agenda. Groups that find their interests well served by current officeholders will pursue an "access" strategy, working to support incumbents of both parties and, via their contributions, to guarantee access to these incumbents so that they can press their agenda. This creates an incentive for incumbent candidates to be responsive to groups to ensure their support during the campaign. Groups that tend to have a more ideological agenda, one further from the average officeholder, will pursue a "replacement" strategy, seeking to replace incumbents with new representatives who share their agenda. These new representatives will typically come from one party or even one ideological faction within the party.[41] The Club for Growth, a group that promotes conservative economic policies, is famous for targeting incumbent "RINOs"—Republicans in Name Only—that it considers too moderate. Of course, incumbent candidates will not sit idly by if they are threatened with such a challenge. They may take new steps to placate the interest groups and convince them not to support their challenger. If that is unsuccessful, they may adjust their own positions on issues to be more in line with their challenger's, thereby negating some of the rationale for replacing them. In the 2010 Arizona Senate race, John McCain, the incumbent, faced a conservative challenger, J. D. Hayworth, in the Republican primary. Hayworth's presence led McCain to take more conservative positions on several issues. McCain soft-pedaled his earlier advocacy for campaign finance reform and the BCRA, even though he had been one of its staunchest advocates.

The agendas of candidates and their interest group supporters may not be well aligned—a very plausible scenario, given that under current campaign finance law, candidates and interest groups are not permitted to coordinate their campaign activities. A supportive interest group may emphasize different issues or themes or adopt a different set of tactics than the candidate it supports. For example, parties and interest groups tend to air far more negative campaign ads than do candidates. At times, this may not bother candidates, who can take the high road and let others do the dirty work. But at other times, candidates may have to disavow a particularly aggressive ad aired by a supporter. In the 1988 presidential election, the National Security Political Action Committee (NSPAC) aired an ad attacking the Democratic candidate, Michael Dukakis, for a Massachusetts program that allowed prisoners to leave jail temporarily for furloughs as part of a rehabilitation effort. The ad focused on one prisoner, William Horton (the ad called him "Willie"), who, while on furlough, raped a woman and assaulted her fiancé. The ad featured a photograph of Horton, who was black, and became controversial after critics argued that it played on racial fears. The campaign of Dukakis's opponent, George H. W. Bush, ultimately requested that NSPAC withdraw it, although some have argued that the Bush campaign knew about the ad in advance

---

[41] See Michael M. Franz. 2008. *Choices and Changes: Interest Groups in the Electoral Process.* Philadelphia: Temple University Press.

and delayed their request for its withdrawal to give the ad time to have an impact.[42]

Ultimately, candidates may find that much of the campaigning that takes place, even on their behalf, is out of their control. As such, it may both help and hurt their campaign, at least as they see it. By expanding the number of actors eligible to raise and spend money, the American system of campaign finance creates loose alliances among candidates, parties, and interest groups that contain significant tensions even as these players seek a common goal.

The Debate over Campaign Finance Reform

The American system of campaign finance is perennially controversial, as the debate over the *Citizens United* decision illustrates. To understand this controversy, it is worth considering the values that underlie the campaign finance system, discussing the tensions among these values, and evaluating proposed reforms to the system. As noted earlier, two important values underlying campaign finance law are freedom of speech, as discussed in Chapter 1 and as enumerated in the First Amendment, and guarding against corruption, in particular the corrupting influence of money. Debate about campaign finance also engages other values discussed in Chapter 1, especially free choice and political equality.

The Supreme Court has weighed those values in different ways when considering the rules imposed on donors and spenders. In *Buckley v. Valeo*, the Court argued that donations to a candidate pose a significant threat of corruption, but that spending on behalf of a candidate (for example, by an interest group) does not. It also argued that donations are not as meaningful as spending in terms of their communicative content. Donations serve only to convey general support but not the reasons for that support. Spending, on the other hand, is central to communicating one's ideas during a campaign. Both of these arguments buttressed the Court's decision in *Buckley* to limit donations but not spending. Concerns about free speech also led to the Court's decision in *Citizens United*, which struck down laws that restricted the spending of independent groups.

---

[42] The Federal Election Commission conducted an investigation into whether there was illicit cooperation between the Bush campaign and the independent group that produced the ad. The commission was deadlocked 3–3 on the question (not surprising, given the presence of three Republicans and three Democrats on the commission) and thus did not produce a conclusive ruling. See www.insidepolitics.org/ps111/independentads.html (accessed 1/4/2015).

The Case against the Status Quo

The chief objection to these legal decisions (and to the American system in general) is that they allow money to have too much influence on politics, which has at least four possible negative consequences. First, it is hard on candidates, who must raise money incessantly, even to the detriment of other, possibly more beneficial activities, such as policy making. It may also discourage some talented individuals from running in the first place, especially ones who have no ability to self-finance as an alternative to raising private donations. In a 2011 survey of potential political candidates, 19 percent of women and 16 percent of men said that the prospect of soliciting campaign contributions would "deter them from running for office."[43]

Second, critics fear that money simply buys elections, meaning that whoever can spend the most wins. They point to the fund-raising disparities between incumbents and challengers and to the extraordinarily high rate at which incumbents win. This criticism is based on the values of free choice and political equality. Voters do not really have a choice, the argument goes, when a well-funded incumbent can scare off many potential challengers and then easily defeat the poorly funded challenger who decides to run. Is it fair that campaign finance rules create such inequality, whereby some candidates have vastly more resources to spend than others?

Third, critics argue, the campaign finance system favors those wealthy enough to donate to campaigns, giving them a greater voice in politics than those who cannot donate and so violating the value of political equality.[44] Wealthy individuals are far more likely than the poor to donate to candidates. Indeed, campaign contributions have become increasingly concentrated among the wealthiest individuals, as overall their wealth has grown and they have become more interested in politics.[45] One analysis of early fund-raising in the 2016 presidential campaign found that fewer than 400 families had donated almost half the money raised.[46] Moreover, critics

---

[43] Jennifer L. Lawless and Richard L. Fox. 2012. "Men Rule: The Continued Under-Representation of Women in U.S. Politics." Washington, D.C.: Women & Politics Institute, School of Public Affairs, American University. www.american.edu/spa/wpi/upload/2012-Men-Rule-Report-final-web.pdf (accessed 9/9/2017).

[44] Richard L. Hasen. 2016. *Plutocrats United: Campaign Money, the Supreme Court, and the Distortion of American Elections*. New Haven, CT: Yale University Press.

[45] Adam Bonica, Nolan McCarty, Keith T. Poole, and Howard Rosenthal. 2013. "Why Hasn't Democracy Slowed Rising Inequality?" *Journal of Economic Perspectives* 27, 3: 103–24.

[46] Nicholas Confessore, Sarah Cohen, and Karen Yourish. 2015. "Small Pool of Rich Donors Dominates Election Giving." *New York Times*, August 1. www.nytimes.com/2015/08/02/us/small-pool-of-rich-donors-dominates-election-giving.html (accessed 10/26/2017).

claim, interest groups that represent wealthy Americans and business or corporate interests are more powerful than groups representing, for example, the poor or working class. In the 2015–16 election cycle, business PACs contributed about $3.4 billion to congressional and presidential candidates, while labor PACs contributed just $205 million.[47]

Fourth, critics point to the fact that some outside groups can raise and spend money without disclosing their donors. This prevents observers and voters from knowing the identities or agendas of the people trying to influence election outcomes. This is all the more problematic, critics argue, since these outside groups are raising donations in unlimited amounts. For example, of the $180 million raised by the 501(c)4 organization Crossroads GPS during the 2012 election cycle, $22.5 million came from a single donor, whose identity is unknown.[48]

Fifth, and perhaps most important, critics argue that the current system does not do enough to combat corruption, or at least the appearance of corruption. Critics note that candidates and political parties still find ways to raise large amounts of money that violate the spirit of campaign finance law. For example, in recent elections candidates and their parties have established "joint fund-raising committees." A donor can write a single check to this committee; this donation is then distributed to the candidate, national party committees, and perhaps state parties. Joint fund-raising committees raise a lot of money, too—$1.2 billion in 2016.[49] Although joint fund-raising committee donations to individual campaigns or party committees cannot exceed contribution limits, critics argue that the overall impact of a single large check gives wealthy donors added clout. Furthermore, committees are established to fund the presidential nominating conventions, to which any individual donor can contribute up to $100,200 per year.[50]

Fundamentally, critics are concerned that the money that donors and organized interests give and spend can influence elected leaders. Stories about the possible influence of money are common. After the mass shooting in Las Vegas on October 1, 2017, some were quick to blame campaign donations by

[47] OpenSecrets.org. "Business-Labor-Ideology Split in PAC & Individual Donations to Candidates, Parties, Super PACs and Outside Spending Groups." www.opensecrets.org/bigpicture/blio.php (accessed 1/4/2015).

[48] Matea Gold. 2013. "One Single Donation to Crossroads GPS in 2012: $22,500,000." *Washington Post*, November 15. www.washingtonpost.com/blogs/the-fix/wp/2013/11/15/one-single-donation-to-crossroads-gps-in-2012-22500000 (accessed 1/4/2015). These figures are in nominal dollars.

[49] See www.opensecrets.org/jfc/ (accessed 9/9/2017).

[50] See www.opensecrets.org/pres16/conventions (accessed 9/9/2017).

the National Rifle Association for the unwillingness of many politicians to support new gun control measures.[51] A 2002 survey of state legislators also found that many believed that campaign contributions had at least some influence on the content and passage of bills in their state's legislature.[52] In the minds of critics, campaign contributions may lead to policies favored by donors, rather than policies that would serve other important goals and perhaps even the general good of the country.

A proposed solution to many of these potential problems with campaign finance rules is public financing, especially a clean elections system like that in Arizona. Clean elections systems can help equalize resources among candidates by providing the same amount of public funding to all candidates and by forbidding any other fund-raising by the recipients of public funding. With equal amounts of funding, campaigns might then be more competitive, improving the quality of information provided to voters and giving them a more meaningful choice. In addition, with almost all campaign financing coming from the government, there is little to no chance that wealthy donors or interest groups will have a disproportionate or corrupting influence. For example, when North Carolina instituted a voluntary public financing system for state Supreme Court candidates, those candidates who opted for public financing were less favorable to attorney donors.[53] Advocates of clean elections have proposed a similar system for federal elections, the Fair Elections Now Act, which could, in the words of one of its proponents, make "elected officials beholden to the people they're supposed to represent instead of the wealthy special interests."[54]

Complicating the Case for Reform

How well do the arguments for campaign finance reform withstand empirical scrutiny? And are there good arguments in support of the system as it stands? Answers to these questions suggest that the American system of campaign finance, however imperfect, may have its merits.

---

[51] Jason Le Miere. 2017. "How the NRA Will React to Las Vegas Shooting: Raise More Money to Donate to Congress to Oppose Gun Controls." *Newsweek*, October 2. www .newsweek.com/las-vegas-shooting-nra-gun-675930 (accessed 10/26/2017).

[52] Lynda W. Powell. 2012. *The Influence of Campaign Contributions in State Legislatures.* Ann Arbor: University of Michigan Press.

[53] Morgan L.W. Hazelton, Jacob M. Montgomery, and Brendan Nyhan. 2016. "Does Public Financing Affect Judicial Behavior? Evidence from the North Carolina Supreme Court." *American Politics Research* 44, 4: 587–617.

[54] Public Campaign. "Bipartisan Fair Elections Now Act Reaches Majority of Majority in U.S. House." www.commondreams.org/newswire/2010/02/04/bipartisan-fair-elections -now-act-reaches-majority-majority-us-house (accessed 10/31/2017).

Two protesters mark the anniversary of the Supreme Court's *Citizens United* decision in 2015. The ongoing consequences of that decision continue to provoke debates about the role of money in politics.

Arguments for reform include two primary claims about the current system: simply stated, money buys elections and money buys legislators' votes. But can we verify that these statements are true? If the first claim means that the candidate who spends the most money will win the election, then this is clearly false. In 2016, Hillary Clinton raised and spent more than Donald Trump, but lost the Electoral College and thus the presidency. A similar point can be made about House elections. House incumbents typically raise much more than challengers, but is this the reason that incumbents tend to win? Or do incumbents raise so much because they are already anticipated to win, and donors often prefer to give to the likely winner? And how do we separate the effects of incumbents' fundraising advantage from the other advantages they have as incumbents, including their work on behalf of constituents and consequent visibility? These sorts of advantages may help explain why incumbents were reelected at such high rates even *before* they were so dominant in fundraising. For example, in the early 1980s, House incumbents were typically spending about 1.5 times as much as challengers; in the 2000s, they typically spent about 2.5 or three times as much. But incumbents' reelection rates in the early 1980s were above 90 percent, slightly higher than in the

2000s, even though their fund-raising advantage increased in the 2000s. Thus, the high reelection rate of incumbents is not necessarily due *only* to their fund-raising advantage.

Incumbents' other advantages may explain why more stringent campaign finance rules do not necessarily transform elections by making them more competitive and incumbents more vulnerable. For example, neither bans on spending by corporations nor different levels of limits on individual donations are associated with incumbent defeats.[55]

The evidence on the effects of clean elections is also somewhat equivocal. Public financing programs appear to reduce the amount of time that candidates spend fund-raising for themselves and thereby to increase the time they spend interacting with voters, but they may also increase the time candidates spend fund-raising for their party. Public financing programs do appear to reduce the advantages of incumbents and make elections more competitive, but they may also make legislatures more polarized by reducing the influence of interest groups that tend to support moderate candidates.[56]

The claim that money buys legislators' votes also needs examination. There is relatively little evidence that this actually occurs. First, because of contribution limits, the amount that any donor or interest group can give is small, relative to the large amounts of money that many candidates routinely raise and spend. Candidates who raise millions of dollars are not likely to "sell" their votes to a PAC for a measly $5,000.

Second, many donations to campaigns are strategic: donors do not want to waste their money on someone who will never support their agenda. Instead, they give to legislators who are already supportive of it, perhaps because these legislators simply have beliefs about policies that are similar to the donors' beliefs or because the legislators work to respond to their

---

[55] Raymond J. La Raja and Brian F. Schaffner. 2014. "The Effects of Campaign Finance Spending Bans on Electoral Outcomes: Evidence from the States about the Potential Impact of *Citizens United v. FEC.*" *Electoral Studies* 33, 1: 102–14; Thomas Stratmann and Francisco J. Aparicio-Castillo. 2006. "Competition Policy for Elections: Do Campaign Contribution Limits Matter?" *Public Choice* 127, 1–2: 177–206.

[56] Peter L. Francia and Paul S. Herrnson. 2003. "The Impact of Public Finance Laws on Fundraising in State Legislative Elections." *American Politics Research* 31, 5: 520–39; Andrew Hall. 2014. "How the Public Funding of Elections Increases Candidate Polarization." Working paper available at www.andrewbenjaminhall.com/Hall _publicfunding.pdf (accessed 1/4/2015); Michael G. Miller. 2013. *Subsidizing Democracy: How Public Funding Changes Elections and How It Can Work in the Future.* Ithaca, NY: Cornell University Press; Powell, *The Influence of Campaign Contributions in State Legislatures.*

constituents, who also share the donors' views. Consider this hypothetical example. The National Farmers Union PAC gives an incumbent congressman $5,000 for his reelection campaign. The congressman represents a rural district in Iowa whose economy revolves around growing corn. After the election, he votes to give additional government subsidies to corn farmers. Did he vote this way because he simply believes that government subsidies are necessary, because many of his constituents are farmers and others who benefit from subsidies, or because he got that PAC contribution?

None of this is to say that campaign donations are ineffectual. Some research suggests that donations are more likely to buy the involvement of an elected official on an issue, if not his vote. Donations appear to motivate representatives to be more active in promoting a given issue on congressional committees, for example. However, this is true only for representatives who already share the donors' positions.[57] Donors may also get more "access" to an elected official—that is, a greater opportunity to advocate for their views in front of a representative or her staff.[58] Of course, this does not imply that the representative will always agree with these views. Ultimately, campaign donations may not be quite as powerful an influence as reformers claim and media coverage often suggests.

The American system of campaign finance can also be defended on philosophical grounds. Two of the features that reformers routinely target—private donations and unlimited spending by candidates—could in fact be considered valuable. By allowing private donations to candidates, the American system creates an opportunity for citizens and interest groups to have a voice and help to elect candidates they believe can best represent them. By allowing unlimited spending, the American system allows for more campaign activity, including advertising that communicates information about the candidates, activities that mobilize citizens to vote, and so on. This point was made in the *Buckley v. Valeo* decision: "A restriction on the amount of money a person or group can spend on political communication during a campaign necessarily reduces the quantity of expression by restricting the number of issues discussed, the depth of their exploration, and the size of the audience reached." And, indeed, there is evidence that campaign spending helps voters learn

---

[57] Richard L. Hall and Frank W. Wayman. 1990. "Buying Time: Moneyed Interests and the Mobilization of Bias in Congressional Committees." *American Political Science Review* 84, 3: 797–820.

[58] Joshua L. Kalla and David E. Broockman. 2016. "Campaign Contributions Facilitate Access to Congressional Officials: A Randomized Field Experiment." *American Journal of Political Science* 60, 3: 545–58.

about political candidates.[59] Given that Americans still do not always know much about the candidates or vote in large numbers, it could be counterproductive to limit campaign spending.

Leaving aside arguments about the merits of the current campaign finance system, there is one further challenge that critics of the system face: there is often little incentive for incumbent leaders to reform the system. Despite the public's complaints about money in elections, polls reveal that opinions about dramatic reforms, such as public financing, depend on how the poll question is worded. For example, a 2010 poll conducted by Common Cause, a group advocating for public funding, found that 63 percent of respondents supported public financing when described this way:

> Under this plan, candidates for Congress could run for office without raising large campaign contributions. Instead they would collect a large number of small contributions from their home state in order to qualify for a limited amount of public funding for their campaign. They would be prohibited from taking any contributions over 100 dollars or any contributions from lobbyists. Contributions of 100 dollars or less would be matched with public funds on a four to one basis, up to a strict limit.[60]

However, a 2007 Gallup poll found that the public actually preferred that presidential candidates *not* accept public financing.[61] Over half of respondents (56 percent) believed that candidates should "opt not to take public financing and spend whatever money they can raise on their own" rather than "agree to take public financing and accept spending limits." Similarly, in 2013 Gallup found that only 50 percent would vote for a "law that would establish a new campaign finance system where federal campaigns are funded by the government and all contributions from individual and private groups are banned." And a November 2015 poll found that 56 percent of Americans believed that candidates should rely on donations, while 26 percent supported full public funding and 17 percent supported a matching system

---

[59] For example, see John J. Coleman and Paul F. Manna. 2003. "Congressional Campaign Spending and the Quality of Democracy." *Journal of Politics* 62, 3: 757–89.

[60] See www.lakeresearch.com/news/MoneyPolitics.publicpresentation.pdf (accessed 1/4/2015).

[61] Lydia Saad. 2007. "Americans Prefer Presidential Candidates to Forgo Public Funding." *Gallup*, April 27. www.gallup.com/poll/27394/Americans-Prefer-Presidential-Candidates-Forgo-Public-Funding.aspx (accessed 1/4/2015).

in which the federal government would match private donations.[62] The public's reluctance to embrace public financing wholeheartedly reflects their ambivalence about using government money—in other words, their taxes—to fund campaigns.

It is actually not clear that the public pays much attention to how candidates finance their campaigns. In an October 2008 Gallup poll, about 70 percent of voters either did not know whether Barack Obama and John McCain had accepted public financing or were mistaken in their view.[63] Little had changed four years later. Despite record spending by outside groups in 2012, only 25 percent of Americans said that they had heard "a lot" about "increased spending in this year's presidential election by outside groups."[64] More generally, the public typically considers campaign finance reform far less important than the economy, foreign affairs and war, health care, education, and a host of other issues. In a May 2015 *New York Times* poll, almost no one ranked campaign finance as the most important issue facing the country.[65] Indeed, the legislation that became the BCRA languished for years until a major scandal involving the energy company Enron—which had developed a close relationship with many elected politicians even as it was covering up financial problems that would eventually lead to bankruptcy—prompted action.

Without a significant push from the public, incumbent leaders are often reluctant to embrace reform. This is entirely rational: they were elected under the status quo. Changing the rules introduces uncertainty into their bids for reelection. Incumbent leaders are especially nervous about public financing because they often believe it will help their opponents to be more competitive—and, of course, this is precisely the outcome desired by some proponents of public financing. The point is not who is wrong or right. The

---

[62] Emily Swanson and Julie Bykowicz. 2015. "AP-NORC Poll: Americans Not Fans of Public Financing." *AP News*, December 8. www.apnews.com/1a0f52ec099d4e82a0f6ed168f9756c9 (accessed 9/9/2017).

[63] Jeffrey M. Jones. 2008. "Campaign Financing Appears to Be Non-Issue for Voters." *Gallup*, October 30. www.gallup.com/poll/111652/Campaign-Financing-Appears-NonIssue -Voters.aspx (accessed 1/4/2015).

[64] The source is a July 2012 *Washington Post* poll: www.washingtonpost.com/politics/polling /americans-unfamiliar-outside-campaign-spending/2012/08/02/gJQA9lWLRX_page.html (accessed 1/4/2015).

[65] Nicholas Confessore and Megan Thee-Brenan. 2015. "Poll Shows Americans Favor an Overhaul of Campaign Financing." *New York Times*, June 2. www.nytimes.com/2015/06/03 /us/politics/poll-shows-americans-favor-overhaul-of-campaign-financing.html?mcubz=3& _r=0 (accessed 9/9/2017).

point is that the implications of campaign finance rules for elected leaders often mean that their best strategy is to not change the rules.

Conclusion

Debates about the efficacy of the current system of campaign finance laws in the United States reinforce the important connections among rules, reality, strategy, and citizens. The American system is unusual among democracies in that candidates and other actors have been given a wide degree of latitude with respect to what they can say, when they can say it, and how they pay for it. Recent changes in campaign finance law have increased the amount of money in federal election campaigns, mostly by allowing interest groups to solicit and spend funds more freely. Some observers have gone so far as to suggest that trying to keep money out of politics is like trying to keep ants out of a kitchen: plugging one hole will only lead the ants to find another as long as there is any sugar around. Nevertheless, proponents of campaign finance reform seek to plug as many holes as possible, even as others defend the current system and do not mourn the failures of regulation. This again highlights the fact that campaign finance rules reflect a fundamental philosophical trade-off between free speech, on the one hand, and the potentially corrupting influence of money, on the other.

KEY TERMS

public funding (p. 84)

Tillman Act (p. 89)

political action committees (PACs) (p. 89)

Federal Election Campaign Act (FECA) (p. 90)

Federal Election Commission (FEC) (p. 90)

Bipartisan Campaign Reform Act (BCRA) (p. 91)

soft money (p. 94)

hard money (p. 94)

express advocacy (p. 94)

magic words (p. 94)

issue advocacy (p. 94)

independent expenditure committees (p. 97)

super PACs (p. 97)

527 organizations (p. 97)

501(c) organizations (p. 98)

Buckley v. Valeo (p. 99)

clean elections systems (p. 101)

Citizens United v. Federal Election Commission (p. 104)

FOR DISCUSSION

1. According to Supreme Court decisions about campaign finance, why are contributions to candidates limited while spending by candidates is unlimited?

2. What are the costs and benefits to a candidate of funding their campaign via (a) money raised from private donors, (b) public funding, and (c) their own money?

3. How did the BCRA and the *Citizens United* decision affect the ways in which political parties and interest groups can raise and spend money in elections?

4. What are arguments for and against the statement that money corrupts politicians?

CHAPTER 5

Modern Campaign Strategies

Lost in much of the surprise over the 2016 election was the fact that Donald Trump had a fairly simple "strategy" that he and his advisers followed throughout his presidential campaign. Early on they decided that Trump would emphasize two words both as a critique of what Washington was lacking and as a rationale for his candidacy: "common sense."

When he started to contemplate a run for political office over two decades ago, Trump sought to cast the complex problems facing the United States as simple dichotomous choices with straightforward implications. His 2016 presidential campaign followed this blueprint from the first day onward.

Shortly after Barack Obama's 2012 reelection, Trump began to plan for the 2016 campaign with his top adviser, Roger Stone. They quickly settled on the phrase "Make America Great Again," which exemplified the larger strategic approach of the campaign. According to Sam Nunberg, one of the advisers who helped Trump launch his 2016 bid:

> Common sense. . . .The Republican primary voter will want it. And Washington will immediately tell you, "You can't do that." That's the elite class telling you, "We're smarter than you and you don't know what's good for you." . . . Further infuriating the voter, and making the voter more dedicated to Trump.[1]

The issues and policy positions that animated Trump's campaign all reflected this broader understanding that voters craved clarity and resisted being told that ineffectiveness and indecisiveness were unavoidable facts in a complex world. For example, Trump's commitment to building a wall on the southern border of the United States demonstrated a simple "solution" to the complex problem of

---

[1] Jeremy Diamond. "CNN's 'Unprecedented': 'Common Sense,' Trump's Campaign Strategy from the Get-Go." CNN *Politics*, November 18. www.cnn.com/2016/11/18/politics/donald -trump-common-sense-campaign-strategy-unprecedented-book/index.html (accessed 8/31/2017).

immigration, while also playing on Trump's experience as a builder and developer. It had the further virtue of casting Trump as a protector in the minds of voters.

Meanwhile, Hillary Clinton's campaign struggled to identify a strategy. Her previous experience made her uniquely qualified to be president, and she would have been the country's first female president. But did she want to run as an expression of gender equality? Or as the heir to Barack Obama? As the heir to Bill Clinton? More concretely, did the Clinton team understand 2016 as a "time for a change" election or as a "building on progress" election? And would they attempt to reach out to independent and Republican voters or would they attempt to reanimate and mobilize the Democratic base? In the end, Clinton's campaign chose to focus on Trump's shortcomings. This seemed prudent at the time—it rallied Democrats and helped counter the perception among independent voters that Clinton wasn't very honest or ethical. However, in failing to provide a positive rationale for her candidacy, many pundits and practitioners contend that Clinton's campaign was fatally flawed.

But how much of this is rewriting history? Did Trump really have a coherent and consistent strategy that guided his campaign's activities? And, if so, how "good" was Trump's campaign strategy in 2016? Was it really a major factor in his successful run to capture the White House? And what about the other side: how "bad" was Hillary Clinton's campaign strategy? Did it cost her the presidency? Or was she simply the victim of an uneven economic recovery and an electorate that wanted something different after eight years of Barack Obama? More generally, how do political scientists define and evaluate campaign strategies as they interpret the results of voting and elections?

Core of the Analysis

- A campaign must develop a strategy in order to compete effectively in a competitive district or state.
- Campaigns try to mobilize supporters and persuade undecided voters.
- Campaign strategy involves decisions about whether to run, which issues to emphasize, what positions to take on issues, whether to attack the opposition, and how to allocate resources to different constituencies and media.
- These strategic decisions depend strongly on the broader rules and realities that candidates confront.
- Campaign organizations have general features in common but vary considerably depending on the size and scope of the campaign.
- Modern political campaigns rely on professionals to devise and execute their strategies, and to organize their campaigns.

The goal of this chapter is to describe and consider the role of strategy (and strategists) in American political campaigns. We begin by defining strategy and discussing how a modern campaign develops a strategy. Next, we outline the important strategic decisions of a campaign, examining both professional practice and academic research. Among other things, we argue that campaigns are selective with respect to what they say and who they say it to. Some voters are critical to victory and they receive most of the campaign's attention. The skill with which a campaign identifies and convinces these voters can be important for the outcome of the election. We then examine what a campaign looks like, how it is organized, and the role of political consultants. Finally, we discuss the normative implications of the rise of more professionalized, strategic campaigns.

How Are Campaign Strategies Constructed?

Assuming a candidate has decided to run—a decision we will consider in greater detail later in this chapter—there are many tasks the campaign must address immediately. The campaign needs a physical space for a headquarters, so that people have a place to work. The candidate has to announce his or her candidacy. There are people who must be contacted, including past candidates and party leaders, whose expertise, advice, and endorsement are all potentially valuable. The campaign needs to identify the main issues the candidate intends to run on and prepare position papers. Finally, the campaign must purchase some of the staples of the modern campaign: computers, computer servers, Wi-Fi and Internet connections, smartphones, and materials for brochures, bumper stickers, buttons, and pamphlets.

But perhaps more than anything else, a campaign needs to quickly develop a **campaign strategy**. Put simply, a strategy is a proposed pathway to victory. It is a plan for how to win, and it is driven by an understanding of who will vote for the candidate and why they will do so. The political scientist Joel Bradshaw posits four key propositions for developing a successful campaign strategy.[2] First, in any election the electorate can be divided into three groups: the candidate's base, the opponent's base, and the undecided. Second, past election results, data from registered voter lists, and survey research make it possible to determine which people fall into each of these three groups. Third, it is neither possible nor necessary to get the support of all people

---

[2] Joel Bradshaw. 2004. "Campaign Strategy," in *Campaigns and Elections American Style*, 2nd ed., eds. James A. Thurber and Candice J. Nelson. Boulder, CO: Westview Press, pp. 38–40.

everywhere to win the election. Research should allow a campaign to determine how best to mobilize the candidate's base and persuade the undecideds. Both mobilization and persuasion are central to a campaign's efforts. Fourth, and last, once a campaign has identified how to win, it can act to create the circumstances to bring about this victory. In order to succeed, campaigns should direct campaign resources—money, time, and message—to key groups of potential voters and nowhere else. Resource allocation is therefore defined by strategy.

Vote Targets

Implicit in these propositions is the need to develop specific **vote targets** (or vote goals). These targets are based on estimates of what the upcoming election will look like: how many total votes the campaign believes will be cast in the election, how many it will need to win, how many votes its candidate can expect no matter what, and how many **persuadable** (or **swing**) **votes** are out there.

Campaigns typically derive vote targets by examining data from recent comparable elections. For example, let us say that our candidate is running for governor in the 2018 general election in Ohio. The simplest way to develop an estimate for the total votes to be cast in the upcoming election is to look across the most recent gubernatorial elections (see Table 5.1).

Notice that we are not looking at turnout in presidential years, which is invariably higher than in midterm elections; we only want to look at data from

TABLE 5.1 Turnout in Ohio Gubernatorial Elections, 2002–14

Year	Registered Voters	Total Votes	Turnout Rate
2002	7,113,826	3,356,285	47%
2006	7,860,052	4,185,597	53%
2010	8,037,806	3,956,045	49%
2014	7,748,201	3,149,876	41%
Average	**7,689,971**	**3,661,950**	**48%**

Source: Ohio Secretary of State. "Voter Turnout: Election Results and Data." www.sos.state.oh.us/elections/election-results-and-data/ (accessed 10/5/2017).

comparable elections. Notice also that the Ohio turnout rate varies a bit from year to year, from a low of about 47 percent in 2002 to a high of about 53 percent in 2006. The number of registered voters, however, increases every year before declining slightly in 2014. It increased by 746,226 from 2002 to 2006, and by 177,754 from 2006 to 2010. It declined by 289,605 from 2010 to 2014. Based on this information, for the 2018 election it is reasonable to assume that (1) turnout will be about 50 percent of registered voters, and (2) the number of registered voters will be between 7.7 and 8.3 million. In a real election campaign, we would be able to access updated registration numbers from the Ohio secretary of state. For illustrative purposes, though, let us assume that there will be 8,000,000 registered voters for the next election. If we assume that 50 percent of those who are registered vote in the governor's race, the total number of votes cast will be about 4,000,000.

How many votes do we need to win? This depends, of course, on the number of candidates in the race. If it is simply a contest between two major party candidates—Republican versus Democrat—our candidate will need slightly more than 50 percent of the vote. If there are minor party or independent candidates, a candidate could conceivably win with less than 50 percent (a plurality, but not a majority). But let us assume that we have a two-party election on our hands. A bare majority (50.1 percent) of our expected electorate would be 2,004,000. Most campaigns round up when estimating a vote target because they want to avoid a situation where they meet their target but lose the election because of unexpectedly high turnout. As a case in point, analysts from Hillary Clinton's 2016 campaign said that she met her vote targets in the critical battleground state of Pennsylvania—including the key Philadelphia collar counties of Bucks and Montgomery—but ultimately lost because of unexpectedly high turnout in the heavily Republican rural counties of central and northern Pennsylvania (the Pennsylvania "T"). So let us be very cautious and set a vote target of 54 percent, or 2.16 million votes.

Next, our campaign should have an expectation about what our candidate's base vote is. In other words, how many votes would a "bad" candidate from the party get in an election in which conditions favored the other side? Again, most campaign strategists turn to past results to estimate this (Table 5.2).

Consider things from the perspective of the Republican candidate. The election results vary a great deal—from a Republican high of 64 percent in 2014 to a low of just under 37 percent in 2006. In many ways, 2006 was a low-water mark for the Republican Party, both in Ohio and across the nation. Republican president George W. Bush was deeply unpopular, a controversial

TABLE 5.2 Votes Won in Ohio Gubernatorial Elections, 2002–14

Year	Republican Candidate	Democratic Candidate	Other Candidates	Republican Candidate's Percentage
2002	1,865,007	1,236,924	127,061	58%
2006	1,474,331	2,435,505	113,019	37%
2010	1,889,186	1,812,059	151,224	49%
2014	1,944,848	1,009,359	101,706	64%

Source: Ohio Secretary of State. "Voter Turnout: Election Results and Data." https://www.sos.state.oh .us/elections/election-results-and-data/ (accessed 10/5/2017).

war was dragging on in Iraq, and the economy was beginning to show signs of recession. Moreover, in Ohio, the Republican gubernatorial candidate, Ken Blackwell, was widely regarded as having run an especially inept campaign. Thus, we can take the 2006 result as an estimate of the Republican base vote: the minimum that a Republican candidate can expect to win. If we use the figure of 37 percent of the expected turnout, our estimate of the Republican base vote in 2018 is 1,480,000.

To generate an estimate of the persuadable vote, we need an upper estimate of what a candidate from our party can achieve. In other words, how many votes would a "good" Republican candidate get in an election in which conditions favored the Republican Party? The 2014 election provides just such an example. The public was angry about the troubled rollout of Obamacare and the slow, uneven economic recovery, and blamed the Democrats in power. Furthermore, the Republican gubernatorial candidate John Kasich was a popular figure who appealed to Democrats and independents as well as Republicans. Let us therefore take his 64 percent result as an estimate of the high potential for a Republican candidate. The difference between these extremes is 64 minus 37 percent, or 27 percent. So our estimate of the persuadable vote for our upcoming Ohio governor's race is 27 percent of the total expected vote of 4 million, or approximately 1,080,000 voters.

This last estimate is critical. To recap, we assume that approximately 4 million voters will cast ballots in the Ohio governor's election in 2018. We have a vote target of 2.16 million, and we estimate that our base vote is slightly under 1.5 million voters. The swing vote in the state is 1.1 million voters. To get from our base (1.5 million) to our target (2.16 million), we need to win 660,000 of the 1,080,000 swing votes (61 percent).

It is important to observe that while this is how many campaigns estimate the number of swing voters, it does not translate into individual "targets"—that is, we have an idea about how many voters can be swayed, but we do not know from these data which individuals are most likely to be persuaded to vote for our candidate. Contemporary campaigns use data from registered voter lists to identify specific individuals to whom directed persuasive communication may be effective (more on this later).

We can also generate vote targets for each county in the state, based on previous election results—for example, we might use the four most recent elections to calculate the average contribution of each county to the total statewide party vote (Table 5.3). Consider Cuyahoga County, where the city of Cleveland is located: it contributed, on average, 7.9 percent of the total Republican vote in Ohio in the past four elections. For the 2018 election, we would multiply this number by the total statewide vote target (2.16 million) to generate a target for Cuyahoga of 170,640 Republican votes. This can be done for every county and even the precincts within a county.

TABLE 5.3 Election Results and Vote Targets for Selected Ohio Counties (Republican Candidates)

County	2014: Kasich Votes	2010: Kasich Votes	2006: Blackwell Votes	2002: Taft Votes	Average Contribution to Republican Vote Total	Vote Target for 2018 Election (based on a statewide target of 2.16 million)
Cuyahoga	172,319	148,611	107,258	142,874	7.90%	170,640
Franklin	161,747	169,487	122,601	156,712	8.45%	188,520
Hamilton	142,066	143,222	141,374	160,223	8.26%	178,416
Montgomery	90,683	89,218	76,189	95,891	4.92%	106,272
Statewide	1,944,848	1,889,186	1,474,331	1,865,007	—	2,160,000

Source: Ohio Secretary of State. "Voter Turnout: Election Results and Data." www.sos.state.oh.us/elections/election-results-and-data/ (accessed 10/5/2017).

Profiling Vote Targets

How can the campaign hope to win over the swing voters it needs to meet its target? First and foremost, the campaign must identify who these voters are. Campaigns typically use surveys and, to a lesser degree, focus groups to do this. Initially, the campaign will conduct surveys to ascertain what sorts of people are persuadable. Most campaign surveys are **probability samples**, in which some number of individuals from a certain population are randomly selected and asked a set of questions. The key to a probability sample is that every individual in the population of interest has a known probability of being selected. Because selection is random, a small number of completed interviews (usually between 400 and 1,000) reveal the general opinions held throughout the population, with a known and relatively small (or at least acceptable) margin of error. In much the same way a doctor can make inferences about your health based on a small sample of your blood, we can make inferences about public opinion based on a small sample of randomly chosen citizens.

Thinking back to our governor's race, a survey (or poll) can thus be used to ask registered voters in Ohio whom they intend to vote for in the upcoming election. For those people with a preference, we can also ask how strongly they prefer their candidate. A survey allows us not only to identify how many people are currently undecided or might be moved from their current preference but also to see if persuadable voters are more common among certain groups, such as women, young people, or Latinos. In addition, we can examine the issue preferences of persuadable voters to develop a plan for winning them over.

Once surveys have been analyzed, many campaigns conduct in-depth interviews with small groups of persuadable voters to gather additional data and test specific issue positions. These are called **focus groups**. They have been a part of political campaigns since the mid-1980s, when campaign consultants noticed that businesses were using them to enhance their understanding of client preferences. They range in size between 8 and 20 participants, and are led by a "facilitator" whose job is to pose questions and encourage full participation from all members. Focus groups differ from polls in that participants are not selected randomly. In fact, they are intentionally recruited on the basis of certain characteristics that the campaign associates with persuadable voters (e.g., gender, age, or ethnicity). Because of this, focus group participants do not necessarily represent what the larger population thinks; they are simply suggestive of how certain subgroups think about politics and the election. And while focus groups do not provide statistically generalizable information, they provide a depth of information that campaigns often find valuable.

Together, polls and focus groups give a campaign a strong sense of what sorts of voters they need to win over and the kinds of appeals that will most effectively accomplish this. This knowledge can be used to craft stump speeches, position papers and press releases, television and radio advertisements, and social media strategies.

The second step to identifying swing voters involves rating the persuadability of all registered voters in the district. This step involves two major tasks. Both tasks represent large and expensive undertakings, and thus they are typically done only in presidential, gubernatorial, U.S. Senate, and hotly contested U.S. House races. Smaller state and local campaigns, as we discuss in Chapter 11, may rely on cheaper and less sophisticated strategies.

The first task is to acquire a list of registered voters and augment it with demographic information on each voter. As we discussed in Chapter 3, the major political parties have compiled extensive databases on voters, including names, addresses, phone numbers, previous voting history, demographic attributes such as gender or race, and financial and consumer data such as home values.

Then, the campaign uses information from the poll that they conducted to determine who is persuadable to estimate how open each voter on the list should be to appeals from its candidate. In other words, the campaign builds a statistical model of persuadability based on the results of the poll, and then uses this to predict the persuadability of every individual in the voter file. The campaign can then isolate specific voters for mailings, phone calls, or in-person visits, all based on a combination of data from the poll and the voter list. This process, called **microtargeting**, was developed in the 2000 and 2002 elections to allow individual-level targeting. Microtargeting avoids the need to make **voter identification** (or **voter ID**) **calls**, in which every voter on the voter list is called and asked his or her preferences for the upcoming race.

It is difficult to microtarget based on a standard campaign poll. A poll of 500 people, for example, will not have a sufficient number of people in certain groups—such as college students—to make reliable inferences about what these groups think. Nor will a standard poll ask enough questions about a respondent's background to take advantage of the information available in voter databases. Thus, microtargeting typically requires a very large poll—say, of 6,000 or more respondents—with additional questions about the respondents' backgrounds and habits. Microtargeting is expensive, but it is much less expensive than a round of statewide voter ID calls.

The Context of Voter Targeting

Targeting voters effectively requires not only polling data and an accurate voter list but also an understanding of the reality associated with the particular election. Perhaps the most important aspect of the reality is whether the candidate is an incumbent or a challenger. For the incumbent, the election is to some degree a referendum on how things have gone on her watch. Citizens will associate prevailing conditions—the state of the economy, crime rates, traffic flow, and so on—with the incumbent candidate and will reward or punish her accordingly. In this context, it is more difficult to persuade voters; people have seen the incumbent in action and have formed opinions. Conversely, if the candidate is a challenger running against an incumbent, he will try to convince people that the incumbent has done a poor job and that it is time for a change. In addition, the challenger will be less familiar to constituents in the district. People prefer someone they know, and they are more likely to recognize the name of the incumbent than that of the challenger. In sum, when an incumbent is running for reelection, most of the campaign is about defending her record. Targeting is thus constrained by real-life conditions.

If there is no incumbent in the race, the central question remains who will do a better job, but candidates do not necessarily have recent and relevant experience by which voters may make assessments. Perhaps more to the point, in an **open-seat** race it is much easier to craft a strategy to persuade people to support your candidate. Other factors can come to the fore.

Another important reality campaigns must consider is the partisan makeup of the district in which the candidate is running. As we discussed in Chapter 2, the characteristics of a candidate's constituency affect nearly every dimension of campaign strategy. If 60 percent of voters in the district are Democratic, 20 percent are Republican, and 20 percent describe themselves as independent, the Democratic candidate will likely emphasize traditionally partisan appeals (and will usually win). The Republican candidate will need to win over some independents and Democrats, and is therefore likely to emphasize candidate-related appeals—experience and background—rather than party. This was the case in the 2016 U.S. Senate race in Pennsylvania between Katie McGinty, a Democrat, and Pat Toomey, the incumbent Republican, in which Toomey pulled off a surprising 49-to-47 percent victory in a state that typically leans Democratic. He focused on voter anger with the status quo and convinced some Democrats that the race was about something besides traditional party labels.

In the 2016 race for one of Democratic-leaning Pennsylvania's U.S. Senate seats, Republican Pat Toomey defeated Democrat Katie McGinty. In addition to turning out Republicans, Toomey targeted independents and moderate Democrats by focusing on voter anger and a pragmatic approach.

But consider another district in which 30 percent of voters are Republican, 30 percent are Democratic, and 40 percent describe themselves as independent. Here the campaign will likely target the broad swath of independents. This was the case in the Colorado U.S. Senate race in 2016, where the incumbent Democrat, Michael Bennet, defeated the Republican challenger, Darryl Glenn. Glenn's fiery conservative rhetoric—he once said Democrats were akin to "evil"—and unorthodox views on several issues helped Bennet paint him as an extremist. Glenn won only 45 percent of independents and Bennet held the seat with a narrow three-point victory.

Although both state and national factors matter, they are not all-powerful. For example, Toomey (a Republican) won in a state that had voted Democratic for president six straight times. Bennet (a Democrat) won in a year when Republicans maintained their hold on the House and took the Senate. The prevalence of the Democratic Party in Pennsylvania and the sour national mood in 2016 (both of which contributed to what we refer to as the political "reality" of a given election) shaped Toomey's and Bennet's respective campaign strategies, but both campaigns were able to target and mobilize electoral majorities.

Strategic Campaign Decisions

Thus far, we have emphasized the broad outlines of strategy but have said little about how it influences the specific decisions that face every political campaign. Much of what we discuss below—especially regarding "what to say" to voters—can be understood as "messaging." Messaging includes the issues that candidates prioritize and the positions they take on them, as well as the broader theme or rationale for the campaign. We think of messaging content as perhaps the foremost example of the strategic decisions that face most campaigns. We now turn to these decisions, paying particular mind to the similarities and differences between the ways in which campaign professionals and political scientists approach them.

The Decision to Run

We are so used to thinking about who wins and loses elections that sometimes we forget an important prior question: who decides to run for office in the first place? Elections are significantly shaped not only by who chooses to run, but also by who sits things out. In 2016, seventeen Republicans decided to run for president, jumbling the field and making it difficult for several of the presumed front-runners to break away. Many have argued that the large GOP field helped Donald Trump by spreading the "conservative" vote among candidates such as Texas senator Ted Cruz and Florida senator Marco Rubio, which allowed Trump to move to the head of the pack with relatively modest early support. On the Democratic side, vice president Joe Biden's decision not to run left Hillary Clinton with minimal opposition— Maryland governor Martin O'Malley, Virginia senator Jim Webb, and Vermont senator Bernie Sanders—for the party's nomination. Sanders's spirited challenge does not obscure the fact that the race would have been quite different had the sitting vice president decided to contest the nomination. The effect of decisions whether or not to run—while most obvious at the presidential level—is felt in races at all levels.

Political consultants and political scientists largely agree that, when thinking about whether to run for office, there are several important factors for a candidate and her advisers to consider. One is *motivation*. Does the candidate want to run for office, or is she being dragged reluctantly into the fray? While we tend to think of politicians as uniformly ambitious, many are ambivalent about moving up the political ladder. For example, an incumbent might prefer his current position to running for higher office and potentially losing. If local and statewide offices are prestigious and attractive, fewer talented politicians will want to seek higher office.[3] Representative Ron Paul, who ran for the Republican nomination for president in 2008, provides a concrete example of such ambivalence. After the election was over, Paul's campaign manager said of his candidate, "We couldn't get him for six months to say that he wanted to be president."[4] For candidates who do want to run, it is also important to understand the reasons that they want to run. Their motivations—duty to country, particular policy goals, and so on—will help inform strategic decisions later on in the campaign.

In gauging motivation, it is also important to know how the candidate's family feels about her candidacy. For example, does she have a spouse who is willing to assist and endure the campaign? Does she have children? Is she willing to move the family around and use them in the campaign? Maybe more to the point, is the candidate willing to endure the potentially embarrassing scrutiny of her immediate and extended family? And does she have secrets that she would like to keep from her family? A concern about separation from his children was one thing that made Barack Obama hesitate before declaring his candidacy in 2008. One of his advisers, David Plouffe, told an audience after the campaign, "He's got young kids and he's very close to them. That was really the biggest hurdle—could he reconcile his desire to see his family a lot?"[5]

A second factor to consider is *resources*. Perhaps the most important question here is whether the candidate can raise money. As we discussed in Chapter 4, the American system of campaign finance puts the onus of fundraising on the candidate, and little can be accomplished without money on hand. Besides money, other resources that affect a candidate's decision to run include credentials (has the potential candidate held an office that gives her relevant experience?) and time (can she take time off work and away from her family to campaign effectively?).

A third factor is whether the candidate can assemble a campaign organization. Does she have an experienced, enthusiastic staff? Is there adequate outside help available, or have the best pollsters, consultants, media people, and field organizers already committed to other campaigns? Modern-day campaign organizations often look like small armies. It is ideal to put an organization in place at the beginning of the campaign.

---

[3] Cherie D. Maestas, Sarah Fulton, L. Sandy Maisel, and Walter J. Stone. 2006. "When to Risk It? Institutions, Ambitions, and the Decision to Run for the U.S. House." *American Political Science Review* 100, 2: 195–208.

[4] Institute of Politics. 2009. *Campaign for President: The Managers Look at 2008*. New York: Rowman & Littlefield, p. 22.

[5] Institute of Politics, *Campaign for President: The Managers Look at 2008*, p. 29.

A final factor for a candidate and advisers to consider in deciding whether to run is the *opportunity* (or lack thereof) presented in the election. Opportunities derive from the realities that candidates face at a particular time and place and are crucial because they often determine *when* a candidate will run, as opposed to whether she has a general inclination to run. Smart candidates will wait until the odds, and the realities of the election, are in their favor. What is the makeup of the electorate? For example, would the candidate be willing to run when the electorate is primarily composed of members of the opposite party? And what is the nature of the competition? Will the candidate face a competitive primary challenger? Will she face a competitive general election opponent? What are the resources that the opponents have? What about conditions in the country? How is the economy doing? How popular is the incumbent president? All of these things may influence whether the candidate feels she can win.

The role of opportunity suggests that candidates can be thought of as "strategic politicians."[6] In some ways, potential candidates are rational actors looking to maximize the chances that they will win. Given the costs of running, and the potential damage to their reputation if they run and lose, they are unlikely to run unless they believe there is a significant chance they will win. Thus, strategic politicians rarely challenge dominant incumbents, rarely run in districts where they are outnumbered by partisans from the other side, and rarely run if the prevailing national mood is against their party.[7] Conversely, they look for races where the incumbent is retiring or weak. They tend to run in districts where most voters share their party affiliation. They tend to run if there is a national tide favoring their party. This mentality creates something of a self-fulfilling prophecy: strategic politicians rarely run unless they calculate favorable odds, so incumbents almost never face tough competition unless other factors are decidedly against

---

[6] Gary C. Jacobson and Samuel Kernell. 1983. *Strategy and Choice in Congressional Elections.* New Haven, CT: Yale University Press.

[7] Candidates will occasionally run for office even though their prospects are not good. Sometimes they run because the upside of victory is enough to offset the downside of a loss. Long-shot presidential candidates fall into this category. At other times, candidates run in order to lay the groundwork for a later run for office. For example, up-and-coming Texas Republican Ted Cruz (the former solicitor general) challenged the much better known and well-financed Lieutenant Governor David Dewhurst for the 2012 GOP Senate nomination, possibly calculating that even a losing effort could enhance his status with the public and fund-raisers. Cruz won the primary and general elections, however, becoming the junior senator from Texas. He then ran for president in 2016 despite having served only three years in the senate and despite the crowded Republican field.

them. To be sure, not every candidate will appear rational. There are plenty of quixotic campaigns waged every election year. But there are still strong incentives for politicians to think strategically about the decision to run.

Political science research on the decision to run suggests that three of these four factors—motivation, resources, and opportunity—matter simultaneously. A good example comes from the research of Jennifer Lawless and Richard Fox on why so few women hold elective office relative to their share of the population. This research has shown that, although women candidates are as likely as male candidates to win elections, they are less likely than men to run in the first place. In part, this is a question of motivation. Women report less enthusiasm for the rigors of campaigning, such as fundraising. They also seem to perceive themselves as lacking in resources. One such resource is their credentials: women are less likely than men to see themselves as qualified. Another resource is time: even women who are employed full time in high-status professions, such as law or business, report spending more time on household tasks and child care than do men in similar professions. Finally, they see fewer opportunities. Relative to men, they are more likely to believe that elections in their community are competitive, that raising money will be difficult, and that female candidates are less likely to win.[8]

Messaging: Issue Priorities

Perhaps the most obvious strategic question of a campaign involves issues and how to talk about them. Which issues should a candidate emphasize? Candidates select issues for their campaign agenda with care and then seek to emphasize only those issues—"staying on **message**," as the saying goes. Choosing issue priorities is a critical strategic decision because candidates want to control the campaign agenda wherever possible. Some issues will work to a candidate's advantage, and some will not. A candidate who keeps the focus on issues on which the public favors her policy positions may win over persuadable voters and perhaps win the election. For example, in the 2016 presidential election Donald Trump wanted to focus attention on immigration, Obamacare, the economy, and the Obama administration's handling of terrorism, while Hillary Clinton wanted to focus on economic inequality, jobs, the environment, and social justice. In some ways, the main fight in the campaign was more about the agenda than specific proposals.

---

[8] Jennifer L. Lawless and Richard L. Fox. 2017. *Women, Men & U.S. Politics: 10 Big Questions.* New York: W. W. Norton.

Once most Americans decided the election was a referendum on the state of the economy and Obamacare, Trump (arguably) had won.

Like the candidates themselves, campaign consultants also believe strongly in the importance of agenda control. Many of them assume that citizens do not care much about politics and only pay attention to the "loudest" moments of the campaign. Thus, while citizens' perceptions are malleable, candidates only have a couple of shots at telling them what the election is about. As a result, consultants structure campaigns so that they focus on one or two issues, **framing** (or presenting) them in simple, easy-to-understand terms. Each side attempts to define what matters.

Why might candidates choose some issues and not others? Here, the reality that candidates confront is crucial. Events outside of their control put certain issues on the agenda, leading the public to prioritize those issues and leaving candidates little choice but to address them. In the 2016 presidential election, both Donald Trump and Hillary Clinton talked a great deal about the economy. The issue was nettlesome for both sides: Clinton was tied to Obama, who had overseen an uneven and slow recovery during his eight years in office, while many still blamed Trump's Republican Party for the collapse of 2008 and were skeptical of a businessman who had several bankruptcies on his ledger. Still, when certain issues become national priorities, as the economy did in 2016, it is common to see opposing candidates with similar agendas.

Candidates also base their agendas on the traditional strengths of their parties. In Chapter 1, we noted that the reputation a political party has developed for attention to a particular issue gives that party greater credibility on the issue. This example of a reality of campaigns and elections is known as **issue ownership**, a term that suggests that parties come to "own" issues because of their reputations.[9] Observers would typically say that the Republican Party owns the issues of national security, taxes, and crime, while the Democratic Party owns health care, education, and entitlement programs like Social Security and Medicare.

If candidates emphasized only the issues their party owns, then we would expect to see them talking past each other, rather than engaging one another on the issues. In reality, although candidates sometimes put greater emphasis on their party's "owned" issues, they often talk about all sorts of other issues, even those "belonging to" the other party.[10] In part, this is because

---

[9] John R. Petrocik. 1996. "Issue Ownership in Presidential Elections, with a 1980 Case Study." *American Journal of Political Science* 40, 3: 825–50.

[10] John Sides. 2006. "The Origins of Campaign Agendas." *British Journal of Political Science* 36, 3: 407–36.

national events demand it. For example, in June 2016, both Donald Trump and Hillary Clinton were forced to address a shooting at an Orlando, Florida, nightclub by a terrorist affiliated with the Islamic State, which left 49 people dead. Both Trump and Clinton had weaknesses on the issues raised by the shooting. For Trump, the lethal attack on a gay nightclub drew attention to his support for an individual's right to bear arms and his ambivalence toward legislation protecting gay rights. For Clinton, the shooter's ties to Islamist extremism drew attention to the rise of ISIS and the devolution of Iraq and Syria during her tenure as secretary of state under Barack Obama. However, the immediacy and power of the event demanded a response. Predictably, Trump's response emphasized the threat of Islamist extremism, while Clinton focused on gun control and the need to combat intolerance toward the LGBTQ community.

Campaign agendas are also influenced by the candidate's own personal experiences and reputation. Regardless of the reputation of their party, candidates often develop areas of policy interest, expertise, and accomplishments, and they can talk credibly about these issues by highlighting their own achievements. For example, in the 2000 presidential election, George W. Bush emphasized education a great deal, even though the Democratic Party usually "owns" this issue. As governor of Texas, he had worked to improve primary and secondary education, and he believed that the state's progress gave him the credibility he needed to "trespass" on the Democrats' territory. Although personal experience can matter, candidates do discuss many issues with which they have limited expertise or experience. This again suggests that candidates are confident that they can frame issues in favorable ways, no matter what the reality is.

Messaging: Issue Positions

While formulating their agendas, candidates also must determine what positions they should take on the issues that they prioritize. In reality, they are not totally free to take any position. Candidates have ideologies that constrain them—liberals are unlikely to take a pro-life position on abortion just to win votes. Candidates also have histories that constrain them; someone who has been conservative her whole life is going to look like a panderer if she suddenly embraces moderate or liberal positions when heading into a tough campaign. Still, even with these limits, candidates for election face a choice: Should they simply take positions that are popular with citizens, or should they seek to persuade citizens to adopt their own point of view?

The logic of taking popular positions can be explained using the **median voter theorem**.[11] This theorem assumes that voters can be arrayed on a spectrum that captures the range of positions on a particular issue—from, say, liberal to conservative. Candidates seek to position themselves on that spectrum nearest to the hypothetical voter who would provide the winning vote for them: the median voter. The median voter is the person who falls in the exact middle of the spectrum. That is, half of all voters are more liberal than this hypothetical person and half are more conservative. The candidate who wins the median voter, as well as all of those voters who are on the same side as the candidate, wins the election.

A diagram may help to illustrate. The bell-shaped curve in Figure 5.1 represents how many voters are positioned at each point along this spectrum, arrayed from left ("L") to right ("R"). The median voter is labeled "M." The two candidates are labeled "A" and "B." Currently, Candidate A appeals to more voters than Candidate B because he is closer to the median voter M. Both candidates could improve their support by adopting policy positions that move them closer to M.

The median voter theorem may seem too abstract to guide campaign strategy. After all, campaigns want to appeal to real voters, not some hypothetical median voter. However, the basic logic of the median voter theorem is quite evident in how campaign professionals and political commentators think about campaigns. For example, we often hear about candidates who

FIGURE 5.1 The Median Voter Theorem

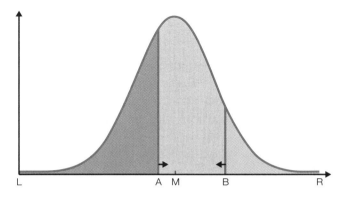

[11] Anthony Downs. 1957. *An Economic Theory of Democracy.* New York: Harper & Row; Harold Hotelling. 1929. "Stability in Competition." *Economic Journal* 39, 153: 41–57.

are "moving to the center," with the presumption that this enables them to appeal to more "moderate," "independent," or "swing" voters whose support would allow them to win the election.

The median voter theorem doesn't always work, for several reasons. For one, as noted earlier, candidates are constrained in the positions they can take. If moving toward the median voter means contradicting some previous position, then the candidate may damage his credibility and risk earning a label like "flip-flopper"—as with John Kerry in 2004 and Mitt Romney in 2012.

Candidates also must appeal to various constituencies, with views that often differ from those of the hypothetical median voter. Donors, activists, and interest groups—all three critical in providing funding, volunteers, and endorsements—tend to have opinions on political issues that are often more ideologically extreme than those of the average citizen. Taking moderate positions on issues may have more costs than benefits if it alienates ideologically driven supporters.

The challenge of appealing to multiple constituencies with different opinions may lead candidates to avoid specific positions on some issues altogether. In Chapter 3, we noted that American campaigns have often centered on biography and personality, offering only vague platitudes about political issues. There may be advantages for candidates in this strategy, even though it seems counter to the conventional wisdom that candidates must take clear stands on the issues. Keeping their positions vague allows candidates to say things that are unobjectionable and popular—"I want to save Social Security" or "Our children need a good education." Various constituencies may interpret such statements as endorsing their particular positions, even when candidates have not done so explicitly. Candidates who take vague positions also provide less for the media and opposing candidates to pick apart. Studies of campaigns find that ambiguity is common and that, consequently, citizens often do not know candidates' positions on specific issues.[12]

This lack of knowledge among citizens points to one final problem with the median voter theorem: it assumes that citizens know where they stand on issues, know where the candidates stand, and vote accordingly. But as we noted earlier, there is reason to suppose that the average citizen is not that attentive to the campaign or to politics generally. Certainly many campaign professionals believe this, and much political science research supports this view. In Chapter 13, we will discuss the assumptions of the median voter theorem, as well as the strategies by which voters choose candidates, in more detail.

---

[12] Michael X. Delli Carpini and Scott Keeter. 1997. *What Americans Know about Politics and Why It Matters*. New Haven, CT: Yale University Press.

If the average citizen does not assess the candidates on the basis of his or her issue positions, then candidates may be empowered to pursue another strategy: attempting to persuade voters to support their positions on issues. Whether candidates can do so speaks to a more general question: the ability of campaigns to affect what citizens think. Just as candidates attempt to frame the election around particular issues, they would also like to persuade citizens to adopt their positions on those issues. In Chapter 13, we will discuss at greater length how successful candidates are in doing this. As we will see, campaign consultants and political scientists come to somewhat different conclusions on this question, with political scientists more skeptical than campaign consultants about how much candidates can change public opinion.

Whether to Attack

Few things attract more attention during campaigns than attacks, which may come from candidates, parties, interest groups, and others. Despite the apparent proliferation of attacks, whether to campaign negatively—or "go negative"—is a complex decision that is largely contingent on the reality of the race.

Negative campaigning can be defined simply as any criticism leveled by supporters of one candidate against the opposing candidate.[13] By contrast, **positive campaigning** (sometimes called *advocacy*) focuses only on the background, record, and views of the sponsored candidate. Of course, campaigns are not limited to one or the other. A campaign message or advertisement may mix positive and negative information. Such advertisements, sometimes called **contrast advertisements**, focus on the differences—in qualifications, record, or issue positions—of the main candidates in the race.

Campaigns make decisions about other specific aspects of a negative message. One aspect is content: Should the negative ads criticize a candidate for her stand on issues that concern voters, or for her personal qualities? Another aspect is civility: Should a negative campaign be critical but respectful, or is it useful to be ugly or mean-spirited? In the discussion that follows, we simply focus on the general question of whether to campaign negatively, and not on specific questions about how to do so.

According to some political scientists and many campaign practitioners, the main factor guiding the decision whether to attack is the political reality surrounding the race—in particular, which candidate is the front-runner and which the underdog. The candidate who is ahead in the polls is less likely to

---

[13] John G. Geer. 2006. *In Defense of Negativity: Attack Ads in Presidential Campaigns.* Chicago: University of Chicago Press, p. 23.

attack than the candidate who is behind. This finding emerges in both academic research and in a survey of campaign consultants.[14] For this reason, incumbents are less likely to attack than their opposition. Only if support for the opposing candidate appears to be increasing would an incumbent seek to define him via negative campaigning. For example, an incumbent with a lot of political baggage who is facing a well-financed, impressive challenger may wish to go negative before the challenger begins campaigning in earnest. This happened in the 2016 Senate race in Missouri, when the incumbent, Roy Blunt, aired early **attack ads** against the challenger, Jason Kander. (Blunt ultimately won the race.) Challengers who are not well known in their districts, or any candidates lagging in the race, may feel they need to attack. The challengers run little risk of further increasing the incumbent's name recognition advantage by airing negative ads because incumbents are already well known in their districts. Moreover, attacking the incumbent raises doubts about his fitness for office and can open the door for a challenger. Attacks on the incumbent are also more likely than positive campaign messages to draw news media coverage, and thus increase the challenger's name recognition.[15]

Although it seems like common sense to advise front-runners to stay positive and underdogs to go negative, large-scale studies of campaign messages and advertisements in American presidential elections suggest that front-runners and underdogs do not always follow this advice.[16] Sometimes incumbents run campaigns that are more negative than the challengers'. Indeed, it is not uncommon for candidates well ahead in the polls to pound away on the underdog. In the 1964 presidential election, for example, Democrat Lyndon Johnson had a commanding lead throughout the campaign, but still relentlessly attacked the Republican candidate, Barry Goldwater.

One potential problem with negative campaigning is that it may not actually win votes. As we will see in Chapters 12 and 13, it is far from certain that negative advertising affects whether citizens vote or for whom they vote. Ultimately, there is enough uncertainty regarding who should go negative, and to what extent negative campaigning influences voters, to produce a wide range of professional opinions on the matter.

[14] Stergios Skaperdas and Bernard Grofman. 1995. "Modeling Negative Campaigning." *American Political Science Review* 89, 1: 49–61; John Theilmann and Allen Wilhite. 1998. "Campaign Tactics and the Decision to Attack." *Journal of Politics* 60, 4: 1050–62.

[15] Travis N. Ridout and Glen R. Smith. 2008. "Free Advertising: How the Media Amplify Campaign Messages." *Political Research Quarterly* 61, 4: 598–608.

[16] Geer, *In Defense of Negativity*; Emmett H. Buell, Jr., and Lee Sigelman. 2009. *Attack Politics: Negativity in Presidential Campaigns since 1960*, 2nd ed. Lawrence: University Press of Kansas.

In 2016, Hillary Clinton based much of her campaign around attacking the fitness of Donald Trump to serve as president. Was Clinton's emphasis on a negative message a fatal strategic mistake?

One final point should be made with respect to the decision to attack: negative communication may come not only from a candidate's campaign but also from independent groups and party organizations that support the candidate. Although coordination between and amongst these groups in federal elections is regulated by law, a strategic campaign might refrain from attacking its opponent but signal to affiliated groups that it would welcome such attacks from outsiders. Some research even suggests that attacks coming from outside groups are more credible—and thus more effective—than those coming from opposing candidates.[17]

Where to Campaign

Whether a candidate is running for president or for city council, decisions about where to deploy precious campaign resources are always hotly debated. Should the presidential candidate go to Florida or to Ohio for that last-minute campaign stop? Should the city council candidate have greeted voters entering

---

[17] Conor M. Dowling and Amber Wichowsky. 2015. "Attacks without Consequences? Candidates, Parties, Groups, and the Changing Face of Negative Advertising." *American Journal of Political Science* 59, 1: 19–36.

the polls in Precinct 1 or in Precinct 4? The assumption shared by consultants and scholars is that a campaign's resources must be allocated strategically to achieve maximum effect.

Generally speaking, there are two models for where to campaign. The first model focuses on mobilizing partisans. The assumption is that a campaign locates and appeals to people who will probably vote for the candidate if they can be persuaded to turn out. Much of the campaign therefore targets supportive areas where turnout and enthusiasm might lag.

The second model focuses on persuading independent and weakly partisan voters. The campaign team develops issue positions that are aimed at the sensibilities of these voters; in fact, these issues and positions may be very narrowly tailored for specific, persuadable constituencies. The campaign is therefore multifaceted, but tends to focus on areas with large numbers of independent voters.

The relative efficacy of these two models may depend on context. A political newcomer, like Donald Trump in 2016, has a chance to reach out to independents and weakly partisan voters and convince them to support his candidacy. A more established candidate, conversely, may have a record that limits her "flexibility" when it comes to winning over independent voters, but may have an advantage in her ability to target and mobilize core supporters. Incumbent candidates, especially those in the more polarized context of today's politics, are therefore more likely to embrace the first model.

There are, of course, combinations of these models. Most campaigns seek to mobilize partisans *and* persuade independents. To do so, they rely on detailed plans for allocating resources. As discussed earlier, most major campaigns use polling and voter identification data to estimate the number of persuadable voters in their state or county. They can then price out the cost of a visit or television ad in that state or county, and calculate the price per persuadable voter. A campaign is thus able to rank-order all states or counties (or precincts) by cost-effectiveness, and can allocate dollars based on this ranking. Other factors may induce a campaign to visit a certain county or advertise in a certain market, but professional campaigns tend to adhere closely to their analytical rankings. Political science research confirms this.[18] For example, research on presidential campaigns from 1992 through 2008 shows that television advertising expenditures were mostly based on price-per-persuadable-voter estimates.[19]

---

[18] Daron R. Shaw. 2006. *The Race to 270: The Electoral College and the Campaign Strategies of 2000 and 2004.* Chicago: University of Chicago Press.

[19] Taofang Huang and Daron Shaw. 2009. "Beyond the Battlegrounds? Electoral College Strategies in the 2008 Presidential Election." *Journal of Political Marketing* 8, 4: 272–91.

Campaigns below the presidential level are not as exacting in their deployment of resources. This is partly because the consulting talent, available data, and allocation options decrease with more localized elections, making it more difficult to develop and execute a rigorous plan for resource allocation.

How to Campaign

Should the campaign use its funds to run television advertisements on the broadcast networks? Or should it purchase cable television advertisements instead? Would radio advertisements be better? Or maybe Facebook or pre-roll advertisements online? What about billboards, lawn signs, bumper stickers, and buttons? And how much time and effort should be spent on the ground game—face-to-face campaigning by the candidate, staff, and volunteers? These are nuts-and-bolts decisions that a campaign strategist must make. In some respects, they are questions of tactics—the means by which strategic goals are accomplished—as opposed to strategy.

Tactics are most affected by available resources. Candidates would prefer to draw on as many tactics as possible—saturating every form of mass media with advertisements, for example—but often they cannot afford to do so. If candidates have enough money to run advertisements on broadcast television, which is not only the most expensive medium but also likely to reach the largest audience, then they will. If they do not, then the question becomes whether other mass media, such as cable television or radio, are affordable. Campaigns with even fewer resources often rely more on the ground game than on media buys, which consists of personal campaigning by the candidate and outreach by volunteers, both door-to-door and over the phone. Well-funded campaigns will combine a ground game with the "air war" of advertising on radio and television.

In the past decade, there has been something of a renaissance of interest in the ground game. Both political consultants and political scientists believe that personal contact with potential voters is effective, especially if the contact is from familiar and credible sources of information, such as friends and neighbors—that old-fashioned door knocks and other forms of personal outreach are often more effective than direct mail or phone banks. Political science studies have confirmed this: personalized contact is much more effective than mail or telephone calls in mobilizing citizens to vote, although phone calls made by professional telemarketers can be effective, especially compared with phone calls with a prerecorded voice.[20]

---

[20] Donald P. Green and Alan S. Gerber. 2004. *Get Out the Vote! How to Increase Voter Turnout.* Washington, D.C.: Brookings Institution Press.

In recent elections, both parties have invested significant resources in developing field organizations that can carry out personalized mobilizations. Union organizations arguably started this move in the 1998 and 2000 campaigns, and Democrats built a get-out-the-vote machine on the unions' initial efforts. Republican Party organizations, spooked by the Democrats, countered with their own volunteer efforts in 2002 and 2004. In 2008 and 2012, the Obama campaign created an extensive field organization of trained volunteers. Somewhat ironically, online forms of social networking—candidate websites, Facebook, and Twitter—are now being used to drive the sorts of in-person outreach that, after the advent of television, had seemed like a thing of the past. In 2016, Hillary Clinton's campaign followed (and even improved on) the Obama playbook for integrating online volunteer outreach and field operations. Michelle Kleppe, national organizing director for Hillary Clinton's 2016 campaign, explained:

> [We are] really pushing our organizers to not only recruit and engage with volunteers on the phones and in their offices and offline, but also organizing online . . . . So an organizer is working with volunteers in their offices and in homes and around kitchen tables, but they are also engaging with volunteers and supporters on Facebook and Twitter. Both in terms of getting them to come offline and actually help build our capacity and talk to additional voters and supporters but also in helping a group of people online engage with their networks. It gives us a broader reach and more opportunities for volunteers to engage in the types of activities that [they] are best suited [for] and that they're most comfortable with.[21]

Thus, offline forms of personal contact will likely continue to be significant, alongside online organizing and, in the case of advertising, on-air messages. For the moment, however, television advertising continues to be the linchpin of contemporary campaigns, especially in statewide and federal races.

Organizing for Strategic Success

The various strategic and tactical decisions we have discussed do not get made by themselves. When a candidate decides to run for office, she needs to

---

[21] Quoted in Philip Bump. 2016. "How Hillary Clinton's 'Happy Volunteer' Strategy Works." *Washington Post*, September 22. www.washingtonpost.com/news/the-fix/wp/2016/09/22/how-hillary-clintons-happy-volunteer-strategy-works/?utm_term=.2fc917f46dea (accessed 7/17/2017).

Can Candidates Control Their Image on the Internet?

Campaigns often try to produce or push content that "goes viral," meaning it is redistributed continuously online and becomes fodder for the news. In the 2016 election, for example, a video of a group of girls called the "USA Freedom Kids" singing and dancing to a rendition of "Freedom's Call"—a pro–Donald Trump take on an old World War I propaganda anthem—was viewed millions of times and shared across the Internet and social media sites. (The group later made headlines again by suing the Trump campaign for breach of contract.[1]) The video reinforced Trump's call for a return to an era of American strength and patriotism. Over the course of the campaign, many such moments went viral with or without a "push" from the Trump or Clinton camps. Furthermore, some of these moments did not show the candidate in a favorable light—even the USA Freedom Kids were seen by some as more negative than positive. But campaigns think these viral moments usually help more than they harm, reinforcing the old adage that any publicity is good publicity.

In addition to engineering and promoting viral content, the 2016 presidential campaigns promoted hashtags that they attempted to get trending with the support of Twitter users. Trump's campaign was enormously effective in this endeavor. Recent research shows that Trump's campaign slogan hashtags appeared nearly 200 times more often than Clinton's.[2] In fact, Trump's main slogan— "#MakeAmericaGreatAgain" or "#MAGA"— was one of the most prolific of all time, while Clinton's "#I'mWithHer" and "#StrongerTogether" hashtags were only moderately successful in penetrating the consciousness of the Twitterverse.

New media are also valuable to candidates because they empower citizens to produce their own content, giving them a sense of ownership in the campaign. In 2016, Jonathan Mann produced an online song and video called "The Hillary Shimmy Song," using footage of Clinton "shimmying" in reaction to a Trump statement during the first presidential debate. The video garnered almost 2.5 million views on YouTube and was referenced several times on broadcast and cable television news shows. Clinton's campaign promoted the video and encouraged supporters to do likewise.

At the same time, the downside of empowering citizens to produce their own content is that candidates may lose some control over their campaign message. One famous historical example occurred in 2008, when an employee of a website development firm working for the Obama campaign produced a video attacking Hillary Clinton that was uploaded to YouTube. The video borrowed from a 1984 Apple Computer ad that portrayed Microsoft as an authoritarian menace. The Obama campaign denied involvement and the employee was forced to resign. In another incident, Barack Obama offered free websites and blogs to his supporters at my.barackobama.com. Some users who objected to Obama's positions on civil liberties issues used these websites to blast Obama. Because the criticisms were coming from Obama supporters, the traditional media gave them more credence.

[1] Emily Shultheis. 2016. "'USA Freedom Kids' sue Trump campaign." *CBS News*, September 7. www.cbsnews.com /news/usa-freedom-kids-sue-trump-campaign (accessed 10/6/2017).
[2] Kareem Darwish, Walid Magdy, and Tahar Zanouda. 2017. "Trump versus Hillary: What Went Viral during the 2016 U.S. Presidential Election." Unpublished manuscript. Cornell University.

identify knowledgeable people to help her design a strategy and set up a campaign organization so that important questions are decided and plans are implemented. But the fact that campaigns face common dilemmas in determining and implementing their strategies does not mean that there is one common solution—in fact, there is no such thing as a "typical" campaign. Campaigns vary in their resources: some have huge budgets and target millions of citizens, and some have tiny budgets and target hundreds or only dozens. Naturally, they will have diverse organizations as well. Moreover, although many campaign organizations include similar positions of authority, these positions do not always have the same job description or the same place in the organization's hierarchy. Campaign managers, who are in charge of organizing the campaign and implementing the strategic plan, are not necessarily at the top of the organization. Chief strategists, who (no surprise) are in charge of developing strategy, usually—but not always—hold centrally important positions. Political directors are typically in charge of organizing the field staff, but some engage in overall messaging strategy as well. Personal relationships can drive the structure of the organization, with positions created to accommodate specific people that the candidate wants for specific purposes.

It is instructive to examine briefly the campaign organizations of Republican Mitt Romney and Democrat Barack Obama in the 2012 presidential race. Although presidential campaigns offer a "deluxe" example of what a campaign can be, smaller campaigns try to do many of the same things, if on a much smaller scale, in terms of people and resources. Romney's presidential campaign evolved throughout the year. Initially, his campaign team (Figure 5.2) moved from state to state as the GOP's primary season unfolded. After clinching the nomination, the organization in Boston was solidified and fleshed out below the top positions; additional senior advisers were added, and fundraising, paid media, and polling became focal points. The team included a finance chair (in charge of overseeing raising campaign money), a political director (in charge of operations, grassroots, outreach, and education), a communications director (in charge of press relations, advertising, and promoting message and image), and a pollster (in charge of identifying target voters and developing appropriate issue and message points). Intent on avoiding the "who's in charge?" problems that plagued Republican presidential nominee John McCain's campaign throughout much of 2008, lines of authority for the Romney team were clearly established, with Stuart Stevens serving as the point person for strategic decisions and Matt Rhoades serving as the final word on organization and staffing.

FIGURE 5.2 Mitt Romney's 2012 Presidential Campaign

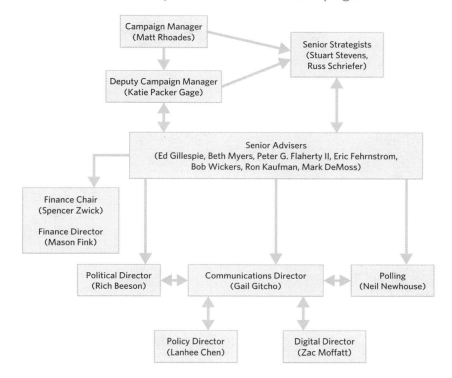

Barack Obama's 2012 presidential campaign, like his 2008 campaign, is best represented as a sort of loop (or circle), in which information flowed in a particular pattern but that also allowed different players to be involved in the decision-making process. Obama had numerous people serving in key positions, and it was not always clear who outranked whom (Figure 5.3). Nevertheless, David Axelrod, senior strategist, had the final say on most important decisions, while Jim Messina, the campaign manager, and David Plouffe, who was able to act as something of an overlord for the organizational apparatus, were usually deferred to on matters involving voter outreach, volunteers, and targeting. The Obama campaign thus maintained the traditional distinction between a campaign strategist and a campaign manager noted earlier: campaign strategists are usually in charge of developing a plan and honing the candidate's message, while campaign managers are usually in charge of running the day-to-day operations of the campaign. The Obama team also featured more specific, task-oriented departments and personnel—most notably, messaging (tasked with ensuring that all elements of the

FIGURE 5.3 Barack Obama's 2012 Presidential Campaign

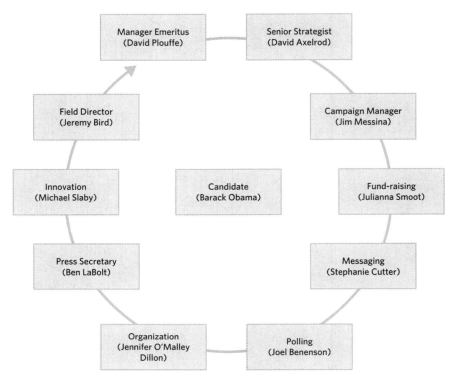

campaign were focused on the same issues and themes), innovation (tasked with e-campaigning, social media, and the development and integration of big data), and field (tasked with coordinating local, regional, and state volunteer and paid staffing work).

Who Are Campaign Strategists?

As described in Chapter 3, the modern American campaign is candidate-centered and dominated by television. This means that candidates recruit and develop their own advisers. A class of professional campaign consultants with expertise in public opinion and television advertising emerged in the 1950s alongside the rise of television as the dominant campaign medium; these professionals have become the main purveyors of strategic advice in American elections.

The Backgrounds of Campaign Strategists

Although the development of professional campaign consultants is relatively new, there have always been strategists in American campaigns. Alexander Hamilton may have been the most famous political consultant in the early days of the new republic, as he constantly schemed and plotted how to win elections for those who shared his Federalist views. James Madison was only slightly less aggressive as Thomas Jefferson's top political strategist, although Jefferson himself was also an active strategist. Indeed, we could put together quite a catalog of campaign strategists from before the modern campaign era.

In today's campaigns, how does someone become a campaign consultant or strategist? First, there are those who become proficient at a specific campaign endeavor, and parlay this into a broader role crafting and overseeing strategy. For example, in the 1960s and 1970s, people with a background in public relations or consumer advertising were much sought after by campaigns, as candidates attempted to develop personal loyalty among constituents through persuasive self-promotion. Public relations and advertising professionals naturally favored using market research to drive messaging, and using mass media (especially television) to deliver these messages. The late Roger Ailes, who worked for Richard Nixon, Ronald Reagan, and George H. W. Bush, and was the long-time president of Fox News, is a good example.

People with a background in journalism or speechwriting have also become successful strategists. Some have moved up by serving as the liaison between the candidates and the news media, while others have served as speechwriters before taking on the broader role of strategist. Democrats Bill Moyers (who served Lyndon Johnson), Bob Shrum (who worked for eight Democratic presidential candidates, including Edward Kennedy and John Kerry), and Ben Rhodes (who served Barack Obama) are prime examples.

Pollsters, who are trained in the art and science of ascertaining what the public is thinking, have also become campaign strategists. Kellyanne Conway, Donald Trump's campaign manager in 2016, ran her own polling and political consulting firm during the 1990s and 2000s. Doug Schoen, Bill Clinton's pollster, later served as Hillary Clinton's presidential campaign strategist. Bob Teeter, a legendary Republican pollster, served as George H. W. Bush's presidential campaign strategist and manager in 1992.

More recently, people who are good at direct mail or telemarketing campaigns have used this success as a way to become general strategists. Both of these activities require a strong sense of which voters the candidate should address and what messages move them. Republican strategist Karl Rove dominated direct mail campaigning in Texas before taking up much broader responsibilities for George W. Bush.

Then there are those with backgrounds in statistics and voter data analytics, which give someone familiarity and experience with targeting, messaging, and budgets and resource allocation. This is perhaps the newest route to power in a campaign. Notable examples include Robby Mook, campaign manager for Hillary Clinton in 2016, and David Plouffe, campaign manager for Barack Obama in 2008, each of whom had extensive backgrounds in data analytics and targeting prior to getting an opportunity to lead a presidential campaign.

Finally, the emergence of campaign management schools has provided another route by which aspiring strategists can hone their craft. As yet, there are few examples of campaign school graduates becoming superstars, but the ranks of congressional and even presidential campaigns are now populated with people who cut their teeth at these academies.

A different path to becoming a campaign strategist consists of developing relationships with particular candidates and marshaling them through their political careers. These individuals may have only a few clients throughout their careers, but they play a major role for those clients. James A. Baker III built his career in law but entered politics at the urging of his friend George H. W. Bush. He served in the Ford, Reagan, and Bush administrations, but only in a handful of campaigns, the most prominent of which involved Bush. Baker's particular value to Bush was as someone who had his best interests at heart, someone who could tell him the unvarnished truth, and someone who knew his strengths and weaknesses inside out.

Regardless of their path into the business, professional campaign strategists have attained much greater visibility in recent decades and are even referred to as *gurus*. Their lionization can be traced to a classic work of campaign journalism, Theodore White's *The Making of the President*.[22] White's narrative of the 1960 campaign details the machinations of Robert Kennedy and other advisers to John F. Kennedy, noting their disciplined targeting of states and voting groups and aggressive voter registration strategy, among other things. White also discusses the opposing side, in particular Richard Nixon's disastrous pledge to campaign in all 50 states, and the challenge of attacking the elusive and charismatic Kennedy. The implication was clear—JFK's victory was due, at least in part, to the cool, methodical, professional campaign strategy developed by his team. The elevation of the strategist had

---

[22] Theodore H. White. 1961. *The Making of the President 1960*. New York: Atheneum.

The "superstar" strategists of recent years have included David Axelrod (left) and Karl Rove (right). Axelrod is credited with helping Obama win in 2008 and 2012 and served in the Obama administration, while Rove is known for devising George W. Bush's strategies in 2000 and 2004 and also went on to work in the White House.

begun, and soon many would become well known: Hamilton Jordan (for Jimmy Carter), Ed Rollins (for Ronald Reagan), James Baker and Lee Atwater (for George H. W. Bush), James Carville and Dick Morris (for Bill Clinton in 1992 and 1996, respectively), Karl Rove (for George W. Bush), David Axelrod (for Barack Obama in 2008 and 2012), and Kellyanne Conway (for Trump in 2016).

Despite the visibility of superstar strategists, we know very little about their actual impact on contemporary elections. Commentaries like *The Selling of the President* have criticized the mass marketing techniques so often employed in contemporary campaigns, on the advice of consultants.[23] But little has been written about how much campaign consultants actually help candidates win. What evidence exists suggests that hiring consultants is no panacea.[24] In part, this may reflect how much both campaign strategy and election outcomes are constrained by the rules governing elections and the reality that candidates face. Political scientists are therefore less likely than campaign professionals to attribute the success of candidates to the strategic genius of their advisers. This skepticism is at the heart of the more general disagreement between campaign consultants and political scientists with respect to whether campaigns "matter."

---

[23] Joe McGinniss. 1969. *The Selling of the President: The Classic Account of the Packaging of a Candidate*. New York: Simon & Schuster.

[24] Stephen K. Medvic. 2001. *Political Consultants in U.S. Congressional Elections*. Columbus: Ohio State University Press.

Conclusion

In this chapter, we have delineated what a campaign strategy is, discussed several key strategic decisions that campaigns make, and considered the perspectives of both campaign consultants and political scientists. We have also discussed how campaigns organize to make strategic decisions, and examined who campaign strategists are. The central notion is straightforward: campaign strategists want to win elections, and everything they do can be understood as a rational, if sometimes imperfect, effort to achieve this goal. Practitioners and academics tend to agree on many of the factors that candidates can and should consider when deciding if they should seek higher office, emphasize a particular issue, run an attack ad, or focus resources on a particular constituency. The central question, however, is how much these strategic decisions matter—a topic we will return to in subsequent chapters.

How should we view campaign strategy in light of the democratic ideals spelled out in Chapter 1? We will explore this topic at greater length in Chapter 14, but we can highlight one issue here. Intrinsic to campaign strategy is this notion: some citizens are more valuable than others. That is, campaigns routinely identify subsets of citizens to target—such as swing voters or voters in a certain geographic area—and ignore many others. This approach may run counter to several ideals. The laserlike focus of campaigns on partisan supporters, swing voters, or any other groups may violate the ideal of political equality. Of course, we are most concerned that citizens be equal in the eyes of the law, not in the eyes of campaign consultants. Nevertheless, this decision involves a trade-off of values. Similarly, targeted voters inevitably receive much more information about the campaign than do other voters, challenging the ideal of deliberation. The information that voters receive clearly differs depending on whether they are the targets of a campaign's strategy. That campaign strategy may fail to live up to these ideals reflects this simple fact: campaign strategy is fundamentally about winning elections, not about upholding civic standards.

KEY TERMS

campaign strategy (p. 126)

vote targets (p. 127)

persuadable (swing) votes (p. 127)

probability samples (p. 131)

focus groups (p. 131)

microtargeting (p. 132)

voter identification (voter ID) calls
    (p. 132)

open seat (p. 133)

message (p. 138)

framing (p. 139)

issue ownership (p. 139)

median voter theorem (p. 141)

negative campaigning (p. 143)

positive campaigning (p. 143)

contrast advertisements (p. 143)

attack ads (p. 144)

FOR DISCUSSION

1. Do campaigns attempt to convince all voters to support their candidate? Why or why not?

2. What factors influence whether or not a candidate chooses to run for an office?

3. Why are challengers more likely than incumbents to run negative advertisements?

4. How has the rise of public opinion polling influenced campaigns?

CHAPTER 6

Political Parties

Beginning an unlikely presidential campaign, Donald Trump descended the escalator of Trump Tower in New York City in June 2015 with his wife Melania. Surrounded by cheering supporters but no Republican Party big-wigs, he took straight aim at immigrants with little restraint: "When Mexico sends its people, they're not sending their best. . . .They're bringing drugs. They're bringing crime. They're rapists. And some, I assume, are good people."[1] His language was "not politically correct,"[2] as he acknowledged, and was worrying for party leaders averse to offending potential voters. He introduced his slogan, taken from Ronald Reagan, "Make America Great Again," but attacked trade and immigration policies that Reagan had supported.

Trump immediately drew the most media coverage and the highest public opinion poll support among the 17 candidates competing for the 2016 Republican nomination, but Republican Party leaders distanced themselves from him. They perceived him as a weak candidate and a stain on the public perception of their party. Although Trump raised traditional Republican Party concerns like national security, taxes, and gun rights—as well as strong opposition to Barack Obama's initiatives—they feared he was not committed to their policy positions or principles. But Republican voters ultimately disagreed, with most states and a large plurality of primary voters supporting Trump.

Political science theory, usually obscure in public debate, played an important role in tamping down expectations of Trump's victory. Journalists regularly cited a prominent political science work, *The Party Decides*, throughout the presidential primary process as evidence that Trump would face near insurmountable odds in

---

[1] Washington Post Staff. 2016. "Full Text: Donald Trump Announces a Presidential Bid." *Washington Post*, June 16. www.washingtonpost.com/news/post-politics/wp/2015/06/16/full-text-donald-trump-announces-a-presidential-bid/?utm_term=.3b61dbf6eeae (accessed 10/7/2017).

[2] Moira Weigel. 2016. "Political Correctness: How the Right Invented a Phantom Enemy." *The Guardian*, November 30. www.theguardian.com/us-news/2016/nov/30/political-correctness-how-the-right-invented-phantom-enemy-donald-trump

his path to winning the nomination.[3] The book argues that party elites select presidential nominees by coordinating on a candidate acceptable to all party factions. The central evidence is that pre-primary endorsements from party leaders predict who becomes a presidential nominee. Yet before the 2016 primary process began, Donald Trump obtained no endorsements from members of Congress or governors. Jeb Bush, Marco Rubio, Ted Cruz, John Kasich, Chris Christie, Mike Huckabee, and Rand Paul had all obtained significantly more party leader endorsements, though most leaders remained publicly neutral. Many other candidates were more widely acceptable; Trump worried key party constituencies.

However, one election does not change a party's fundamental role. Political parties have a permanent place in American politics, helping to structure and order the competition between candidates in American elections. Party organizations have diverse roles in campaigns—recruiting candidates, running advertisements, and mobilizing voters—but citizens have to support a party's decisions to enforce the party's will, and votes ultimately determine election results. By Election Day, the vast majority of Republican elected officials and voters had committed to supporting Trump. For most people, decisions about whom to support in any one election follow from the more basic political decision of selecting a party, one of the two major sides of American political competition. Despite lacking full control of their presidential nominations, America's two major parties are remarkably stable and resilient: even in 2016, endorsements still helped to predict the winners of House and Senate primaries, and the party-favored candidate, Hillary Clinton, won the Democratic primary.

Core of the Analysis

- Political parties strategically participate in elections by recruiting candidates, airing advertisements, and mobilizing voters.
- Political parties still play a central role in elections, despite attempts by some reformers to weaken them.
- The two major political parties have adapted to new issues and slowly changed their voting coalitions, in the process becoming more ideologically polarized.
- Political parties fall short of achieving some democratic values, but it is unlikely that democracy could function without them.

---

[3] Marty Cohen, David Karol, Hans Noel, and John Zaller. 2008. *The Party Decides: Presidential Nominations before and after Reform.* Chicago: University of Chicago Press. The authors of the book discussed Trump and the popularity of their theory in 2016 in Steve Kolowich. 2016. "The Life of 'The Party Decides.'" *Chronicle of Higher Education*, May 16.

In this chapter, we will address several questions about the role of political parties in campaigns. What are political parties and why do we have them? Why only the Democrats and the Republicans? How is their role in campaigns evolving? We also consider broader questions about how parties fit into American politics. How do electoral rules and political and economic realities constrain parties? Are parties contributing to ideological polarization or just adapting to a changing society and policy issue agenda? Each of these questions raises key philosophical concerns: Do parties serve or undermine democratic values in campaigns? Even if Americans are dissatisfied with parties, do viable alternatives exist? To evaluate parties, we first have to understand why they behave as they do.

What Are Political Parties?

Political parties are groups of people with the shared interest of electing public officials under a common label. Supporters of the two major political parties in the United States, the Democrats and the Republicans, each share the goal of winning elections. Each party has policy goals as well, but it is their electoral goals that unite parties and distinguish them from other kinds of groups.

To make sense of political parties, the political scientist V. O. Key suggested three manifestations of political parties: the **party-in-the-electorate**, the **party-as-organization**, and the **party-in-government** (see Table 6.1).[4] The party-in-the-electorate includes all citizens who identify with the party. The party-as-organization comprises the institutions that administer party affairs, including the official bodies that raise funds and create the rules for the party. The party-in-government consists of the elected leaders and appointed government officials who shape party policy goals. Each of these manifestations of the party is somewhat independent of the others. Partisans in the electorate do not directly decide how party leaders operate. Organizational leaders cannot tell a party's senators how to vote.

In studying campaigns and elections, we pay most attention to the party-as-organization, which assists the candidates, and the party-in-the-electorate, which votes for them. Some scholars have expanded the definition of the party-as-organization to include political action committees and interest groups that usually support one party, calling the parties "multilayered coalitions" of diverse actors that share mutual goals and collaborate

---

[4] V. O. Key, Jr. 1952. *Politics, Parties, and Pressure Groups*, 3rd ed. New York: Thomas Y. Crowell.

TABLE 6.1 Three Aspects of the Major American Parties		
Aspect of Party	**Democrats**	**Republicans**
Party-in-the-electorate	• Democratic registrants • People who identify themselves as Democrats • Democratic primary voters • Democratic general election voters • Democratic campaign volunteers and activists	• Republican registrants • People who identify themselves as Republicans • Republican primary voters • Republican general election voters • Republican campaign volunteers and activists
Party-as-organization	• Democratic National Committee • Democratic Senatorial Campaign Committee • Democratic Congressional Campaign Committee • State and local party committees • Liberal/Democratic political action committees	• Republican National Committee • National Republican Senatorial Committee • National Republican Congressional Committee • State and local party committees • Conservative/Republican political action committees
Party-in-government	• Senate Minority Leader (Charles Schumer) • House Minority Leader (Nancy Pelosi) • Democratic state and local elected officials	• President (Donald Trump) • Senate Majority Leader (Mitch McConnell) • Speaker of the House (Paul Ryan) • Republican state and local elected officials

regularly.[5] The parties, for example, share mailing lists across an "extended party network" with individual candidates, allied interest groups, and ideological news outlets.[6]

The extent of these networks means that American political parties can be amorphous groups. Even basic questions, like who is in charge of the Democratic and Republican parties, often do not have straightforward answers. The president is usually the most prominent spokesperson for his or her party; during presidential campaigns, the presidential nominees generally

---

[5] Paul S. Herrnson. 1999. "The Roles of Party Organizations, Party-Connected Committees, and Party Allies in Elections." *Journal of Politics* 71, 4: 1207–24.

[6] Gregory Koger, Seth Masket, and Hans Noel. 2009. "Partisan Webs: Information Exchange and Party Networks." *British Journal of Political Science* 39: 633–53.

have this role. But this is not always the case: for example, when President Donald Trump is unpopular, Republican congressional leaders such as House Speaker Paul Ryan and Senate Majority Leader Mitch McConnell have often tried to distance themselves from his actions. When a party loses a presidential election, like the Democrats in 2016, it often creates a leadership vacuum that is not filled until four years later. The closest to an official head of the Democratic Party, Democratic National Committee (DNC) chairman Tom Perez, was elected in 2017 in a rare, closely contested race against Keith Ellison. The race largely replayed the contest between Democratic factions that lined up behind Hillary Clinton and Bernie Sanders in the Democratic primary, with Sanders supporting Ellison. Perez still lacks the full support of some of Sanders's supporters. Like most party leaders, he does not run any government departments, vote in Congress, or appear on voter ballots. Senate Minority Leader Chuck Schumer and House Minority Leader Nancy Pelosi are the heads of the Democratic Party-in-government. Yet reporters often look to former or potential future presidential candidates to represent the party's views on policy.

Like party hierarchy, party membership is also unclear. If your friend says that she is a Republican, this does not necessarily mean that she is officially registered with the party. In many states, individuals do not need to register with a political party in order to vote in that party's primary; in some states, there is no official party registration at all. Political scientists have found that even people who view themselves as independents—meaning they are unaffiliated with either party—often vote consistently for one party's candidates. The same is true of elected officials who call themselves independent. Even Bernie Sanders is still listed as an independent, but ran for the Democratic nomination for president and works closely with the Democratic leadership in the U.S. Senate.

Why Do We Have Parties?

Most of the American Founders feared parties, even as they later participated in them. As he left office, George Washington warned of "the baneful effects of the spirit of party." Nevertheless, political parties quickly developed and took on increasingly important roles in American government. The first political parties, the Federalists and the Democratic-Republicans, coalesced around different views of federal government strength and regional economic interests (see Chapter 3). Early parties almost immediately structured voting in Congress and created electoral coalitions for and against early presidents. But

Who speaks for the Democratic Party? a. 2016 presidential candidates Hillary Clinton and Bernie Sanders; b. former president Barack Obama; c. House Minority Leader Nancy Pelosi and Senate Minority Leader Chuck Schumer; d. Democratic National Committee Chairman Tom Perez and Deputy Chair Keith Ellison; or someone else?

these parties developed even before they had clear identities in public opinion; voters did not start calling themselves partisans before politicians organized themselves into competing coalitions. In fact, parties have developed in all democracies across the world because politicians find them useful in legislative and electoral politics.

Political parties serve the needs of politicians who want durable legislative majorities in order to pass legislation.[7] Politicians also benefit from a reputation or "brand" that citizens recognize and can rely on when voting, and they need an infrastructure that helps persuade and mobilize voters during elections. Parties serve all of these functions. Political parties also help promote the policy goals of various interest groups, which often affiliate with parties in order to advance their policy goals. By working through a party, interest groups seek to influence policy by helping to choose candidates and assist them in elections. The alternative to a political

[7] John H. Aldrich. 1995. *Why Parties? The Origin and Transformation of Political Parties in America*. Chicago: University of Chicago Press.

party—negotiating with individual candidates and legislators to support a group's agenda—is more costly.

Political parties can also help make democratic government work better. First, they aggregate and articulate interests. Every citizen and politician has his or her own interests and ideas, but democracy requires that they work with others in order to achieve these goals. Parties help individuals to decide which of their goals are most important and to find people who agree with them. Second, parties organize coalitions. If every ethnic, religious, and economic group nominated its own candidates, it would be difficult for any group to obtain a majority of the vote. Parties enable groups to unite under broader umbrellas. Third, parties coordinate elections and mobilize voters. Without them, candidates would have to convince voters individually that they share their views; and they would have to mobilize their own constituencies. Party labels make it easier for voters to form opinions about the candidates. Fourth, parties coordinate the legislative process. This role helps voters learn how their vote will likely translate into public policy. Finally, parties facilitate collective political action. Both electing candidates and governing require individuals to work together, and parties provide a crucial means by which people join together in pursuit of shared goals.

The Democratic and Republican Parties

Two major political parties have long dominated the U.S. political system. The Democratic Party traces its history to the 1828 election of Andrew Jackson. The Republicans emerged as their major challenger with the 1860 election of Abraham Lincoln. Since the 1920s, the two major parties combined have always controlled at least 95 percent of House and Senate seats and won at least 90 percent of Electoral College votes for the presidency.

Ideologically, the Republican Party is more conservative and the Democratic Party is more liberal. Internationally, political competition is usually organized on the ideological spectrum from left (liberal) to right (conservative), although other countries use alternative labels. These ideologies can be generally defined by their views on the size and scope of government responsibility: the Democratic Party favors more government intervention in the economy than the Republican Party, often in an attempt to ameliorate inequality. But American parties have also divided on issues surrounding social or moral concerns, with Republicans more favorable toward social traditions and Democrats more favorable to social diversity, as well as international concerns, with Republicans prioritizing American military strength and Democrats prioritizing international cooperation. Republicans more uniformly share an ideological self-identification: 82 percent of Republicans identify as conservatives, but only 62 percent of Democrats identify as liberal (see Figure 6.1). In both parties, activists (those who volunteer or work in campaigns) and donors (those who provide money to a party or its candidates) are more ideologically consistent with their party than those who merely identify with it.

FIGURE 6.1 Ideological Distribution of Party Members, Activists, and Donors

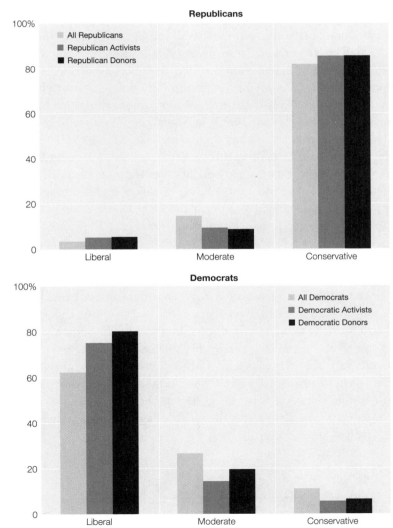

The Democratic voting coalition is largely made up of minority groups that vote for them by large margins, such as African Americans, Jews, professionals, and union members. The Republican Party usually wins by smaller margins among larger groups, such as whites and married voters. The largest change in the party coalitions has been the move of the southern states from solid Democratic voting in the early and mid-twentieth century to Republican voting in recent elections, but the parties are also increasingly divided along racial, educational, and gender lines (as discussed in Chapters 3 and 13).

The American electorate as a whole contains more self-identified Democrats than Republicans, but neither group is a majority. Curiously, the electorate also contains more self-identified conservatives than liberals. The Democrats have the advantage in party identification, but the Republicans have the advantage in ideological conflict. Republicans also tend to explain party competition as an ideological battle between left and right, whereas Democrats are more likely to see politics as a group competition between the rich on one side and the vulnerable on the other.[8] As a result, Republicans usually benefit from framing their opponents as liberals but face regular pressure from their base to conform to conservative orthodoxy and symbolism (see Box 6.1). Democrats instead benefit from framing elections as a battle between the people and the powerful. Nationally, Republicans need to win a greater share of independents than do the Democrats, whereas Democrats have to win more votes than Republicans among moderates because they have a smaller liberal ideological base.

The United States has tended to have strong two-party competition throughout its history, though different historical eras have favored one party or the other. The Democratic Party continuously controlled a majority in the House of Representatives from 1955 to 1994, but the Republicans have had a majority for all but four years since 1995. The Senate has switched control more often but has usually been closely divided; since 1955, the Democrats have always held at least 44 U.S. Senate seats and the Republicans have always held at least 32 seats. There have also been many party transitions in the presidency; since the 1930s, neither party has had more than two consecutive presidents, and the parties have alternated back-and-forth for the last five presidencies.

---

[8] Matt Grossmann and David A. Hopkins. 2016. *Asymmetric Politics: Ideological Republicans and Group Interest Democrats.* New York: Oxford University Press.

BOX 6.1

What Is the Tea Party?

In 2009, thousands of activists organized protests and attended congressional town hall meetings to oppose President Barack Obama's policy agenda, including health care reform legislation. They called themselves the "Tea Party movement," emphasizing their link to the values of the American founders by evoking the Boston Tea Party. Where does the Tea Party fit within the major party landscape?

In the 2010, 2012, and 2014 elections, Tea Partiers supported several candidates and were credited with changing election outcomes. They frequently opposed the Republican Party's preferred candidate in primary elections in favor of a more conservative choice with fewer ties to government service—occasionally to disastrous effect for the Republicans. In the 2012 U.S. Senate primary in Indiana, Tea Party favorite Richard Mourdock defeated incumbent Senator Richard Lugar. Following Mourdock's comments that "if life begins in that horrible situation of rape, that it is something that God intended to happen," he went on to lose the seat—one that had been held by a Republican for 36 years—to Democrat Joe Donnelly.[1] In 2014 and 2016, however, self-identified Tea Party candidates running against party favorites were successful less often in Senate races.

The Tea Party's overall goal has not been to replace the Republican Party but to move it in a conservative direction and replace existing party leaders. Attendees at Tea Party events were far more likely to consider themselves Republicans than Democrats. Republican respondents to public opinion polls were consistently more supportive of Tea Party activities.[2] Republican Party activists and consultants helped organize the group's protests and campaigns. Republican officeholders and candidates spoke at their events. Most Tea Party activists want to support Republican candidates rather than organize a third party.[3]

Washington interest groups like FreedomWorks and Americans for Tax Reform provided logistical support for initial Tea Party protests and their town hall meeting attendance strategy. Tea Party activists have also created several nonprofit organizations and political action committees to fund candidates and intervene in elections.

In 2017, in the wake of Donald Trump's election, Democratic Party activists copied the tactical innovations of the Tea Party, usually following an "Indivisible Guide" produced by former congressional staffers. They created local action groups, often organized on Facebook, and attended town hall meetings and contacted elected officials. The groups succeeded in replicating some of the 2009 spectacles at congressional town hall meetings, this time with activists mobilizing against the Affordable Care Act's repeal rather than against the act's enactment.

---

[1] The comments can be viewed here: www.politico.com/blogs/on-congress/2012/10/richard-mourdock-under-fire-for-rape-remarks-139411 (accessed 10/8/2017).
[2] Vanessa Williamson, Theda Skocpol, and John Coggin. 2011. "The Tea Party and the Remaking of Republican Conservatism." *Perspectives on Politics* 9, 1: 25–43.
[3] Kate Zernike and Megan Thee-Brenan. 2010. "Poll Finds Tea Party Backers Wealthier and More Educated." *New York Times*, April 15, p. A1.

What about Third Parties?

It is rare for any candidate not affiliated with either major party to get elected to federal office. At the presidential level, the most successful third-party or independent candidates have won at best a handful of states and thus come up woefully short in the Electoral College. Theodore Roosevelt ran as the Progressive Party nominee in 1912 but won only six states. Strom Thurmond ran as the States' Rights Democratic Party (or Dixiecrat) nominee in 1948 and George Wallace ran as the American Independent Party's nominee in 1968; neither won any states outside the Deep South. In 1992, an independent candidate, Ross Perot, won 19 percent of the popular vote but no electoral votes. Consumer advocate Ralph Nader received 2.7 percent of the popular vote as the Green Party candidate in 2000. Libertarian Party nominee Gary Johnson won 3.3 percent of the popular vote in 2016, improving on his 0.9 percent in 2012; Green Party nominee Jill Stein won 1.1 percent in 2016, improving on her 0.4 percent in 2012. Neither won any electoral votes.

The largest obstacles third parties face in U.S. elections are the rules of the electoral system. As discussed in Chapter 2, the use of single-member districts and plurality elections favors congressional candidates from the two major parties. Plurality voting within the Electoral College—whereby the candidate who wins the most votes in each state wins all of that state's electoral votes—hurts the chances of national third parties or independent candidates at the presidential level. These electoral rules tend to make voters, activists, and candidates wary that encouraging third-party support will "waste" potential votes or serve as a "spoiler," taking potential votes away from a major party candidate. For example, if most Nader voters in 2000 had voted for their second choices instead, Al Gore would likely have been elected instead of George W. Bush. There are other legal hurdles for third parties, including requirements for getting on the ballot (see Chapter 2). With the playing field tilted so strongly against them, third parties routinely find it difficult to attract media coverage, raise money, recruit experienced candidates, or earn a place in candidate debates. Despite these difficulties, third parties and independent candidates are sometimes successful. The Green Party and the Libertarian Party have elected more than 200 officeholders between them, mostly in local elections. Third parties and independent candidates can also influence the issues discussed in campaigns. For example, both the Democrats and the Republicans felt compelled to respond to Perot's concerns about the federal budget deficit in 1992. But this small amount of policy influence also makes third parties short-lived. One or both of the two major parties can adopt their issue positions and lure third-party supporters away.

What Roles Do Parties Play in Campaigns?

Political parties play central roles in contemporary campaigns, with the party-in-the-electorate, the party-as-organization, and the party-in-government all having some impact on the electoral process.

The Role of the Party-in-the-Electorate

The vast majority of Americans identify with or lean toward either the Democratic Party or the Republican Party and vote loyally for candidates from their preferred party. This makes the partisan complexion of a district or state a central feature of the reality that candidates confront. Candidates and campaign consultants carefully count partisans of both camps as well as independent or undecided voters when planning their campaign strategy (see Chapter 5). The party-in-the-electorate is as important as the volunteer base and cheering section for each party. Party supporters contact their friends, family, and neighbors—both formally in partnership with the candidates or party organizations and informally in their communities and online social networks—to try to convince them to support their party's candidates and encourage participation. In local elections for city council, the school board, or county commission, volunteer networks and party activists are often the only visible party involvement. Because the United States is becoming more geographically polarized, with Democrats increasingly concentrated in cities and inner-ring suburbs (especially along the two coasts), many areas no longer support viable two-party competition and each set of partisans is now likely to be surrounded by others who share and reinforce their partisanship.

The Role of the Party-as-Organization

The party-as-organization plays a central role in political campaigns. Party organizations such as the national committees, state committees, and legislative campaign committees recruit candidates and raise money for them. Recruiting candidates is harder than it might seem: in 2016, 42 percent of state legislative candidates faced no opposition candidate from the other major party.[9] Parties try to recruit quality candidates who are well known to the electorate and have relevant experience for the office they seek. Candidates who have previously held elected office are much more likely to win

---

[9] An analysis of all state legislative candidacies is available at https://ballotpedia.org/2016 _state_legislative_elections_analyzed_using_a_Competitiveness_Index (accessed 10/8/2017).

future elections, so they are often the first people party organizations try to draft. For instance, the Republican-affiliated organization GOPAC recruits and trains candidates to run for state and local offices. Under the leadership of Newt Gingrich, it was credited with helping to build the team of candidates that enabled the 1994 Republican takeover of Congress. In addition to recruiting candidates, parties also work to minimize retirements within their ranks because incumbents are more likely to win elections than newcomers.

Traditionally, the party organization also selected the party's nominees for general elections. Before 1972, unpledged party delegates selected presidential nominees at the national conventions (see Chapter 3). That changed with reforms to the presidential nomination system that emphasized primaries and caucuses. Primary elections became more important in nominations for lower-level offices as well, although party nominees for some statewide or local offices are still selected at party conventions or by party leaders. In many states, party organizations can also replace candidates who are no longer able to run or select nominees for special elections. For example, after incumbent senator Paul Wellstone was killed in a plane crash in October 2002, the Minnesota state party quickly put former vice president Walter Mondale on the ballot as a replacement. And even where party organizations no longer officially nominate their own candidates, party officials can influence primary results with their money or endorsements. They often discourage primary challengers, leaving only one candidate. When party leaders unite behind one front-runner, their preferred candidate usually wins the primary election.[10]

The other main task of party organizations is to raise money for their candidates. As discussed in Chapter 4, parties are quite successful at raising money, despite the ban on soft money contributions. They contribute some of this money directly to individual campaigns. They sometimes pay campaign consultants, pollsters, and other vendors of campaign goods and services. Parties also spend money to produce and broadcast television advertisements, build local party organizations and pay for get-out-the-vote drives.

Parties are now spending considerable sums on candidates' behalf, much of it on television advertisements. During the 2004 election cycle, party expenditures increased dramatically and shifted away from **coordinated expenditures**, which allow parties to cooperate with candidates in developing messages and communicating them to voters, toward independent expenditures (Figure 6.2). As we discussed in Chapter 4, court rulings on campaign finance

---

[10] Hans J. G. Hassell. 2016. "Party Control of Party Primaries: Party Influence in Nominations for the US Senate." *Journal of Politics* 78, 1: 75–87.

FIGURE 6.2 Party Committee Coordinated and Independent Expenditures

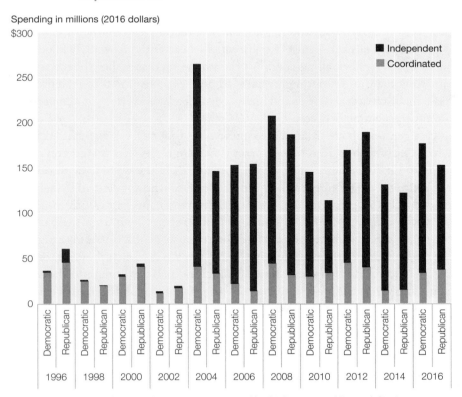

Spending in millions (2016 dollars)

Source: Data from Federal Election Commission, summarized by the Congressional Research Service

opened the way for unlimited independent expenditures. Parties' initial use of this option was circumscribed but both Democrats and Republicans now use it extensively. Democratic committees had the overall spending advantage in 2004, 2008, and 2016, but Republican committees spent more in 2012.

Party organizations also play an important role in mobilizing voters to participate in elections. People who are contacted by a political party during a campaign are more likely to vote, more likely to persuade others how to vote, more likely to work on behalf of their candidate, and more likely to contribute money.[11] Yet the parties consistently fail to contact most citizens. According to the American National Election Studies, the percentage of citizens

---

[11] Steven J. Rosenstone and John Mark Hansen. 1993. *Mobilization, Participation, and Democracy in America*. New York: Macmillan.

who reported contact from either of the political parties went from 31 percent in 1982 to a low of 19 percent in 1990. From 2002 to 2012, at least 40 percent of citizens were contacted by one of the parties, but only 32 percent were contacted in 2016 (with the Republicans contacting fewer citizens than the Democrats). Political science experiments consistently show that knocking on voters' doors or calling them on the phone increases their likelihood of participation; these experiments have led political consultants to recommend more mobilization activities and seem to have had some effect on the parties' resource allocation decisions.[12]

One reason not all citizens are contacted is that party organizations tend to concentrate their resources on races that are closely contested and most likely to tip the balance of power in legislatures. They want their resources to maximize the number of their representatives who get elected by helping candidates who can win. This means that many candidates with minimal resources and little chance of winning do not receive help from the parties. The way a party distributes its resources also sends important signals to other actors. Politicians who have leadership PACs, which they may establish to help fund other candidates' campaigns, usually donate to the same candidates that the parties invest in. Interest groups affiliated with the parties also follow their lead. Party organizations make their priorities explicit by distributing lists of targeted districts or winnable elections to guide other actors.

Parties can also direct resources to where their needs are greatest. For example, in 2008, Obama did not need party expenditures to compete with John McCain due to a substantial fund-raising advantage; as a result, the Democrats could direct more resources to their congressional candidates. Republican Party organizations were critical to helping McCain but their intervention was less important in 2012, when Mitt Romney was helped by a substantial super PAC spending advantage. In 2016, Hillary Clinton and the Democrats had a fund-raising advantage in the presidential race, and fewer super PAC resources were available to help Donald Trump close the gap.

Of course, parties are not necessarily unified when developing a campaign strategy. As mentioned in Chapter 4, former Democratic Party leaders Howard Dean and Rahm Emanuel regularly battled over whether the party should devote resources to all of the states or only to competitive races. Another traditional conflict within party organizations is the trade-off between ideological purity and electability. Parties want elected officials who support their

---

[12] Donald P. Green and Alan S. Gerber. 2008. *Get Out the Vote! How to Increase Voter Turnout*, 2nd ed. Washington, D.C.: Brookings Institution Press.

party's agenda. Yet sometimes candidates who are more ideologically moderate and less consistently partisan are more likely to win elections, especially in swing districts where voters are evenly divided along partisan lines.

In 2006, Congressman Joe Schwarz of Michigan's 7th U.S. House District was challenged in the Republican primary by Tim Walberg, a former state representative. Republican politicians and party organizations supported the moderate Schwarz, but many interest groups supported the more conservative Walberg. Walberg beat Schwarz in the primary and prevailed in the general election. But two years later, he lost the congressional seat to Mark Schauer, a Democratic state senator. In 2010, Walberg sought to challenge Schauer in the congressional race, but the National Republican Congressional Committee (NRCC) recruited Brian Rooney, the brother of a Florida congressman, to run against Walberg in the Republican primary. Most observers saw the primary as pitting ideological consistency against electability: Walberg was conservative but, given his 2008 loss, perhaps not electable. In 2010, however—a better year for conservatives and Republicans—Walberg won the Republican primary and the general election and returned to Congress. It is rare that intraparty feuding reaches this level, but such cases show how decentralized parties sometimes fail to reach consensus.

The Role of the Party-in-Government

The party-in-government also influences campaigns and election outcomes. For better or worse, candidates with a party label are tied to the party's elected leaders. With Donald Trump as president, other Republican politicians are seen as favoring his agenda, and Democratic politicians are seen as opposing it. If Trump's approval rating is low, it may hurt all Republican candidates. If the party leadership in Congress advances a legislative program, it will also reflect on that party's candidates. Many Republican candidates, for example, will have to defend their president's proposals as well as those of their congressional leaders. The same dynamics play out in state races, where candidates are seen as favoring or opposing their current governor's agenda. In legislative races, candidates are also affected by the current balance of power between the parties. The party with a majority in the legislature gets to set the agenda, typically earns more donations from access-oriented contributors, and can time legislation to maximize its impact on elections.

Candidates associated with the political party in power, especially incumbents, are judged on the basis of almost anything that occurs during their party's reign. Even adverse weather conditions like the dust storms of the 1930s, or events that have nothing to do with public policy, such as the

Choosing a Gubernatorial Nominee

At the beginning of the 2010 Michigan gubernatorial campaign, the Republican Party was confident. State public opinion had moved against the Democrats, including Governor Jennifer Granholm, who was retiring. The most popular potential Democratic candidate, the lieutenant governor, decided not to run. The expected Republican victory brought several quality candidates into the primary field. Early primary polls showed the race divided between Mike Cox, the popular attorney general from the Detroit area, and Congressman Pete Hoekstra, from the more conservative western part of the state.

Republican leaders and interest groups tried to unify behind a candidate. Cox received endorsements from Right to Life of Michigan and the Michigan Chamber of Commerce as well as that of the previous Republican candidate for governor. Yet western Michigan voters still supported Hoekstra.

Rick Snyder, a businessman in the race with no ties to state party or interest group leaders, began with almost no public support but took advantage of the dissension. At the state's largest party gathering, the Mackinac Republican Leadership Conference, Snyder unexpectedly won the straw poll. Newspapers explained the victory by reporting that Snyder had paid for many college Republicans to enjoy the splendid conference weekend on Mackinac Island, which they used for partying of the more traditional variety.

By using his own wealth, Snyder was also able to advertise directly to voters rather than court the state's interest groups. His folksy advertising campaign, begun with a television ad during the Super Bowl, christened him as "one tough nerd," a successful outsider and accountant who would shake up the state's politics.

The state's party establishment and interest groups, meanwhile, did not take him seriously. Republican leaders continued to decide between Hoekstra and Cox because they were seen as more ideologically conservative and loyal to the party than Snyder. Shadowy groups designed to avoid recognition also waged a two-way battle on the airwaves. A group calling itself the Michigan Taxpayers Alert ran ads in support of Cox, attacking Hoekstra for supposed support of tax increases. Another group calling itself the Foundation for a Secure and Prosperous America ran misleading ads on behalf of Hoekstra, attacking Cox for alleged ties to the disgraced Detroit mayor Kwame Kilpatrick. While Cox and Hoekstra responded to attacks from one another, Snyder ran only positive ads and remained largely unscathed.

Snyder benefited not only from lack of consensus among Republican leaders but also from state election law. Because Michigan does not ask voters to register by party, independents and Democrats can decide to vote in the Republican primary. In 2010, nearly twice as many people voted in the Republican primary as the Democratic primary, including many who did not identify as Republicans. Snyder, seen as the most moderate candidate, received many of their crossover votes and won the primary.

Republican leaders ended up with a nominee with few ties to the party. Snyder had taken advantage of an opening produced by conservatives who failed to rally behind one alternative. In November, Snyder was elected governor in a landslide. As the incumbent in 2014, he won again—this time with no primary opposition and the support of Republican leaders.

1916 Jersey Shore shark attacks that inspired the movie *Jaws*, move the mood of the electorate against the incumbent party.[13]

Legislators also must work through their party to pass bills that benefit their districts, such as legislation to support local road projects. Bringing federal money or other benefits to their districts can help increase an incumbent's popularity and prospects for reelection. Legislative party leaders know of this power; they often decide which of their incumbents to favor with local goods or legislative achievements, based on the importance of their district in the next election.

How Rules and Reality Constrain Parties

Like candidates, political parties are strategic actors that must make decisions within the context of both the reality on the ground and the rules set by government. The major rules that affect the parties are election laws (Chapter 2) and campaign finance laws (Chapter 4). The most relevant election laws for parties involve those affecting primary elections. There are long-running legal disputes about the extent to which parties can control their own nomination processes. Some states mandate open primaries, where independents can vote in either party's election, but many party organizations prefer closed primaries, where only party members can vote. Parties have also attempted to set their own dates for primary elections and administer the voting, but most states demand that party rules conform to state laws and procedures (often meaning that the two parties have to hold their elections on the same day). Parties still set many of their own rules, and changes to their nomination processes are closely contested by potential candidates and their supporters.

The State of California has implemented a series of reforms intended to weaken the influence of party organizations in primary elections. In 1996 voters enacted a "blanket primary": all of the candidates from both parties were listed on the ballot, allowing voters to vote in the Democratic primary for one office and in the Republican primary for another (see Chapter 2). The Supreme Court struck down this practice in 2000, finding that it violated a political party's First Amendment freedom of association. In 2010, California voters passed another initiative that created a new system: candidates from all parties run together in the first round of voting, and the

---

[13] Christopher H. Achen and Larry M. Bartels. 2016. *Democracy for Realists: Why Elections Do Not Produce Responsive Government.* Princeton: Princeton University Press.

two candidates with the most votes advance to the general election. This means that two Democrats (or two Republicans) might be the only candidates on the final ballot. Under this system, party organizations that convince fewer of their candidates to run for each office have an advantage.

Campaign finance rules affect how parties can raise and spend money. As discussed in Chapter 4, before the Bipartisan Campaign Reform Act (BCRA) of 2002 political parties could accept unlimited contributions—or "soft money"—to spend on party-building activities and issue advertising. The BCRA made soft money contributions illegal, but donors reacted by creating so-called 527 organizations to channel the money that they had previously directed to parties. The BCRA's ban on soft money has not yet been overturned, despite several rulings weakening its restrictions on independent groups and corporations.

Federal campaign finance law does benefit political parties in one sense: unlike other organizations, such as super PACs, parties are allowed to coordinate their campaign expenditures with the candidates they support. Party organizations also make independent expenditures that are not coordinated with candidates (see Figure 6.2 on p. 171). A party can thus intervene in a federal election by donating money to the candidate, donating money to state party organizations, coordinating expenditures with the candidate, and running its own advertisements.

Parties are not only affected by rules but are also constrained by the same realities that candidates face. For example, **party identification** is one reality: the party ID of voters is relatively stable (see Chapter 13), and parties cannot easily convince citizens to change their identification and "join" another party. Similarly, parties cannot easily change how the public perceives them and their leaders. "Issue ownership," discussed in Chapter 5, means that the public trusts one party more than another to deal with certain problems. For example, voters have traditionally trusted Democrats more than Republicans to handle education, while Republicans have typically been trusted to handle taxes.

Parties are also constrained by the reality of the prevailing economy. Many citizens come to disapprove of the party that presides over an economic recession and support the party that presides over an economic boom. Parties will often find it harder to recruit quality candidates and prevent incumbents from retiring when economic conditions are unfavorable.

A party's ability to win seats in an election can also depend on its recent success or failure. A party that has won recent elections and developed a strong majority may find that there are few remaining seats that it can win because its candidates have already won so many of the closely divided seats. Meanwhile, a minority that lost the most recent elections can some-times win back lots of seats with a small swing in the national electorate. In 2010, one of the reasons the Republicans were able to win 63 more seats in the House of Representatives than they previously held was that they had lost so many seats in competitive districts in the 2006 and 2008 elections.

Finally, parties may find themselves constrained by the decisions of other actors, including candidates and interest groups. At times, these actors may work at cross-purposes with the party they support. Candidates who are fearful of losing independent voters may renounce aspects of their party's accomplishments and agenda. Interest groups that are otherwise allied with the party may even work against that party's incumbents. But parties and their allies among interest groups, consultants, and candidates typically strive to develop similar agendas and to target a similar set of competitive races.

Are Political Parties in Decline?

Although some observers have suggested that political parties are in decline, political scientists are skeptical of these claims. Political parties are cer-tainly not in decline in government: research shows that they have become more, not less, unified in the last 40 years and are able to exert better con-trol of the legislative process. Partisan voting has become increasingly com-mon in state legislatures and even in the courts.

Most arguments for party decline emphasize the apparent disregard for parties within the electorate; substantial percentages of the public iden-tify as "independent," profess to dislike the major parties and their lead-ers, and favor a system with competitive third parties or independent candidacies. But reading too much into these sentiments is a mistake. As we noted earlier, most citizens who claim to be "independent" still favor one of the major parties and tend to vote for that party. These voters are really "closet partisans" who may seek to avoid public acknowledgment of their party.[14] Only one in 10 voters is a pure independent with no prefer-ence for either party. Moreover, party identification is actually becoming *more* important in congressional, presidential, and state elections. This does not mean that most citizens are familiar with the platforms of the political

---

[14] Samara Klar and Yanna Krupnikov. 2016. *Independent Politics: How American Disdain for Parties Leads to Political Inaction*. New York: Cambridge University Press.

parties or have political opinions that are always closely aligned with their preferred party. These things are true of only the most well-informed citizens. Party identification, however, is a useful shortcut that voters use to reach judgments on candidates with or without detailed information.

Perhaps the best evidence for party decline comes from the decreasing role of party organizations in elections. In Chapter 3, we discussed how a certain kind of strong party organization known as a "party machine" gradually declined after the nineteenth century because of reforms such as the secret ballot. The rise of candidate-centered elections in the latter half of the twentieth century created a relationship whereby parties service candidates rather than having control over them.[15] There is indeed some evidence that candidates position themselves as independent of parties and create their own constituencies, donors, and volunteer networks—although parties still provide important resources that help with fund-raising, polling, and get-out-the-vote operations, including shared and integrated voter data operations.[16]

As we have seen, today's party organizations also have less control over selecting nominees to run in the general election than they did several decades ago. In presidential elections, the national party conventions used to select the presidential nominees largely independent of the voters. State parties once performed similar roles. With the rise of direct primaries for presidential and legislative elections, party organization leaders no longer have complete control over who becomes a party nominee. After all, Trump was the least preferred party nominee of most Republican elected officials.

Party leaders can try to coordinate their support for a candidate during the "invisible primary"—the period of time before the actual presidential primaries begin, when party leaders can observe and interact with potential candidates and each other. As we noted at the beginning of the chapter, according to *The Party Decides*, party leader endorsements normally predict which candidate wins the nomination, even after taking into account the candidates' support in polls, the amount of money they raise, and the amount of media coverage they receive.[17] But Trump's case, though dramatic, is not the only instance of party consensus failure. Neither Barack Obama nor John McCain won the support of enough party leaders to make the 2008 primary election results a foregone conclusion. In both 2008 and 2016, both parties

---

[15] Aldrich, *Why Parties?*

[16] Rebecca S. Hatch. 2016. "Party Organizational Strength and Technological Capacity." *Party Politics* 22, 2: 191–202.

[17] Cohen et al., *The Party Decides*.

experienced a lengthy and intensely competitive primary season. But in many other presidential election years, the nominee with the most support from party leaders has quickly emerged as the winner. In 2012, Mitt Romney led the endorsement race and Obama faced no primary challenger.

Debates over the rise and decline of parties often return to definitional controversies. Who constitutes the party? If it is anyone who endorses candidates, it includes affiliated interest groups, celebrities, and others with access to money or organizations. If it is anyone who gives money, it includes PACs, business leaders, professionals, and activists. The more narrowly the party organization is defined—for instance, as only including official party committees—the more evidence there is for its decline. By contrast, the more broadly parties are defined, the more it becomes clear that two broad, competing coalitions still strive for power under the Democratic and Republican umbrellas.

Party Evolution and Polarization

Although there is little evidence of partisan decline, there have been some changes in the issue positions and social coalitions of the Democrats and the Republicans. The most important geographic change, the transformation of the South from solidly Democratic to a mostly Republican region, coincided with a sorting of voters into partisan camps based on their ideologies. Conservative Democrats, concentrated in but not exclusively from the South, slowly left the party. Liberal Republicans, largely from the northern states, changed parties or became more conservative. Ideological sorting was also helped by religious coalition change. Catholic voters, once a part of the Democratic coalition, became more evenly divided; white evangelicals gravitated toward Republicans.[18] The growing population of nonreligious voters is mostly Democratic. Less-educated white voters have become less tied to the Democratic Party over time, with white-collar professionals and single women becoming more Democratic. As the nation has diversified, Latinos and Asian Americans have become larger components of the Democratic Party coalition. (We will discuss party ID further in Chapter 13.)

Some political scientists have argued that many of these changes were brought about by the rising salience of racial issues in American politics.[19]

---

[18] Jeff Manza and Clem Brooks. 1999. *Social Cleavages and Political Change: Voter Alignments and U.S. Party Coalitions.* New York: Oxford University Press.

[19] Edward G. Carmines and James A. Stimson. 1989. *Issue Evolution: Race and the Transformation of American Politics.* Princeton, NJ: Princeton University Press.

The civil rights movement of the 1960s split the parties' electoral coalitions, especially the uneasy alliance of white segregationists and African Americans in the Democratic Party. As a result, voters' feelings on civil rights policies, such as school integration and affirmative action, became more important to their overall partisan identification—leading some to switch parties and others to align their racial and economic policy views with their party. This has led to concerns that Republican politicians' campaign messages include "coded racial appeals," discussing immigration, crime, and welfare to tap underlying white racial resentment.[20] Trump's campaign, with its more open hostility to Muslim and Latino immigrants, only accelerated these concerns.

Other scholars argue that the parties have extended their liberal-conservative ideological conflicts on economic issues to an array of new issues, including race and gender as well as moral issues like abortion.[21] When the Supreme Court struck down antiabortion laws in the 1973 *Roe v. Wade* decision, Republicans and Democrats (in both Congress and the electorate) were almost evenly divided between pro-choice and pro-life positions. Today, pro-choice Republicans and pro-life Democrats are rare. The same is true of other issues that formerly divided each party. As a result, citizens now learn a lot more about candidates based on their party affiliation alone and partisans of either stripe find it harder to admire any candidates in the other party.

Increasing party-line voting in Congress (with most Democrats on one side and most Republicans on the other) demonstrates elite polarization: the two parties are moving further apart from one another on an underlying ideological spectrum. As legislators have sorted into two parties with diametrically opposed views on most issues, Democrats and Republicans in the American public also seem to be lining up against one another on more issues. Within each issue area, fewer members of each party now agree with the other party. This hardly means that we are a nation of extremists: many voters still express moderation and relatively few have consistently conservative or liberal views on every topic or hold more extreme positions than they did before. Increasing consistency in divisions across the issue spectrum, however, has made it more difficult for politicians to campaign on issue positions likely to draw in voters from the other camp. Since Republicans and

---

[20] Ian Haney López. 2015. *Dog Whistle Politics: How Coded Racial Appeals Have Reinvented Racism and Wrecked the Middle Class.* New York: Oxford University Press.

[21] Geoffrey C. Layman, Thomas M. Carsey, and Juliana Menasce Horowitz. 2006. "Party Polarization in American Politics: Characteristics, Causes, and Consequences." *Annual Review of Political Science* 9: 83–110.

Party polarization across the spectrum of social, economic, and political issues has contributed to the rise of negative partianship in recent elections. Research has shown that voters hold increasingly negative opinions of members and candidates of the opposing party.

Democrats are now more segregated geographically, many legislative districts are also now less competitive.

Polarization has also led voters to dislike the other party, and the groups associated with it, more intensely than before. Negative partisanship is on the rise: people increasingly dislike the other party, even if they feel no more favorable toward their own.[22] Some citizens even fear their children marrying members of the other party or believe the other party is a threat to the nation's well-being. This may be one reason why partisans now accept nearly anything that their side does; in 2016, most Republican voters who said they disliked Trump's views and behaviors still voted for him over the even-more-dreaded Hillary Clinton. Partisans see nearly everything through the lens of their positive attitude toward one party and negative attitude toward the other, with sometimes comical results: directly before the 2016 election (with Obama still presiding), Democrats thought the economy was in good shape while Republicans feared the worst; but one week later, the pattern had completely reversed, with

---

[22] Alan I. Abramowitz and Steven Webster. 2016. "The Rise of Negative Partisanship and the Nationalization of U.S. Elections in the 21st Century." *Electoral Studies* 41, 1: 12–22.

Republicans excited after Trump's victory and Democrats seeing the economy more gloomily, despite no underlying change in the real economy.

Polarized parties also affect which candidates run for office, with more moderate candidates often afraid to put their names forward.[23] As the parties move apart, they tend to stimulate candidates who are consistent supporters of their agendas, making each generation of politicians even more polarized than the one before.

Evaluating Political Parties

Political parties play important roles in elections but they are also frequently criticized. The major parties tend to have low approval ratings. To evaluate whether parties are helpful or harmful for democracy, we can use the standards for evaluating campaigns that we set out in Chapter 1.

First, do parties help voters make informed choices, or do they manipulate voters? On the one hand, parties and the platforms they create provide voters with clear choices and information about those choices, which help voters select the candidate with whom they agree on most issues. In fact, simply voting on the basis of party affiliation can be an effective way for some people to identify the candidate whose views accord more with their own.[24] Yet voters with different priorities than the major parties may find the information provided by parties less helpful. As for manipulation, there is evidence that when citizens hold a policy preference different from that of a trusted party leader, they change their own preferences rather than oppose their party.[25] In addition to manipulation, this may simply reflect citizens following elite views.

Second, do parties contribute to free choice? Here too the picture is mixed. The two major political parties provide for competitive elections in many places, especially at the national level. They are roughly equal in their resources, the quality of their candidates (as judged by experience), and the support they command from voters. Clearly this is better than the one-party systems in some authoritarian regimes. At the same time, the Democratic

---

[23] Danielle M. Thomsen. 2017. *Opting Out of Congress: Partisan Polarization and the Decline of Moderate Candidates*. New York: Cambridge University Press.

[24] Richard R. Lau and David P. Redlawsk. 2001. "Advantages and Disadvantages of Cognitive Heuristics in Political Decision Making." *American Journal of Political Science* 45, 4: 951–71.

[25] Gabriel S. Lenz. 2009. "Learning and Opinion Change, Not Priming: Reconsidering the Priming Hypothesis." *American Journal of Political Science* 53, 4: 821–37.

and Republican parties certainly do nothing to alter the American system's bias against third parties and independent candidates who might represent other preferences among the public; indeed, the major parties may collude to exclude third-party competition.

Third, do parties contribute to deliberation? In one sense, they do. Competition between the major parties helps to clarify similarities and differences in what candidates and parties believe. But in other ways, parties do not contribute to healthy deliberation. Much like candidates, parties try to persuade voters, not promote conversation. They also tend to focus on the narrow range of issues that will appeal to swing voters. Multiparty systems encourage a much broader range of issue discussion.

Even if we are dissatisfied with the current role of parties, we should ask whether there is a viable alternative to them. Our criticisms of political parties do not always recognize what downsides the alternative might entail. In the 1950s, many political scientists and activists criticized the parties for not offering clear alternatives to voters; now that they do, we complain of polarization.

Because most major democracies feature parties, it is hard to know what elections would look like without them. It is true that many local elections are nonpartisan (see Chapter 11), but this does not necessarily stop parties from forming, if only informally. Even without official parties, candidates tend to develop stable alliances. One could argue that this is good, in that identifiable "teams" of candidates are easier for voters to evaluate than a mass of Lone Rangers. A multiparty system would provide voters more diverse options and better represent the range of views in the public. But multiparty systems may also make it more difficult for elected leaders to coordinate after elections.[26]

Conclusion

Political parties are key features of American campaigns. Candidates and voters usually have preexisting ties to the Democrats or Republicans, and campaigns usually replicate partisan divisions on public policy issues. Party organizations often recruit the candidates and determine their viability, directing resources to those most likely to win. Primary elections are usually internal party battles, with partisan leaders and activists helping to determine

---

[26] Keena Lipsitz. 2004. "Democratic Theory and Political Campaigns." *Journal of Political Philosophy* 12, 2: 163–89.

the nominees. General elections are largely fought along partisan lines, with each party's candidate presenting the party's issue positions and philosophy to voters already predisposed to choose one side in the battle.

But parties are also decentralized, not top-down, organizations. Members of Congress and party organizational leaders may say they oppose a candidate like Donald Trump, but conservative talk radio hosts and rally attendees may decide to ignore their advice—or even take it as a badge of honor, seeing it as evidence that Trump will shake up the political system. Partisan activists and individual voters also shape the party's image and help decide its representatives; unfortunately for Jeb Bush and the other traditional candidates in the race, they preferred a bombastic billionaire over practiced politicians in 2016.

Political science theories of nomination politics fared no better than Bush in 2016, but they enabled journalists to understand how much of an aberration Trump represented. Nonetheless, we should not assume that the party, or its network of elites, dies with one election. Despite some trepidation, Republicans won the presidency and did well in House and Senate elections in 2016; Trump supporters largely accepted the party's other candidates, and most Republican leaders eventually accepted Trump.

In the abstract, most citizens disdain parties. But despite persistent claims of decline, America's two major political parties are here to stay. As groups of citizens, officeholders, and organizations, parties guide voters, they train and organize candidates, and they govern. Attempts to regulate their influence typically succeed only in redirecting it. Whatever burdens parties create, it is difficult to imagine that democracy could work without them.

KEY TERMS

political parties (p. 160)

party-in-the-electorate (p. 160)

party-as-organization (p. 160)

party-in-government (p. 160)

coordinated expenditures (p. 170)

party identification (p. 176)

FOR DISCUSSION

1. Would American elections improve if party organizations were more involved in selecting party nominees and informing voters about the differences between candidates, or would it be better to leave campaigning to the candidates? How would elections change with more or less party involvement?

2. Democratic and Republican candidates (and voters) now take distinct positions on most issues. Is this a positive trend, because voters can now more easily tell the parties apart and elect candidates who share their views, or a negative trend, because the two parties are too extreme to compete for moderate voters?

3. Should political parties seek to maximize the seats that they control in Congress, running less loyal and less ideologically consistent candidates in the districts where they have fewer identifiers, or support only those candidates who adhere to the party's platform? Why?

4. What are the most significant changes in the role of political parties in American elections since the 1960s? Have they gained or lost influence? How have their coalitions and issue positions evolved?

CHAPTER 7

Interest Groups

Charles and David Koch, the primary owners of a manufacturing, energy, and mining firm called Koch Industries, have a long history of promoting conservative and libertarian political causes. Through their family foundations, they helped build the main think tanks of the American right: the Heritage Foundation, the American Enterprise Institute, and the Cato Institute. They helped found organizations that became key promoters of the Tea Party movement, including Americans for Prosperity and FreedomWorks. As individuals and through their company, they have long been major donors to political candidates.

In the 2012 election cycle, they substantially increased their political spending in the hopes of defeating President Obama. A large network of interest groups they helped create and facilitate spent $170 million on federal campaigns, more than half of which was directly provided by Koch-linked grants.[1] Charles and David Koch, and Koch Industries, also provided more than $5 million in campaign contributions, more than 90 percent on the Republican side. In 2016, they were less enthusiastic about Republican presidential candidate Donald Trump, and shifted their focus to down-ballot candidates. They spent about $250 million on political activities in the 2016 cycle and pledged to spend more than $300 million leading up to 2018, but because their network funnels money through opaque organizations, their specific targets are difficult to track. They have also been increasingly focused on grassroots lobbying and organization building at the state level, rather than influencing presidential campaigns.

Democrats criticize their efforts as self-interested and extreme. Even though neither Koch brother is a candidate or a party official, they have become the subject of attack ads. A Democratic super PAC ran television ads directly attacking them as "out-of-state billionaires" fighting to "rig the system," "end Medicare as

---

[1] Robert Macguire. 2013. "At Least 1 in 4 Dark Money Dollars in 2012 Had Koch Links." Center for Responsive Politics, December 3. www.opensecrets.org/news/2013/12/1-in-4 -dark-money-dollars-in-2012-c (accessed 10/27/2017).

we know it," and even "cut off hurricane relief."[2] Their donation patterns and elaborate network of organizations, sometimes difficult to trace back to them, influence the finances available to candidates and the content of their advertising campaigns.

Although the amount of money they spend on campaigns is far beyond the norm, several aspects of their political activities are emblematic of interest group participation in campaigns. First, the Kochs personify the most common type of big donors to interest groups: well-off business officials with clear ties to one party. Second, some of their organizations are traditional interest groups that lobby Congress and produce research, but others are part of a new breed of entities that are developed to take advantage of some feature of tax or campaign finance law. Americans for Prosperity mobilizes voters and lobbies state legislatures, but the American Future Fund and Americans for Responsible Leadership may simply be accounts for collecting money and paying for television ads. Even if the Kochs do not like a major candidate such as Trump, they have plenty of other places to put their money to work—especially since campaigns are only one place for interest groups to be active. Third, the Koch brothers are motivated by a combination of financial interest and ideology. Their companies can gain from federal contracts and low regulation, but their political spending is far beyond their direct foreseeable gain. They also provide considerable charitable contributions for art and education (with no obvious company benefit); politics is another outlet for using their money to advance their ideas.

Core of the Analysis

- Interest groups are varied actors, only some of which get involved in campaigns. They have proliferated, while changing form in response to changes in law.

- Interest groups donate money, run advertisements, and help mobilize voters, but their motives are distinct from those of the candidates and parties they support.

- Interest group spending can affect voters' choices, but there is only limited evidence that they redirect campaign agendas or deliver specific constituency votes.

- Interest group activity is at odds with some of our hopes for campaigns, although it can increase the diversity of voices in campaigns beyond those of the candidates.

---

[2] Rachel Finkel. 2014. "2014 Players Guide: Senate Majority PAC." FactCheck.org, February 7. www.factcheck.org/2014/02/senate-majority-pac (accessed 10/27/2017).

Interest groups play important roles in American campaigns, but the most involved groups are often adjuncts of political parties or creations of rich patrons. This chapter explores their roles, focusing both on the traditional role of interest groups in mobilizing segments of the electorate and their contemporary role as vehicles for campaign spending independent of candidates and parties. We first discuss the various types of interest groups and why they have proliferated. The chapter then looks at their involvement in campaigns and how it has coevolved with changes in campaign finance law. We also focus on their unique roles in initiative campaigns and note that the majority of interest groups still avoid campaigns in favor of lobbying. The chapter then addresses interest group campaign strategy in the context of the rules and realities they face, and assesses whether interest groups succeed in changing campaign debates or delivering constituency votes. Finally, we evaluate their role: Are interest groups meddling liars that divert candidates from their messages and mislead voters, or do they add important voices to American campaigns? Are the Koch brothers best seen, as their spokesman has suggested, as "patriotic Americans that have devoted their lives to advancing tolerance and freedom in America" or, as former senator Harry Reid has argued, as "two power-drunk billionaires" running the Republican Party?[3] Their true role may be more pedestrian: motivated by conservative ideas (and aligned business interests), the Koch brothers have created a network of interest groups to help Republicans win elections—just as other rich individuals fund groups supporting Democrats.

Types of Interest Groups

An **interest group** is a collection of people acting toward the shared goal of influencing public policy. Although political parties also have policy goals, interest groups differ from parties in key respects. Most important, interest groups do not run their own candidates for office. Interest groups usually seek more particular policy goals than do parties, often directly in line with the goals of their supporters. Interest groups are not always aligned with any one party, and many groups attempt to influence members of both parties. Even in campaigns, some groups will support candidates from both parties. Other interest groups do not participate in elections at all, focusing instead on lobbying policy makers after they are elected. But election

---

[3] Kenneth P. Vogel. 2014. "Behind Reid's War against the Kochs." *Politico*, July 7. www.politico.com/story/2014/07/harry-reid-koch-brothers-108632.html (accessed 10/27/2017).

results influence policy outcomes, so many interest groups do participate in campaigns and can be important actors in elections.

There are several major types of interest groups. The largest sector of groups represents businesses. More than 3,000 individual corporations or trade associations have political offices in or near Washington, D.C. These include large groups such as the National Association of Manufacturers and the American Farm Bureau Federation that, through affiliates, regularly give money to campaigns and participate directly in them. Yet most corporations do not have political action committees (PACs), make campaign contributions, or air their own campaign advertisements. Another large sector of interest groups, professional associations, represents occupations; examples include the American Medical Association and the American Bar Association. The largest of these groups participate in elections, but most are small and do not participate in campaigns. A third sector of interest groups, labor unions, regularly participates in campaigns. Most labor unions—for example, the American Federation of State, County, and Municipal Employees (AFSCME) and the Service Employees International Union (SEIU)—usually support Democratic candidates. A smaller number of unions, such as the Teamsters Union, sometimes endorse candidates from both parties.

Rather than the direct economic concerns of corporations, unions, and professionals, some interest groups seek to represent broader social groups or ideological perspectives. Groups that represent a social group include the National Association for the Advancement of Colored People (NAACP), which works on behalf of African Americans. Some groups, such as the American Conservative Union, represent a general ideological orientation. These groups usually refer to themselves as *public interest groups*. Other groups advocate for a single issue. The National Rifle Association (NRA), for example, promotes the rights of gun owners (see Box 7.1). Public interest and single-issue groups are more likely to participate in elections than are economic groups, but they are less numerous and have fewer resources.[4] In 2012, the number of ideological groups created only to advertise in that year's campaign, rather than for ongoing lobbying, increased significantly.

Interest groups differ in the extent of their ties to political parties. Unions like the National Education Association have endorsed the Democratic Party candidate in every presidential election of the past few decades; others, like the Fraternal Order of Police, lean toward the Republicans. Many interest groups share close ties to a party, exchanging mailing lists and voter targets,

---

[4] Jack L. Walker, Jr. 1991. *Mobilizing Interest Groups in America: Patrons, Professions, and Social Movements*. Ann Arbor: University of Michigan Press.

BOX 7.1

How the National Rifle Association Holds Elected Officials Accountable on Gun Rights

The National Rifle Association's political influence is legendary. The 1994 congressional elections sealed its reputation: many incumbents that the group opposed lost their bids for reelection, thereby shifting control of Congress to the Republicans. Several of these members had defected from supporting gun rights on only one significant occasion—by supporting the assault weapons ban in a crime bill—but that was enough to earn the NRA's retaliation. According to many observers, including former president Bill Clinton, the NRA's advertising and voter mobilization cost these members their seats in Congress. "The gun lobby claimed to have defeated nineteen of the twenty-four members on its hit list," Clinton reported in his autobiography, "They did at least that much damage and could rightly claim to have made [Newt] Gingrich the House Speaker."[1]

Political scientists are more cautious about attributing influence on election outcomes to interest groups. Many other factors contributed to the Republican Party's victories in 1994, and there is little evidence that the NRA's television ads or the votes of gun rights supporters were the deciding factors. For the NRA's purposes, however, it may not matter. Their reputation as a group with clout benefited regardless, enabling them to exert more influence on members of both parties. The group's influential reputation continues today: NRA-backed candidates, including Donald Trump and several senators competing in close races, mostly emerged victorious in 2016. The NRA does not win every battle it enters, but it wins enough to make an impression on politicians wavering in their support of gun rights.

The NRA's CEO, Wayne LaPierre, regularly presides over rallies that highlight the organization's goals.

Can the NRA's influence be neutralized? In 2014, former New York Mayor Michael Bloomberg said he would donate $50 million to build interest groups in favor of gun control. The goal, according to Bloomberg, was to "make [the NRA] afraid of us."[2] Bloomberg is satisfied that he is doing the right thing: "I have earned my place in heaven. It's not even close," he said. Nevertheless, Bloomberg's initial efforts to counteract the NRA did not result in much success: federal gun control is no closer to enactment, and few, if any, candidates have changed their views or gone down to defeat as a result of Bloomberg's campaigns. The NRA's reputation as an influential political force with a solid constituency behind it has stayed intact despite a continued string of mass shootings and associated upsurges in public complaints.

[1] Bill Clinton. 2005. *My Life, Vol. II: The Presidential Years.* New York: Vintage Books, p. 215.
[2] Adam O'Neal. 2014. "Bloomberg: 'I've Earned My Place in Heaven.'" *Real Clear Politics*, April 16. www.realclearpolitics.com/articles/2014/04/16/bloomberg_i_have_earned_my_place_in_heaven_122299.html (accessed 10/27/2017).

even if they officially claim to be nonpartisan. Groups may have some incentive to maintain allies in the opposing party: the NRA still gives money to some Democrats, even though the Republican National Committee was a top recipient of its largesse.

Why Does the United States Have So Many Interest Groups?

The United States has a large and growing number of interest groups. Citizens tend to bemoan groups as narrow "special interests," but the large number also reflects the country's increasing diversity of ideas and backgrounds. The proliferation of interest groups has been particularly dramatic since the 1960s. One important reason why is the expansion of government. As all levels of government in the United States, particularly the federal government, have taken on more responsibilities, they now regulate more entities and provide resources to more people. This creates an incentive for groups to organize to advocate for receiving more favorable regulations and additional resources.

A second reason for interest group expansion is improved strategies for organizational maintenance. A key innovation was direct mail fund-raising, by which an organization could regularly solicit contributions from an expanding list of like-minded Americans. Today, organizations maintain e-mail lists, social media accounts, and websites to further facilitate fund-raising appeals.

A third reason is that prominent social movements have served as models for other groups to mobilize. After the success of the African American civil rights movement, for example, other minority groups mobilized. The increasing ethnic and religious diversity of the United States has furthered this trend. Successful mobilization by one side can also stimulate mobilization by the other. For example, a conservative group called the American Action Network was founded in 2010 in response to the liberal Center for American Progress, which was originally founded to counter conservative think tanks like the Heritage Foundation. The Heritage Foundation was itself founded to counter the liberal Brookings Institution. This pattern of response and counterresponse is common.

A fourth factor driving the proliferation of interest groups is the federal tax and campaign finance rules that encourage organizations to create separate affiliated groups for distinct purposes. As noted in Chapter 4, many

This advertisement, run by the True Republican PAC during Alabama's 2010 gubernatorial primary elections, attacked the incumbent Republican candidate for his belief in evolution. However, reports later surfaced that tied the PAC to the state teachers' association, whose members were unlikely to be concerned about teaching evolution.

interest groups are registered with the Internal Revenue Service (IRS) as 501(c) nonprofit corporations or as 527 groups. Interest groups also create PACs to accept contributions and donate them directly to political candidates. Some organizations have a combination of affiliates of different types. For example, EMILY's List, a supporter of female Democratic candidates, is a PAC with affiliated 527s. Progress for America is a conservative 501(c)4 organization with a 527 affiliate. The Center for American Progress is a 501(c)3 with a 501(c)4 affiliate. The NRA is a 501(c)4 with a PAC. State and local laws differ in how these organizations are treated and whether they can participate in state and local elections. As a result, organizations with state or local affiliates can have even more complicated structures.

Campaign finance rules drive the formation of new groups in another way: because laws require that the sponsors of advertisements be disclosed in the advertisements themselves, some groups create new organizations with names designed specifically to appeal to the electorate. In a 2010 California ballot initiative campaign dealing with auto insurance, the side funded by insurance companies called itself "Californians for Fair Auto Insurance Rates" and created the "California Senior Advocates League" to promote its cause. In 2010, the Alabama Education Association, a liberal teachers association, even funded the "True Republican PAC." This PAC disingenuously ran advertisements during Alabama's gubernatorial primaries critical of the incumbent Republican candidate's belief in evolution in an attempt to weaken conservative voters' support for him in the Republican primary. Campaign finance laws, in other words, encourage the same groups of people to create multiple organizations for legal and public relations purposes.

An increase in campaign activity by interest groups has accompanied the general increase in the number of groups; more interest groups have meant more interest group campaigning. Yet, as Figure 7.1 illustrates, not all of these trends have followed the same trajectory. The largest increase in PACs occurred in the late 1970s and early 1980s. The numbers of lobbyists and PACs have changed only slightly in the past eight election cycles, but they have been accompanied by new types of groups: 527s and super PACs. Expenditures by 527s were concentrated in the 2004 election cycle. Independent spending has increased most dramatically since 2006, with notable spending by super PACs in 2012. 501(c) organizations also began spending considerable sums on election-related activities in the last few election cycles.

Figure 7.2 illustrates trends in the total amounts of money that interest groups donate in federal campaign contributions and how much they directly spend in campaigns (including several types of expenditures). Since PAC contributions go disproportionately to incumbents who often lack competition, direct spending can be more influential than campaign contributions in close elections. It also has some disadvantages for interest groups, since independent spenders cannot coordinate with candidates and often have to pay higher rates for television advertising. In 2012, independent expenditures in federal elections eclipsed total PAC contributions for the first time, tripling the totals from the previous campaign. These trends were caused more by changes in campaign finance laws than by changes in the number of groups trying to influence campaigns (as Figure 7.1 shows). As discussed in Chapter 4, Supreme Court rulings and Federal Election Commission (FEC) interpretations enabled new super PACs to accept unlimited contributions and spend unlimited amounts to influence elections. In 2012, a small number of them, disproportionately favoring Republicans, directed the large increase in direct group spending. The Republican super PAC advantage in 2012 allowed Republican candidate Mitt Romney to remain competitive in total advertising volume, even though Barack Obama's

FIGURE 7.1 Number of Lobbyists, Contributing Political Action Committees, Super PACs, and 527s, 1998–2016

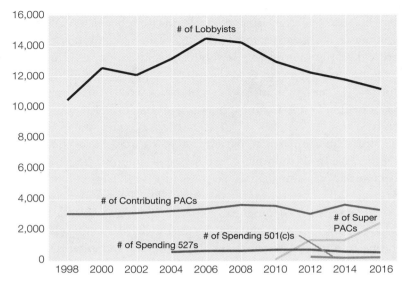

Source: Lobbyist data are from the Center for Responsive Politics, based on data from the Senate Office of Public Records. PAC data are from the Federal Election Commission. Super PAC and 527 data are from the Center for Responsive Politics, based on Federal Election Commission and Internal Revenue Service data.

campaign substantially outraised the Romney campaign. In 2014, Democrats were more effective at mobilizing super PAC dollars than in previous elections. In 2016, outside spending in the presidential race was more even; Republican-supporting groups outspent Democrats in Senate races, but Democratic-aligned groups outspent Republicans in House races. Outside groups also outspent the candidates themselves in 26 congressional races.

How Are Interest Groups Involved in Campaigns?

Although the majority of interest groups do not get involved in campaigns, many groups contribute money and endorse candidates. Organizations with members commonly communicate with and attempt to mobilize their members to volunteer and turn out to vote for their preferred candidates. A small number of interest groups engage in their own advertising, including an increasing number that are founded exclusively for this purpose.

FIGURE 7.2 Total Interest Group Campaign Contributions and Direct Campaign Spending, 1998–2016

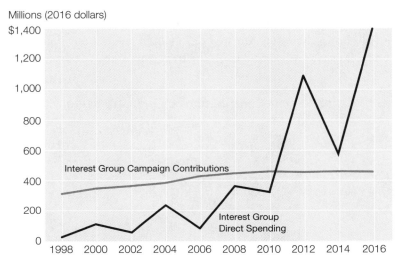

Source: Data are from the Center for Responsive Politics (OpenSecrets.org), based on data from the Federal Election Commission. Campaign contributions include only PAC contributions. Direct spending includes independent expenditures, electioneering communications, and communication costs.

Because of donor disclosure requirements, campaign contributions are the type of interest group electioneering that is easiest to track. Interest groups often donate money to candidates and parties through their affiliated PACs. Total PAC contributions have been increasing since the 1970s (rising from $126 million in 1978 to $441 million in 2016; see Figure 7.2), even as the number of PACs has held relatively steady (see Figure 7.1).[5] Most PACs are associated with professional associations, unions, or corporations. Corporate, union, and association executives also make individual contributions to candidates. The Center for Responsive Politics combines PAC giving with donations from individuals associated with an organization in its tracking of total giving by industries over time. In 2016, according to their data, total giving by entities affiliated with business accounted for 59.9 percent of large federal campaign contributions, labor unions contributed 4.6 percent, and ideological interest groups contributed 13.4 percent. Ideological and single-issue PACs are becoming more numerous, but their contributions still

---

[5] Campaign Finance Institute. 2016. Data (in constant 2016 dollars). http://www.cfinst.org /data.aspx (accessed 11/1/2017).

account for a small portion of total PAC giving. Within the corporate sector, the financial industry donates more money than any other corporate sector, with companies in law, energy, health, and communications also accounting for a large portion of contributions (see Figure 7.3). Corporate sectors differ not only in how much they donate but in who receives their donations. The building materials and oil and gas industries consistently favor Republicans,

FIGURE 7.3 **Total Political Contributions by Industry Sector**

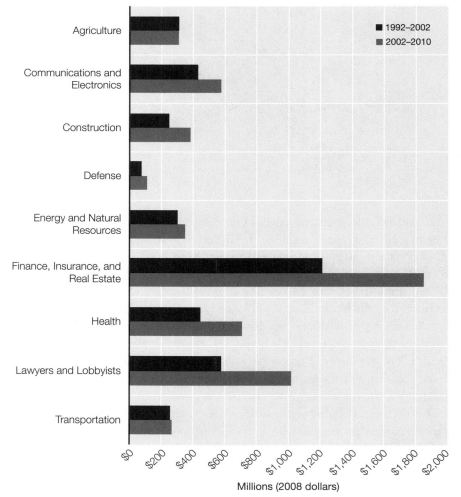

Source: Data are from the Center for Responsive Politics (OpenSecrets.org). Included are individual contributions, PAC contributions, and soft money.

while the entertainment and publishing industries consistently favor Democrats. Unions are bigger supporters of Democratic candidates than any industry sector. Despite their different party preferences, most corporate and labor PACs donate overwhelmingly to incumbents. Although PACs are clearly important donors, their contributions must be put in context: as we discussed in Chapter 4, PACs donate less money to American political campaigns than do individuals, although many of these individuals are employees of corporations with political interests.

Interest groups can also participate in elections by running their own advertising campaigns. In 2016, super PACs dominated outside campaign intervention, spending more than $1 billion. Table 7.1 reports the top interest group spenders in the 2016 federal elections. The top super PACs were broadly conservative or liberal groups, designed to supplement party spending. New 501(c) organizations officially claiming to advance social welfare, rather than focus on politics, were nonetheless also funneling money toward campaign advertising. Traditional interest groups like the U.S. Chamber of Commerce, the SEIU, and the NRA also continued to spend at high levels. Together, 2016 interest groups allocated nearly six times as much as political parties to independent spending—but many were closely associated with party leaders and allocated money to the same races.

In 2016, interest groups accounted for 28 percent of ads in federal races, matching their role in 2012 and 2014. But campaign advertisements aired by interest groups have consistently been much more likely to be negative than those aired by candidates across House, Senate, and presidential races. In particular, ads favoring Hillary Clinton in 2016 were overwhelmingly negative toward Trump across all ad sponsors.[6] Interest groups are less concerned than candidates or parties with protecting their reputation and are willing to risk any backlash from negative advertising. Interest group ads are less obviously tied to the candidate that they are supporting, although voters may not necessarily distinguish interest group ads from candidate ads. Interest group advertisements are also more likely to focus on policy issues than are candidate advertisements. Candidates are more concerned with sharing their biographies, whereas interest groups often want to make the issues that concern them more central to the campaign.

Contributions and independent expenditures may be the easiest way to measure interest group involvement in campaigns, but they are not the only

---

[6] Erika Franklin Fowler, Travis N. Ridout, and Michael M. Franz. 2016. "Political Advertising in 2016: The Presidential Election as Outlier." *Forum* 14, 4: 445–69.

TABLE 7.1 Top Interest Group Spenders in 2016 Elections

Group Name	Amount Spent	Partisan Tilt
Priorities USA/Priorities USA Action	$133,407,972	Democratic
Right to Rise USA	$86,817,138	Republican
Senate Leadership Fund	$85,994,270	Republican
Senate Majority PAC	$75,413,426	Democratic
Conservative Solutions PAC	$55,443,483	Republican
National Rifle Association	$54,398,558	Republican
House Majority PAC	$47,470,121	Democratic
Congressional Leadership Fund	$40,125,691	Republican
EMILY's List	$33,167,285	Democratic
Freedom Partners	$29,728,798	Republican
U.S. Chamber of Commerce	$29,106,034	Republican
Service Employees International Union	$24,545,408	Democratic
Granite State Solutions	$24,267,135	Republican
Future45	$24,264,009	Republican
Great America PAC	$23,608,264	Republican

Source: Data from Center for Responsive Politics (OpenSecrets.org).

ways in which interest groups try to influence elections. Interest groups also use other media to get their campaign messages out and support specific candidates. Many groups have large e-mail lists and groups of online supporters on social networking sites like Facebook and Twitter. Many groups mobilize their members to support causes or candidates via donations or other forms of activism. At times, online activists and blogs, such as the liberal *Daily Kos*, become interest groups in themselves, raising money and endorsing candidates.

Interest groups also sometimes pursue independent efforts to mobilize and persuade voters. Unions, for example, have long engaged in grassroots mobilization of their members. In 2004, 527s on the Democratic side, such as America Coming Together, also worked to mobilize voters. Many interest groups produce voter guides or endorse slates of candidates. The Christian Coalition handed out millions of voter guides outside churches in 1994, making it clear that they believed Republican candidates were pro-life and pro-family whereas Democratic candidates were not. These kinds of activities were less important in 2016—but in local races, groups still often place door-hangers throughout a district, listing all of the candidates that they support.

Interest groups that undertake these campaign activities often claim to speak for broader **constituencies**, such as all voters from a particular ethnic or religious group. Organizations and leaders that represent a particular group can help to reinforce the allegiance of group members in the voting public to a party or set of candidates. Arguably, the loyalty of African American voters to the Democratic Party arises in part because most black leaders are allied with the party.[7] Republican candidates also sometimes attend NAACP conventions, if only to avoid appearing to ignore African Americans. Candidates may also sign on to a group's policy agenda, such as Americans for Tax Reform's "Taxpayer Protection Pledge," which entails a promise not to raise taxes. Candidates signing the pledge expect not only to gain the support of individuals affiliated with the interest group, but also to signal to all voters opposed to taxes that they share their views.

Interest Groups in Initiative Campaigns

In **ballot initiative campaigns**, where voters are given a choice to support or oppose specific policy changes, interest groups replace the candidates as the main actors. In states and localities where initiatives and referenda are allowed, coalitions of individuals and interest groups often form to pay firms to gather enough signatures from registered voters to meet requirements to get an issue on the ballot. In California, proponents of initiatives routinely pay millions of dollars just for the signature-gathering effort before the real campaign begins. Legislatures can also directly put questions on the ballot, and local governing authorities are sometimes required to put measures like tax increases to the voters. No matter how they make their way onto the ballot, committees often form to support or oppose these issues.

---

[7] Paul Frymer. 1999. *Uneasy Alliances: Race and Party Competition in America*. Princeton, NJ: Princeton University Press.

Statewide initiatives, especially those that will impact the bottom line of businesses, are more likely to generate active campaigns.

Interest group endorsements and advertising can provide clues to initiative voters who might not otherwise understand the complex legislative language of initiatives. A study of California voters deciding on five complicated insurance initiatives found that knowing whether the insurance industry, trial lawyers, and consumer activists supported the measures was enough to help voters who could not understand the initiatives emulate the votes of those who did have full information.[8] Voters just had to know whether they favored the position of the insurance industry or the trial lawyers, not which particular law they preferred.

With enough money, even obscure interest groups can put their issues to the voters. In 2014, a wealthy technology businessman tried to qualify an initiative to divide California into six separate states including one named "Silicon Valley," even though polls showed little support for the proposal and legal experts said voters lacked the authority to break up the state. Because too many signatures were invalid, the initiative was kept off the ballot. Interest group spending can also help defeat initiatives, especially if opponents outspend proponents by a 2–1 margin, but there is little evidence that outsized spending on the positive side can move voters to support a proposition.[9] Money might eventually buy this businessman a place on the ballot, but California is in little danger of splitting up anytime soon.

Why Do Some Interest Groups Avoid Campaigns?

Many traditional interest groups avoid spending money on political campaigns. Most businesses that hire lobbyists fail to start PACs. Even some huge firms like Apple and Berkshire Hathaway lack PACs. All of the major industries that do donate to candidates still spend considerably more on lobbying and charitable contributions than on campaigns.[10] Few interest groups give the maximum amounts allowed by law to candidates, and even fewer spend their own money directly in campaigns.

This points to a difference in the goals of interest groups as compared with those of political parties and candidates. Interest groups' primary concerns are policy outcomes, rather than who holds power. They care about elections

---

[8] Arthur Lupia. 1994. "Shortcuts versus Encyclopedias: Information and Voting Behavior in California Insurance Reform Elections." *American Political Science Review* 88, 1: 63–76.

[9] Elisabeth R. Gerber. 1999. *The Populist Paradox: Interest Group Influence and the Promise of Direct Legislation*. Princeton, NJ: Princeton University Press.

[10] Jeffrey Milyo, David Primo, and Timothy Groseclose. 2000. "Corporate PAC Campaign Contributions in Perspective." *Business and Politics* 2, 1: 75–88.

because the party that controls government influences whether legislatures pass the laws they favor or oppose and how administrations implement those laws. Groups may also be able to identify the particular candidates most likely to support their policy goals. But elections are not interest groups' only opportunities to influence policy: they can also lobby whoever is elected or appointed. If a group plans to talk to members of both parties to advance its goals, it may be disadvantageous to have a firm tie to either the Democrats or the Republicans.

As judged by their spending habits, most interest groups view spending money on lobbying as a better strategy than spending on campaigns. The issues of interest to many corporations, such as a specific tax exemption or a small appropriation, never come up in campaigns. Interest groups also like to present an apolitical image of expertise and a willingness to work with anyone to achieve shared goals. Appearing to stay above the fray, rather than intervening in elections, may better serve that image.

The combination of some interest groups averse to campaigns and some interest groups invented for the sole purpose of running ads in campaigns means that the most involved groups in elections are not representative of all the groups trying to influence policy. The campaigning groups are much more likely to take a clear partisan side and be motivated by ideology than those who sit on the sidelines.

Rules, Reality, and Interest Group Strategies

Interest groups decide their campaign role in the context of the rules set by government. As we have seen, campaign finance laws set limits on how much any group can donate and encourage groups to establish multiple subsidiaries—501(c) organizations, 527 organizations, PACs—in order to stay within the law. Groups are also prohibited from coordinating their advertising or mobilization efforts with candidates. Candidates cannot use the resources of interest groups, even office space or printed materials, without counting those resources as in-kind contributions, subject to disclosure and contribution limits. Furthermore, tax law limits the activities of many interest groups if they are organized as tax-exempt nonprofit organizations. Depending on their tax status, interest groups may be prohibited from publicly endorsing candidates or engaging in campaign activity.

Interest group strategies are also constrained by certain realities that they may not be able to change during any particular campaign. Some interest groups represent more popular issue positions than others. Some represent issues that are already of great concern to voters, but others need to stimulate interest in their issue areas. Some groups find it easier to raise money and thus have more resources to use in elections than others. Candidates inevitably cater to the wealthiest groups and those most able to deliver large numbers of votes.

Interest group strategies also depend on how their agenda and issue positions correspond to those of incumbent politicians.[11] Groups whose agendas are well served by incumbent politicians will typically support them, regardless of party, and will seek to maintain their access to these politicians and thus ensure that government policy continues to match their preferences. Evidence of this strategy can be seen among interest groups that give to members of both parties. For example, the defense and aerospace industry—which has earned many billions of dollars in government contracts—routinely gives considerable sums to both parties. In 2016, the top donors in the industry, Lockheed Martin and Boeing, gave $3.1 million to Democrats and $3.7 million to Republicans. By contrast, interest groups whose views are not well represented among incumbents—typically, ideological and single-issue groups—will seek to replace these incumbents, often with representatives who are more liberal or conservative than the average legislator. The actions of the Club for Growth exemplify this strategy, as the group often seeks to replace Republican and Democratic incumbents with more conservative alternatives. But most ideological groups still support incumbent candidates of their preferred party.

Substantial interest group resources—particularly in the form of independent expenditures—are often targeted at a few competitive races. Interest group involvement can complicate life for the candidates in these races, as groups often emphasize messages different from those of the candidates they support. Interest groups' messages may center on their narrow agendas rather than the concerns of the average voter and may also be more controversial than the candidate's. The Willie Horton advertisement discussed in Chapter 4, for example, was broadcast by an interest group and ultimately disavowed by the candidate, George H. W. Bush, that it was meant to support.

Interest Group Campaign Influence

Interest groups largely engage in the same activities as candidates and parties, meaning that their ultimate influence is tied to similar factors. If voters know little about the candidates, one side spends considerably more than the

---

[11] Michael M. Franz. 2008. *Choices and Changes: Interest Groups in the Electoral Process.* Philadelphia: Temple University Press.

other, and a close race is otherwise projected, interest group activities can help tip the balance. In races with well-known contenders or balanced levels of spending, interest group activities—just like candidate and party campaigns—will have a hard time affecting election outcomes. If ads or get-out-the-vote efforts are successful in the hands of parties or candidates, interest groups can use the same strategies to achieve similar effects. But interest groups face the same environment as their candidate and party allies: most favored Romney over Obama in 2012, but had no more luck than the Republican Party or Romney in convincing voters to reject Obama. And most favored Clinton in 2016, but voters in critical states still supported Trump.

The large increase in interest group campaign activity has stimulated some research on its impact. In the 2012 Republican presidential primary, during which super PACs outspent candidates in many states, research has shown that super PACs extended the viability of Rick Santorum, who had limited money, and reduced the influence of candidate wins in the early states on the contests that followed them.[12] In an experiment in which researchers showed 2012 super PAC ads to voters, they found that the ads reduced voters' evaluations of Romney, indirectly helping Obama even though they were meant to support Romney's primary opponents.[13] Interest group expenditures may also be less valuable at the beginning of a candidate's primary campaign, when the actual campaign organization needs direct donations just to build a competent organization and enable regular travel. For example, despite pledged super PAC support, Wisconsin Governor Scott Walker decided to drop out of the 2016 presidential race in part due to lack of direct donations.

Many reformers are concerned that interest group influence will grow with unlimited spending by super PACs. Some have even fought back by forming their own. In 2011, comedian Stephen Colbert started a super PAC to dramatize the potential for unlimited and hidden political spending. He raised $1 million, increasing awareness of campaign finance laws among his television viewers but failing to influence many voters with his advertising. In 2014, Harvard professor Lawrence Lessig started the Mayday PAC with an odd purpose: to support candidates who want to eliminate super PACs. He recommends that citizens "embrace the irony" of using super PACs to fight against super PACs, but the effort faced an uphill battle: making the issue matter to electable candidates without stimulating overwhelming opposition

---

[12] Dino P. Christenson and Corwin D. Smidt. 2014. "Following the Money: Super PACs and the 2012 Presidential Nomination." *Presidential Studies Quarterly* 44, 3: 410–30.

[13] David Lynn Painter. 2014. "Collateral Damage: Involvement and the Effects of Negative Super PAC Advertising." *American Behavioral Scientist* 58, 4: 510–23.

spending.[14] Thus far, Lessig's operation has spent considerable sums (often on long-shot candidacies) to little effect.

Interest groups may be especially likely to influence outcomes when other campaigning is limited, such as in ballot initiative campaigns. In one field experiment, researchers worked with an advocacy group supporting and opposing statewide initiatives in Oregon to send persuasive mailers to randomly selected households, and found that precincts that received the materials were more likely to support initiatives favored by the group and oppose those that the group sought to defeat.[15]

Can Interest Groups Deliver Constituency Votes?

As noted earlier, interest groups often claim to represent constituencies like gun owners, union members, and African Americans. They offer candidates a deal: support our groups' goals and you will win the votes of our members and sympathetic fans in the electorate. But can interest groups actually deliver the votes? Gaining the support of interest groups is likely to translate into votes for a given candidate only if group members perceive a common fate, believe that an organization best represents their interests, and tend to vote together consistently. Securing a Farm Bureau organizational endorsement, for example, matters more if farmers see themselves as a group that will rise and fall based on support for particular agricultural policies. The endorsement efforts of interest groups and their leaders may be especially important for candidates in local elections, where voters know more about their neighborhood association, union, or business association than they know about many of the candidates. In local elections, there will often be a direct negotiation between candidates and local group leaders over which candidates will receive the votes of group members. For example, all of the local African American neighborhood leaders may endorse one of the mayoral candidates, sending a message to potential voters that the candidate supports African American interests and promising the candidate that they will mobilize local African Americans through churches and community associations on their behalf.

Yet candidates cannot be certain that earning the endorsement of groups or their leaders will lead group members to vote for them. For instance, former Florida governor Jeb Bush gained the support of politicians and

---

[14] Nicholas Confessore. 2014. "Big Money to Fight Big Donors." *New York Times*, September 7, A1.

[15] Todd Rogers and Joel Middleton. 2015. "Are Ballot Initiative Outcomes Influenced by the Campaigns of Independent Groups? A Precinct-Randomized Field Experiment Showing That They Are." *Political Behavior* 37, 3: 567–93.

group leaders as the 2016 campaign approached, but never caught fire with voters. More generally, interest groups sometimes exaggerate their ability to "deliver" votes for a candidate. The views of group leaders are often more consistently ideological or strongly partisan than are the views of group members. Members may also be more divided than leaders in their loyalties to parties or candidates. Ultimately, although candidates typically seek the support of sympathetic interest groups, the number of voters any group can deliver is uncertain.

For example, Democratic candidates often seek the support of unions, which have traditionally been a major force in Democratic Party politics. Much of the campaigning in Democratic primaries consists of traveling from union hall to union hall, gathering endorsements by talking at open meetings or negotiating with leadership. National labor groups like the AFL-CIO and the SEIU are still among the top Democratic Party donors and spend considerably on their own advertising and get-out-the-vote strategies. They also serve as national volunteer networks for Democratic campaigns. But Republican politicians regularly complain that union leadership fails to represent the views of their significant, but minority, Republican membership. Unions

Hillary Clinton, like most Democratic candidates, gained the support of major unions in 2016. Clinton, who spoke at an AFL-CIO convention in Philadelphia during the 2016 primary season, won the union's endorsement for the Democratic nomination for president over rival Bernie Sanders.

also face a declining membership and they increasingly represent government employees rather than private sector workers, making it harder to reach out to the broader working class that they hope to mobilize on behalf of Democrats. In 2016, union efforts to spread Clinton's message faltered even among many of their own members; some trusted Trump rather than their own union leaders, as he spoke directly to them about concerns over trade and immigration.

When a constituency is easily identifiable, motivated, and ascendant, interest groups can help channel members' energies toward candidates who share their views. Conservative and Tea Party–affiliated organizations often support the same candidates in Republican Party primaries, stamping them with the moniker of "consistent conservative" and helping to direct conservative voters to the candidates they support. Although not many Americans are official members of these interest groups, many more are sympathetic to their broader aims. Interest group endorsements help codify one candidate as the favorite of the right, a notion often amplified by talk radio hosts and reported in local media coverage.

Can Interest Groups Change the Campaign Agenda?

Some interest groups have goals beyond electing a particular candidate; they hope to change the **campaign agenda**: the issues at the heart of a campaign. Environmental organizations, for example, usually support Democratic candidates, but they also want issues like pollution and climate change to play a generally more prominent role in campaigns. They may advertise directly on the issues that most concern them, hoping to stimulate candidate and voter discussion on these issues. The League of Conservation Voters targets 12 candidates it calls the "dirty dozen" that it says oppose clean energy. It funds television ads, voter contact operations, and online videos focused on these candidates' environmental records.

As interest group activity in campaigns has come to be dominated less by single-issue groups and more by ideological and partisan organizations established to funnel money toward advertising, group advertising has become less distinctive. If interest groups use the same political consulting firms, run similar focus groups, and use similar survey data to design their advertising, the output is likely to look the same as candidates' own advertisements. There is also little evidence that candidates follow the lead of interest groups when they choose to advertise on different issues. Candidates choose their own issue focus and often respond to the issues that their opponents raise, but do not necessarily shift their advertising on the basis of issues raised only by interest groups.

Even with limited resources for advertising, interest groups may help focus their supporters' attention on the candidates' records on the issues that concern them. Many interest groups issue scorecards for elected officials, outlining their votes for and against the groups' positions. Abortion rights groups regularly declare that Republicans have waged a "war on women" and highlight candidate statements that oppose legal abortion even in cases of rape or incest. Candidates are sometimes forced to respond to these interest group efforts, with reporters asking why they have a poor voting record according to a particular group or asking them to clarify a statement highlighted by a group.

Evaluating Interest Groups

Interest groups are often labeled "special interests" by politicians and even citizens—suggesting that they are opposed to the broader public interest. Some interest group advertising is notoriously misleading, and interest groups cannot be held as accountable as candidates for their deceptions. Interest groups do represent a diversity of perspectives, which helps to ensure that Americans from a variety of backgrounds have a voice. But they are most likely to represent constituencies that are wealthier and have more to gain from government policy, which tends to heighten inequalities in political influence.

The independent role of interest groups can be especially important. Interest groups advance the democratic ideal of free speech, empowering individuals and organizations other than the candidates to express their opinions. They highlight some concerns from voters, advocating views other than those that the candidates themselves articulate. Interest groups help serve the standards of free choice, but do not always contribute to the ideal of equality. They add voices to campaign deliberation, but intend to persuade rather than inform voters.

Would we be better off without interest groups? There have been numerous attempts to limit interest group involvement in American campaigns, most prominently via campaign finance law. However, courts have invalidated some of these laws, arguing that interest groups deserve free speech protection because they advocate for the concerns of their supporters. Even if the courts had not ruled in this way, it seems unlikely that interest groups could be significantly weakened. There will always be incentives for advocates of a cause to band together and seek to influence parties and candidates. In fact, this may benefit democracy, inasmuch as citizens have political views that

Education Politics

A 2017 election for the Los Angeles School Board was hardly a local affair, attracting more than $15 million in spending, with donors like former New York Mayor Michael Bloomberg, Netflix CEO Reed Hastings, and heirs to the Wal-Mart, GAP, and Apple fortunes facing off against national unions. The races served as a national proxy fight between education interest groups, with proponents of district-level reform and charter schools (including Bloomberg and Hastings) supporting one set of candidates and their opponents (especially teachers' unions) supporting an alternative slate. The charter-supporting candidates won their first majority on the board, defeating the incumbent school board president.

The battle over education reform often plays out within the Democratic Party, the primary home to both teachers' unions and many charter school enthusiasts, but the combatants have not limited themselves to (largely non-partisan) school board elections. Mayors guide education policy in their cities, meaning that mayoral elections can sometimes determine the fate of school reform efforts.

Neither side limits its fight to the local level, either. Interest groups in Washington State helped legalize charter schools via a 2012 statewide ballot initiative campaign that gathered bipartisan support. Betsy DeVos was nominated to serve as secretary of education by President Trump on the basis of her philanthropy and political donations on behalf of charter schools in Michigan and other states.

Two national-level interest groups exemplify the divide within the Democratic Party: Democrats for Education Reform, which often supports pro-charter candidates; and the Network for Public Education, which was founded by Diane Ravitch, an education historian who has become the leader of charter school opponents. The partisan politics of education have become even stranger with the fight over the Common Core, a set of national education standards promoted by business groups, unions, and the Obama administration and adopted by nearly all states before becoming a lightning rod, attracting opposition from Tea Party Republicans as well as criticism from Ravitch and those on the ideological left.

The motives of education interest groups are different from those of parties or candidates. They seek to change policies through whatever venues are available. That sometimes means lobbying a school board or state legislature, but it also can mean running an initiative campaign, endorsing candidates in a local or state race, or backing a national effort to influence Congress or the administration. Education reform battles have divided each party. Both the Bush and Obama administrations sought to nationalize education standards and support charter schools and faced opposition from both the left and the right. Trump has again empowered DeVos to influence state and local policy from Washington, but also railed against federal control of education.

According to Ravitch and other critics, recent education reforms are the pet projects of billionaire philanthropists like DeVos and Bill Gates: they are using their resources to disrupt public education and impose their untested ideas. The reformers, in turn, say teachers' unions have controlled local education policy making for too long, blocking competition and protecting bad teachers. In other words, both sets of interest groups claim to be fighting the special interests—they are willing to intervene in many types of election campaigns to change policies in their favor while decrying their opponents' efforts to do the same.

they want to share with politicians. Interest groups help citizens get politicians' attention. Hillary Clinton was roundly booed in 2007 when she told an audience of liberal bloggers that "lobbyists, whether you like it or not, represent real Americans," citing associations of nurses and teachers.[16] But sometimes, that is true.

Interest group involvement in campaigns also raises some unique concerns. Candidates may feel beholden to interest groups that donate to them or advertise on their behalf. Regardless of whether these groups change election outcomes, politicians may exchange favors or moderate their positions to stay on their good side. If candidates believe that casino magnate Sheldon Adelson is likely to spend millions on a single presidential campaign, for example, they may be less likely to criticize gambling or they may look for other ways to impress him. At a gathering in Las Vegas led by Adelson in 2014, potential 2016 presidential contenders were careful to emphasize their positions in favor of military support for Israel and trade with China, two issues about which Adelson cares deeply. Perhaps the downsides of interest group campaigning will not show up in campaigns at all, but in one-sided policies advanced by parties or candidates trying to curry interest groups' favor.

Conclusion

Citizens are not kind to the "special interests" they believe are corrupting campaigns. Candidates encourage their condemnation by christening their opponents as supporters of nefarious groups. But one person's special interest is another person's professional association, advocacy group, workplace, or church. Interest groups can help to focus campaigns on policies designed to solve people's problems, rather than vacuous debates about personality and patriotism.

Interest groups regularly donate to candidates, air advertisements, and mobilize their followers. They are likely to play increasingly important roles in driving campaigns. Voters in competitive districts may see more ads from interest groups than from the candidates. Although many groups that lobby still steer clear of campaigns, changes in campaign finance law and regulation are enabling more groups to play in campaigns—including many groups created for that express purpose.

---

[16] Katherine Seelye. 2007. "Clinton and the Lobbyists." August 6, https://thecaucus.blogs.nytimes.com/2007/08/06/clinton-and-the-lobbyists/?_r=0 (accessed 10/28/2017).

In 2012 and 2014, some ideological interest groups considerably upped their ante, waging millions on the candidates they supported and advertising nationwide. The Koch brothers alone helped create new organizations and funneled millions through their network of supportive groups. After running attack ads, they became the subject of competing ads run by Democratic interest groups. Democrats lashed out against their undue influence, but also helped to build groups that could play similar roles in favor of Democratic candidates. In 2016, the Koch network moved its focus away from the presidential contest, but continued to build organizations and support candidates in state races.

Some interest groups are extensions of the political parties, not only raising similar concerns but also playing similar roles in voter mobilization and education. Other groups play unique roles in ballot initiative campaigns, in representing ethnic or religious constituencies, or in making sure that the candidates address the issues they care about most. They all see elections as an important method of advancing their policy goals, but not always the only method; even Koch Industries still spends money on traditional lobbying.

As interest groups spend considerable sums on campaigns, there is some fear that candidates may lose control of their own messages. The experience so far suggests that interest group campaigning looks a lot like candidate campaigning. Where candidate and interest group goals diverge, we should expect some different emphases. However, because winning elections still requires convincing the same voters, no matter who is running the campaign, interest groups are subject to the same constraints as candidates in convincing the voters to support their side.

KEY TERMS

interest group (p. 188)
constituencies (p. 199)
ballot initiative campaigns (p. 199)
campaign agenda (p. 206)

FOR DISCUSSION

1. Would American elections improve if interest groups left campaigning to the candidates? How would elections change if they donated less to candidates or spent less directly in campaigns?

2. If you were working for an interest group, how would you suggest attempting to influence elections in your state? Would you provide money to candidate campaigns, work to mobilize your own membership, or seek to influence voters directly through an advertising campaign? What are the advantages and disadvantages of each approach?

3. Should interest groups act as adjuncts to the campaign, funding the same types of advertisements and voter contact efforts as candidates, or should they focus more on the issues that most concern them and target their resources on the voters most sympathetic to their specific positions? How would each strategy help advance interest group goals?

4. Is it better for voters to hear only directly from the candidates about their positions on the issues, or do interest groups help force candidates to take clear positions and better inform the voters about which candidates support their views?

CHAPTER 8

Media

In an outtake from a 2005 appearance on the entertainment news show *Access Hollywood*, Donald Trump was caught on tape bragging about his aggressive pursuit of sexual contact with women. While approaching the actress Arianne Zucker with cohost Billy Bush, Trump said:

> I better use some Tic Tacs just in case I start kissing her. You know, I'm automatically attracted to beautiful—I just start kissing them. It's like a magnet. Just kiss. I don't even wait. And when you're a star, they let you do it. You can do anything. . . . Grab 'em by the pussy. You can do anything.[1]

The video had not been widely seen until the *Washington Post* released it online on October 7, 2016—two days before a presidential debate and one month before Election Day.

Trump's comments garnered immediate condemnation from across the political spectrum, with most lawyers describing them as a threat of sexual assault. Many Republican governors and members of Congress called on Trump to withdraw from the campaign, and dozens publicly rescinded their support of Trump. The story dominated headlines, and the video aired thousands of times on television news. While Trump at first dismissed the comments as "locker room talk," claiming that Bill Clinton had "said far worse to [him] on the golf course," he released a video later that night, and acknowledged, "I said it. I was wrong. And I apologize."

The tape fit a common media narrative suggesting that Trump was lewd, sexist, and disrespectful. In a series of prior campaign events, Trump's comments helped advance this storyline: he accused Mexican immigrants of being "rapists," John McCain of not being a war hero, Megyn Kelly of having "blood coming out of her wherever," Ted Cruz's father of consulting with John F. Kennedy's

---

[1] The video is available at www.nytimes.com/2016/10/08/us/donald-trump-tape-transcript.html?_r=0 (accessed 9/14/2017).

assassin, and a federal judge of being unfair due to his Mexican ancestry. During the campaign, he also mocked a disabled reporter, asked Russia to hack Hillary Clinton's e-mail account, and told his crowds to "knock the crap out of" protesters.[2] All of these incidents were widely believed to undermine Trump's presidential stature. And all were replayed over and over again as media sound bites.

Yet there is little evidence that the coverage of any of these comments—even the *Access Hollywood* video—made much difference in the public's perception of Trump. Even though many women came forward to report sexual assault allegations against Trump (stimulated by the video and Trump's denials that it reflected his true intentions), most Trump supporters dismissed the allegations. Some voters did momentarily shift from supporting Trump to declaring themselves undecided, but they largely returned to Trump within a few weeks. Voters who already opposed Trump only found additional reasons to oppose him. By Election Day, many normally Republican voters who said they personally disliked Trump still voted for him, reporting that they disliked Clinton even more.

The media's coverage of the *Access Hollywood* video highlights several important features of the news media and their role in contemporary American campaigns. First, the media's interest illustrates their news values, or the criteria

Core of the Analysis

- The news media typically seek to be objective but also to generate stories that will interest their audience.
- Candidates seek to persuade the public by influencing news content.
- The incentives of candidates and the news media often diverge, creating conflict between them, but candidates can take advantage of the news media's need for compelling stories.
- Media coverage can affect citizens, but its impact is often limited because citizens' attitudes are difficult to change.
- The news media do not always live up to democratic ideals, but citizens share some of the responsibility for the shortcomings in media coverage of campaigns.

---

[2] The media coverage of all of these events is reviewed in Michael Kruse and Taylor Gee. 2016. "The 37 Fatal Gaffes That Didn't Kill Donald Trump." *Politico*, September 25. www.politico.com/magazine/story/2016/09/trump-biggest-fatal-gaffes-mistakes-offensive -214289 (accessed 11/1/2017).

Many observers expected the media's coverage of the *Access Hollywood* tape, in which Donald Trump was recorded making crude comments about women, to be detrimental to Trump's campaign. How much of an effect do the media ultimately have on election outcomes?

by which they judge stories to be newsworthy. In this case, this story had video of the candidate—an inside look at an unguarded moment—and fit with a pre-existing narrative about Trump's debauchery. Although Republicans assume that the news media targeted Trump to derail his candidacy, in 2008 reporters were similarly attracted to a video that many observers believed was detrimental to Barack Obama: the remarks of Obama's retired pastor, Jeremiah Wright, that included the words "God damn America" were played on a nearly nonstop television loop. The news media do not so much champion one candidate or party as seek out stories that they deem newsworthy, especially ones that include video content ready for television or the Web.

Second, the media's coverage diverged sharply from what the implicated candidate, Donald Trump, wanted to discuss. Although candidates attempt to shape media coverage to benefit themselves, media outlets often pursue a different agenda. Reporters view their job as sharing useful information and analyzing factors that may affect elections or government, rather than passing along unfiltered campaign messages. By contrast, candidates repeat their campaign messages again and again, frustrating reporters who want new information. These conflicting agendas create tension between the candidates and news media.

Third, candidates often feel forced to respond to media coverage, no matter how much they may want to repeat their preferred message. Candidates believe that the news media are an important source of information for the public and thus a platform that they must use to deliver their message. So rather than ignore the media, candidates attempt to reshape media coverage. In the case of the *Access Hollywood* tapes, the Trump campaign first minimized the incident, then apologized, and then went on offense. Immediately before the second presidential debate on October 9, they held a surprise press conference with four women who had accused Bill Clinton of sexual harassment or assault (and Hillary Clinton of silencing their accusations) and invited them to attend the debate. Since the media were going to be discussing Trump's attitudes and actions toward women, the Trump campaign wanted to elevate a similar negative story about the Clintons.

Fourth, despite the media's extensive coverage of the *Access Hollywood* episode, it is unclear that the video or the accusations had much effect on the public. This lack of impact reflects two key facts: many citizens do not pay close attention to politics in the news, failing to learn and evaluate the full details of news stories, and it is often difficult to sway those who do pay attention, as they have already made up their minds.

Fifth, the episode raises important questions about the news media's role in campaigns and whether it is conducive to democratic values like deliberation. One might easily criticize the media's focus on this story as excessive. Aren't there more important issues than what Trump said over a decade ago before an entertainment program? On the other hand, perhaps the story was useful, if one believes it revealed the "real" Trump in an unguarded moment. The incident raises the broader question of whether the news media uphold or undermine the ideals we have for campaigns.

In this chapter, we begin by discussing the various types of news media outlets and comparing the size of their audiences. We then describe how both rules and reality structure the campaign coverage that the news media produce. We emphasize how the economics of the news business shape the content of the news. We next consider how the news media and candidates interact, noting the necessity of this relationship for both but also the tensions within this relationship. We then evaluate how much news coverage actually affects public opinion, considering that the media's impact is constrained by the public's interest in the news and willingness to believe what they read, see, or hear. Finally, we examine how well the news media help campaigns meet democratic values.

Who Are the News Media?

Most people learn about political campaigns from the **news media**: regular communicators of information designed to reach large audiences. Historically, the daily newspaper was the primary source of news for most Americans. Newspaper stories allow regular and in-depth coverage of candidates, issues, and campaign events. Although newspapers are still a popular source of information, especially for older Americans, the audience for the printed product has been shrinking. In 2016, on average 34.7 million copies of print newspapers were distributed every day, compared with a peak of 63.3 million in 1984.[3] Newspapers' websites are still among the most popular online news sources. The top American newspapers, the *Wall Street Journal* and the *New York Times*, each now have more than one million paid online subscribers. Even if newspapers no longer dominate campaign news coverage, they are still a source of information for citizens, politicians, and journalists and often shape the coverage of other media outlets. Newspapers are also the main source of coverage for many smaller campaigns. A nice illustration of this point comes from a study of Pittsburgh during a 1992 newspaper strike. Without access to a newspaper, Pittsburgh residents did find other sources of information on that year's presidential and Senate elections, but they lacked information on congressional races.[4]

The most popular source of news today is television newscasts. Local news averages almost 21 million viewers per day in its early evening time slot (between 5 and 7:30 P.M.), more than 20 million viewers in its later time slot (10 P.M. to 12 A.M.), and nearly 11 million in the mornings. Although local news offers only limited campaign coverage—with sports and weather accounting for a large share of local broadcasts—it is still the main news source for many Americans. National network television news also reaches a large audience. In 2016, the nightly news on ABC, CBS, and NBC together averaged 23.8 million viewers per day, though that is down from more than 40 million in 1980. Morning news shows, such as NBC's *Today* and ABC's *Good Morning America*, averaged a total of 13.2 million daily viewers in 2016.[5]

---

[3] The data derive from the Newspaper Association of America (now called News Media Alliance) and are available via the Pew Research Center's Journalism Project at www .journalism.org/fact-sheet/newspapers (accessed 9/14/2017).

[4] Jeffery J. Mondak. 1995. *Nothing to Read: Newspapers and Elections in a Social Experiment.* Ann Arbor: University of Michigan Press.

[5] These figures are based on Nielsen ratings for ABC, NBC, CBS, and Fox and their affiliates. All viewership numbers are available from the Pew Research Center at www .journalism.org/datasets/ (accessed 9/14/2017).

Network news coverage favors stories with better visuals and less depth than newspapers. The average **sound bite** from presidential candidates broadcast on television news is only nine seconds long.[6] The public television channel PBS, funded in small part by the federal government, offers more coverage and longer sound bites.

Cable news has a smaller viewership on average than either local or network news but offers hours of continuous coverage. The average prime-time audience reached nearly 4.8 million in 2016, with daytime viewership exceeding 2.7 million. Fox News Channel dominates CNN, HLN, and MSNBC in each time period throughout the day, in part because many Fox News viewers watch repeatedly. Fox News Channel's average evening viewership was 2.4 million per night in 2016. All three networks' ratings spiked dramatically during the election year, but, unusually, their ratings gains extended into 2017 as they began to cover the new administration. (Love him or hate him, viewers cannot get enough of Trump.) In the evenings, cable news channels are dominated by commentary, with Fox News offering mostly conservatives and MSNBC offering mostly liberals. Since viewers can watch endlessly, the cable audience is larger in terms of total minutes watched, but cable networks reach fewer people overall than network broadcasts. Approximately seven percent of Americans watch Fox News at least one hour per week; even fewer watch MSNBC (4 percent) or CNN (5 percent).[7]

Radio news also serves a niche audience. The United States has nearly 1,500 commercial news or talk radio stations and 900 National Public Radio (NPR) member stations, which are partially funded by listeners. NPR's two daily news shows, *Morning Edition* and *All Things Considered*, average more than 14 million listeners per week, while a total of 53 million listeners per week tune in to commercial news and talk radio.[8] (Because these numbers are weekly, rather than daily, and include people who listen only sporadically, they cannot be compared directly with the television audience estimates.) In 2016, the top political talk radio hosts were all conservatives: Rush Limbaugh, Sean Hannity, Michael Savage, Glenn Beck, and Mark Levin. Commercial radio news features content similar to cable television, especially in its commentary and its regular updates of news headlines. NPR, by contrast, is known for in-depth coverage and longer interviews; its audience is more liberal.

---

[6] Stephen J. Farnsworth and S. Robert Lichter. 2010. *The Nightly News Nightmare: Media Coverage of U.S. Presidential Elections: 1988–2008*. Lanham, MD: Rowman & Littlefield.

[7] Markus Prior. 2013. "Media and Political Polarization." *Annual Review of Political Science* 16: 101–27.

[8] These figures are based on Arbitron ratings. Listenership numbers are available from the Pew Research Center, at www.journalism.org/datasets/ (accessed 9/14/2017).

While online-only news outlets have also become an important source of news, most campaign stories still originate from traditional news providers. The most popular news websites include CNN, the *New York Times*, Fox News, and NBC News along with aggregators of traditional news stories like *Yahoo News* and *Google News*. Some online-only outlets, like *HuffPost*, are just as prominent (although some of their content recycles or adds commentary to stories originally reported by newspapers or television networks). Political **blogs** are mostly sources of opinionated commentary on mainstream news (see Box 8.1), though some conservative sites like *Breitbart* and the *Daily Caller* and some liberal sites like *Daily Kos* and *Think Progress* produce original news for large audiences. Nearly all these sites have mobile editions and/or mobile apps, with increasing shares of the online audience accessing the news through smartphones.

News stories shared on social networking sites also usually link to news that originates in traditional reporting. Even though Facebook, Pinterest, and Twitter have become major sources of traffic for news sites, most original political news stories that users circulate on these platforms, especially about state or local campaigns, still come from newspapers.[9] However, the share of social media content that comes from avowedly conservative and liberal sources is increasing. Candidates, exemplified by Donald Trump, also use Twitter and other social media to directly communicate with supporters and drive mainstream media coverage of their campaigns.

Because stories are usually shared on social media by one's friends or compatriots, online content can generate audiences even without a preexisting branded provider. You might not have heard of westernjournalism.com or truthdig.com, for example, but trust your friend enough to believe a story they shared from these websites. This disregard for a source's reputation allows sites designed to support particular candidates or parties to gain a broad audience. In 2016, "fake news" websites—mostly supporting Donald Trump—constantly churned out content designed for sharing on Facebook, spreading conspiracy theories, and gaining audiences toward the end of the campaign.

Beyond official news outlets, some entertainment programming also offers political content. During his career at the *Tonight Show*, Jay Leno made more than 20,000 jokes about politicians, with Bill Clinton and George W. Bush his most frequent targets.[10] Political satirist Jon Stewart, who was watched

---

[9] Robert W. McChesney and John Nichols. 2010. *The Death and Life of American Journalism: The Media Revolution Will Begin the World Again*. New York: Nation Books.

[10] Kathryn Davis. 2014. "Study: Leno's Top Joke Target Was Bill Clinton." Center for Media and Public Affairs, February 4. https://cmpa.gmu.edu/study-lenos-top-joke-target-was-bill -clinton/ (accessed 11/1/2017).

BOX 8.1

Political Blogs

Blogs, which are websites with regularly updated news in reverse chronological order, have been touted as a form of "citizen media" in which individuals can become reporters and commentators. But the universe of blogs, or the blogosphere, is dominated not by ordinary citizens but by traditional media organizations. Relatively few blogs generate large audiences, and many of those that do are hosted by large news outlets, such as the *Washington Post* or the *New York Times*. By adding blogs to their sites, traditional media outlets have imitated the behavior of new outlets and blurred the boundaries between journalism by individual citizens and media companies.[1]

Some commentators hoped that blogs would become alternative sources of news, challenging the dominance of the big newspapers and television networks. This has happened from time to time, particularly when blogs pushed a story first, leading traditional media to report on it. During the 2004 presidential campaign, Dan Rather of *CBS Evening News* questioned the U.S. National Guard service record of George W. Bush, holding up memos that supposedly came from Bush's superiors at the time of his service. Conservative blogs questioned the authenticity of those memos, arguing that their typeface was not available on typewriters used by the military at the time. *CBS Evening News* eventually retracted the report and asked Rather to leave the show.[2]

Such cases are the exception, however. Blogs rely on newspapers and television stations for news, in part because few bloggers have the resources to report their own stories. In fact, most political blog posts are links to articles from other outlets with limited commentary.[3] Moreover, to gain traction for their stories, bloggers need them to be picked up by television and newspapers. The influence of blogs is tied not to their readership among the public but to their influence on reporters from traditional media outlets.[4]

Bloggers make a unique contribution not so much as news reporters but as commentators and activists. Many of the most prominent political blogs are ideological or partisan in nature. Political bloggers tend to self-segregate, with both liberal and conservative bloggers linking and responding mainly to bloggers with similar views.[5] Their audiences are also self-segregated, with people reading blogs they agree with. Few people read both conservative and liberal blogs.[6] Thus, blogs are more effective at reinforcing people's existing political beliefs, and perhaps spurring them to act on those beliefs, than they are at changing anyone's mind.

[1] Matthew Hindman. 2009. *The Myth of Digital Democracy.* Princeton, NJ: Princeton University Press.
[2] Associated Press. 2005. "CBS Ousts Four for Roles in Bush Guard Story." January 10. www.nbcnews.com/id /6807825/#.Wfp_iWhSyUk (accessed 11/1/2017).
[3] Laura McKenna and Antoinette Pole. 2008. "What Do Bloggers Do: An Average Day on an Average Political Blog." *Public Choice* 134, 1–2: 97–108.
[4] Henry Farrell and Daniel W. Drezner. 2008. "The Power and Politics of Blogs." *Public Choice* 134, 1–2: 15–30.
[5] Eszter Hargittai, Jason Gallo, and Matthew Kane. 2008. "Cross-Ideological Discussions among Conservative and Liberal Bloggers." *Public Choice* 134, 1–2: 67–86.
[6] Eric Lawrence, John Sides, and Henry Farrell. 2010. "Self-Segregation or Deliberation? Blog Readership, Participation, and Polarization in American Politics." *Perspectives on Politics* 8, 1: 141–57.

by 2.5 million viewers per night on Comedy Central, devoted substantial coverage to political campaigns. *Last Week Tonight with John Oliver* has a niche audience on HBO, but his YouTube videos have garnered more than 1 billion views.

These aggregate statistics on the audience for media largely comport with surveys that ask individuals where they get their news (although Americans do tend to overreport how much news they watch and read). Figure 8.1 shows the percentage of people who said they "got news yesterday" from television, newspapers, radio, and the Internet. Reported newspaper readership and radio listenership declined throughout the 1990s and 2000s, while television news viewership declined less rapidly. At the same time, the number of people receiving news online is increasing, particularly among young people. Although those under 30 are only half as likely as those over 60 to report that they generally follow the news, they are much likelier to prefer reading online news to watching news on television.[11] Younger people are also more likely to share and receive news via social networks. This does not mean that online news consumers are ignoring newspapers or television: they are often seeing the same stories in a repackaged or redistributed format.[12] But viral content from online-only providers now makes up a larger share of campaign news, with *Breitbart* playing a central role in driving conservative media coverage and social media sharing in 2016.[13]

Americans vary greatly in their news consumption habits. Some citizens follow news regularly, reading a newspaper, watching cable news, and sharing news stories online. But this is far from the norm: most Americans, when given the option, prefer sports and entertainment to news.[14] As Election Day approaches, citizens do watch more news, but the levels are still somewhat low. Americans who are news junkies tend to be stronger partisans. For politicians, this means it is hard to reach potential voters via news media coverage who are not already on their side. For news media outlets, it means their readers, listeners, and viewers are the minority of Americans who hold stronger views on politics.

---

[11] Pew Research Center's Journalism Project. www.journalism.org/2016/07/07/pathways-to-news (accessed 11/1/ 2017).

[12] Matthew Hindman. 2008. *The Myth of Digital Democracy*. Princeton, NJ: Princeton University Press.

[13] Rob Faris, Hal Roberts, Bruce Etling, Nikki Bourassa, Ethan Zuckerman, and Yochai Benkler. 2017. "Partisanship, Propaganda, and Disinformation: Online Media and the 2016 U.S. Presidential Election." Berkman Klein Center, August 16. https://cyber.harvard.edu/publications/2017/08/mediacloud (accessed November 1, 2017).

[14] Markus Prior. 2007. *Post-Broadcast Democracy: How Media Choice Increases Inequality in Political Involvement and Polarizes Elections*. New York: Cambridge University Press.

FIGURE 8.1 Where People Get Their News

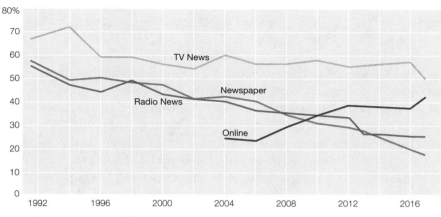

Source: Pew Research Center. 2017. "American Trends Panel." www.pewresearch.org/topics/american-trends -panel/2017 (accessed 9/11/2017).

Trends in media consumption demonstrate how both the media and their audience have changed in recent years. They also hint at some of the challenges that the news media face today, particularly declining audiences for some types of media. The need to attract an audience is crucial and, as we will see, profoundly affects how the media cover campaigns.

Government's Limited Oversight of the News Media

Like other actors in campaigns, such as candidates, parties, and interest groups, the news media are influenced by rules. In this case, rules include constitutional doctrine and government policies that affect—or, more important, do not affect—the content of media coverage. The First Amendment's guarantee of a free press means that there are relatively few rules that constrain media coverage. Given that Supreme Court interpretations of the First Amendment have allowed the media to publish stories about classified government programs, where the stakes are much higher than in political campaigns, the media can largely report on political campaigns as they see fit.

The restrictions that do exist pertain mainly to broadcast (AM/FM) radio and broadcast television, which includes the major networks (ABC, NBC, CBS, and Fox) and their affiliates but not cable television networks. The Federal Communications Commission (FCC) regulates broadcast radio and television because there is limited space on the broadcast spectrum—think of the FM radio dial, which has space only between 87.5 and 108.0 megahertz. The Supreme Court ruled in *Red Lion Broadcasting Co., Inc. v. FCC* (1969) that this scarce spectrum provided a rationale for regulation of broadcasting, but decided in *Miami Herald Publishing Co. v. Tornillo* (1974) that newspapers could not be subject to the same restrictions.

The FCC rule that is most relevant to political campaigns is the **right to equal time**. Stations with FCC licenses are required to provide "equal time" to all candidates for office. They cannot simply devote attention to a favored candidate and ignore the others. This means that if a TV station sells time to a candidate who wants to air ads on that station, it must make the same opportunity available to all candidates for that office.

However, important loopholes allow unequal time. Certain events are exempt from this rule, including news interviews and on-the-spot news events. The incumbent president, whether or not he is running for re-election, gets news coverage simply for doing things like giving press conferences and traveling to foreign countries. The FCC also exempts presidential debates from the equal time rule. Debate organizers, who include representatives of the major parties and media companies, can thus exclude third-party candidates without breaking the rule.

Even though debates do provide relatively equal platforms for candidates, the news media still cover the candidates who have the best shot to win or generate the most viewer interest. The 2016 Republican presidential primary debates featured so many candidates that lower-tier contenders were forced to compete in a "warm-up debate" in an earlier time slot. Even during the main debates, Trump received a disproportionate share of attention, not only in the debates themselves but directly afterward, when he was often immediately interviewed about his performance just off the debate stage. Trump was always available for questions, and cable news took full advantage.

Even when the right to equal time does apply, it does not require media outlets to broadcast significant coverage of campaigns or political news generally. In some situations, television news outlets have not carried presidential debates. They certainly do not feel obligated to carry every gubernatorial, Senate, or House candidate debate; often, interested viewers have to watch online or on a public television channel.

Media regulation is much weaker in the United States than in other democratic countries. Many nations have strong and well-funded public media outlets and more requirements for private media companies that are also covering campaigns. One consequence is that other countries tend to provide more free time for parties and candidates to speak directly to voters.[15]

---

[15] Shanto Iyengar. 2016. *Media Politics: A Citizen's Guide*, 3rd ed. New York: W. W. Norton.

The Business of News and the Norm of Objectivity

The minimal requirements that the government places on news media outlets mean that these outlets can cover—or not cover—politics and campaigns largely as they see fit. News outlets are thus free to base decisions about coverage on other factors, and coverage of campaigns is powerfully shaped by the prevailing reality or context in which the media operate. News outlets have practical constraints of time, space, and personnel. They cannot cover every potentially newsworthy event and must make choices. These choices are guided by two aspects of their reality: the profit motive of business and the norm of objectivity.

News as a Business

The economics of the news business demand that the news be profitable, first and foremost. The need to turn a profit is not new, but it has grown more imperative with time. Today, large corporations traded on public stock exchanges own many news outlets; these firms do not have the same personal investment in the news product as a family that owns a newspaper might have had (and families owned most of the country's major newspapers until recently). Corporations are not content to lose money maintaining a news operation simply for the satisfaction of creating a quality news product. Thus, news outlets are expected to generate revenue and keep costs down.

This is a significant challenge. Many of the most prestigious news outlets—including major newspapers and television networks—are losing audience share and thus losing advertising dollars. Newspapers in particular are suffering, as their classified advertising revenue has declined sharply due in part to the advent of websites like Craigslist. Online audiences for newspapers are growing, but, as yet, newspapers have not figured out a way to make as much money from their online content as they did from their print editions (Figure 8.2). At the same time, covering political campaigns is not cheap. The length of many American campaigns means that news outlets must commit significant resources if they want to provide continuous coverage.

One strategy that media outlets use to maintain viability in the face of these challenges is to cut their operating costs. Newspapers and television news organizations have cut costs by eliminating reporting positions and other staff, and newspapers have cut back on the size of their print editions. Some newspapers, such as Denver's *Rocky Mountain News*, have closed outright, and others, such as the *Seattle Post-Intelligencer*, now publish only online

FIGURE 8.2 Newspaper Advertising Revenue

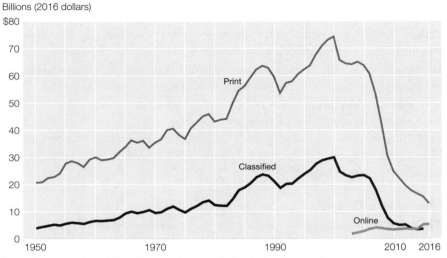

Source: Newspaper Association of America data, compiled by the Pew Research Center.

editions. News outlets have also changed the kinds of news they gather firsthand. Many have closed news bureaus, reducing the number of reporters who are based in places outside of the outlet's hometown. They are also reconsidering whether to use resources for relatively "expensive" stories—for example, whether to send reporters with the president on his travels.[16]

These sorts of cuts can affect coverage of campaigns. News outlets may simply devote less time to covering campaigns, especially state and local campaigns that generate minimal attention. News organizations also look for more cost-effective ways to cover campaigns. One tactic is to employ part-time reporters who carry handheld video cameras and follow the candidates around, waiting for something to happen. This is much cheaper than employing a full-time reporter and a camera crew.

A second strategy for economic success is raising revenue. Some news outlets charge for access to their news online, but most have sought to raise revenue by increasing the size of their online audience. News media often appeal to the public with stories that are laden with emotion, have

[16] Brian Stelter. 2010. "When the President Travels, It's Cheaper for Reporters to Stay Home." *New York Times*, May 23. www.nytimes.com/2010/05/24/business/media/24press .html (accessed 5/22/2014).

stimulating visual images and clickable headlines, or are simply sensa-tionalistic. This is nothing new, of course. As we discussed in Chapter 3, newspapers in the nineteenth century began covering scandals, sports, crime, politics, and other stories in an often lurid way. But the continued rise of **infotainment**—a combination of informational and entertainment programming—is evident today. For example, nightly news broadcasts have increased their coverage of celebrities, athletes, and famous criminals but not their coverage of business leaders and political figures. They have decreased the fraction of important congressional votes that they cover.[17] It is easy to criticize the news media for this, but news consumers may also bear some responsibility. These sorts of decisions often reflect careful monitoring of what the audience reads, watches, or hears. News outlets also pay close attention to what stories are shared on Facebook and Twitter, leading to a proliferation of funny lists, heartwarming stories, viral videos, and coverage of gaffes.

However, some news media organizations have established more highbrow outlets that are distinguished by their use of data, statistics, and background information to better explain the news. Traditional media companies have established separate brands—such as ESPN's *FiveThirtyEight* and the *New York Times's The Upshot*—to play this role, and online-only sites like Vox.com have emerged as part of this trend. These sites merge scholarly analysis from political science and other disciplines with traditional journalism and opin-ion columns, though much of their campaign content is focused on predict-ing election outcomes or analyzing polling movements in real time. Most citizens may stick with funny lists and videos, but political junkies can now consume even more polling data and demographic analysis.

The Norm of Objectivity

Economic pressures are not the only influence on the contemporary news media. Most reporters, editors, and other news professionals subscribe to a set of norms that inform how they do their jobs. The most important norm is objectivity, a relatively recent feature of the news media. In Chapter 3, we described how the American print media were largely partisan until well into the twentieth century. Newspapers used to be directly allied with political parties (some newspapers still retain their old "Democrat" or "Republican" in their titles), which in turn helped to fund their costs of production.

---

[17] James T. Hamilton. 2003. *All the News That's Fit to Sell: How the Market Transforms Information into News.* Princeton, NJ: Princeton University Press.

The decline of the partisan press and the rise of objectivity came about partly because newspaper owners sought to build larger and broader audiences by producing an objective news product that would appeal to many different kinds of readers. They sent journalists to report on events firsthand by seeking out information and interviewing sources.

Journalists then began to see it as their job to report on events fairly and accurately, with appropriate attention to all sides of controversial issues. The norm of objectivity became codified in the guidelines of news organizations. For example, the code of the American Society of Newspaper Editors, which was founded in 1922, included a principle of "impartiality": "News reports should be free from opinion or bias of any kind." This principle was taught to aspiring·journalists in newly founded journalism schools; the first, at Columbia University, was founded by Joseph Pulitzer in 1902. Technology also enabled the spread of more objective journalism. The development of the telegraph in the 1830s led to the creation of **wire services** like the Associated Press, which produce content that is shared among news outlets. Wire services—named for the wires used to send messages via telegraph—allowed stories to be disseminated quickly to many outlets. A similar pattern evolved in radio and television news, where local stations chose to affiliate with national networks and reuse their news products.

An autonomous and impartial press also began scrutinizing the government and politicians more closely. Often this meant looking for evidence of scandal and malfeasance. Events such as the Vietnam War and the Watergate scandal weakened trust in political leaders and fueled the rise of investigative reporting. Some things that journalists knew about but did not report on—such as the extramarital affairs of Presidents Franklin Roosevelt and John F. Kennedy—became fair game for later generations of journalists.

This talk of objectivity might seem dated to today's media consumers. After all, with the proliferation of cable news talk shows and blogs, is objective journalism a thing of the past? The short answer is "no." There is a larger audience for traditional news outlets, which generally strive to be ideologically neutral, than for outlets with an ideological or partisan agenda.

Reporters dedicated to appearing impartial are even sometimes criticized for "false balance," the tendency to treat statements from each candidate's campaign equally even when one side is clearly stretching the truth.

Reporters seek to cover each side in the debate between the candidates rather than to arbitrate between them and decide who is right—perhaps providing a disincentive for the candidates to tell the truth as their less honest statements will merely be repeated faithfully along with those of the opposition. Many commentators blamed the news media and "false balance" for helping to "normalize" Donald Trump's 2016 campaign (which they felt violated norms of civility) and for treating Hillary Clinton's scandals more seriously than those associated with Trump. Indeed, coverage of Clinton's use of a private e-mail server while secretary of state, and the ties between her family foundation and foreign countries, exceeded coverage of any of Trump's scandals,[18] leading voters to report that they heard more about Clinton's e-mails than anything else related to her campaign. Trump instead received coverage of his substantive views on immigration, though much of it was also negative.

Nonetheless, ideological and partisan outlets are flourishing, as the growth in the audience for Fox News, MSNBC, and online-only ideological sites suggests. One reason has to do with economic incentives, which can take precedence over the norm of objectivity. With news outlets seeking to appeal to an audience, it is natural that some may choose an ideological approach. This strategy will not earn them the loyalty of the majority of news consumers, some of whom are on the opposite side ideologically and others of whom prefer impartial news. But it can earn them a niche audience that is sizable enough to produce subscription and advertising revenues. Furthermore, advances in technology make niche broadcasting—sometimes called **narrow-casting**—financially viable. Many niche media products, such as blogs, can be produced relatively cheaply.

In sum, the rules and reality that affect the news media present something of a paradox. On the one hand, the government does relatively little to regulate the media, which gives them considerable discretion to write and publish what they wish. On the other hand, the news media face significant constraints of time and resources, even with the Internet providing essentially infinite space for news. Indeed, those resources have been shrinking for many outlets. The news media must therefore continue to find ways to cut costs or increase revenue by attracting a larger audience, or at least an audience that is desirable to advertisers. This has led to an increasingly diverse media landscape, with most outlets continuing to observe the traditional norm of objectivity but other outlets pursuing a partisan or ideological agenda for a smaller but loyal audience. These constraints affect how the news media cover campaigns.

---

[18] Thomas E. Patterson. 2016. "News Coverage of the 2016 General Election: How the Press Failed the Voters." Shorenstein Center, December 7. https://shorensteincenter.org/news -coverage-2016-general-election/ (accessed 11/1/2017).

What Gets Covered, and How?

A top priority for most campaigns is to get the news media to cover their candidate and their message. This is often easier said than done. Campaigns vie with other candidates, other races, and the events of the day for the media's attention. Getting the media to communicate the campaign's message is partly a matter of skill and partly a matter of conditions and luck.

Which Races Get Covered?

In deciding which campaigns to cover, the media must allocate their limited resources while stimulating interest among their audience. The media are more likely to cover a campaign when the race is competitive, because races in which one candidate cruises to easy victory rarely generate stories that the media consider newsworthy. The front-runner can campaign conservatively, never risking an event where she might slip up and say something controversial. The challenger, if there is one, most likely lacks the resources to promote his candidacy or draw unfavorable attention to the front-runner. If new polls are conducted and released, they show little change. In sum, nothing dramatic happens. Of course, an uncompetitive race might become more competitive if voters learned about the challenger through news coverage.

The media are also more likely to cover a campaign when the office at stake has more authority. The national news media cover the presidential campaigns extensively, as well as a few campaigns for governor and senator. They rarely cover campaigns for state legislature or local offices, or even the House of Representatives. To the extent that they cover House races, the national news media focus on the broader competition between Democrats and Republicans for majority control, rather than on the particular candidates or issues in each race. Local media, especially newspapers, cover more state and local elections, but they also report on the presidential campaign and the battle for control of Congress.

When the media do cover a campaign other than the presidential campaign or a particularly competitive race, it is often because it has some feature that appeals to their audience. Media outlets are more likely to cover a congressional race when more of their readers live in that particular congressional district and can vote in that election.[19] The media are also drawn to celebrity candidates, like Trump and former California governor

---

[19] James M. Snyder, Jr. and David Strömberg. 2010. "Press Coverage and Political Accountability." *Journal of Political Economy* 118, 2: 355–408.

Arnold Schwarzenegger. They are drawn to scandals, particularly if sex or money—or, even better, money for sex—is involved. Reporters covered Anthony Weiner's long-shot bid for New York mayor in 2013 because he had resigned from Congress following the release of sexually suggestive photos he had sent to several female Twitter followers. He went on to place only fifth in the Democratic primary but not before generating yet more news coverage: he admitted that—after apologizing for the earlier incidents—he had sent lurid pictures to another woman, this time calling himself "Carlos Danger." Weiner even managed to indirectly influence the 2016 presidential campaign, when federal agents investigating his case found e-mails originating from Hillary Clinton on Weiner's laptop (his wife, Huma Abedin, worked for Clinton for years). These e-mails were the impetus for FBI director James Comey to re-open the FBI's investigation of Clinton's e-mail server 11 days before Election Day.

Which Aspects of Campaigns Get Covered?

When news media do cover election campaigns, what do they cover? Although newspapers typically run general profiles of the candidates and the campaign, the vast majority of news is driven by events. What kinds of events do the media judge to be particularly newsworthy? We speak of their criteria for newsworthiness as **news values**.

The first and most important news value is *novelty*. The term *news* does contain the word *new*, after all. Typically, this means that the news follows what happened recently—that is, since the last edition, newscast, or online update. Candidates and their advisers know this, of course, so they organize a continuous stream of new events to gain the media's attention. Consider the events that take place before the actual campaign begins. Potential candidates coyly suggest that they might enter the race in order to generate speculation in the media. When a politician formally announces her candidacy, it is treated as news, even when it is a foregone conclusion that she will be running. Politicians sometimes even hold multiple "announcements" in different media markets, as well as issuing press releases and online videos.

The media also value *personality*. Newsworthy stories often involve compelling people, and news audiences are presumed to be engaged by the "characters" in the campaign—whether they are good or bad. During the campaign, the news media will repeatedly dwell on the biographies of candidates in an attempt to understand what they are "really like." There are stories about where the candidates grew up, whether they were popular in high school, and so on.

The media also attempt to characterize a candidate's personality. Journalists play amateur psychologists, looking for evidence of candidates' personality traits in their words and deeds. Barack Obama was portrayed as intellectual and emotionally unflappable. John McCain was described as angry. Mitt Romney was regularly characterized as out of touch as a result of his wealth. Hillary Clinton was seen by journalists as overly guarded and insincere, while Trump was sometimes portrayed as a bigoted playboy. All of these characterizations may have some truth to them, and clearly reporters try to document them with information from sources—although the sources are often described simply as "some" people or "observers" so that reporters do not appear to be passing judgment themselves.

Another news value in campaign coverage is *conflict*. It is easier to generate newsworthy stories when the candidates, their surrogates, the parties, interest groups, and other campaign actors are at each other's throats. (Fortunately, all of these actors often comply.) The media's emphasis on negativity is evident in how it portrays campaign advertisements: negative ads, especially ones with outlandish claims, are discussed to a far greater extent than positive ads—even when positive ads are actually more numerous.[20] Candidates can sometimes get the media to cover negative ads simply by releasing them on the Internet, without ever paying to air them on television. The media also focus on internal conflict within the Democratic and Republican parties, highlighting dissenters even when most party members are in agreement.[21]

The media cover candidate debates or other joint appearances with a similar hope for conflict. When the candidates do not disagree, the event is less newsworthy, perhaps frustratingly so from the media's perspective. In February 2008, a debate between Hillary Clinton and Barack Obama was billed as "fight night" on CNN. CNN commentator Jack Cafferty previewed the debate by saying: "Remember last week, the heated debate in South Carolina? Tonight could make that seem like a garden party." But Clinton and Obama, fearful that the South Carolina debate was too rancorous, came out and played nice, much to the media's disappointment. A *New York Times* reporter who was behind the scenes with CNN staff observed their exasperation.[22] One CNN producer complained that the debate was "like a press conference" rather than the brawl they apparently wanted to see. Rarely does one see reporters reveal news values so explicitly.

---

[20] Travis N. Ridout and Glen R. Smith. 2008. "Free Advertising: How the Media Amplify Campaign Messages." *Political Research Quarterly* 61, 4: 598–608.

[21] Tim Groeling. 2010. *When Politicians Attack: Party Cohesion in the Media.* New York: Cambridge University Press.

[22] Brian Stelter. 2008. "Even as the Candidates Make Nice, the TV Crew Hopes for a Fight." *New York Times*, February 4, p. 1.

Covering Donald Trump

Real estate mogul and reality television star Donald Trump toyed with running for president for decades before he announced his 2016 candidacy. Oprah Winfrey asked him whether he would run in the 1980s. He ran a six-month exploratory campaign for the Reform Party's 2000 nomination, appearing at campaign events and on television programs. He almost jumped in the 2012 race, appearing as the front-runner in several polls. Reporters suspected that he was engaged in publicity stunts to promote his television program, yet they still covered him.

When Trump did jump into the 2016 race, he generated little support from Republican politicians or party leaders, but he did have a national following—not only of supporters but of gawking onlookers. Reporters knew that interviews with Trump would generate high ratings.

Meanwhile, other candidates had to decide how to respond to Trump's sudden rise. In 2016, several candidates thought that public support for Trump would fade early, and they wanted to avoid offending him or his supporters in the event that Trump dropped out of the race and his backers needed to find new candidates to support. That Trump immediately outpolled many of the other Republican challengers did not look good—but they did not expect him to ultimately be a serious competitor. Many Republican leaders were concerned that Trump, and not more supposedly electable candidates, was dominating coverage and recommended that other candidates avoid giving him the attention he craved. By the time they decided to take him seriously, he was completely dominating television news, debate performances, and polls. He came up with nicknames for his competitors, such as "little Marco" and "low-energy Jeb," eventually goading them into responding.

Reporters reacted to every Trump gaffe with more rounds of news cycle domination—and Trump knew how to generate attention with every tweet and every interview. Living by the adage that all publicity is good publicity, Trump was willing to insult and shock his way to more coverage than all of the other GOP candidates combined. As he generated coverage, voters learned his stances on immigration and crime, heard his critiques of Obama and the Washington establishment, and gave Trump alone credit for raising many of the same issues that other candidates were discussing.

Trump's rallies became bigger, his campaign started to be taken more seriously by political elites, and he was eventually seen as the front-runner for the Republican nomination. Although prior candidates had lost support after being overloaded with media criticism, Trump held his support among his core supporters. He took every opportunity to speak through the media even while critiquing their coverage (he claimed he saved millions of dollars in unneeded advertising because his message was delivered for free). His opponents ultimately agreed that Trump's free coverage was beneficial, and constantly complained of unfair media treatment.

Even when reporters suspect a candidate is not playing by the normal rules, they can rarely turn away from a spectacle. If politicians appeal to news values, they can take advantage of more coverage. Trump took this strategy to a whole new level, possibly stimulating some future imitators. This strategy puts competitors in a quandary: should they attempt to make crazier statements to generate attention, or toil at traditional forums away from the spotlight?

A fourth news value is *skepticism*. Today's professional journalists are trained to be dubious about the claims that politicians make, and perhaps for good reason. Thus, what candidates say is rarely taken at face value. At a minimum, the norm of objectivity requires news outlets to engage in "he said, she said" journalism, pairing claims by one candidate with responses from the opponent. Reporters sometimes engage in fact-checking, evaluating candidates' claims in advertisements and elsewhere for their accuracy. Some news outlets have even created fact-checking websites, like the *Tampa Bay Times*'s PolitiFact.com, which regularly monitors the statements of politicians and ranks them on a scale from "true" to "pants on fire."

Journalists also have another kind of news value: assumptions about American national values that shape their coverage. They believe their audience is nationalistic, prizing the United States above all other nations, and that it shares a widespread belief in grassroots democracy, a capitalist economy, individualism, and small-town values.[23] The media often portray politicians as out of touch with these values or as seeking to reconnect with Americans who seem to embody them. But journalists also seek to protect democratic norms, especially those that involve freedom of the press and the access of journalists, and will defend other media organizations when they are attacked by politicians (with even CNN defending Fox News when the latter was attacked by Trump). In 2016, journalists were caught between these impulses: they saw Trump as stepping over the line in threatening the press's ability to question his claims and inciting his supporters' distrust of the media, but they also saw him connecting with heartland voters. His nostalgic campaign elaborated long-standing American themes that journalists traditionally like to highlight, but Trump broke key norms important to them by calling any negative story about him "fake" and threatening to retaliate against reporters.

Perhaps the preeminent focus of coverage across all campaigns, however, is *strategy*. This kind of campaign coverage is sometimes known as **horse race journalism**. Horse race campaign coverage focuses on which candidate is ahead or behind, who is gaining or losing ground, and what the candidates are trying to do to win (their strategies), much the way the announcer at a horse race describes which horse is winning, surging, or faltering. A study of print, broadcast, and Internet news outlets during the 2016 general election found that 42 percent of coverage of the presidential campaign was about the horse race, while only 10 percent dealt with policy issues. The horse race

---

[23] Herbert J. Gans. 1979. *Deciding What's News: A Study of CBS Evening News, NBC Nightly News,* Newsweek, *and* Time. New York: Random House.

was also the focus of the 2008 and 2012 campaigns, but policy coverage was more prominent in these prior campaigns.[24] It is easy to see why horse race coverage is so appealing. For one, there are many ways to determine who is ahead or behind: fund-raising, endorsements, polls, the size of rallies, and so on. These indicators can be frequently updated, as candidates release fund-raising numbers or as media outlets field new polls, creating fresh grist for a story. Similarly, candidate debates are scored in terms of who "won" or "lost." Stories about undecided voters also generate horse race coverage, as these voters can be canvassed again and again to see if they have moved toward a candidate.

Television networks sometimes convene small groups of undecided voters to watch presidential debates and then interview them after the debate. One experiment, however, showed that viewers' opinions of a debate are often more influenced by the media's tone following it than by their own interpretation of the candidates.[25] Clinton was largely judged the winner of the 2016 presidential debates by both media pundits and voters—though that does not mean her performance in the three exchanges earned her votes that she wouldn't have otherwise won. (Mike Pence was judged the winner of the vice presidential debate, but Trump still seemed displeased with his performance.)

Within the context of horse race coverage, the media's discussion of strategy allows them to engage in what is sometimes called **interpretive journalism**. Reporters do not simply report on what the candidates do and say. They provide further analysis and interpretation. That is, they attempt to tell their audience why the candidates are doing what they are doing and thereby reveal the candidates' underlying strategy. Journalists see their obligation as not just to narrate events but to provide context. Reporters draw on their perceived expertise to read between the lines and to help their audience understand what is "really going on."

Is Campaign Coverage Biased?

Thus far, we have focused on how news values shape campaign coverage. But the most frequent public criticism of campaign coverage is that it is ideologically biased. One version of this complaint singles out specific news outlets as biased. Some of these complaints may have merit, as newspaper coverage tends to favor incumbent candidates that the newspaper supports

---

[24] Patterson, "News Coverage of the 2016 General Election."

[25] Michael I. Norton and George R. Goethals. 2004. "Spin (and Pitch) Doctors: Campaign Strategies in Televised Political Debates." *Political Behavior* 26, 3: 227–48.

on its editorial page.[26] Analyses that compare the word usage of Democratic and Republican members of Congress with that of news outlets also classify some outlets as more liberal (more closely matching Democratic rhetoric) and some as more conservative.[27] But it is difficult to know whether this kind of bias simply reflects the preferences of the media outlets' audiences. Any bias may be coming from the "demand side," which is based on what the audience wants, rather than the "supply side," which is based on what the news media provides. Some of the programming decisions on the more conservative Fox News and the more liberal MSNBC may be driven by the partisan biases of each network's audience.

The more important complaint about bias targets all news outlets. Supporters on both sides complain that "the media" as a whole favor someone other than their preferred candidate. President George H. W. Bush's 1992 campaign made this claim, producing bumper stickers that said "Annoy the Media: Re-Elect Bush!" Some people even assert that this bias is chronic and that the media favor the Republican or Democratic Party in election after election. Of course, it is easy to find examples of news coverage that seem more favorable to one candidate or the other. Yet it has been difficult to prove that candidate coverage is consistently biased toward one party or ideology. Despite persistent claims of many conservatives, traditional news coverage is not consistently more favorable toward liberal or Democratic candidates. Although journalists tend to be more liberal than the general public, studies examining the actual content of coverage have found little evidence of consistent bias in either direction.[28] This is likely because the norm of impartiality is so strongly ingrained in journalists.

Of course, many media outlets produce editorials and commentary in addition to news content, as well as more opinionated pieces framed as "news analysis." Avowedly conservative or liberal outlets may also produce and share news. But most partisan bias in traditional media is in the minds of citizens, rather than in the news. Even when members of the two parties are watching the same coverage, Democrats believe that media coverage is more favorable

---

[26] Kim Fridkin Kahn and Patrick J. Kenney. 2002. "The Slant of the News: How Editorial Endorsements Influence Campaign Coverage and Citizens' Views of Candidates." *American Political Science Review* 96, 2: 381–94.

[27] Matthew Gentzkow and Jesse M. Shapiro. 2010. "What Drives Media Slant? Evidence from U.S. Daily Newspapers." *Econometrica* 78, 1: 35–71.

[28] David H. Weaver, Randal A. Beam, Bonnie J. Brownlee, Paul S. Voakes, and G. Cleveland Wilhoit. 2006. *The American Journalist in the 21st Century: U.S. News People at the Dawn of a New Millennium.* New York: Routledge; D. D'Alessio and M. Allen. 2000. "Media Bias in Presidential Elections: A Meta-Analysis." *Journal of Communication* 50, 4: 133–56.

toward the Republican candidate and vice versa.[29] Nonetheless, Republican politicians and activists have repeatedly characterized the news media as liberal and raised concerns about its role in helping Democrats. Trump dramatically upped the ante on this strategy in 2016, repeatedly calling mainstream news stories he disliked "fake" and calling journalists "dishonest people" who "don't like our country." The long-term conservative challenge has reduced public confidence in the press, especially among Republicans, and made it harder for citizens to learn facts from media coverage.[30]

This is not to say that the media are not biased in other ways. Most important, news coverage tends to be more favorable to candidates who are ahead in the polls. Reporters write stories about how the losing campaign is "in disarray" and "floundering," while extolling the strategic prowess of the winning campaign. This bias was evident during the 2012 and 2016 presidential campaigns. In 2012, there were four negative stories about Mitt Romney for every positive story from late August to early October. Following Obama's poor performance in the first presidential debate, however, coverage of Obama turned much more negative and coverage of Romney was more positive. In 2016, 77 percent of stories about the Trump campaign were negative overall, but they became less negative in the final two weeks of the campaign when Trump gained ground; 64 percent of Clinton stories were negative, but her coverage became more negative in the final two weeks.[31]

In other words, horse race coverage is more favorable when candidates are doing better in the horse race. The moral of the story is that whatever their personal political preferences, reporters have an incentive to appear balanced while favoring dramatic coverage of the changing fortunes of each candidate.

How Do Candidates and the News Media Interact?

Campaigns seek to influence news media coverage and to use the news media to reach potential voters. Political consultants speak about "earned media" or "free media," meaning news coverage given to the candidates, as distinct

[29] William P. Eveland, Jr., and Dhavan V. Shah. 2003. "The Impact of Individual and Interpersonal Factors on Perceived News Media Bias." *Political Psychology* 24, 1: 101–17.

[30] Jonathan M. Ladd. 2012. *Why Americans Hate the Media and How It Matters*. Princeton, NJ: Princeton University Press.

[31] Patterson, "News Coverage of the 2016 General Election"; and Pew Research Center's Project for Excellence in Journalism. 2012. "Winning the Media Campaign 2012." www.journalism.org/2012/11/02/winning-media-campaign-2012/ (accessed 11/1/2017).

from their "paid media," or advertising. There are many ways in which candidates seek to transmit messages via the news media. They interact directly with the media in interviews, meetings with newspaper editorial boards, and press conferences. They hold public events and give speeches, and invite reporters to attend. They issue press releases, report polling data, publish policy position papers, and announce endorsements. They also leak stories to selected reporters. Nearly everything a candidate does is designed to be picked up in the next day's newspaper, the night's television broadcast, the next hour's update to a website, or the next minute's tweet.

Candidates want every interaction with the news media to be on their terms. They seek to control when and where the interaction takes place, whom they interact with, and what they talk about. Thus, candidates often prefer to avoid the unexpected. For example, candidates cannot anticipate every question that will be asked at a press conference or television interview, and unexpected questions are more likely to trip them up and lead to some misstatement or gaffe. In 2008, Sarah Palin, the Republican vice presidential nominee, had a disastrous interview with *CBS Evening News* anchor Katie Couric. Palin seemed unable to answer simple questions—such as which newspapers she read—and generally appeared hesitant and apprehensive. Candidates fearful of negative news coverage sometimes eschew interviews or press conferences, limiting their interactions with reporters. In 2017, Republican Roy Moore, candidate for U.S. Senate in Alabama, came under withering criticism when several women came forward to report that he had sexually harassed or assaulted them while they were teenagers. Moore sought to avoid mainstream media interviews and instead addressed the allegations in an interview with his conservative ally, Sean Hannity. But several senators who saw the interview came out against Moore. Even Hannity was initially unsatisfied with his explanations, though he eventually supported Moore. Moore went on to lose a close election in a normally reliably Republican state. Campaigns sometimes take further steps to ensure that rallies and speeches lead to good media coverage—for example, by screening the attendees to guarantee that only cheering supporters, and not jeering opponents, are in the audience.

Candidates also plan their advertising around its anticipated media exposure. Many ads are replayed more often by news shows, at no cost to candidates, than during air time that candidates purchase. President Lyndon Johnson's 1964 "Daisy" ad, which featured a little girl counting flower petals before seamlessly shifting to a countdown for the detonation of a nuclear weapon, aired only once but generated significant media coverage and controversy because of its implication that Johnson's opponent, Barry Goldwater, would lead the country into nuclear war. In 2004, ads purchased by a new

Rather than rethinking their support in the wake of sexual misconduct allegations, Roy Moore's supporters lashed out against liberal journalists for what they perceived as a smear campaign against the candidate.

group calling itself Swift Boat Veterans for Truth criticized John Kerry's military service and antiwar activism; they were aired sparingly but became fodder for newscasts. After an initial flurry of coverage, the group was able to raise enough money to run the ads more widely, stimulating additional news coverage and eventually forcing Kerry to respond.

The media strategies of campaigns can help reporters do their jobs. The media want to tell their audience how day-to-day events might affect election outcomes, and campaigns strive to provide something eventful every day. The media are also always looking for a good story, preferably one with drama and conflict. The candidates are often only too happy to leak scandalous tidbits of information about each other.

But there are fundamental conflicts between the agendas of candidates and the news media. Candidates may schedule new events every day, but the content of those events is often repetitive because candidates want to present a consistent message. The audience at any given speech will not have heard it—in fact, the candidate will have just flown into their town an hour before. But the reporters who traveled with the candidate on that plane have been to dozens of towns and heard the speech dozens of times. The day-to-day routine of a campaign does not usually satisfy the media's desire for fresh new story lines every day. Rallies with supporters rarely supply the sort of drama and conflict that the media want. If everybody is cheering for the candidate, nobody is arguing.

Trump's innovation in 2016—whether accidental or intended—was to constantly supply news through outlandish remarks and made-for-television events. Even his rallies were dramatic, as they provoked protests and occasional fistfights. He often went off script in freewheeling comments, attacking opponents and reporters. The cost of such antics is that the stories they produce are often about how a candidate is out of control or unprepared to hold office. But they did gain an audience: cable news networks often carried Trump's speeches live (in anticipation of the next outrage), enabling him to spread his message more widely.

The national party conventions are another example of normally staid events that became more newsworthy in 2016. The media have long complained that live coverage of the conventions is not newsworthy. In 1996, ABC News anchor Ted Koppel actually left the Republican convention midway through the proceedings, declaring, "This convention is more of an infomercial than a news event. Nothing surprising has happened; nothing surprising is anticipated."[32] From the perspective of the party, this is what is supposed to happen. Parties would like the media to report that conflict is limited and the party has a consistent message—but that does not make for much of a news story. Both 2016 conventions gave the media more of what they wanted (to the detriment of the candidates). Supporters of Bernie Sanders's candidacy for the Democratic nomination protested throughout the Democratic convention, with some even interrupting speeches and pledging to defect to third parties. At the Republican convention, Senator Ted Cruz refused to endorse Trump from the stage, arguing that his supporters should "vote their conscience" and provoking crowd-wide boos. The dissent distracted from the candidates' messages but made for good television.

Perhaps the most fundamental conflict between reporters and campaign organizations is that reporters do not want to simply deliver the candidate's message. This is what a professionalized press does: it makes its own decisions about what is important, rather than simply repeating what the candidate thinks is important. For example, although candidates spend most of their speeches talking, even if vaguely, about their policy agendas and goals, the media often talk about the horse race, especially when polls suggest that the race is becoming more competitive.[33] Even when journalists and commentators focus on what the candidates are talking about, they typically subject the candidates' messages to their own analysis. They comment

---

[32] *Nightline.* 1996. Transcript, August 13.

[33] Danny Hayes. 2010. "The Dynamics of Agenda Convergence and the Paradox of Competitiveness in Presidential Campaigns." *Political Research Quarterly* 63, 3: 594–611.

on a candidate's statement or compare it with previous statements or opposition views. Often, the story the reporter writes is not the same one that the candidate hoped she would write.

Reporters are influenced by factors other than the candidates' messages. Newsworthy events such as the financial crisis of 2008 drive the news media's agenda and force candidates to respond accordingly. Frequently, reporters follow the story lines developed by other reporters or commentators. This is the phenomenon of **pack journalism**. Reporters who cover campaigns tend to travel together, talk to each other, and read each other's stories. Because they fear missing an important story, they tend to converge on similar ideas and themes. Beltway denizens like Mark Halperin and daily digests like *Politico*'s "Playbook" summarize what reporters are thinking and talking about and are read widely within the media. On a day-to-day basis, even MSNBC and Fox News generally highlight the same campaign events and candidate statements. Needless to say, candidates are not convinced that these insiders get the story right: "If Politico and Halperin say we're winning, we're losing," Obama's campaign manager David Plouffe said repeatedly during the 2008 campaign.[34]

As a result of these differences, the relationship between candidates and the media is a lot like a marriage: sometimes cozy and sometimes combative. In *Journeys with George*, a documentary about George W. Bush's 2000 presidential campaign, Bush is depicted playing games with the reporters covering him. He gives them nicknames, spends time in their section of the plane, and attempts to make friends with many of them. He even kisses the cheek of the movie's producer, who happens to be the daughter of Representative Nancy Pelosi (D-Calif.). But Bush's relations with the news media were sometimes more frosty. At one campaign event, he was overheard telling running mate Dick Cheney, "There's Adam Clymer—major league asshole—from the *New York Times*." This contradictory behavior reflects the tension in the relationship between candidates and the news media. They need to stay on good terms with one another but they have differing goals and incentives.

The Effects of Media Coverage on Citizens

Campaigns seek to influence media coverage because they believe it will influence what the public thinks about the candidates and thus the election's

---

[34] Mark Leibovich. 2008. "Between Obama and the Press." *New York Times Magazine*, December 17. www.nytimes.com/2008/12/21/magazine/21Gibbs-t.html (accessed 11/1/2017).

outcome. But the effects of media coverage are often not that dramatic because the media cannot easily move public opinion.

Many people fear that partisan media outlets are contributing to political polarization, though evidence is mixed.[35] In experiments, some consumers do gravitate to news sources associated with their partisan slant, but others seek information from both sides. A study of Web browsing found that ideological and partisan segregation in online media is limited in comparison with face-to-face interactions: conservative Republicans talk mostly to others who share their views but visit some liberal websites (and vice versa).[36] Most MSNBC viewers watch some Fox News, though the most dedicated Fox viewers rarely watch a full MSNBC or CNN program.[37] Cable news watchers also tend to watch considerable local news, which usually lacks an ideological or partisan slant.

However, the evidence that Fox News has contributed to both polarization and Republican electoral gains is building. Although researchers have long known that Fox News viewers tend to skew conservative and Republican, that fact alone was not enough to conclude that the channel changed attitudes: its viewers may have instead been attracted to the network because of their prior partisanship and ideology. But recent studies using external factors that influence viewing, like the geographic availability of the channel or its position on the dial (because lower numbered channels are watched more), have enabled better causal inferences. They show that easier access to Fox News was associated with increased Republican voting; MSNBC had no effect on its viewers in this study in part because of its much lower viewership (though its ratings have since risen).[38]

These studies are surprising because it is difficult for information presented by the media to *persuade* people to change their opinions. As news coverage of a candidate becomes more favorable, one might expect the public's view of that candidate to become more favorable as well. But this is not so common for two reasons. First, many people do not follow politics very closely. They are unlikely to read, see, or hear much about a political campaign, and thus their opinions about the candidates, if they have any opinions, will not change.

---

[35] Prior, "Media and Political Polarization."

[36] Matthew Gentzkow and Jesse M. Shapiro. 2011. "Ideological Segregation Online and Offline." *Quarterly Journal of Economics* 126, 4: 1799–839.

[37] Natalie Jomini Stroud. 2011. *Niche News: The Politics of News Choice.* New York: Oxford University Press.

[38] Stefano DellaVigna and Ethan Kaplan. 2007. "The Fox News Effect: Media Bias and Voting." *Quarterly Journal of Economics* 122, 3: 1187–234; Gregory J. Martin and Ali Yurukoglu. 2017. "Bias in Cable News: Persuasion and Polarization." *American Economic Review* 107, 9: 2565–99.

Second, among those who do follow politics, relatively few people are undecided about political candidates, especially at higher levels of office. Instead, these people tend to interpret information from the news media in ways that support the choice they have already made.[39] People are motivated reasoners, meaning they are emotionally invested in a desired conclusion; they learn, recall, and interpret information in a biased fashion to make it more consistent with their prior views.

Because of this, a much more common effect of media coverage is to strengthen or *reinforce* people's preexisting views. This happens not so much because people deliberately ignore contrary news. Instead, people simply interpret information in ways that confirm what they already think. Supporters of two different candidates who see a news report on the campaign will each see yet more reasons to support their favored candidate and oppose the other candidate. Even a news report that is highly unfavorable to a particular candidate is unlikely to change the opinions of that candidate's supporters. People have an impressive ability to ignore, rationalize, or argue against information that is contrary to their views.[40] They find reasons to dispute such a report or dismiss its importance. Fact checking can provoke a similar reaction. By repeating false claims, even to debunk them, fact checkers may only reinforce misperceptions among those predisposed to hold them.[41]

Persuasion is thus more common when people do not have strong preexisting opinions and are more susceptible to new information. A good example of this type of situation is primaries. When voters are choosing among candidates from the same party, whether voters are Democrats or Republicans themselves does not help them make a choice. Moreover, many primary candidates are not familiar figures, and so voters may not know much about them. Under these conditions, media coverage can affect opinions. For example, throughout the 2012 Republican presidential primary, there were sudden increases in media coverage of several different candidates, usually following the sort of novel or dramatic event that attracts media attention.

---

[39] David O. Sears and Richard Kosterman. 1994. "Political Persuasion," in *Persuasion: Psychological Insights and Perspectives*, eds. Sharon Shavitt and Timothy C. Brock. Boston: Allyn & Bacon, pp. 251–78.

[40] Michael F. Meffert, Sungeun Chung, Amber J. Joiner, Leah Waks, and Jennifer Garst. 2006. "The Effects of Negativity and Motivated Information Processing during a Political Campaign." *Journal of Communication* 56, 1: 27–35.

[41] R. Kelly Garrett, Erik C. Nisbet, and Emily K. Lynch. 2013. "Undermining the Corrective Effects of Media-Based Political Fact Checking? The Role of Contextual Cues and Naïve Theory." *Journal of Communication* 63, 4: 617–37.

In one case, news coverage of a candidate that few observers believed viable, businessman Herman Cain, increased after he won a nonbinding straw poll among Republican activists in Florida. This media coverage then increased the candidate's standing in the polls.[42]

Although the media are often less effective at persuasion—or changing what people think—they are more effective at changing what people think *about*. One way in which the media does this is **agenda setting**. The idea is simple: the more the media report on something, the more the public regards it as important. If the media talk a lot about health care, citizens are more likely to cite health care as an issue of concern. Early studies showed that the issues emphasized in the newspapers were those that the public considered important.[43] Subsequent studies that use experimental manipulations of media coverage have demonstrated the same finding: people who are randomly assigned to view newscasts with several stories about a given issue will believe that issue to be more important than will people who watch newscasts with no stories about the issue.[44] These findings provide candidates even more reason to try to shape the media's agenda. The 2016 cycle saw increased media coverage of the candidates' positions on immigration and trade, increasing the salience of those issues among voters.

Related to agenda setting is a process called **priming**. The media influence or "prime" the criteria citizens use to make judgments by the degree of emphasis issues receive, even if the media are not explicitly telling the public to make judgments in this manner. In fact, priming occurs even when media reports do not mention the candidates in the context of discussing an issue. The more reporters discuss an ongoing war, the more the public will judge the president for his performance on the war, even if reporters do not explicitly credit or blame the president for the war.

An example of priming during a political campaign involved Senator Gary Hart (D-Colo.), who ran in the 1988 presidential primary. Hart, who was married, was caught having an affair with a young woman named Donna Rice. Reporters discovered a picture of Rice sitting on Hart's lap aboard a yacht named, appropriately enough, *Monkey Business*. Because of this scandal, people's own moral values became stronger predictors of their attitudes toward Hart as the campaign progressed, with those who were morally

---

[42] John Sides and Lynn Vavreck, *The Gamble: Choice and Chance in the 2012 Presidential Election*. Princeton, NJ: Princeton University Press.

[43] Maxwell E. McCombs and Donald L. Shaw. 1972. "The Agenda-Setting Function of Mass Media." *Public Opinion Quarterly* 36, 2: 176–87.

[44] Shanto Iyengar and Donald R. Kinder. *News That Matters*. 1987. Chicago: Chicago University Press.

conservative being less favorable to Hart. In other words, news media coverage of Hart's affair "primed" moral values, making them an important factor in the public's judgments of Hart.[45] Similarly in 2016, the continuous focus on Trump's negative comments about immigrants and women—in both news reports and Clinton's campaign ads—may have made voters' attitudes toward those groups a more significant factor in their voting decisions.

Finally, the news media affect citizens by *informing*. News coverage of campaigns can help citizens learn relevant facts about the candidates, including candidate biographies and issue positions (even if issues are generally not the main focus of campaign coverage). As campaigns attract more media coverage, citizens are more likely to recognize and recall the names of the candidates and to identify the issues that the candidates are discussing.[46] Although it can be difficult to separate the informing effect of the media from that of other information sources, such as campaign advertising, media coverage plays an important role.

None of these effects are mutually exclusive. The information conveyed in the news media could simultaneously educate people about a candidate's position on an issue (informing), make them feel that the issue is an important problem (agenda setting), and lead them to draw on that issue when deciding whom to vote for (priming). Candidates' attempts to influence news media coverage, if they are successful, might also have multiple effects simultaneously.

There are, however, inherent limits to how much the media influence opinions. Many people do not pay attention to political news or already have well-defined viewpoints that are unlikely to change. Since the rise of cable television and the Internet, Americans who do not want to watch news have been able to choose from an increasing array of other programming, such as sports, cooking shows, and movies. With more channels, most people can avoid the news. The result is an increasingly divided electorate, where some people pay attention to news, learn about politics, and participate in political activities, while the rest of the population largely tunes out and is less likely to vote.[47]

[45] Laura Stoker. 1993. "Judging Presidential Character: The Demise of Gary Hart." *Political Behavior* 15, 2: 193–223.

[46] Kim Fridkin Kahn and Patrick J. Kenney. 1999. *The Spectacle of U.S. Senate Campaigns.* Princeton, NJ: Princeton University Press.

[47] Prior, *Post-Broadcast Democracy.*

Evaluating the News Media's Role in Campaigns

How well do the news media uphold the democratic ideals of free choice, equality, and deliberation by which we might judge political campaigns? In some ways, the media work to support the standard of free choice, as media coverage helps citizens learn who the candidates are and what they stand for, so that they can make an informed choice when they cast their vote. But news coverage is not created with education in mind. It is designed by companies trying to maximize the attention of the audiences coveted by advertisers. As a result, most campaigns receive little attention from the news media. For those that do get attention, media coverage often emphasizes what is new, dramatic, or scandalous. This is not due to partisan or ideological biases. Unlike the candidates themselves, the news media—or at least those outlets that strive for objectivity—are not seeking to manipulate citizens into voting for particular candidates. Instead, they are seeking to build and maintain an audience. If juicy revelations surrounding a candidate's divorce emerge, then the media will feature these revelations regardless of whether this is the most important information for citizens to learn.

We can also ask whether news media contribute to equality. A central question here is whether news media coverage helps to address information inequality, whereby those citizens who are habitually attentive to politics learn a great deal about campaigns, but those who are inattentive to politics learn very little. There is always the potential for information in the news media to reach a wide and diverse audience, but this rarely happens— usually only when a big story breaks and receives nonstop coverage by multiple outlets. More often, the many channels and websites available to consumers encourage segmentation, with political junkies getting their fill of campaign news, and most other people watching entertainment and sports programming. This information inequality reflects and may reinforce a broader economic inequality: people with lower incomes and education levels are less likely to see political news.

A third standard is deliberation. In a large democracy, deliberation must be mediated: Americans cannot all talk to one another or to the candidates face-to-face. Thus, it is up to the media to convey information that clarifies the views of each side. The media's interest in conflict means that they will often report on the differences among the candidates. At times they play referee, intervening as if moderating a debate, investigating the claims that candidates make, and helping citizens understand what the candidates are saying, and whether it is truthful. But the prevalence of "fake news" websites in 2016 raises concerns about whether traditional objective news can still dominate public knowledge, especially if voters would rather seek out and circulate positive news about their candidate and negative news about their opponent, without considering the credibility of the source. One rumor that Hillary Clinton's campaign was running a pedophilia ring out of a pizza parlor actually led one man to show up and fire his rifle in the restaurant. Although these conspiracy theories are spread easily online, traditional news coverage still dominates campaign information. Ultimately, the news media's ability to serve as a watchdog depends in part on the economic prospects for the news business. Cuts in newsroom budgets tend to limit investigative journalism and lead outlets to rely on less experienced journalists.

There is mixed evidence that the media facilitate person-to-person deliberation among citizens. Blogs, online communities, and social networks have the potential to allow millions to communicate and respond to one another's views. Yet partisans may be speaking mainly to one another, and disinterested citizens are mostly opting out of the conversation. Online communities can still promote involvement in campaigns: large experiments on Facebook found that users who saw that their friends had reported voting were themselves a bit more likely to turn out to vote.[48] But there is also evidence that offering token public support for a cause on Facebook or Twitter may make one less likely to be involved in offline campaign activities.[49]

Commentators raise other ethical concerns about media coverage. Some argue that the media are too adversarial and thus too quick to criticize candidates or seize on any hint of scandal, no matter how minor.[50] Some fear that negative media coverage of campaigns may have made people more cynical about politics generally.[51] But there is a delicate balance here. Some accuse the media of trying too hard to be evenhanded, either by treating each candidate's scandals as equivalent or by reporting each side's accusations about the other, even if the facts behind the claims do not warrant equal alarm. In a democracy, we also need the news media to hold candidates accountable, and many media outlets see this as one of their roles. So critical coverage of candidates may be necessary, but it is often in the eye of the beholder where accountability ends and cynicism begins.

---

[48] Robert M. Bond, Christopher J. Fariss, Jason J. Jones, Adam D. I. Kramer, Cameron Marlow, Jaime E. Settle, and James H. Fowler. 2012. "A 61-Million-Person Experiment in Social Influence and Political Mobilization." *Nature* 489: 295–98.

[49] Kirk Kristofferson, Katherine White, and John Peloza. 2014. "The Nature of Slacktivism: How the Social Observability of an Initial Act of Token Support Affects Subsequent Prosocial Action." *Journal of Consumer Research* 40, 6: 1149–66.

[50] Thomas E. Patterson. 1993. *Out of Order.* New York: Knopf.

[51] Joseph N. Cappella and Kathleen Hall Jamieson. 1996. "News Frames, Political Cynicism, and Media Cynicism." *Annals of the American Academy of Political and Social Science* 546, 1: 71–84.

Furthermore, blaming the media for the campaign coverage we see gets us only so far. Studies in which people are given a variety of information about candidates, including their biographies, their views on issues, their strategies, and their horse race positions, show that they gravitate to the stories about polls and strategy—precisely the kinds of topics that the news media are so often criticized for emphasizing.[52] In fact, people who pay a lot of attention to politics, and are thus likely to be regular readers of the news, are more likely to read these kinds of stories. Thus, the news media's focus on campaign strategy and the horse race may simply give consumers the information they want. This is what we would expect when news organizations need to maintain and build an audience in order to sell advertising. It is not always easy to tell how much blame media outlets and their consumers each deserve.

Conclusion

The media play an important role in communicating information about campaigns, determining the issues discussed in them, and shaping the images that voters develop of each candidate. The frenzy surrounding the video of Donald Trump's remarks on the set of *Access Hollywood* illustrates how the news media cover campaigns, as well as the potential for and the limits to their influence on voters. The attention to the video reflected the news values of journalists. The story was new. It involved drama and controversy. It had inflammatory rhetoric. This is why it featured so heavily in news coverage.

The story's salience demonstrates how the news media's agenda may diverge from the candidate's agenda. Certainly Trump did not want to talk about his remarks. But he was forced to engage nonetheless, and even raised decades-old accusations regarding his opponent's husband in response. Candidates cannot avoid interacting with the media, because it is an important way in which they speak to the public. Trump did not react by simply criticizing the media (although he did so constantly throughout his campaign). He had to apologize, and he attempted to deflect by raising equivalent concerns about his opponent.

The episode also shows us how difficult it is for the news media to affect public opinion. When the video first appeared, the campaign had been under way for months. Those paying attention to politics had already formed opinions of Trump and Clinton, and the revelation of Trump's *Access Hollywood* comments did little to change them. News coverage of political campaigns

---

[52] Shanto Iyengar, Helmut Norpoth, and Kyu S. Hahn. 2004. "Consumer Demand for Election News: The Horse Race Sells." *Journal of Politics* 66, 1: 157–75.

often implies that campaign events have a powerful impact on the public. In essence, the news media seem to believe in their own power. In reality, although the media do help determine the issue content of campaigns and the criteria by which candidates are judged, their effect on the political attitudes of Americans is much more limited.

At their best, the news media can uphold the ideals we would like political campaigns to embody. Journalists can convey messages from candidates while also serving as watchdogs. News coverage can contrast the views of the parties, correct untruths, and direct attention to important issues and to the candidates' strengths and weaknesses. At the same time, the coverage also focuses on sideshows and horse race trivia, while ignoring the bigger picture—a fact that must be blamed not only on the news media themselves but on citizens who consume news. Campaigns show us the best and worst of the contemporary news media.

KEY TERMS

news media (p. 216)

sound bite (p. 217)

blogs (p. 218)

right to equal time (p. 222)

infotainment (p. 225)

wire services (p. 226)

narrow-casting (p. 227)

news values (p. 229)

horse race journalism (p. 232)

interpretive journalism (p. 233)

pack journalism (p. 239)

agenda setting (p. 242)

priming (p. 242)

FOR DISCUSSION

1. Who is more responsible for the weaknesses of campaign coverage in the American news media: reporters or consumers?

2. If you were starting a blog about campaigns in your state, what would you cover? How would you generate an audience? Would the need to build your audience change the types of stories that you covered?

3. How should the media have covered the release of the Trump *Access Hollywood* video? Could they have ignored it? Was it a legitimate campaign issue?

4. With Trump as a model, are any changes likely to occur in how candidates interact with the media?

CHAPTER 9

Presidential Campaigns

During the last weekend of the 2016 presidential election campaign, it seemed to many as if Donald Trump and his running mate, Mike Pence of Indiana, were engaged in a desperate attempt to transform an electoral map that had turned against them. On Friday, Trump gave a speech in Reno, Nevada, where early voting totals showed Democratic nominee Hillary Clinton with a commanding lead. Later that day, he held a rally in Denver, Colorado, where Clinton's campaign was so confident they would win that they had pulled their television ads in early September. On Saturday, Trump campaigned in Virginia, a state where polls showed Clinton up by double digits. He also visited Minnesota, a state that has been reliably Democratic since the Great Depression. Meanwhile, Clinton seemed to be expanding her list of targeted states, visiting the traditional Republican stronghold of Arizona and keeping the pressure on in Iowa and Ohio, nonessential states where Trump's polling numbers were relatively rosy.

But there were signs that Trump's strategy was more savvy than chaotic. On Saturday, at the same time as Trump's rally in Minnesota, Pence held a major event in Wisconsin alongside Speaker of the House Paul Ryan and GOP Senate candidate Ron Johnson. Later that Saturday and throughout Sunday and Monday, both Trump and Pence made multiple appearances in Michigan and Pennsylvania, long regarded as essential (and safe) bricks in the Democrats' "Blue Wall"—states that had gone Democratic in every presidential election from 1992 through 2012. These visits were a hot ticket locally, and garnered tremendous regional television and newspaper coverage. The late activities of the Clinton team seem to validate the notion that the vote in these upper Midwest states might be very close. Clinton added last-minute stops in Michigan and Pennsylvania on Monday, the day before the election. Clinton's running mate, Tim Kaine of Virginia, spent part of Sunday stumping in Wisconsin. Clinton's campaign even had President Obama and the First Lady campaign in Ann Arbor and Detroit on Monday afternoon and evening. As the votes were tallied, it became clear that the Trump campaign's late flurry of activity was justified: Trump defeated Clinton by a mere 44,000 votes in Pennsylvania, 22,000 votes in Wisconsin, and 10,000 votes in

Michigan. Many commentators, as well as some Democrats, argued that Clinton's campaign had blown the election by ignoring telltale signs and neglecting states that proved to be decisive.

It is far from clear, however, that personal appearances in Pennsylvania, Wisconsin, and Michigan won Trump and Pence these three states. In fact, it is far from clear that Trump's campaign itinerary was more prescient than Clinton's. After all, he did spend considerable time in states that Clinton carried, such as Colorado, Nevada, New Hampshire, and Virginia. And his late-October forays into Minnesota and New Mexico did little to help his standing in either of those long-shot states. Furthermore, it is not the case that Clinton ignored the upper Midwest states that ultimately proved her undoing; between Labor Day and Election Day, Clinton made 14 appearances in Michigan, Pennsylvania, and Wisconsin, while Kaine made 18. Still, the Democrats' decision to attempt to expand the map and the Republicans' decision to continue their efforts in the upper Midwest illustrate the strategic choices that animate modern presidential campaigns. And in close elections, these strategic choices might be critical.

The phrase *"might* be critical" reflects the skepticism among political scientists about the extent to which presidential campaigns affect election outcomes. This is not to say that academics believe presidential campaigns do not matter. They reinforce citizens' underlying partisan loyalties and raise the salience of other fundamental factors that affect who gets elected, such as the state of the economy. But campaigns do not necessarily decide who wins; broader political and economic realities may be more significant. Political scientists often observe that just because certain campaign strategies are correlated

Core of the Analysis

- Presidential candidates have two goals: to secure their party's nomination and then to win a majority of Electoral College votes.
- Electoral rules structure the presidential nomination process, and as candidates campaign for their party's nomination, they encounter a variety of election formats in different states.
- Nominating conventions may provide significant boosts to the presidential candidates, as can events that occur later in the campaign.
- The Electoral College structures the general election campaign, and candidates target particular states in order to win the necessary electoral votes.
- Political reality—especially the state of the economy—has an enormous influence on presidential elections.

In November 2016, Republican vice-presidential candidate Mike Pence (center) campaigned in Wisconsin with Speaker of the House Paul Ryan (second from left) and Senate candidate Ron Johnson (second from right). This last-minute trip may have increased support for the Republican ticket among key constituencies.

with victory does not mean that they *cause* victory. Campaign consultants, by contrast, are much more confident that presidential campaigns affect public opinion and therefore the outcome of the election. Consultants tend to believe that campaign strategy is often decisive in determining who wins.

In this chapter, we explain how political scientists and campaign strategists understand the role of presidential campaigns in the electoral process and seek to reconcile their somewhat different views. We argue that campaigns act strategically to maximize the chances that their candidate will win the White House. In developing strategies, presidential campaigns are influenced by two institutional arrangements. First, there is the series of statewide nominating contests—primaries and caucuses—during the first five months of a presidential election year. Second, there is the Electoral College, in which electors cast the deciding ballots for president. The electors are determined largely by winner-take-all statewide popular vote outcomes. Both arrangements demonstrate how electoral rules affect campaign strategy. Maximizing the prospects for victory also means acknowledging the political reality of a given presidential election cycle. Candidates are likely to pursue different strategies depending on whether the economy is strong or weak, whether the country is at war or peace, and which party presently holds the White House.

We first examine a presidential campaign's basic goals. We then turn to the three major stages of presidential elections—the nomination contest, the national convention, and the general election—taking care to consider the important rules and broader realities that affect strategy at each stage. We also discuss the effects that conventions and debates typically have on public opinion. We conclude by considering how well modern presidential campaigns serve American democracy.

Goals of Presidential Campaigns

Two goals have to be met to win the White House. The first goal is to amass a sufficient number of delegates to secure a party's nomination at the national convention. Most delegates (roughly 75 percent) are selected in statewide primary elections, caucuses, and conventions. Of these methods, primary elections are the most common.

The second goal is to win enough states in the general election to garner at least 270—a majority—of the 538 available Electoral College votes and thus win the presidency. Note that the goal is *not* to win a majority of the popular vote; this is usually necessary to claim enough states to win 270 electoral votes, but not always. In fact, there have been presidents who lost the popular vote but still won the election: John Quincy Adams (1824), Rutherford B. Hayes (1876), Benjamin Harrison (1888), George W. Bush (2000), and Donald Trump (2016). There is even some evidence that John F. Kennedy lost the popular vote in 1960.[1]

The problem is that these two goals can be somewhat incompatible. To win the nomination a candidate must win the votes of a plurality of partisans. But partisans, whether Republican or Democrat, tend to be more ideological than the average voter in the general election. This gives candidates the incentive to move away from the political center during primary and caucus season in order to cater to ideologues and win the nomination, and then back toward the center to win the election. (This is related to the median voter theorem introduced in Chapter 5. More will be said about this and the broader spatial theory of voting in Chapter 13.) One could certainly argue that this is what happened to the campaigns of Bob Dole (1996), John Kerry (2004), John McCain (2008), and Mitt Romney (2012), all of whom shifted their positions on certain issues between the primary and general elections.

---

[1] Brian J. Gaines. 2001. "Popular Myths about Popular Vote–Electoral College Splits." *PS: Political Science and Politics* 34, 1: 70–75.

Some recent candidates have sought to avoid the inconsistency of following strident partisan appeals during presidential primaries with more inclusive, moderate policy appeals. George W. Bush (2000) and Hillary Clinton (2008 and 2016) were careful not to embrace primary strategies that were inconsistent with their longer-term plans for the general election. But this strategy is risky too: appealing to more centrist, general election voters can alienate hard-core partisans who play a major role in primaries and caucuses.

Winning the Nomination

Before the convention and the general election campaign, presidential candidates have several important tasks to accomplish. We focus on two of the most important: contesting the party's primaries and caucuses, and selecting a vice-presidential candidate to be his or her running mate.

Primaries and Caucuses

In Chapters 3 and 6, we discussed how the political parties no longer directly control the nominating process.[2] As a consequence, individual candidates must campaign state by state, in primary elections and party caucuses. These elections determine who the state party will send to represent the state at the national party nominating convention. These representatives are called **delegates**. To win the nomination at the convention, a candidate has to accumulate delegates by winning an array of statewide elections, each with distinct rules, over a period of several months. This makes four different kinds of rules important: how states structure these elections, how delegates are allocated to candidates, how delegates are selected to attend the national convention, and the order in which states hold their elections.

States typically employ either caucuses or primary elections to determine who their delegates will be. **Caucuses** are relatively closed affairs in which registered partisans attend meetings at election precinct locations and vote

---

[2] Although most scholars agree that the political parties no longer control the presidential nomination process, Cohen and colleagues contend that higher-level party officials and donors remain the dominant forces in the selection of candidates. Their analysis features a case study of George W. Bush's rise in 1999, based on the preferences of the Republican Party's power-brokers. See Marty Cohen, David Karol, Hans Noel, and John Zaller. 2008. *The Party Decides: Presidential Nominations before and after Reform.* Chicago: University of Chicago Press. More recent research, however, suggests that consultants (at least on the Republican side in 2012) do not behave in this manner (see Sean A. Cain. 2015. "Polls and Elections: Leviathan's Reach? The Impact of Political Consultants on the Outcomes of the 2012 Republican Primaries and Caucuses." *Presidential Studies Quarterly* 45, 1: 132–56).

to select delegates to the county or state party conventions. Typically, these delegates are "pledged" to support a particular presidential candidate at the next level. The actual delegates to the national convention are then selected at the state convention. To be successful in a caucus state, a candidate must have a committed group of followers and an organization that can deliver these followers to the caucus locations. The first contest of the presidential nomination process is the Iowa caucuses.

More commonly, states use some form of **primary election** to determine delegates to the national convention. The form of the primary election affects the kinds of voters who can participate. As we discussed in Chapter 2, primaries can be closed, open, or semi-closed. In closed primaries, only registered partisans can vote. That is, only registered Democrats can vote in the Democratic primary, and only registered Republicans can vote in the Republican primary. In open primaries, voters can choose the primary in which they will vote, regardless of their party, but they may vote only in one party's primary.[3] In semi-closed primaries, both unaffiliated voters and those registered as members of a party can vote in that party's primary—so, for example, registered Republicans and independents may vote in the Republican primary. Candidates will thus face more or less ideological electorates depending on the type of primary. For example, a socially conservative candidate who appeals to the Republican base would stand a better chance in a closed primary state than in an open primary state in which independents and Democrats are allowed to vote. The first primary of the presidential election year, in New Hampshire, is a semi-closed primary.

Most states allocate delegates in proportion to the percentage of the vote won by a candidate in the primary or caucuses.[4] Under this system, a candidate with 40 percent of the vote in a state's primary gets 40 percent of the delegates from that state. The Democratic Party mandates a proportionality rule for its nomination process. In the Republican nomination process, some states have historically used a winner-take-all rule, allocating all delegates from the state to the winning candidate regardless of the vote margin. As recently as 2012, the winner-take-all rule was being phased out on the Republican side as well, in favor of a proportional rule. In 2016, however, states that held their primaries later in the Republican nomination process (after March 15) were allowed to use winner-take-all rules; the assumption was

---

[3] In fact, most open primary states do not have registration by party.

[4] It is important to note that a candidate usually must reach a threshold—often 15 percent of the vote—before earning a proportional allocation of delegates. Candidates not reaching this threshold do not receive any delegates.

that this would allow the front-runner to wrap up the nomination and avoid a protracted struggle that might damage the candidate in the fall election. In hindsight, it is unclear whether this assumption was borne out by events in 2016.

To select the individual delegates, some states (such as New York) use a direct vote, others (such as California) allow the candidates to select as many delegates as they are entitled to on the basis of the primary or caucus results, and still others (such as Texas) allow delegates to pledge themselves to candidates and then stand for election at the state convention. These differing arrangements affect what a campaign must do to maximize the number of delegates it can obtain. For example, in Texas, delegates are allocated in proportion to the vote a candidate gets statewide and by the proportion won in each of the state's congressional districts. Precinct caucuses (which occur on the night of the primary election; coupling substantively important primary elections and caucus meetings is known as the "Texas Two-Step") select delegates to county conventions; the delegates at the county conventions select delegates to the state conventions; and delegates at the state convention select delegates to the national convention. This multistage process means that candidates need committed supporters in as many parts of the state as possible. In 2008, the Obama campaign was able to maximize delegate totals in several states through a mastery of complex caucus and convention selection processes.

In addition to the delegates selected through the competitive processes of these statewide nomination contests, roughly one-quarter of delegates to the national nominating conventions achieve that status because they are officeholders or occupy certain positions within the party. These are referred to as *at-large* delegates (or *superdelegates*) and are not pledged to support any particular candidate based on a statewide vote. They are free agents who must be persuaded, one by one, by the candidate and campaign. Bernie Sanders's 2016 campaign worked long and hard to convince the at-large delegates to ignore Hillary Clinton's edge in pledged delegates and to vote for him at the convention. In the end, however, at-large delegates sided with Clinton, who had won more total votes in all the primaries and caucuses and thus more pledged delegates.

The primaries and consequent delegate selection occur in a sequence, with some states' primaries or caucuses held as early as February and others as late as June. The early contests—especially the Iowa caucuses and the New Hampshire and South Carolina primaries—can have an effect on the process that is disproportionate to the actual number of delegates from those states. This is because their results are seen by both the news media and citizens as conveying important information about the **viability** of the candidates, or their chances for winning the nomination.[5] Because the choice between candidates is often complex and may require more resources than some are willing or able to invest, the news media and citizens seek ways to simplify the choice, especially when many candidates are running for a party's nomination. The early races thus serve to winnow (that is, narrow) the field. Some candidates drop out because their performance in Iowa, New Hampshire, or South Carolina indicates they have no chance of winning the nomination. In late 2015, five Democrats and 17 Republicans sought their parties' nominations for the 2016 election; after the March 15, 2016, primaries, only two Democrats (Hillary Clinton and Bernie Sanders) and three Republicans (Donald Trump, Ted Cruz, and John Kasich) remained active candidates.

The importance of early contests gives state legislatures the incentive to schedule their primaries and caucuses earlier in the calendar so that they will exert greater influence on the nominating process. This is known as **front-loading**. The national party organizations, aware that a system in which all states hold early primaries might help a charismatic but still relatively unknown and flawed candidate to win the nomination, have discouraged front-loading in order to provide additional time for citizens to learn about the candidates. The Republican National Committee (RNC), for example, adopted a "preferred" calendar for 2016, with no primaries or caucuses scheduled before February 1, and specified that states jumping to the front of the calendar must use a proportional allocation method (which minimizes the delegate totals for a "winning" candidate compared with a winner-take-all system). The RNC's preferences were somewhat realized, although state legislatures remain the ultimate authorities for election rules and dates.

Taken together, these features of the presidential nominating process have important implications for campaign strategy. Candidates face a demanding task. They must develop a campaign organization that can compete in a rapid-fire sequence of contests with different eligible voters and different rules: the precinct caucuses in Iowa, the semi-closed primary election in New Hampshire a week later, the open primary election in South Carolina two or three weeks after that, and then the numerous primaries (including Georgia, Texas, and Virginia) that mark "Super Tuesday." It is a significant test

---

[5] John H. Aldrich. 1980. *Before the Convention: Strategies and Choices in Presidential Nomination Campaigns.* Chicago: University of Chicago Press; Larry M. Bartels. 1988. *Presidential Primaries and the Dynamics of Public Choice.* Princeton, NJ: Princeton University Press; Stephen M. Utych and Cindy D. Kam. 2013. "Viability, Information Seeking and Vote Choice." *Journal of Politics* 76, 1: 152–66.

and one that requires money, attention from news media, and the support of at least some within the party organization.

Thus, the first strategic decision we discussed in Chapter 5—whether to run in the first place—entails a calculation about whether the candidate can muster the resources needed to compete. Candidates must ask themselves whether they can raise the money necessary to assemble campaign organizations across the many states holding nominating contests. If they cannot, then they must answer a different question: whether they can convince enough voters in one of the early states to support them, thereby earning greater attention and ensuring that they remain relevant in subsequent contests. At this early stage of the election season, some lesser-known candidates craft issue-based or ideological appeals and hammer their message home, hoping to attract wider attention. For example, in 2016 Vermont Senator Bernie Sanders presented himself as more liberal and more vehement in his denunciations of Wall Street and income inequality than the other Democratic contenders. In the 2016 Republican primaries, brain surgeon Ben Carson focused his campaign on social issues such as abortion and offered an extremely conservative agenda that appealed to core elements of the Republican Party. Both candidates generated enough support and attention early on to sustain lengthy campaigns.

For candidates who do run, subsequent decisions will depend on their level of prominence. **Front-runners**—candidates with a lot of money and who are well known by the electorate—must decide how much time and money to spend in the early states, since some of them are small and thus have fewer delegates than the large states whose primaries fall on Super Tuesday and later in the calendar. Hillary Clinton's national campaign in 2008 emphasized the early contests in Iowa and New Hampshire, which was a controversial strategy. She could have ignored Iowa, for example, and perhaps minimized the significance of an upset victory by Barack Obama or John Edwards, who both campaigned and organized tirelessly there. But ignoring Iowa would have raised questions about her front-runner status: Was she afraid of losing? How dominant was she really?

As alluded to earlier, lesser-known candidates face a different strategic challenge: Which of the early contests are the most promising targets for pulling off an upset and thereby generating important publicity for the campaign? Surpassing low expectations and thereby triggering favorable media coverage generates momentum. Candidates with momentum can build on early victories to win later primaries and ultimately the nomination. Candidates who benefited from momentum include Jimmy Carter in 1976,

George H. W. Bush in 1980, Gary Hart in 1984, John McCain in 2000, Howard Dean in 2004, Barack Obama in 2008, and Bernie Sanders and Ted Cruz in 2016. Only one of these candidates won the nomination, however, illustrating that early victories are usually not enough.

Given the importance of fund-raising, primary contenders must also decide whether to accept public funds. As we discussed in Chapter 4, the Federal Election Campaign Act (FECA) provides public money for presidential candidates who meet fairly attainable thresholds—$5,000 in contributions of $250 or less across at least 20 states. But the money comes with conditions: the recipient must abide by state-by-state as well as overall spending limits. In 2016, the overall limits were about $48.07 million. Ever since multimillionaire Steve Forbes targeted Bob Dole with millions of dollars in negative ads in the 1996 New Hampshire Republican primary, many candidates have been reticent to accept public funds and the limits they entail. In fact, in 2016 only Democrat Martin O'Malley accepted public funding. This has made recent elections increasingly expensive.

For all intents and purposes, the nominating contest is over when one candidate has earned a sufficient number of delegates to claim a majority at the convention. Oftentimes, this threshold is determined by the news media, or even the candidates themselves, who update their "delegate counts" after every contest. The result, of course, is not official until the **roll-call vote** at the convention. Still, there is pressure on the other candidates to drop out and rally behind the winner after the result begins to look clear.

Choosing a Running Mate

After the nominations are clinched, the presidential campaign enters the preconvention phase. The 2016 nomination contests were unusual because they lasted so long; typically, the delegate contest is decided by the end of March and the nominee has until mid- or late summer to prepare for the convention. An important part of this phase is the selection of the vice-presidential nominee. Despite the fact that there is little evidence that the vice president has any direct effect on the outcome of the general election, this decision drives media coverage before and during the convention. There are at least five strategic options for the vice-presidential pick. The first is to select someone whose knowledge and expertise compensate for the shortcomings of the presidential candidate. In 2008, Barack Obama, a first-term senator from Illinois with almost no foreign policy experience, selected Joe Biden, a six-term senator who served as chairman of the Foreign Relations Committee. In 2000, Texas governor George W. Bush also sought to bolster

National conventions used to be the setting in which the party's presidential nominee was selected. Today, the nominee is almost always determined in advance of the convention through primary elections and caucuses, as was the case for Donald Trump and his running mate, Mike Pence, in 2016.

the foreign policy credentials of his presidential campaign by selecting former defense secretary Dick Cheney.[6] In 2016, Donald Trump's selection of Mike Pence, a former U.S. senator and a senior member of the Foreign Relations Committee, can be seen as an effort to help him on foreign policy issues.

A second option is to choose someone who can help the candidate carry a state or region. For example, John F. Kennedy's selection of Texas senator Lyndon Johnson in 1960 helped win the state for the Democrats. Many believe that Hillary Clinton's choice of Tim Kaine was made in part to lock down the state of Virginia, where Kaine had served as governor, for the Democrats. Some even thought it would help her compete in the neighboring battleground state of North Carolina. More generally, presidential nominees often select running mates from large states, like Texas, where there are more electoral votes in play.

---

[6] Lee Sigelman and Paul J. Wahlbeck. 1997. "The 'Veepstakes': Strategic Choice in Presidential Running Mate Selection." *American Political Science Review* 91, 4: 855–64.

A third option is to select someone from a political or demographic group whose support the candidate needs. In 2012, Mitt Romney was viewed unenthusiastically by conservatives because of his support of health care reform in Massachusetts and his formerly pro-choice position on abortion. To win over conservatives, he selected Wisconsin representative Paul Ryan, who was the architect of the House Republicans' aggressive deficit reduction plan. Many observers believe that Trump's selection of Pence was designed to help him with Republicans who doubted the New York mogul's commitment to conservative Republican principles.

A fourth option is to select someone to heal intraparty wounds. In 1980, Ronald Reagan reached out to his chief rival from the primaries, George H. W. Bush. In 1976, Gerald Ford almost asked Reagan to be his running mate even though the two had had a bruising struggle for the nomination. In 2008, many Democrats urged Obama to ask Hillary Clinton to join the ticket despite their nomination fight. In the end, however, both Ford and Obama saw more downside than upside to this strategy.

Finally, a fifth option would be to select someone who reinforces the image of the candidate. Although it may seem counterintuitive, the vice-presidential selection need not always be about shoring up weaknesses. In 1992, Bill Clinton asked Tennessee senator Al Gore to be his running mate. Both were young, white, and southern. But Clinton's campaign strategists saw the virtue of reinforcing their candidate's image as a new, fresh face.

Presidential candidates must also decide when to announce their choice of a running mate. Announcing several weeks before the convention maximizes the time that both the presidential and vice-presidential nominees are on the trail and ensures that there will be two media "hits" (the announcement plus the convention). In contrast, announcing the pick right before the convention helps to maximize the impact of the convention. In recent years, major-party candidates have typically opted for the second strategy. In 2008, both Obama and McCain, for example, named their running mates within the week before their nominating conventions.

The National Conventions

The Republican and Democratic national conventions mark the formal transition from the nominating process to the general election campaign, even though the general election is always the ultimate goal as the nominating contest unfolds. Like the nominating process, today's conventions are quite different than they were through the 1960s. Until the 1970s, the political parties exercised a great deal of control over the nomination, and the conventions were deliberative bodies where party officials and state delegates bargained and cut deals to arrive at a consensus choice for the nomination. But the role of political caucuses and primaries, which had been slowly building over the course of the twentieth century, became decisive following rule changes made before the 1972 election cycle. These rule changes—most notably those mandated by the Democrats' McGovern-Fraser Commission—were aimed at increasing the say of rank-and-file partisans in determining the votes of statewide delegations. As a result, the Republican and Democratic nominees are now typically known well in advance of the national conventions; delegate totals based on primary and caucus results, as well as on the commitments of unelected delegates, are easily calculated. Today's conventions have thus transformed from determinative political events into four-day public-relations spectacles, during which the nominees present themselves and their policies to the American electorate.

Conventions as Showcase Events

The candidate's travel to the convention is itself a part of the convention process. Candidates publicly preview the message of their nomination acceptance speech, as well as their entire fall campaign. In 2016, Hillary Clinton spent the days before the Democratic convention defending the economic growth seen during the Obama presidency, but also touting her plans to make college more affordable and to go after Wall Street interests that enriched themselves at the expense of the middle class. This tricky mix of defending progress but promising to improve on the status quo defined her autumn strategy. Candidates also reveal the constituencies and states that they believe are critical to victory. In the three days before the opening gavel for her nominating convention, the Clinton campaign's presumed road map to victory was clear; she traveled to Miami Beach, Tampa, and Orlando, Florida, and then stopped to make a speech in Charlotte, North Carolina, before moving on to Philadelphia, Pennsylvania.

Despite the attention the campaigns and the news media give to these appearances, their impact is typically modest. Both the timing and the location of the conventions have greater potential influence. Unfortunately for the candidates, the parties choose the location well in advance of the actual campaign, after a selective bidding process. Parties also set the timing in advance. Traditionally, the party that is not in power holds its convention first, and sometimes there is a significant gap between the two conventions. For example, in 1992, seven weeks separated the conventions—the

Democrats held theirs in mid-July and the Republicans held theirs in late August. More recently, both parties have attempted to hold their conventions as late as possible in order to maximize television audiences and the presumed impact of coverage on voters: after the Summer Olympics but before Labor Day.

Campaign strategists have three goals at the convention: tell voters what the past four years have been about, identify how the current candidates are different, and offer a vision for the country. Most conventions thus begin with a narrative of what has happened over the past four years. Speakers at the convention of the party out of power (the "out-party") talk about what has gone wrong and why there is a need for change. Speakers at the convention of the incumbent party talk about what has been successfully accomplished and how it occurred. These contrasting narratives are usually conveyed by well-known politicians on Monday and Tuesday nights of the convention week. Then conventions tend to focus on the contrasts between the candidates, with convention speakers describing the choice before the nation: What are the stakes and options the party faces? What would the party's candidate do, and how does that differ from the opposing candidate? This is usually accomplished in the Wednesday speech of the vice-presidential nominee. Last, the party and its candidate have to offer a vision for the future: Where is the country headed, and how will it get there? This is the goal of the presidential nominee's speech on Thursday night.

Convention Effects

Do conventions actually affect what the public thinks of the two candidates? They certainly seem to, although it should be noted that the magnitude of these effects appears to have decreased in recent years. Still, each party's nominee appears to garner additional support from the public after the convention. This is commonly referred to as the **convention bump** (or **convention bounce**). More precisely, the convention bump is defined as the candidate's share of the two-party vote in trial-heat polls conducted 1 to 7 days after the convention minus his or her share of the two-party vote in polls conducted 1 to 7 days before the convention. The average convention bump is about five points, as measured by polling data from Gallup (see Table 9.1). As we will see, conventions have tended to have larger effects than other presidential campaign events, such as the debates. Political scientists believe that convention effects are often larger for two main reasons. First, conventions occur relatively early in the general election campaign, when there are a larger number of citizens who are undecided or only weakly committed to a candidate. There is thus a greater potential for persuasion.

TABLE 9.1 Convention Bumps, 1972–2016

Year	Candidate	Democratic Convention City	Bump	Candidate	Republican Convention City	Bump
2016	H. R. Clinton	Philadelphia	+2	Trump	Cleveland	0
2012	Obama	Charlotte	+3	Romney	Tampa	−1
2008	Obama	Denver	+4	McCain	St. Paul	+6
2004	Kerry	Boston	−1	G. W. Bush	New York City	+2
2000	Gore	Los Angeles	+8	G. W. Bush	Philadelphia	+8
1996	W. J. Clinton	Chicago	+5	Dole	San Diego	+3
1992	W. J. Clinton	New York City	+16	G. H. W. Bush	Houston	+5
1988	Dukakis	Atlanta	+7	G. H. W. Bush	New Orleans	+6
1984	Mondale	San Francisco	+9	Reagan	Dallas	+4
1980	Carter	New York City	+10	Reagan	Detroit	+8
1976	Carter	New York City	+9	Ford	Kansas City	+5
1972	McGovern	Miami Beach	0	Nixon	Miami Beach	+7

Source: www.gallup.com/poll/109702/conventions-typically-result-fivepoint-bounce.aspx (accessed 5/5/2011); 2012 estimates calculated by authors, using Gallup Poll figures; see www.gallup.com/video/109906/obama-sees-convention-bounce.aspx (accessed 5/5/2011); 2016 estimates are based on a comparison of results from the polling aggregator, RealClearPolitics; see www.realclearpolitics.com/epolls/2016/president/us/general_election_trump_vs_clinton-5491.html (accessed 10/28/2017).

Later in the campaign, with fewer undecided voters, events serve mainly to reinforce preexisting opinions about the candidates. Second, conventions produce news stories that tend to be favorable to the candidate being nominated. This is what the hoopla of conventions is designed to do. This effect is amplified by the fact that the candidate from the opposition party is likely to campaign less vigorously during this period, knowing that it is not easy to compete with the speeches and images of the other party's convention.

Of course, not all conventions give candidates the same size bump. Bill Clinton's 1992 convention stands out as the most effective since 1964, although it was due mostly to an unusual occurrence: on the last day of the Democratic convention, Ross Perot, who had run as an independent candidate, dropped out of the race, thus leaving his supporters, about one-third of likely voters, looking for a new candidate to support. More often, the size of the convention bump depends on how well the candidate is doing given prevailing political realities, such as the state of the economy and approval of the incumbent president.[7] Candidates who are favored by these realities but are for other reasons underperforming in the polls will tend to get a larger bump—in part because convention messages often include messages about the economy and the incumbent president.

Not everyone thinks that convention bounces are consequential. Some political scientists believe that convention bounces—especially those associated with recent elections—are both minimal and ephemeral. Political scientists Doug Rivers and Ben Lauderdale argue that the surge in support for a candidate after the convention is mostly a function of "response bias" in polls. That is, supporters of the other candidate are less likely to agree to take a poll during this time, inflating the estimated support for the candidate whose convention just concluded. This response bias fades after 10 days or so, leaving the race roughly where it was before the convention.[8] Other political scientists point to reduced news media coverage of the conventions, as well as the hyper-partisanship of today's politics that leaves relatively fewer voters available for persuasion today compared with 20 years ago. The consensus among both academics and practitioners is that conventions remain important campaign events, but that they are rarely the game changers they once were.

The General Election

After the convention balloons have popped and the confetti has been swept up, the presidential candidates and their running mates hit the campaign trail, followed by a gaggle of reporters. At the same time, the campaigns blanket the airwaves with radio and television advertisements. But the states and media markets where the candidates travel and broadcast advertisements are not chosen at random. Moreover, candidates assiduously court some citizens more than others. Understanding contemporary presidential campaigning requires an understanding of the rules and reality that govern it.

---

[7] Thomas M. Holbrook. 1996. *Do Campaigns Matter?* Thousand Oaks, CA: Sage Publications.

[8] Benjamin Lauderdale and Douglas Rivers. 2016. "Beware the Phantom Swings: Why Dramatic Bounces in the Polls Aren't Always What They Seem." *YouGov*, November 1. https://today.yougov.com/news/2016/11/01/beware-phantom-swings-why-dramatic-swings -in-the-p/ (accessed 9/12/2017).

The resulting system, though often criticized, has positive as well as negative implications for democratic values.

The Electoral College

The strategic context of the general election is dominated by the institutional reality of the Electoral College. According to Article II of the Constitution, each state has a number of electoral votes equal to its total number of representatives to the U.S. Congress—that is, its members in the House plus its two senators. The passage of the Twenty-third Amendment gave the District of Columbia three electoral votes. In sum, there are 538 electors (based on 435 House members plus 100 senators plus three electors from Washington, D.C.).[9] As noted earlier, the strategic goal is thus to win some combination of states whose electoral votes total at least 270.

The Electoral College has often been the subject of controversy. One criticism involves the method for determining electoral votes. The formula—the total number of representatives plus the total number of senators—was derived to secure the support of small states in the fight over the ratification of the Constitution; it creates a bias in favor of those smaller states. For example, Wyoming has one elector for every 195,167 residents, while California has one for every 713,637. However, some argue that the Electoral College actually benefits large states because carrying a large state by a tiny margin creates an Electoral College windfall due to the winner-take-all rule. For example, Bill Clinton won 70 percent of the electoral vote despite getting only 49 percent of the popular vote in 1996.

Concern about the representation of states has led to various attempts for reform. For instance, a group called National Popular Vote has called for state legislatures to commit their state's electoral votes to the candidate who receives the most popular votes nationwide. These bills would take effect only when enough states passed them to represent a majority of electoral votes—that is, sufficient votes to elect a president. As of 2017, ten states (plus Washington, D.C.) have passed such bills into law and several others have bills pending in the current legislative session. The laws would in effect create a system under which the president wins by a plurality of the popular vote. Support for this proposal is buttressed by public opinion polls, which indicate that Americans would prefer to have the president elected via a simple

---

[9] Most states use a winner-take-all rule in assigning Electoral College votes to candidates: the candidate with the most votes in the state gets all of the state's electoral votes. This is a matter of state law, however, and Maine and Nebraska allocate two votes based on the statewide vote and then allow votes in the congressional districts to determine the remaining electors.

national vote, and by controversies like the ones after the 2000 and 2016 presidential elections, when some questioned the legitimacy of George W. Bush's and Donald Trump's victories, given that they lost the popular vote. The reform is also designed to circumvent the difficulties in actually amending the Constitution to replace the Electoral College with another system. However, at this point in time, National Popular Vote bills seem unlikely to pass in enough states to affect presidential elections in the near future.

Recent Trends in Electoral College Outcomes The Electoral College's role makes it important for presidential candidates to understand the partisan complexion of individual states. Some states tend to produce close presidential elections, while others are predictably Republican or Democratic. Furthermore, some states are more likely to actually swing from one party to the other in different presidential elections. Figure 9.1 shows how states might be categorized, based on the 2000, 2004, 2008, 2012, and 2016 elections, with states that voted the same way every time ("base states") distinguished from those that produced mixed results ("battleground states"). The Democrats start off with a slight advantage in the Electoral College because they dominate large states such as California, New York, New Jersey, and Illinois. In these elections, Democrats have dominated the northeastern, upper Midwest, and Pacific coast states. Republican candidates have dominated in the southern and mountain west states, creating what analysts call the **Republican L**.

The outcomes of recent elections have thus hinged on the results in a handful of states. As shown in Figure 9.1, 37 states (and Washington, D.C.) voted for the same party in the 2000, 2004, 2008, 2012, and 2016 presidential elections, while 13 states did not: Colorado, Florida, Indiana, Iowa, Michigan, Nevada, New Hampshire, New Mexico, North Carolina, Ohio, Pennsylvania, Virginia, and Wisconsin. These **battleground** (or **swing**) **states** combined for 162 electoral votes in 2016, and when they have favored a single candidate, as they did Obama in 2008, they provide that candidate with a comfortable margin of victory. Other states are sometimes considered battleground (or swing) states by campaign experts even though they have consistently (but narrowly) favored one party or the other. Although knowledgeable people may differ with respect to which states are battleground states, the main point is that battleground states are targeted in presidential campaigns.

The decennial U.S. census can change the playing field. As mandated by the Constitution, House seats, and therefore electoral votes, are reapportioned according to changes in state populations. Based on estimates of the 2020 census, in the 2024 election states that were safely Democratic in 2016 are projected to lose three or four seats and those that were safely

FIGURE 9.1 Presidential Election Results, 2000–16

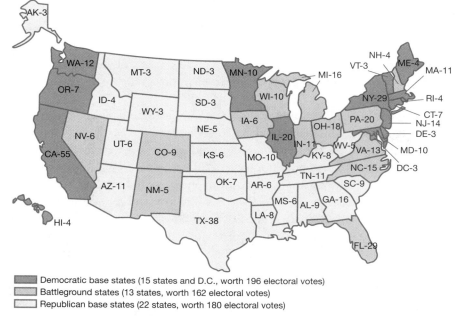

Democratic base states (15 states and D.C., worth 196 electoral votes)
Battleground states (13 states, worth 162 electoral votes)
Republican base states (22 states, worth 180 electoral votes)

Note: 2016 electoral votes presented after state abbreviations.

Republican are projected to gain between two and four seats (Table 9.2). This may not help Democratic candidates in the 2024 election and beyond, but it might not hurt them very much either. In 2012, for example, Barack Obama would have won by a healthy margin even if that election had been conducted with the projected post-2020 allocation of electoral votes.

Strategic Impact of the Electoral College We have emphasized the effects of rules on campaign strategy, and the presidential election is an obvious example. In particular, the Electoral College affects how and where candidates campaign. Presidential campaigns begin with a list of targeted states that are necessary for them to get 270 electoral votes. Whether (and how much) to campaign depends not only on how competitive a state is and whether it is critical to achieving 270 votes but also on the relative cost of campaigning in that state compared with other target states. Thus, candidates concentrate their television ads and in-person visits on the most cost-effective states and media markets on their list.[10]

---

[10] Daron R. Shaw. 2006. *The Race to 270: The Electoral College and the Campaign Strategies of 2000 and 2004.* Chicago: University of Chicago Press.

TABLE 9.2 Projected Electoral Vote Changes Based on the 2020 Census

Safe Democratic States	Battleground States	Safe Republican States
Illinois (–1 or –2)	Colorado (+1)	Alabama (–1)
Minnesota (–1)	Florida (+2)	Arizona (+1)
New York (–1)	Michigan (–1)	Montana (0 or +1)
Oregon (+1)	North Carolina (+1)	Texas (+3 or +4)
Rhode Island (–1)	Ohio (–1)	West Virginia (–1)
	Pennsylvania (–1)	
Overall: –3 or –4	Overall: +1	Overall: +2, +3, or +4

Source: Projections are from Election Data Services and are derived from census estimates. Other states' electoral votes are not expected to change.

In 2016, both the Trump and Clinton campaigns focused on television advertising and visits to states the campaigns determined to be critical to the election outcome. Trump spent 37 percent of his total advertising budget, an estimated $97.4 million, on ads in 10 media markets that his campaign deemed crucial. Clinton spent approximately 43 percent of her total television advertising budget, an estimated $148.1 million, on her top 10 markets (Table 9.3). Their visits were also concentrated on battleground states, with the top five most-visited states receiving nearly 70 percent of all presidential visits (Table 9.4). Furthermore, visits to nonbattleground states were typically to hold fund-raising events.

In 2016, Hillary Clinton and Democratic groups raised and spent more money than Donald Trump and Republican groups. The advantage wasn't as great as it had been for Barack Obama in his campaign versus John McCain in 2008, but it was substantial. Indeed, the data show that while Trump made more personal appearances during the campaign than Clinton, Clinton and the Democratic Party vastly outspent Trump and the Republicans on television advertising. This disadvantage made it imperative for Trump to deploy his resources as strategically as possible. Conversely, Clinton's advantage allowed her to advertise in places normally considered out of reach for Democratic candidates, such as Arizona and even Texas—states that she nevertheless could not swing.

TABLE 9.3 Trump and Clinton TV Ad Airings: Top Eleven Media Markets

Trump and Republican Groups		Clinton and Democratic Groups	
Tampa-St. Petersburg, FL	4,963	Orlando-Daytona Beach, FL	17,710
Orlando-Daytona Beach, FL	4,386	Tampa-St. Petersburg, FL	16,668
Cleveland-Akron, OH	4,027	Las Vegas, NV	14,469
Columbus, OH	3,784	Charlotte, NC	13,155
Denver, CO	3,292	West Palm Beach, FL	11,633
Charlotte, NC	3,282	Cleveland-Akron, OH	10,645
Cincinnati, OH	3,265	Greensboro, NC	10,289
West Palm Beach, FL	3,193	Raleigh-Durham, NC	9,887
Greensboro, NC	3,064	Reno, NV	9,881
Pittsburgh, PA	2,935	Columbus, OH	9,852
Raleigh-Durham, NC	2,892	Philadelphia, PA	9,804

Source: Data are from Kantar Media/CMAG and reflect advertising from June 8, 2016 to October 30, 2016.

Although all presidential campaigns target battleground states, they differ in how ambitious their targeting is. Some campaigns, such as George H. W. Bush's 1988 and Hillary Clinton's 2016 campaigns, play "offense" by targeting a number of states that usually vote for the other party. Other campaigns, such as Bill Clinton's in 1996, play "defense" by looking to solidify states that voted for them last time or that look "safe" in the current election. Still other campaigns, such as Al Gore's in 2000, concentrate on a very small number of highly competitive battleground states in an attempt to create a narrow Electoral College majority—a tactic referred to as "threading the needle." Finally, campaigns can employ a "mixed" strategy—emphasizing defensive campaigning at one stage of the campaign, and then offensive campaigning at another stage. George W. Bush's campaign organization did this in 2000, casting a very broad net early and then narrowing it considerably when data showed progress in some states but not

TABLE 9.4 Trump/Pence and Clinton/Kaine Appearances: The Top Eleven States

Trump/Pence		Clinton/Kaine	
State	**Appearances**	**State**	**Appearances**
Pennsylvania	38	Florida	37
Ohio	38	North Carolina	27
Florida	34	New York	25
North Carolina	30	Pennsylvania	20
New York	17	Ohio	18
New Hampshire	16	Iowa	10
Michigan	15	California	9
Iowa	15	Nevada	8
Virginia	14	New Hampshire	8
Colorado	13	Michigan	7
Nevada	9	Arizona	6
TOTAL	**239**	**TOTAL**	**175**

Notes: Candidate appearances include all events, including fund-raisers, from Sept. 1 to Nov. 6, 2016.

in others.[11] There is some evidence that Donald Trump's campaign pursued a mixed strategy in 2016.

Electoral College strategies are not set in stone, however. Campaigns may adjust these strategies during the campaign itself. By the month before the general election, the campaigns should have enough polling information to abandon some states, add others, or simply narrow the battlefield to those states that are absolutely essential to victory. In 2008, the Obama campaign added Indiana and North Carolina to its list of targets based on late September polling that showed Obama was ahead in those traditionally Republican states. (Obama won both.) In 2000, George W. Bush decided to make a concerted effort to win Tennessee (the home state of his opponent, Al Gore) and West Virginia (which had not voted for a Republican presidential

---

[11] Shaw, *The Race to 270*.

Putting Together an Electoral College Plan

In the 2016 presidential election, Donald Trump won 46.1 percent of the national popular vote to Hillary Clinton's 48.2 percent. More important, based on the statewide tallies Trump won 306 electoral votes to Clinton's 232.[1] Trump's electoral coalition included Republican strongholds, such as Texas, Georgia, and Arizona, as well as traditionally Democratic states, such as Wisconsin and Michigan. These results—and the issues and attitudes that drove them—will fascinate political scientists for years. But for Team Trump, the results of the 2012 election constituted the baseline for drawing up the 2016 battle plan. Presidential campaign strategists, like meteorologists, assume that tomorrow will look a lot like today, with modest changes driven by factors such as the census, the performance of the incumbent president, and the particular candidates. Understanding how those changes influence the relative competitiveness of states compared to the last election is critical to a successful Electoral College plan.

In devising their plan for the 2016 election, the starting point for Trump's team was Mitt Romney's loss to Barack Obama in 2012. Romney won 206 electoral votes, but lost every battleground state with the exception of North Carolina. Trump needed to add another 64 electoral votes to Romney's coalition to win. The most logical starting point was to focus on maintaining the Tar Heel State and adding Iowa, Ohio, and Florida to the Republican column. Not only were these states often battlegrounds during the Bush and Obama elections, but Iowa and Ohio also had large proportions of

less-well-educated white voters, with whom Trump had a particular rapport. The trifecta of Iowa, Ohio, and Florida would contribute 53 of the 64 electoral votes necessary to win the White House, but it would still leave the New York billionaire short. Where would the 11 remaining votes (10 for a tie) come from? Trump strategists began referring to a "3 Plus 1" strategy: Iowa, Ohio, and Florida plus one additional state from a list that included Pennsylvania (20 electoral votes), Michigan (16 electoral votes), Virginia (13 electoral votes), and Wisconsin (10 electoral votes). The "Plus 1" could also become a "Plus 2" to encompass plausible combinations of smaller states, such as Colorado (nine electoral votes), Nevada (six electoral votes), or New Hampshire (four electoral votes).

After several meetings in late August, Kellyanne Conway and other leaders from the Trump campaign began to quietly refer to their broader battleground strategy as the "14-State Plan." They decided to allocate resources—television and digital advertising, as well as candidate and surrogate appearances—into a relatively wide range of states so that they maximized their pathways to 270 electoral votes. The 14 states included obvious battleground states (Florida, New Hampshire, Nevada, North Carolina, and Pennsylvania), as well as states that many thought leaned toward Trump (Iowa and Ohio) and states that many thought leaned toward Clinton (Colorado, Maine, Michigan, Virginia, and Wisconsin). Finally, at the outer edges of Trump's 14-State Plan were the deeply Democratic states of Minnesota and New Mexico, which demonstrated either the vision or the foolhardiness (depending on your perspective) of his expansive view of the electoral map.

Of course, Trump's campaign monitored the movements of Hillary Clinton's campaign,

---

[1] Seven electors ultimately cast their votes for other candidates, leaving the official Electoral College vote at 304 for Trump and 227 for Clinton.

which had its own Electoral College strategy. The Clinton team's initial targeting was loosely based on the "Blue Wall" strategy: this held that the Democratic base consisted of 17 states (plus the District of Columbia) that had gone Democratic in every election since 1992. Clinton's "Blue Wall" states total 222 electoral votes and put her within 48 electoral votes of a 270-vote majority. Adding the Clinton-friendly states of Virginia (13 electoral votes), Colorado (nine electoral votes), and New Mexico (five electoral votes) to this total, the Democrats could count on 249 electoral votes, only 21 shy of victory. But how to get these 21 electoral votes? The Clinton team valued flexibility, and sketched out a "Florida Path" (29 electoral votes), a "Pennsylvania Path" (20 electoral votes plus any other state), and a "North Carolina + Nevada Path" (21 electoral votes). Despite the initial assumption that Michigan was part of the "Blue Wall," Clinton's data analytics chief, Elan Kriegel, modeled the various pathways to 270 in mid-October and concluded that Michigan and Pennsylvania were the most likely "tipping point" states; that is, states that would ultimately prove decisive for the election outcome.

Of course, in the end, Trump was able to execute his "3 Plus 1" strategy for winning the Electoral College. But both he and Clinton followed their plans, allocating personal appearances and advertising dollars in a handful of states as they fought to win the White House.

The targeting strategies of presidential candidates create self-fulfilling prophecies: rules that govern the election process cause campaigns to target most of their resources to the handful of states that they think will prove crucial, such that voters in these states (as predicted!) have decided the most recent presidential elections. Advocates of Electoral College reform argue that this strategy may be neither smart nor fair. Perhaps other states could become competitive if resources were routinely allocated to win over their voters. And might it be that certain states receive disproportionate public policy commitments and advertising revenue because of their status as "battleground states"? In any case, criticism of the candidates or their campaigns for this reality is misplaced: they are simply responding to the rules of the current system.

candidate since 1964) after early October polls revealed competitive contests. (Bush won both.)

Political and Economic Realities

Presidential campaigns are substantially constrained not only by the rules of the elections but also by political reality. In any given election, a campaign is dealt a deck of cards. How the campaign plays the cards is important, but the luck of the draw has a major impact on who wins the hand. Three factors in a presidential election are particularly important: incumbency, war, and the economy. Of these, the economy is usually considered paramount.

Incumbent presidents have natural advantages. They have the advantage of experience, having run a previous presidential campaign. They have the trappings of the office of the presidency, including the pomp and circumstance and an enhanced ability to make news, communicate with the public, and shape the national agenda. They also have an easier road to the party's nomination, with typically no opposition or only token opposition. It is no surprise, then, that two-thirds of incumbent presidents who seek reelection win. Typically, they begin the campaign with a larger lead than non-incumbent candidates and hold on to a larger portion of this lead during the campaign.[12]

Ongoing wars matter in both positive and negative ways. An incumbent president up for reelection at the outset of a war will likely benefit from the public's tendency to rally behind the president in times of crisis. But it has been rare for an election to occur just as a conflict is getting under way. At the same time, it is often thought that presidents will seek to create such a crisis right before the election—sometimes referred to as an "October Surprise." This, too, is rare. Historically, wars have more often had a negative impact on the incumbent president's reelection bid. The number of American military personnel killed in action during war tends to sour voters on the mission, producing more negative evaluations of the president's job performance, and reducing his support at the polls.[13] This was particularly consequential for the Democratic Party in both 1952 and 1968, when Presidents Truman and Johnson were presiding over the wars in Korea and Vietnam, respectively.

The economy wields the most powerful influence on presidential elections. The candidate of the incumbent party, and especially an incumbent president, is much more likely to win if the economy is growing strongly. In recent presidential elections, there has been a powerful relationship between the incumbent party's share of the vote and economic indicators like the growth in average disposable income in the year before the election. The upward sloping line of Figure 9.2 captures the trend: as economic growth increases, so does the incumbent party's share of the vote. Jimmy Carter, who ran for reelection when incomes were shrinking, won only 45 percent of the two-party vote. But his successor, Ronald Reagan, was reelected easily, thanks to the booming economy of 1984. Hillary Clinton received just over 51 percent of the two-party vote share in 2016; almost exactly what one would predict given 2.1 percent growth in personal income during the preceding year.

The powerful impact of the economy creates strategic imperatives for the candidates. Candidates who benefit politically from the state of the economy

---

[12] James E. Campbell. 2000. *The American Campaign: U.S. Presidential Campaigns and the National Vote.* College Station, TX: Texas A&M University Press.

[13] Douglas A. Hibbs, Jr. 2000. "Bread and Peace Voting in U.S. Presidential Elections." *Public Choice* 104, 1/2: 149–80.

FIGURE 9.2 Election Year Income Growth

Incumbent Party's Share of Two-Party Vote

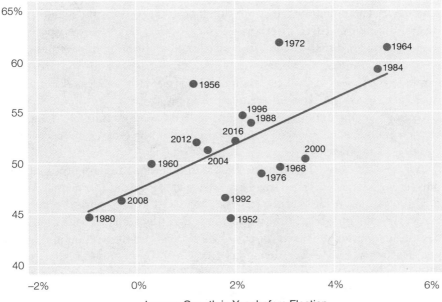

Income Growth in Year before Election

tend to make it the central issue of their campaign. Thus, an incumbent president or incumbent party candidate will emphasize the economy during periods of economic growth. Conversely, the opposition party will emphasize the economy during an economic downturn. Candidates who are not favored by the economy need to change the subject by emphasizing other issues.[14] This dynamic was evident in the 2016 presidential campaign, as Hillary Clinton argued that the economy was "doing well but could be better," while Donald Trump campaigned against an economy that was "failing people like you."

The Fall Campaign

As the campaign gets under way after the conventions, candidates must make a series of strategic decisions within the context of Electoral College math and broader realities. We discuss several important parts of that process: message development, the timing of campaign activity, the candidate debates, and mobilizing supporters to vote.

---

[14] Lynn Vavreck. 2009. *The Message Matters: The Economy and Presidential Campaigns.* Princeton, NJ: Princeton University Press.

Message Development As presidential candidates shift from the primary campaign to the general election campaign, they often refine their message, particularly to address contrasts with their opponent. As we discussed in Chapter 5, campaign messages are designed to appeal to undecided voters or mobilize sympathetic partisans. Typically, campaigns rely on polls and focus groups to discern which issues are salient to the public, which issue positions are most popular, and how issues can be framed to improve the campaign's chances for success. Candidates have their own ideas about political issues, of course, but no serious presidential campaign makes a move without surveying public opinion. Campaigns do not always follow the results of their polls, but they need to know how the public will likely react to the campaign's message.

As candidates decide what issues to emphasize, they are thinking not only about the broader political realities but about any other factor that might advantage or disadvantage them. One factor is the political reputation of their party. In 2016, Hillary Clinton's team decided that she would do best if her message focused on issues directly affecting women and young people, such as education and civil rights. They were confident that Americans would trust their candidate to handle these issues more effectively than Donald Trump. A second factor is the particular positions of "swing voters." As we discussed in Chapter 5, campaigns have an incentive to locate themselves close to the so-called median voter, so that candidates will maximize their appeal to the public. In the United States, this incentive pushes candidates to the center of the political spectrum because many Americans hold fairly centrist positions on political issues.

But calculations about issue agendas and positions are fraught with difficulties. What if a candidate would prefer to ignore an issue that is a top priority of the party's base? What if a candidate's position appeals to a slim majority of voters overall but is unpopular with the base? And what if the popular position contradicts the candidate's previous position? Candidates naturally want to avoid contradicting themselves. In 2004, for example, Democrat John Kerry attempted to explain how in 2003 he had supported a bill allocating $87 billion for the troops fighting the Iraq War, but then ended up opposing the funding bill that ultimately was passed. He famously said, "I actually did vote for the $87 billion before I voted against it." This quote was later used by the Bush campaign to portray Kerry as a flip-flopper.

Presidential campaigns can sometimes finesse the challenges of message development by delivering different messages via different media. In television ads and public speeches, candidates focus on broadly salient issues and popular positions. In direct mail, phone calls, and e-mails, candidates focus on issues and positions popular with their party's base. This is because they can use **narrow-casting**, targeting a smaller audience using these media, without the visibility that mass media entail. In 2008, for example, John McCain used direct mail to Republican households to emphasize his pro-life position on abortion, even as he made no mention of this issue in his television advertising. Similarly, Obama never mentioned race in his television or radio advertising; telephone calls to black households, though, focused on his being the first black major-party candidate.

When asked about his opponent's claim that he "had a plan" to defeat him, the former heavyweight boxing champion Mike Tyson said, "Everyone has a plan until they get hit in the mouth." This statement applies to every presidential campaign ever run. Despite all of the planning that goes into developing a message, life intervenes. Campaigns are particularly sensitive to the harsh judgments of the electorate, and they have up-to-the-minute feedback loops in the form of polls from all of their battleground states. By mid- to late September, they have enough information about public opinion to know whether they need to change course or not.

Front-runners have less need to make adjustments, unless their lead is shrinking. The trailing candidate, however, may decide to do something different. The most common major strategic adjustment is often to "go negative." In 1988, George H. W. Bush was trailing by double digits when his campaign made a strategic decision to attack Michael Dukakis's record as governor of Massachusetts. This was deemed easier and more effective than rebuilding Bush's image. After all, Bush had been in the public eye for over two decades, while Dukakis was a newcomer and had received little scrutiny during the Democratic primaries. In August, Bush strongly criticized Dukakis's record on crime and the environment. By early September, Bush had pulled ahead strongly, and the entire dynamic of the election had changed.

In general, incumbent presidents are much more likely to engage in negative campaigning than their opponents, mostly because they are well-known and people have formed opinions about the president that are difficult to change. It is therefore difficult to "re-set" their image or "move the dial" in a positive manner. Conversely, challengers tend to be new on the scene and often come to the fray with mostly positive images borne of winning the nomination. They are a blank slate; the public views them positively but these positive attitudes are typically shallow and easily changed, especially among members of the opposite party. Bill Clinton, George W. Bush, and Barack Obama were much more negative in their reelection campaigns than their opponents, not because they were dirty campaigners but because they recognized that they could drive up the negative ratings on their challengers much more easily than they could recast their own images in a more positive light.

As noted in Chapter 3, both Donald Trump and Hillary Clinton went negative early and often in 2016. Clinton's negativity is somewhat easy to understand and contextualize. Her favorability ratings dropped substantially during late 2015 and early 2016 because of questions about her use of a personal e-mail server as secretary of state under President Obama. Meanwhile, Donald Trump provided lots of fodder for Clinton by saying controversial things about women (most notably, journalist Megyn Kelly and former beauty pageant queen, Alicia Machado), Latinos (Machado and U.S. District Court Judge Gonzalo Curiel), and war heroes (Arizona Senator John McCain and Captain Humayun Khan). Then, in early October 2016, it was revealed that Trump had made several particularly offensive and outrageous statements about women on the set of *Access Hollywood* in 2005 (see Chapter 8). This presented Clinton with an obvious opportunity to frame the election as a choice between an experienced, steady, and knowledgeable candidate versus a "loose cannon." Still, after the election many criticized her campaign for focusing too much on Trump and neglecting a positive message.

For Trump, the strategic thinking behind the decision to attack is less obvious. Hillary Clinton's negative ratings were already high by the spring of 2016: why not focus on the positive case for change (in general) and Trump (in particular)? The answer seems to be that Trump was less strategic and more instinctual than any other major party presidential candidate in recent memory. When Clinton (or anyone else) hit him, he would hit back harder. The veracity of his claims was often questionable, but it seemed that the tone was more important to voters than the content of his message. In this way, he accomplished something strategically, perhaps without even knowing it—his image as a brash, fight-back, don't-care-what-elites-think-of-me "winner" was reinforced (especially among his supporters) even as his honesty and character ratings declined. It is unclear whether Trump's unique messaging strategy—focusing on negative, personal attacks via Twitter and other social media—is a unique anomaly or a preview of the future of political campaigns.

Timing Although the Electoral College dominates decision making about *where* campaign activity occurs, *when* that activity occurs is a separate question. Some campaigns prefer to stockpile their resources and end the campaign with a massive advertising blitz, presumably when more citizens are paying attention. In 2016, Donald Trump's campaign spent much of its resources in the final 10 days. His campaign strategists assumed that citizens are more affected by the last thing they see or hear, and that the best strategy was to conserve its money for the home stretch. Other campaigns like to spend more of their resources earlier, hoping to define the race at the opening of the campaign. Still others expend resources during such high-profile events as the conventions and debates. For example, George W. Bush increased his television advertising during the 2000 presidential debates, while Al Gore significantly decreased his advertising on those days. Bush wanted to reinforce the themes he articulated during the debates, whereas Gore believed the debates and their attendant news coverage rendered additional campaigning superfluous.

There is no conclusive evidence that any particular timing strategy is best. The relatively large size of convention bumps is consistent with the notion that it is easier to influence the public's preferences early in the campaign when more people have yet to develop strong opinions of the candidates. In the last four presidential elections, polling showed that citizens made up their minds about the candidates quite early in the campaign season, and much earlier than they had in 2000. However, other evidence suggests that many citizens do not pay attention to the campaign until late in the process and that the effects of a television advertisement or candidate visit usually dissipate after only a few days.[15]

Candidate Debates Every fall campaign has its share of important events. But televised candidate debates stand out as the only potentially significant events that a campaign knows are coming. These are the most-watched events of the campaign, and underdog candidates often look to them with the hope that they will reshape a race.

The bipartisan Commission on Presidential Debates was established in 1987 to ensure that debates are a part of every presidential campaign. The commission sponsors the debates, varying their geographic location and format in an effort to engage as much of the public and to provide as much information as possible. After the major-party candidates accept their nominations, the commission produces a debate schedule and the campaigns are obliged either to accept or decline their recommendations. If they decline— or even suggest direct negotiations between the campaigns, as George H. W.

---

[15] Alan S. Gerber, James G. Gimpel, Donald P. Green, and Daron R. Shaw. 2011. "How Large and Long-lasting Are the Persuasive Effects of Televised Campaign Ads? Results from a Randomized Field Experiment." *American Political Science Review* 105, 1: 135–50; Daron R. Shaw and James G. Gimpel. 2012. "What If We Randomized the Governor's Schedule? Evidence on Campaign Appearance Effects from a Texas Field Experiment." *Political Communication* 29, 2: 137–59.

In the first televised presidential debate, in 1960 (left), John F. Kennedy delivered a surprisingly strong performance against the more experienced Richard Nixon. Hillary Clinton was judged by many to have won the presidential debates in 2016 (right), but Donald Trump quickly rebounded.

Bush did in 1992 and George W. Bush did in 2000—they must explain their reasoning to the news media and the public. Any campaign that does not immediately accept the commission's recommendations will surely face the accusation that their candidate is dodging the debates, and so the standard in recent years has been to accept.

During the debates, campaigns have several goals. The first and most obvious goal is to "do no harm"—that is, avoid the sort of gaffe that drives subsequent news media coverage and undermines the campaign's effort to control messaging. To minimize the chances of a major mistake, presidential candidates prepare well in advance, usually for an hour or two each week during the summer and early fall and then all day for three to four days before the debate itself. Campaigns run mock debates for the candidate, using stand-ins for the opposition and staging the aggressive questioning that sometimes occurs. These efforts are videotaped and then critiqued on the basis of style and substance. Campaign staff makes sure the candidates absorb voluminous briefing books on issues; candidates are then quizzed and asked to redress substantive weaknesses. In 2016, Hillary Clinton devoted days to debate preparation and was widely judged to have dominated her three encounters with Donald Trump, who reportedly engaged in only very minimal debate prep.

During the debate, candidates essentially seek to implement a miniature version of their overall campaign strategy. They emphasize issues and appeals that benefit them, avoiding issues on which their opponent has the advantage. Viewers may not tune in to the debate for very long and may not be paying much attention, so candidates want to broadcast the strongest case for their candidacy. This is why candidates often seem to be answering questions besides the ones that were actually asked. When challenged, candidates tend to respond to every charge made by the opposition. They do this because it has been shown that viewers may assume that any charge, no matter how outrageous, is true if not contradicted. However, focusing on the issues while not letting a charge go unanswered is a tricky thing to do. Trump's advisors admitted that he made a mistake by allowing himself to be drawn into a discussion of his personal taxes during the debates; he wanted to respond to a charge made by Clinton, but ended up wasting precious time on a subject with little or no upside.

Candidates also address their answers to the television audience and not to the other candidate or the audience in the hall (unless the debate is held in a town hall format, with actual citizens asking questions). The reaction of those in the auditorium is much less important than the reaction of those watching on television, and especially the news media. Media coverage of the debates is actually more important for influencing public opinion than the debates themselves.[16] For example, immediately after the first debate of the 2000 presidential campaign, Al Gore was judged to have scored a slight victory over George W. Bush, but subsequent media coverage of several questionable claims he made during the debate, as well as mocking coverage of his colorful makeup, turned opinion around. One week after the debate, Bush was judged to have been the winner. The lesson here reinforces the main goal of debates (do no harm) but also emphasizes the need for the campaign to defend its candidate's performance in order to shape news media interpretations.

Despite all the preparation and strategizing that goes into debates, and despite the public's opinions about who did or did not win a particular debate, there are rarely large changes in public support for the candidates after a debate. Simply put, most debates have little impact on the polls and on the election's outcome. Because debates occur relatively late in the campaign, most people have already made up their minds by the time the debates air. People then view debates through partisan lenses: the vast majority of partisans believe that their candidate won. An example from the 2008 race is illustrative: according to a CNN poll conducted after the first 2008 presidential debate, 85 percent of Democrats thought Obama had won and 64 percent of Republicans thought McCain had won. Moreover, whereas during each convention one party dominates the news, debates consist of

---

[16] Richard Johnston, Michael G. Hagen, and Kathleen Hall Jamieson. 2004. *The 2000 Presidential Election and the Foundations of Party Politics.* New York: Cambridge University Press.

opposing messages from both parties. In a sense, these messages tend to cancel each other out, making it difficult for either party's candidate to get much of a boost in the polls from the debate.

Even when debates do seem to move the electorate a point or two, as happened after the first presidential debate of 2016 when Hillary Clinton scored a clear victory in the view of voters and the news media over Donald Trump, the effect is usually ephemeral. Sometimes the debate bounce simply fades, as in 2016, and other times subsequent debates even things out, as in 2004 when George W. Bush rebounded in his second debate with John Kerry or in 2012 when Barack Obama rebounded in his second debate with Mitt Romney.

Mobilizing Citizens At the end of the campaign, the candidate's staff works furiously to reach out to supporters and encourage them to vote. Complicating this effort is the rise of **convenience voting**, a term that includes a variety of ways in which citizens can vote without actually going to their polls on Election Day (Figure 9.3). Methods of convenience voting include early voting, voting by mail, and voting by absentee ballot. In 2016, approximately 30 percent of Americans cast their presidential votes before Election Day. Presidential campaigns must therefore ensure that supporters get absentee ballot applications or information about early voting locations well in advance of the relevant deadlines.

Campaigns have to time their outreach appropriately. In 2016, over 50 percent of Florida voters voted early, so it would have been foolish to

FIGURE 9.3 Convenience Voting across the United States, 1992–2016

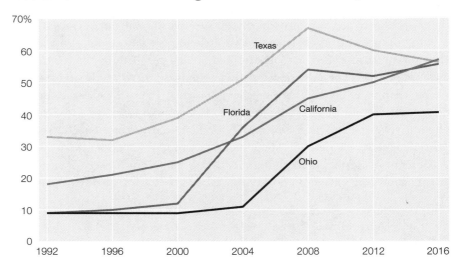

launch an extensive get-out-the-vote operation in late October. Campaigns must also monitor early voting records from the states to see which of their targets have failed to vote (these individuals receive additional outreach) and which have voted (these individuals may be asked to contribute to or volunteer for the campaign). We'll discuss convenience voting in more detail in Chapter 12.

As Election Day draws near, candidates visit the most critical locales and groups. As described earlier, in 2016 Donald Trump held large rallies in Florida, North Carolina, Michigan, and Pennsylvania over the last weekend before the election. Moreover, these rallies tended to be in suburban or even rural areas, where Trump most needed a massive turnout of the party's faithful. In an effort to drive more (and more favorable) coverage, campaigns sometimes try gimmicks to get the news media's attention. In 2000, for example, Al Gore vowed to campaign without sleep for the final 72 hours of the campaign. His midnight and early morning events produced large crowds and extensive media coverage.

Gore's personal efforts and the perceived success of the Democratic Party's last-minute organizational outreach prompted a comparable effort by the Republicans in 2002 and 2004. This "72-hour plan" featured extensive door-to-door campaigning and phone calls in the three days before the election. It was credited with mobilizing the Republican base in key areas. Naturally, Democrats responded in kind. In 2008 and 2012, Obama and the Democrats flooded neighborhoods with volunteer workers and also used e-mail lists and social networking websites to greatly extend the range and scope of their outreach. In 2016, Trump and the Republicans spent fully half of their media budget on digital outreach, targeting likely GOP voters with personalized e-mails, texts, and Instagram and Snapchat messages. Political science scholarship has confirmed that contact with a campaign does raise the likelihood of an individual turning out to vote.

On Election Day, citizens have to be contacted (via phone and e-mail) and mobilized to vote (using buses, cars, walks, and so on). As the day wears on, reports from precincts allow campaign staff to know where they are "light" (getting fewer targeted votes) and "heavy" (getting all or most targeted votes). Campaign attention can be refocused accordingly. Lawyers are also employed to file motions to keep the polls open in places where candidates expect to win and where there might be "irregularities," such as too few ballots or long lines. This has become a standard tactic in recent elections, especially among Democrats, who want to ensure that lower-income and minority precincts are properly equipped. Of course, the 2000 presidential election showed that the election may not end on Election Day. In

2004, 2008, 2012, and 2016, Democratic and Republican campaigns allocated money not only for election night parties for staff and supporters but also for media operations to influence news media reportage of close contests and for legal teams in case of recounts.

Conclusion

American presidential elections illustrate a crucial feature of elections everywhere: they depend a great deal on the rules and realities that candidates confront. For presidential candidates, the rules of the nomination process and the Electoral College strongly affect strategies—the decision to run, the states to target, and so on. Candidates are also constrained by the realities of whether an incumbent is running, whether the country is at war or at peace, and whether the economy is prospering or struggling. As a result, candidates will often find it difficult to persuade the public. Political scientists and campaign professionals have different perspectives on how much these factors constrain campaign effects: academics emphasize the limits to what electioneering can accomplish, while practitioners emphasize the small effects that a good campaign can produce—effects that could decide a close election.

   Do American presidential elections meet democratic ideals? Both the nominations and the general election processes frequently elicit criticisms. For one, some claim that the nominating process produces unrepresentative candidates. Specifically, the complaint is that the sequence of primaries and caucuses allows small and ideologically extreme groups to exercise disproportionate influence by electing their favored candidates in states such as Iowa or New Hampshire. A cursory examination of the historical record casts doubt on this claim. Republicans John McCain, Robert Dole, George W. Bush, George H. W. Bush, and Mitt Romney and Democrats Bill Clinton, Hillary Clinton, Al Gore, John Kerry, and Barack Obama hardly seem out of the mainstream. One could argue that Ronald Reagan was more conservative than the average Republican or that Michael Dukakis was more liberal than the average Democrat, but their records as governors offer many examples of pragmatism. Moreover, this is consistent with political science research demonstrating that while presidential primary electorates tend to be older and slightly more ideological than the party electorate as a whole, they are not necessarily ideologically extreme.[17]

---

[17] John G. Geer. 1988. "Assessing the Representativeness of Electorates in Presidential Primaries." *American Journal of Political Science* 32, 4: 929–45.

A second complaint is that the national conventions are just public relations events. There is no deliberation about the candidates and little meaningful debate about the parties' platforms. This complaint is undoubtedly justified. It is less clear, however, that conventions themselves are simply fluff. Conventions help to unify parties after divisive primaries. They also allow the candidates to present themselves and their campaigns to a wide swath of citizens. The nominees' speeches are often rich in information about their policy agendas and goals.[18] After the conventions, citizens typically express more interest in the campaign.[19] The television networks may claim that the conventions are staged, but it may not be a bad thing to allow the parties to speak directly to the American people once every four years.

A third complaint is similar to the second: debates are uninspired and scripted. This may be true at times, although one would be hard-pressed to see the 2016 presidential debates as "scripted." But even if many presidential debates have been tedious and predictable, they still have positive consequences. After the debates, citizens tend to be more interested in the campaign, feel more favorably about the candidates, and be more knowledgeable about the candidates in some ways.[20] However, the knowledge they've gained is not always about the candidates' positions on issues. Thus, it is quite possible that debates could be reformed to become more informative or empowering. Citizens seem especially impressed by the town hall debate format, suggesting that more direct citizen involvement in the debates would be desirable. There are also those who would like to see more debates, spread out over the entirety of the campaign.

A final set of complaints concerns the Electoral College. As mentioned earlier, perhaps the most prominent of these is that the Electoral College is not as democratic as a direct popular vote and can produce a winner who did not win the popular vote. Other complaints center on the perceived built-in biases of the Electoral College—most notably, that it favors smaller states and leads candidates to focus on battleground states and ignore others. In

---

[18] Marion Just, Tami Buhr, and Ann Crigler. 2000. "Shifting the Balance: Journalist versus Candidate Communication in the 1996 Presidential Campaign," in *Campaign Reform: Insights and Evidence*, eds. Larry M. Bartels and Lynn Vavreck. Ann Arbor: University of Michigan Press.

[19] For data from the 2000 campaign, see Johnston et al., *The 2000 Presidential Election and the Foundations of Party Politics*.

[20] Larry M. Bartels. 2000. "Campaign Quality: Standards for Evaluation, Benchmarks for Reform," in *Campaign Reform: Insights and Evidence*, eds. Larry M. Bartels and Lynn Vavreck; Thomas M. Holbrook. 1999. "Political Learning from Presidential Debates." *Political Behavior* 21, 1: 67–89.

particular, critics fear that this focus on battleground states leads citizens in other states to be less motivated to vote on Election Day.

Defenders of the Electoral College respond that discrepancies between the Electoral College and popular vote are rare. They also note that battleground states are actually quite representative of the country as a whole.[21] Moreover, although voters in battleground states, and particularly those with lower incomes, have relatively higher turnout rates, this is due to a surge in interest and engagement amongst those battleground electorates, and not because those in nonbattleground states are demobilized, as some Electoral College critics maintain.[22]

Would a new presidential election system have comparable or even greater drawbacks? A direct national vote would have the virtue of enhancing legitimacy: a popularly elected president would automatically be able to lay claim to a mandate from the people, and we would never again have to deal with a split between the Electoral College and the national vote. This is the most obvious upside to changing the system, although some might object to an executive with a claim to representing the people beyond that envisioned by the framers. In other respects, the virtues of a direct popular vote are more contentious. For instance, it may not stop candidates from campaigning selectively. In a national election, Democrats would be tempted to spend a lot of time in major urban areas such as New York, Chicago, and Los Angeles, mobilizing reliably Democratic constituents. Republicans, meanwhile, would have incentives to concentrate in suburban areas around cities such as Dallas, Atlanta, and Phoenix. For candidates to campaign nationally, they might also have to work harder and spend more money than they currently do. This would make presidential campaigns even more arduous and expensive than they currently are—and the challenges and costs of campaigns are already criticized as discouraging potential candidates from running and allowing too much money into politics.

Of course, it is entirely possible that the presidential election system could be improved. But alternatives entail trade-offs among competing values, with any improvements creating new and even unforeseen problems. This is not an excuse for inaction; rather, it is a reminder that the words *perfection* and *democracy* rarely appear in the same sentence.

---

[21] Darshan J. Goux and David A. Hopkins. 2008. "The Empirical Implications of Electoral College Reform." *American Politics Research* 36, 6: 857–79.

[22] James G. Gimpel, Karen M. Kaufmann, and Shanna Pearson-Merkowitz. 2007. "Battleground States versus Blackout States: The Behavioral Implications of Modern Presidential Campaigns." *Journal of Politics* 69, 3: 786–97; Keena Lipsitz. 2009. "The Consequences of Battleground and 'Spectator' State Residency for Political Participation." *Political Behavior* 31, 2: 187–209.

KEY TERMS

delegates (p. 252)

caucuses (p. 252)

primary election (p. 253)

viability (p. 255)

front-loading (p. 255)

front-runners (p. 256)

roll-call vote (p. 257)

convention bump/convention bounce (p. 261)

Republican L (p. 265)

battleground (or swing) states (p. 265)

narrow-casting (p. 275)

convenience voting (p. 280)

FOR DISCUSSION

1. Why do states want to move their primary dates up in the election calendar? What is this process called? What is the effect of this process on campaigning?

2. How are the national party conventions different today compared with conventions in the 1950s?

3. How does the Electoral College affect the strategies of presidential campaigns?

4. Why might a presidential candidate want to campaign relatively early in the fall? Why might she want to campaign relatively late?

CHAPTER 10

Congressional Campaigns

As the 2016 campaign got under way, Democrats were the minority party in Congress. After the 2014 midterm election gave Republicans their largest majority in decades, the Democrats found themselves in a major hole in the House. Although winning the House back was a long shot, Democrats had higher hopes in the Senate. They controlled 46 seats after the 2014 election, including the two independent senators who typically voted with the Democrats. It would not take but a handful of victories to get them to a Senate majority.

As the 2016 campaign progressed, the news for Democrats seemed to get better and better. Many political observers thought that the nomination of Donald Trump and the controversies that engulfed his campaign would hurt Republican candidates running downballot, including those in Senate and House races. The only question was, as one headline put it, "How Many Republicans Will Trump Take Down with Him?"[1]

Democrats were particularly hopeful about their chances of winning a Senate seat in Pennsylvania. Democratic presidential candidates had won the state in every election since 1992, including Barack Obama, who beat Mitt Romney by five points in 2012. According to polls taken throughout the fall of the 2016 campaign, Clinton led Trump in the state by about four points. The incumbent Republican senator up for reelection, Pat Toomey, had a reliably conservative voting record that seemed out of step with a state that routinely tilted blue. His Democratic challenger, Katie McGinty, had served in positions under two different governors and had run for governor herself in 2014. Even though she did not win that election, she still seemed to be the kind of experienced candidate who could mount a successful challenge to Toomey. By the end of the campaign, she was leading Toomey in the polls by an average of three points.

---

[1] Alan Greenblatt. 2016. "How Many Republicans Will Trump Take Down with Him?" *Governing*, October 14. www.governing.com/topics/elections/gov-trump-downballot-republicans.html (accessed 10/25/2017).

On Election Day, however, the news for Democrats took a disastrous turn. Not only did Trump win the presidency, defying many forecasts, Democratic gains in both the House and Senate were meager. Compared with their numbers after the 2014 election, Democrats gained only six seats in the House and two seats in the Senate. Pennsylvania was not one of those Senate seats: Toomey edged McGinty by just over one point. This was about the same margin by which Trump ultimately beat Clinton in Pennsylvania, which gave Trump crucial Electoral College votes that helped him overcome Clinton's popular vote victory.

In many ways, the outcomes in Pennsylvania and elsewhere were a surprise. But nevertheless, they illustrate predictable features of how congressional elections work. Congressional elections are increasingly shaped by trends and forces at the national level. Voters who choose a presidential candidate in one party are unlikely to "split" their ticket and vote for a congressional candidate in the other party. For this reason, the forces that propelled Trump to victory in Pennsylvania also helped Toomey. Moreover, incumbent members of Congress like Toomey retain key advantages that help them stave off even experienced challengers like McGinty.

These facts illustrate an important truth about congressional elections: their outcomes are often driven by factors beyond candidates' control. There was little that Democratic Senate candidates like McGinty could do about the fact that shifts in the turnout and preferences of voters at the presidential level had such important effects on congressional races. McGinty could not do much to change the fact that Toomey vastly outspent her—$31 million to $16 million—as incumbents typically outspend challengers. Democrats ultimately found that it was

Core of the Analysis

- The rules governing congressional elections and campaign finance directly shape the strategies of House and Senate candidates.
- The political fortunes of congressional candidates often hinge on factors beyond their control, such as the popularity of the president and the state of the economy.
- Potential congressional candidates are ambitious and are strategic about when they run.
- Voters typically know little about congressional candidates, especially challengers.
- Incumbents have substantial advantages over challengers in congressional races.

In 2016, Pennsylvania Senator Pat Toomey, a Republican, won a narrow victory over Democrat Katie McGinty as Democrats struggled to make substantial gains in the U.S. Congress.

difficult to knock off many other Republican incumbents. Altogether, 20 of the 22 Republican incumbents who ran for reelection in 2016 won.

In this chapter, we explore the nature and effects of congressional campaigns. As with presidential campaigns, we find that the impact of congressional campaigns depends on the particular rules governing the elections. Constitutional provisions and campaign finance law are especially important. We also find that incumbents have a substantial advantage over challengers in most congressional races. Consequently, challengers typically need fortuitous circumstances and strong campaigns to beat incumbents. Recent elections illustrate this point: in 2010, for example, an unusually large number of House incumbents were defeated, owing to voter frustration with the economy and President Obama. These conditions made it easier for the minority party to recruit and fund challenger candidates. At the same time, even in 2010, about 85 percent of incumbents who ran won reelection, signaling the advantages of incumbency even in potentially difficult conditions. This raises an important question: are congressional elections competitive enough to meet the standards we might want for a democracy?

Rules, Reality, and Who Runs for Congress

If you decide to run for Congress, few legal obstacles stand in your way. As we discussed in Chapter 2, the constitutional requirements entail only a minimum age, U.S. citizenship for a number of years, and residency in the state that you want to represent. If you satisfy these requirements and meet state requirements for having your name appear on the ballot, such as paying a filing fee or collecting a certain number of signatures, you can run for Congress. Because the bar for running is so low, one might assume that people from all walks of life can and do run for office. If this were the case, Congress would be representative of the electorate in terms of demographics, such as age, income, race, and gender. However, both those who run and those who win are quite unrepresentative of the broader electorate.

Most individuals who run for office are ambitious and strategic. Politicians are rarely content to hold one job for long and are always looking for opportunities to advance. Congressional candidates have usually held a lower political office that has provided them with experience and connections that are helpful to their campaign. Serious candidates will also enter a race only when their prospects of winning are good. If a candidate runs and loses, then the connections and resources that they once enjoyed may dry up.

The person with the best odds of winning an election is the **incumbent**, or the person who already occupies the office. Figure 10.1 shows the percentage of House and Senate incumbents seeking reelection who then won. From 1946 to 2016, the average percentage of House incumbents running who were reelected was 92 percent, while the average for Senate incumbents was 80 percent. Even in relatively challenging years for incumbents, such as 2010, they are much more likely to be reelected than defeated.

Because the odds of their winning are so high, only extraordinary circumstances such as poor health will keep incumbents from running for reelection. Incumbents may also step down because of scandal. Sixty-six members of the House decided to retire after the 1992 House banking scandal, in which many representatives had written checks from their House bank accounts without the funds to cover those checks.

House incumbents may also decide to retire when their districts change after redistricting and they must court new constituents. Districts can be drawn to protect incumbents of both parties, but partisan redistricting can endanger incumbents in the party that does not get to draw the new district boundaries. In Chapter 2, we described an unusual mid-decade redistricting undertaken by Texas Republicans in 2003. Their plan targeted 10

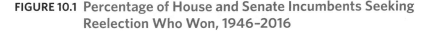

FIGURE 10.1 Percentage of House and Senate Incumbents Seeking Reelection Who Won, 1946–2016

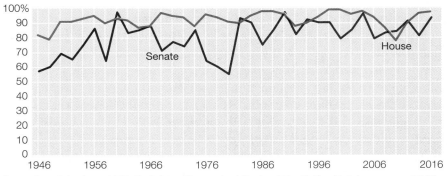

Source: Gary C. Jacobson. 2008. *The Politics of Congressional Elections* (7th ed.). New York: Longman, pp. 28–29. Additional data for 2008–16 collected by the authors.

Democratic incumbents, most of whom faced the prospect of competing in the 2004 election in substantially changed districts.[2] Although many of these incumbents decided to run in their new districts and lost, one incumbent—Congressman Jim Turner, a Democrat who had served Texas's 2nd District for six years—saw the writing on the wall. Republican state legislators had moved most of Turner's former district into the 8th District, leaving him in the solidly conservative 6th District, which was represented by a 10-term Republican incumbent, Joe Barton. As a result, Turner decided to retire rather than run for reelection in 2004.

In addition, House and Senate incumbents may also retire if they feel that the country is experiencing a wave of anti-incumbent sentiment or a wave of sentiment that favors the opposing party. During the 2015–16 election cycle, there were more Republican than Democratic retirements in the House of Representatives, perhaps because the presidential election climate was initially seen as unfavorable to Republicans.

When incumbents decide to retire, their decision creates an **open seat**, allowing for a contest between nonincumbents. Open seats are significant because they attract **quality challengers**, candidates with the experience and backing necessary to run a competitive campaign and who recognize that their chances of winning are higher with the incumbent out of the picture. In contrast, **political amateurs** are candidates who have no political

---

[2] Steve Bickerstaff. 2007. *Lines in the Sand: Congressional Redistricting in Texas and the Downfall of Tom DeLay.* Austin: University of Texas Press.

experience and are less likely to win an election. Quality challengers are strategic candidates, basing their decision to run on whether the incumbent is running or is vulnerable because of a scandal or a national political tide. Quality challengers also assess the incumbent's ability to attract votes and money. For example, if an incumbent has been winning by smaller margins or is struggling to raise money, potential challengers may assume that the incumbent is vulnerable.

Challengers must consider whether they will be supported by their own party. The clearest indication of the party's support is whether the party has recruited a person to run. The "**Hill committees**"—the National Republican Senatorial Committee (NRSC), Democratic Senatorial Campaign Committee (DSCC), National Republican Congressional Committee (NRCC), and Democratic Congressional Campaign Committee (DCCC)—encourage prospective candidates throughout the country to run for office. Much like scouts in sports, the parties are always looking for leaders who might make successful candidates for office. These individuals are courted by party leaders and sent to workshops to learn how to run campaigns. They may also be provided with lists of potential contributors. Without such support, an ambitious and strategic individual might make the rational calculation that it is better to keep her current job than to run for Congress.

Because winning a congressional election requires resources and connections, certain types of individuals are more likely to run. On average, those who choose to run are more educated and wealthier than most Americans. They are also overwhelmingly white and male. Quality challengers tend to work in business, the law, or politics, with large networks that can be tapped for campaign resources. Thus, members of Congress are unrepresentative of the nation in terms of their education, wealth, race, and gender because the people who run for office are unrepresentative of the nation.

Campaign Organization and Funding

Once candidates have decided to run for Congress, they need to put together a campaign staff. Because campaigns in the United States are candidate-centered, candidates, rather than parties, are almost entirely responsible for raising money and putting together a campaign organization. This is true even if a party has recruited the candidate. The party might provide the candidate with a list of political consultants who have worked with other

What It Takes to Get Women to Run

The underrepresentation of women in Congress is a chronic feature of American politics. After the 2016 elections, only 19 percent of U.S. House members were women. Only 21 percent of U.S. senators were women. And although women's representation in Congress has increased over time, the trend is very slow. Why?

The most straightforward answer—that the women who run for office are more likely than men to lose—is not actually true. Indeed, women who run are often very strong candidates who mount professionalized campaigns. Women in congressional elections are not clearly penalized by either the media or voters for their gender. Systematic analysis of media coverage in the 2010 and 2014 House elections did not find that women were covered more unfavorably than men.[1] Similarly, recent analysis of voter behavior identifies some differences in what voters think of male and female candidates—including some perceptions that fit with traditional gender stereotypes—but voters are much more likely to rely on party than gender when choosing whom to vote for.[2]

Instead, the bigger problem is that women are not running for office in the first place.[3] Surveys of men and women in the professions that feed into politics, like business, education, and law, find that women are less likely than men to express political ambition. Women report more trepidation about aspects of campaigning like fund-raising and negative attacks. (High-profile attacks on female candidates like Hillary Clinton and Sarah Palin only exacerbate women's concerns.) Women also report that they receive less encouragement to run from political leaders and other people. And these patterns are visible even among male and female college students, suggesting that gender gaps in political ambition emerge relatively early in life.[4] This makes it less likely that young women will take the early steps, such as getting involved in student politics or running for local offices, that can make a later run for Congress more successful.

Complicating things further is that women still take on far more household and childcare responsibilities than men do. Although this does not appear correlated with whether women express political ambition, it may affect their decision to run. One study has found that state legislative districts far from the state capital are less likely to have female representatives or candidates than districts closer to the state capital.[5] This fact, and some other evidence, suggests that women may be more reluctant to run when serving in office would entail a long commute from their life and family at home.

Thus, the problem of women's underrepresentation is not easily solved. The most obvious step, however, is for political parties and other groups to work harder to identify and encourage promising women to run. Putting more women in office requires putting more women in the pipeline. Not every new female candidate will win, but their presence on the ballot can help change women's perceptions about their potential to hold elective office.

[1] Danny Hayes and Jennifer L. Lawless. 2016. *Women on the Run: Gender, Media, and Political Campaigns in a Polarized Era.* New York: Cambridge University Press.
[2] Kathleen Dolan. 2014. *When Does Gender Matter? Women Candidates and Gender Stereotypes in American Elections.* New York: Oxford University Press.
[3] Jennifer L. Lawless and Richard L. Fox. 2010. *It Still Takes a Candidate: Why Women Don't Run for Office.* New York: Cambridge University Press.
[4] Jennifer L. Lawless and Richard L. Fox. 2015. *Running from Office: Why Young Americans Are Turned Off to Politics.* New York: Oxford University Press.
[5] Rachel Silbermann. 2015. "Gender Roles, Work-Life Balance, and Running for Office." *Quarterly Journal of Political Science* 10, 2: 123–53.

party candidates, but the candidate still must choose consultants that she feels will best help her win. And many candidates are left entirely to their own devices. They have to piece together a campaign staff as best they can.

Congressional campaign organizations range widely from bare-bones operations that are run by unpaid volunteers to big organizations that are run by paid professional consultants. Amateurs with no prior political experience, and thus fewer contacts and resources, are more likely to have the former, while incumbents often have the latter. A well-funded congressional campaign typically has a campaign manager, who oversees the day-to-day operations of the campaign and helps develop strategy. There may be a separate campaign strategist, as well as staff to deal with press relations, issue and opposition research, fund-raising, accounting, and grassroots organizing. The best-funded candidates, who include many House and Senate incumbents, may also hire consultants to conduct polls, develop radio and television advertisements, create direct-mail pieces, and operate phone banks. An example of a campaign at this end of the spectrum was Hillary Clinton's 2006 Senate reelection bid in New York, in which she spent nearly $41 million despite having only token opposition. In addition to the tens of thousands of dollars paid each month to consultants, her campaign spent $27,000 on valet parking, $160,000 on private jet travel, and almost $750,000—more than the cost of most House campaigns—on catering and entertainment.[3]

The size and shape of congressional campaign organizations depend almost entirely on how much money they can raise. In 2016, the average House incumbent raised $1.6 million, while the average House challenger raised $232,000; the average Senate incumbent raised $13 million, while the average Senate challenger raised $1.6 million.[4] Congressional candidates differ greatly in how much they raise and spend, however. For instance, in 2016, incumbent senator Mike Lee (R-Utah) easily won reelection after spending just under $6 million. In contrast, Patrick Murphy, the Democratic Senate candidate in Florida, lost against incumbent Marco Rubio despite spending $19 million.[5]

---

[3] Anne E. Kornblut and Jeff Zeleny. 2006. "Clinton Won Easily, but Bankroll Shows the Toll." *New York Times*, November 21. www.nytimes.com/2006/11/21/us/politics/21donate .html (accessed 1/13/2015).

[4] Center for Responsive Politics. 2017. "Incumbent Advantage." www.opensecrets.org /overview/incumbs.php (accessed 10/25/2017).

[5] Center for Responsive Politics. 2017. "Who's Raised the Least." www.opensecrets.org /overview/topraise.php?display=A&memb=S&sort=A&view=btmraise (accessed 10/25/2017).

The funding sources for congressional candidates are different from those for presidential candidates. First, unlike presidential candidates, congressional candidates are not eligible for public financing (although, as we discussed in Chapter 4, few presidential candidates now take public funding). Congressional candidates must raise money from individuals and political action committees (PACs). Compared with presidential candidates, congressional candidates rely more on PAC contributions and less on individual contributions. Figure 10.2 shows that House candidates in 2016 raised 52 percent of their funds from individual contributions and 39 percent of their funds from PACs. The comparable figures for Senate candidates were 68 percent and 16 percent, respectively. In contrast, Clinton and Trump raised virtually nothing from PACs—0.22 percent of their funding, which is too small to be visible in Figure 10.2—relying mainly on individual contributions and joint fund-raising committees (labeled "Other" in the Presidential Candidates pie chart). PACs are limited to a contribution of $5,000 per candidate for each election cycle, making total PAC contributions a drop in the bucket for a presidential campaign but a more significant amount for congressional candidates.

Despite these differences, congressional candidates, like presidential candidates, raise a majority of their funds from individuals. But these individual contributions do not necessarily come from the candidates' districts or states, especially in competitive races. For example, House candidates in 2004 received an average of two-thirds of their individual contributions from nonresidents.[6] Citizens who give to out-of-district (or out-of-state) candidates appear to be chiefly motivated by partisanship, seeking to increase their party's share of congressional seats.

Beyond individual and PAC contributions, House and Senate candidates sometimes self-finance most or part of their campaigns and rely on spending by outside groups that will campaign on their behalf, such as the super PACs and 501(c)4s discussed in Chapter 4. In 2016, 21 House and Senate candidates wrote themselves checks of $1,000,000.[7] Self-financed candidates do not always win, but they can give their opponents a run for their money. In 2016, outside groups unaffiliated with the parties spent $682 million in House and Senate races combined. Their spending amounted to approximately 40 percent of the amount that all House and

---

[6] James G. Gimpel, Frances E. Lee, and Shanna Pearson-Merkowitz. 2008. "The Check Is in the Mail: Interdistrict Funding Flows in Congressional Elections." *American Journal of Political Science* 52, 2: 373–94.

[7] Center for Responsive Politics. 2017. "Self-Funding Candidates." www.opensecrets.org /overview/topself.php?cycle=2016 (accessed 10/25/2017).

FIGURE 10.2 Comparison of House, Senate, and Presidential Candidate Funding Sources in 2016

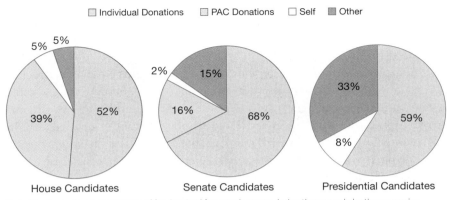

Note: Pie charts depict percentage of funds raised from each source during the general election campaign.
Source: Campaign Finance Institute (http://www.cfinst.org/pdf/vital/VitalStats_t8.pdf); Center for Responsive Politics (www.opensecrets.org/pres16/candidate?id=N00000019 and www.opensecrets.org/pres16/candidate?id=N00023864).

Senate candidates spent on the election.[8] Like candidates, outside groups are strategic, which means they target races where their money is likely to make a difference. For example, with control of the Senate at stake in 2016, outside groups focused their spending on the closest races, spending $104 million alone in the Pennsylvania Senate race discussed in the chapter opener.[9]

The Nomination Process

Like all candidates who run for a partisan office in the United States, congressional candidates must first compete for their party's nomination in a primary election. In the United States, it is not uncommon for congressional primaries to be uncontested. Such primaries usually feature a popular incumbent, whose seniority, power, and connections discourage would-be

---

[8] Center for Responsive Politics. 2017. "2016 Outside Spending, by Race." www.opensecrets.org/outsidespending/summ.php?cycle=2016&disp=R&pty=N&type=A (accessed 10/25/2017); Center for Responsive Politics. 2017. "Election Overview." www.opensecrets.org/overview/index.php?display=T&type=A&cycle=2016 (accessed 10/25/2017).

[9] Center for Responsive Politics. 2017. "2016 Outside Spending, by Super PAC." www.opensecrets.org/outsidespending/summ.php?cycle=2016&disp=R&pty=N&type=S (accessed 11/18/2017).

challengers. When incumbents do face primary challenges, they usually win for the same reasons. Thus, recent high-profile challenges to congressional incumbents do not suggest a broader trend. There has not been an increase in the number of incumbents drawing challengers or in the number of successful primary challenges. In 2014 and 2016, for example, no incumbent senator lost his or her primary.[10]

Open-seat primaries occur when a party's incumbent has retired or when the party that is out of power must choose a candidate to challenge the incumbent in the general election. These are typically the most competitive primaries and the most likely to attract quality challengers. In such contests, the party normally remains neutral and lets the voters decide who the party should back in the general election. From time to time, however, party leaders back an open-seat primary candidate who they believe has a good chance of winning the general election. In 2014, Democrats saw an opportunity in Virginia's 10th U.S. House District, where there was an open seat after the retirement of Republican Frank Wolf. So Democrats worked to "clear the field" for Fairfax County supervisor John Foust, leading another Democratic candidate to suspend his campaign.[11] Party leaders likely wanted to save Foust from a bruising primary so that he would have sufficient standing and resources to run in the general election. Regardless, Foust lost to Republican Barbara Comstock. This example is more the exception than the rule, however. Parties rarely get involved in congressional primaries because they prefer to save their limited resources for the general election.

Just like candidates in presidential primaries, candidates in House and Senate primaries must compete for votes from an electorate that is more ideological than the electorate in a general election. Thus, they must appeal to party stalwarts without jeopardizing their ability to attract the votes of moderates in the general election. One way to do this is to emphasize issues in the primary election that are ideological in nature—issues on which they can adopt positions that might be described as "modestly extreme," positions that appeal to ideological primary voters but are not as extreme as the views

---

[10] Robert G. Boatright. 2013. *Getting Primaried: The Changing Politics of Congressional Primary Challenges.* Ann Arbor: University of Michigan Press. See also Robert Boatright. 2014. "Who Won the Republican Civil War?" *Monkey Cage*, August 13. www.washingtonpost.com/blogs/monkey-cage/wp/2014/08/13/who-won-the-republican-civil-war/ (accessed 2/13/2015).

[11] Emily Cahn. 2014. "Democrats Clear Primary Field in Competitive Virginia House Race." *Roll Call*, March 14. http://atr.rollcall.com/democrats-clear-primary-fieldr-competitive-virginia-house-race/ (accessed 2/13/2015).

Todd Akin's comments about rape and pregnancy incited widespread outrage during his 2012 campaign for the U.S. Senate. Here, protesters at one of his campaign stops hold signs condemning Akin's remarks.

of some primary voters.[12] Then, in the general election, candidates move toward the center by emphasizing nonideological issues, such as personal character. They must be careful, however, not to change their agendas or positions too dramatically or else they might be criticized for "flip-flopping."

The fate of Todd Akin, the Republican Senate candidate in Missouri in 2012, illustrates the potential difficulty of shifting from a primary to a general election constituency. As we mentioned in Chapter 8, Akin brought on the ire of Democrats and even some Republican leaders when, shortly after defeating more moderate GOP candidates in the primary, he explained in an interview that he opposed allowing women who have become pregnant as the result of rape to have an abortion because such pregnancies are "really rare." They are rare, he explained, because "if it's a legitimate rape, the female body has ways to try to shut that whole thing down."[13] Although Akin apologized for his comments and claimed he "misspoke," he forfeited his lead in the

---

[12] Barry C. Burden. 2004. "Candidate Positioning in US Congressional Elections." *British Journal of Political Science* 34, 2: 211–27; Samuel Merrill III and Bernard Grofman. 1999. *A Unified Theory of Voting: Directional and Proximity Spatial Models.* New York: Cambridge University Press.

[13] John Eligon and Michael Schwirtz. 2012. "Senate Candidate Provokes Ire with 'Legitimate Rape' Comment." *New York Times*, August 19. www.nytimes.com/2012/08/20/us/politics /todd-akin-provokes-ire-with-legitimate-rape-comment.html (accessed 2/13/2015).

polls and ultimately lost to Democratic senator Claire McCaskill, who was one of the most vulnerable Democratic incumbents in 2012.

On the other hand, Republican Barbara Comstock, mentioned above, provides a good example of how a candidate may try to appeal to primary voters but not necessarily turn off general election voters. The 10th District is located in northern Virginia and tilts only slightly Republican, which makes appealing to moderate voters more important. Comstock's position on reproductive rights therefore reflects a balancing act. She takes a more conservative, but not the most conservative, position on abortion: allowing it only in cases of rape, incest, and danger to the mother's life. At the same time, she takes a more liberal position on birth control, supporting the sale of contraceptives over the counter. Similarly, after the *Access Hollywood* tape was released in October of the 2016 election (see Chapter 8), Comstock distanced herself from Donald Trump and condemned his behavior as "disgusting, vile, and disqualifying." She ended up winning the seat again by six points.

The General Election

Once candidates have secured their party's nomination, they must quickly turn their attention to the general election campaign. Some candidates who were uncontested in the primary or did not have any serious challengers may even start their general election campaign earlier if they have the resources to do so. Incumbents typically have these resources, so challengers face a particularly difficult path: while they are battling for the nomination, the incumbent has already started appealing to the general-election electorate.

Voters often know far less about House and Senate candidates than they do about candidates for president. According to a 2002 study, after an uncompetitive House election featuring an incumbent and a challenger, less than 15 percent of the people living in the district could remember the names of both candidates. After a competitive House election, approximately 40 percent of the electorate could remember the candidates' names. Citizens are typically more familiar with Senate candidates. Approximately one-third could remember their names after a noncompetitive election, while two-thirds could remember the names of both candidates after a competitive open-seat race.[14] These numbers suggest that many citizens vote for congressional candidates without knowing their names, let alone anything

---

[14] Paul S. Herrnson. 2004. *Congressional Elections: Campaigning at Home and in Washington*, 4th ed. Washington, DC: CQ Press, p. 190.

substantive about them. Congressional candidates and their political consultants are well aware of voters' lack of knowledge. Challengers, in particular, are well aware that people rarely vote for someone they do not know. Thus, many congressional candidates spend their entire campaign simply introducing themselves to voters. They do this by communicating with potential supporters and working to ensure that supporters turn out on Election Day.

Developing a Campaign Message

As we discussed in Chapter 5, a key to winning an election is knowing the electorate. Candidates need to know who their supporters are and where they live. They also need to know who the persuadable voters are in their district or state and how to get their message to these voters.

The next step is to develop a message that appeals to the target audience, which requires understanding the issues that are important to the potential voters in the district or state. Candidates acquire this knowledge in several ways. Congressional candidates are often community leaders or have prior political experience that has given them knowledge of the state or district in which they are running. They may be business leaders who know the state's economy, or state legislators who have passed bills designed to address problems in the state. Candidates also have extensive social and professional networks that can provide a sense of the issues affecting their communities. Furthermore, they have help in developing their message from the organizations whose endorsements they seek. These groups not only help candidates contact their members but also provide the candidate with information about their members' concerns. Finally, if candidates have enough money they can also hire a pollster to survey voters. If the race is competitive, one of the congressional campaign committees or state party organizations may conduct polls and share the results with their party's candidates.

Unlike presidential candidates, whose messages are focused almost exclusively on national politics, congressional candidates face the challenge of crafting a campaign message that addresses both local and national issues. The conventional wisdom is that local issues should predominate—a sentiment best captured by former speaker of the House Thomas "Tip" O'Neill's famous assertion that "All politics is local." Yet, when local issues dominate a campaign, both the Democratic and Republican candidates may end up taking very similar positions. For instance, candidates running to represent a rural House district whose economy depends on farming may be united in their support of federal agricultural subsidies. When national issues dominate, candidates may have similar agendas—such as the need for jobs in a weak economy—but may take quite different positions. For example, to create jobs,

Republican candidates may emphasize the need to cut taxes on businesses to encourage them to hire workers, while Democrats may emphasize the need for government spending to stimulate job growth. The positions of individual congressional candidates will often be similar to the positions of their respective national parties. Studies of congressional campaign messages have found that national issues are more prevalent than local issues. As a result, candidates often take different positions, a strategy that contrasts with the assumptions of the median voter theorem discussed in Chapter 5.[15]

Communicating the Message

Once candidates have determined what they want to say to voters, they communicate that message in several ways. Like presidential candidates, congressional candidates rely on direct mail as well as newspaper, radio, and television advertisements, but the extent to which they rely on each of these is different. For example, although presidential campaigns typically spend more than half of their budget on television advertising, the typical Senate campaign spends one-third of its budget, and the average House campaign spends just 20 percent of its budget, on television ads.[16] House candidates rely the least on television ads because they are expensive, and they typically have less money to spend per voter than Senate candidates. In fact, many House races feature no television advertising whatsoever.

Another problem for House and Senate candidates is that television advertisements are purchased in predefined media markets. Large media markets often serve more than one congressional district, which means that a House candidate who purchases television ads may be paying for people in neighboring districts to see those ads. Media markets do not necessarily respect state borders either. If a state has a competitive Senate race, voters in neighboring states that share media markets with the competitive state may see ads in races in which they cannot vote. For example, New Jersey has no television media markets of its own. Its northern half lies in the New York City market and its southern half in the Philadelphia market. Thus, congressional candidates in New Jersey must purchase airtime in one or both of these extremely expensive media markets if they want to run television ads. For these reasons, congressional candidates may rely more on radio and newspaper advertisements, billboards, and yard signs.

---

[15] Stephen Ansolabehere, James M. Snyder, Jr., and Charles Stewart III. 2001. "Candidate Positioning in U.S. House Elections." *American Journal of Political Science* 45, 1: 136–59; Burden, "Candidate Positioning in US Congressional Elections."

[16] Herrnson, *Congressional Elections*, p. 85.

Congressional candidates, especially House candidates, can also rely more than presidential candidates on communicating with citizens directly. Presidential candidates have no personal contact with most Americans; the population is simply too large. Citizens "experience" presidential candidates mainly as talking heads on their television screens. In contrast, House candidates can have direct, unmediated contact with a larger portion of their constituency. They attend parades, sporting events, or any type of event where large numbers of potential voters gather. This kind of contact is intended to increase name recognition and to make a favorable impression, not to convey substantive information about policy agendas or proposals.

House challengers rely heavily on personal contacts to get their name out. It is not unheard of for House challengers to literally walk across their district to meet voters and generate publicity. For example, in preparation for the 2018 election Ian Golden, a Democratic candidate for New York's 23rd Congressional District, embarked on a walking tour as part of his primary campaign.[17] This was no small feat: the district is 450 miles long. Though such tactics might seem gimmicky, they are often one of the few means by which an underfunded challenger can generate name recognition. Apart from House candidates running in the seven states that have only one representative, meaning that the state and congressional district have identical boundaries, Senate candidates usually have a much larger territory to cover than House candidates. As a result, it is often more practical for senators to rely on television and radio than on personal contact with voters.

Congressional candidates also differ from presidential candidates in how much they depend on earned media. **Earned media (or free media)** is the publicity that candidates get by engaging in promotional activities. For example, candidates frequently hold press conferences or give speeches, hoping that these events will be covered by the local media. Candidate appearances, such as walking tours, have the same goal. Congressional candidates sometimes use gimmicks to attract attention. For example, in 2016, Greg Evers, a Republican candidate for Florida's 1st Congressional District, started a contest to give away an assault rifle in the wake of a mass shooting at an Orlando nightclub in June 2015.[18] (Evers eventually came in second in the primary.)

---

[17] Cody Carlson. 2017. "Local Congressional Candidate Walking across NY 23rd District." *WENY*, September 27. www.weny.com/story/36462799/local-congressional-candidate -walking-across-ny-23rd-district (accessed 10/25/2017).

[18] Associated Press. 2016. "Florida Congressional Candidate Greg Evers to Give Away AR-15." *NBC News*, June 21. www.nbcnews.com/news/us-news/florida-congressional -candidate-greg-evers-give-away-ar-15-n596211 (accessed 11/11/2017).

Mobilizing Voters

Congressional candidates use the same basic tactics that presidential candidates do to get their supporters to the polls on Election Day, including mailers, phone calls, and neighborhood canvassing. The main differences are the size and sophistication of their mobilization drives. Presidential candidates have vast resources at their disposal, which enable them to develop extensive field organizations. In presidential election years, congressional candidates benefit from the presidential campaigns' mobilization efforts because most voters who go to the polls to cast a ballot for the president usually cast a ballot for candidates in other races at the same time. In midterm election years, however, congressional candidates must turn out voters themselves, assisted by other organizations, including state and national party committees and interest groups. Despite those efforts, congressional campaigns rarely generate the kind of interest that presidential campaigns do. As a result, voter turnout in midterm elections is lower than in presidential elections.

The Role of the Parties and the Hill Committees

Political parties can play a significant role in congressional campaigns. The Hill committees defined earlier in this chapter focus exclusively on electing party members to Congress. They accomplish this by targeting the handful of House and Senate races that are closely contested in each election cycle and ignoring the rest. Their first priority is to protect incumbents who are in jeopardy of losing their seats. For example, the Democratic Congressional Campaign Committee has an effort called "Frontline" that seeks to protect their most vulnerable incumbents. Their second priority is to defend the seats of members of the party who are leaving office. Finally, when national political and economic conditions favor one party, that party may also target seats that have been controlled by the other party. In 2014, for example, the National Republican Congressional Committee launched a "Drive to 245" campaign, which reflected their goal of picking up enough seats to control 245 seats in the House (they eventually won 247).

The Hill committees do not rigidly adhere to campaign plans. In response to campaign events, they may redirect resources to crucial races. They typically begin the election season with a longer list of competitive races and whittle that number down as the campaigns evolve and it becomes clear which ones will be the most fiercely contested. They may decide some races are not worth their involvement. In the races where they are involved, the committees can make direct contributions, coordinate expenditures with the candidate, or make independent expenditures without a candidate's involvement. **Coordinated expenditures** involve collaboration between the committee and the candidate or a representative of the candidate. They are usually spent on services that are given to a candidate directly or performed by a political consultant on behalf of a candidate. The services might include the purchase of airtime on television and radio, direct mail, polling, or the organization of fund-raising events. Campaign finance law treats coordinated expenditures the same way it treats direct contributions to a candidate, which means they are subject to strict limits.

As a result, the Hill committees usually rely on **independent expenditures** to fund their campaign efforts. As discussed Chapter 4, these expenditures cannot be limited but must be made without consulting or coordinating with a candidate. This allows the committees to spend large sums of money on a race. For example, in 2016 both the DCCC and the NRCC spent heavily in Colorado's 6th District. The NRCC spent $4.8 million to support its candidate, Rep. Mike Coffman, while the DCCC spent $3.2 million to help elect the Democratic challenger Morgan Carroll. To put this amount of money in perspective, consider that Coffman himself raised $3.5 million for his bid, while Carroll raised $3.1 million for hers. Thus, the DCCC and the NRCC collectively spent more than the candidates did in this race. (Coffman eventually won by six points.)

While the Hill committees tend to help candidates purchase campaign communications and provide technical expertise, state and local party committees more often help candidates with grassroots activities, such as voter registration and mobilization drives designed to get voters to the polls. In addition, they organize phone banks and neighborhood canvassing campaigns to knock on doors and provide voters with campaign literature.

The Incumbency Advantage

A defining feature of congressional elections is the electoral advantage that incumbents enjoy over challengers. The **incumbency advantage** is defined as the vote share earned by an incumbent compared with what a nonincumbent would have earned if he or she had run.

The incumbency advantage can be attributed to several factors. For one thing, incumbents have greater political experience. They also have an easier time soliciting campaign donations than challengers do. Contributors like to back winners and know that challengers lose most elections. Only challengers in competitive races or candidates in open-seat races can typically raise anything close to what incumbents raise. Similarly, parties and interest groups funnel resources to candidates who have a greater chance of winning.

As a result, in 2016 the average House incumbent raised about seven times what the average challenger raised. The average Senate incumbent raised about eight times as much as the average challenger.[19] Quality challengers fare better than the average challenger, but they typically cannot match incumbents dollar for dollar.

Another important source of incumbents' advantage is their familiarity to voters. For example, in the 115th Congress (2017–18), the average House member had served nine years and the average senator had served 10 years.[20] Incumbents have had the chance to establish a relationship with the citizens they represent. Citizens see them in the news and around the district or state. Incumbents can also make use of certain perquisites of office to get publicity. For example, the **franking privilege**, which has existed since colonial times, allows members of Congress to send mail to constituents without postage. Although it cannot be used for campaigning purposes, to send holiday greetings, or to provide biographical information about representatives and their families, it can be used to send out newsletters and other informational mailings. The volume of franked mail increases in election years, suggesting that the mailings are being used for campaign purposes. In addition, members of Congress can employ staff for **casework**, which typically involves helping constituents deal with government bureaucracies. Whenever a staff member solves a constituent's problem, that constituent is likely to view the congressperson more favorably. The **personal vote**—that portion of an elected official's vote share that can be attributed to their relationship with constituents—is one component of the incumbency advantage.

Contrast the situation of incumbents with that of challengers. Unless challengers are well known for other reasons, most citizens in their districts or may not even be able to recognize their faces or names. And challengers have only limited resources to make themselves better known. Moreover, even if an incumbent is unpopular, many voters may still feel it is better to cast a ballot for the devil they know than the devil they don't know.

The size of the incumbency advantage is not, however, a constant. It has changed over time. The incumbency advantage increased substantially beginning in the 1960s and continuing through the 1980s—from about two points to eight points in the House, and from one point to nearly 10 points in the

---

[19] Center for Responsive Politics. 2017. "Incumbent Advantage." www.opensecrets.org /overview/incumbs.php (accessed 10/25/2017).

[20] Jennifer E. Manning. 2017. "Membership of the 115th Congress: A Profile." Congressional Research Service, March 13. https://fas.org/sgp/crs/misc/R44762.pdf (accessed 11/11/2017).

Senate.[21] Why did the incumbency advantage increase during this period? There are several partial explanations. For one, the increase in House incumbents' advantage in the 1960s has been linked to the growth in local television stations across the country.[22] At that time, local news broadcasts were widely watched, and, unlike today's broadcasts, they emphasized news stories about politics. Local television stations even relied on members of Congress to produce reports about their activities, which the stations then inserted into their local newscasts. In the 1970s, local television news began to focus less on political stories, and in the late 1970s audiences began watching local news broadcasts less often as their attention shifted to emerging cable television stations. Despite these changes, local news stations continued to cover incumbent activities and to do so in a largely positive manner, which helped maintain the incumbency advantage for House members. However, similar analysis of Senate elections has not found much connection between television and the incumbency advantage.[23]

Second, members of Congress have given themselves more official resources over the years, such as increased funds for franked mail, larger salaries for staff, and bigger travel budgets. These have allowed them to communicate more with their constituents and have potentially increased their advantages over challengers. On top of this, incumbents became more successful at campaign fund-raising, further increasing their financial advantage.[24]

Third, the Supreme Court decisions in the early 1960s that reformed the redistricting process may also have contributed to the incumbency advantage. These decisions require that virtually every district in the country change every 10 years through the processes of reapportionment and redistricting (which we discussed in Chapter 2). As a result, many candidates wait until the election following redistricting to determine whether they will run. Incumbents must decide how the new boundaries of their district affect their electoral prospects, and they may decide to retire if their

---

[21] Stephen Ansolabehere and James M. Snyder, Jr. 2004. "The Incumbency Advantage in U.S. Elections: An Analysis of State and Federal Offices, 1942–2000." *Election Law Journal* 1, 3: 315–38.

[22] Markus Prior. 2006. "The Incumbent in the Living Room: The Rise of Television and the Incumbency Advantage in U.S. House Elections." *Journal of Politics* 68, 3: 657–73.

[23] Stephen Ansolabehere, Erik C. Snowberg, and James M. Snyder, Jr. 2006. "Television and the Incumbency Advantage in U.S. Elections." *Legislative Studies Quarterly* 31, 4: 469–90.

[24] Jacobson, *The Politics of Congressional Elections*, p. 30; Alan I. Abramowitz, Brad Alexander, and Matthew Gunning. 2006. Incumbency, Redistricting, and the Decline of Competition in U.S. House Elections. *Journal of Politics* 68, 1: 75–88.

new districts are very different from their old districts.[25] Thus, the increase in the incumbency advantage for House members after the 1960s can be partly explained by changes in the reapportionment and redistricting processes and their influence on incumbent retirements.

However, the incumbency advantage has waned somewhat since the 1990s.[26] This shrinking advantage may reflect the growing "nationalization" of congressional elections—whereby congressional elections are influenced less by local factors, such as the personal vote accrued by an incumbent, and more by national political factors, like the popularity of the president. One consequence of nationalization is that voters are more consistently partisan—voting loyally for their party's candidates at all levels of office.[27] If part of the incumbency advantage depended on appealing to voters in the other party—perhaps because incumbents could demonstrate the good work they had done in the district—then cross-party appeals have become a difficult sell to a more partisan electorate.

Although the incumbency advantage may have declined, it certainly still exists. Nevertheless, despite the many advantages incumbents have, they rarely act as if they are confident about winning. This creates a paradox in congressional elections: many incumbents are "running scared" even though incumbents rarely lose.[28] Why? For one, incumbents do occasionally lose—especially when they are vulnerable because of personal scandals or a national political climate that is not favorable to their party. Moreover, the cost of losing is high. When incumbents lose elections, they also lose their jobs and the political power and reputation that they have amassed. The loss might even mean the end of their political careers.

Thus, despite the high chance of victory, incumbents in campaigns often behave as if they are fighting for their political lives. This is one reason that they are constantly raising money: amassing a huge war chest

---

[25] Gary W. Cox and Jonathan N. Katz. 2002. *Elbridge Gerry's Salamander: The Electoral Consequences of the Reapportionment Revolution.* Cambridge: Cambridge University Press.

[26] Andrew Gelman and Zaiying Huang. 2008. "Estimating Incumbency Advantage and Its Variation, as an Example of a Before-After Study." *Journal of the American Statistical Association* 103, 482: 437–46.

[27] Joseph Bafumi and Robert Y. Shapiro. 2009. "A New Partisan Voter." *Journal of Politics* 71, 1: 1–24; Marc J. Hetherington. 2001. "Resurgent Mass Partisanship: The Role of Elite Polarization." *American Political Science Review* 95, 3: 619–31; Larry M. Bartels. 2000. "Partisanship and Voting Behavior, 1952–1996." *American Journal of Political Science* 44, 1: 35–50; Alan I. Abramowitz and Kyle L. Saunders. 1998. "Ideological Realignment in the U.S. Electorate." *Journal of Politics* 60, 3: 634–52.

[28] Anthony King. 1997. *Running Scared: Why America's Politicians Campaign Too Much and Govern Too Little.* New York: Free Press.

helps scare off serious competitors. They want to avoid sending any signal that they may be vulnerable. Serious competitors know better than to compete with incumbents under most circumstances, so they bide their time until the district boundaries are redrawn or the incumbent decides to retire. As a result, most congressional elections pit incumbents against political novices, and, unsurprisingly, incumbents tend to win.

The Declining Competitiveness of Congressional Elections

Since the middle of the twentieth century, competitive congressional elections have become somewhat rarer. A simple measure of competitiveness is the number of House seats won by less than 10 percent (Figure 10.3).

The decline in electoral competitiveness is most visible from 1952 to 1988. Two likely causes are the increased power of incumbency and increasing party loyalty. Electoral competitiveness has decreased only in House elections that feature an incumbent. It has not decreased in open-seat House races. At the same time, as we have discussed, Americans have become less willing to vote for political candidates from a different party. To understand why this leads to declining competition, consider a district in which 60 percent of the voters are Democratic and 40 percent are Republican. If Democratic voters are willing to cross party lines, then a strong Republican

FIGURE 10.3 Number of House Elections Won by 10 Points or Less, 1952–2016

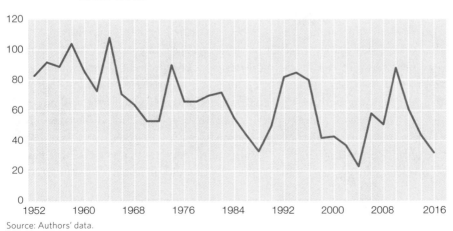

Source: Authors' data.

candidate could make the election competitive. But if Democratic voters are unwilling to cross party lines, then this district would rarely have a competitive election. Interestingly, redistricting appears to play little role in the declining competitiveness in House elections. There appears to be little change in competitiveness before and after redistricting cycles.[29]

At the same time, there are clearly years in which a larger number of House elections are competitive—such as 1992, 1994, and 2010. In 1992, there was the previously mentioned scandal of House incumbents' overdrawing their House bank accounts. In 1994 and 2010, the national political climate produced conditions very favorable to one party—in this case, the Republicans—which gave them a good opportunity to defeat Democratic incumbents. This made many more seats competitive.

Nevertheless, there does appear to be a decline in competitiveness overall, which raises at least three concerns about the American electoral system. First, a decline in competitiveness can undermine democratic accountability. In a representative democracy, the main way to ensure that politicians respond to citizens is to hold frequent elections; if the public is unhappy with a politician, voters can replace that person. But if representatives know that their reelection is virtually guaranteed, they respond less to citizens, relying more on their own views or on those of interest groups and lobbyists. Second, declining competitiveness can prevent the demographics of Congress from changing to reflect the electorate. This is a major problem for women and minorities, both of whom are underrepresented in Congress. Finally, the demographics of a state or district can change during an incumbent's tenure. If so, then incumbents may grow out of touch with constituents. Without a competitive election, incumbents have less incentive to bring their views into line with those of a changing electorate.

At the same time, declining competition may not be a serious problem. It may be less important whether party control of a congressional district changes regularly than whether party control of Congress as a whole changes regularly. Despite the declining number of competitive districts, party control of Congress has changed frequently in the last three decades. Critics of the current system argue that the framers of the Constitution did not want the legislature to represent parties at all—in fact, political parties did not exist in this country at that time—but to represent the diverse interests of the public. For example, the Constitution specifies that representatives are to be elected every two years so that they would be sensitive to the needs of

---

[29] Abramowitz, Alexander, and Gunning, "Incumbency, Redistricting, and the Decline of Competition in U.S. House Elections."

their constituents. Thus, the rotation of power between the parties is irrelevant to critics, who believe that declining competitiveness undermines the theory of representation enshrined in the Constitution.

Another argument for why declining competitiveness may be of little concern is that even if incumbents almost always win the general election, they must fight for the party's nomination. Direct primaries were adopted precisely because they would introduce contested elections into jurisdictions dominated by a single party. And primaries do appear to provide some accountability for incumbents.[30] Critics point out that most primaries are closed, meaning that only registered members of the party can vote in them, and independent voters or opposite partisans have no say in who will represent them. Moreover, most primaries are not competitive; most House incumbents do not face any primary opposition. In 2016, less than half of House Democratic and Republican primaries were contested.[31]

Among the reforms that have been proposed to improve the competitiveness of congressional elections are term limits, public financing, and redistricting. In a 2013 Gallup poll, 75 percent of Americans embraced term limits, which require incumbents to leave office after having served a certain number of terms. But, the Supreme Court has ruled that term limits are unconstitutional for federal officeholders, so term limits could be adopted only through a constitutional amendment.

Public financing for congressional candidates would entail providing all candidates with a minimum amount of money to help get their campaigns off the ground. As we noted in Chapter 4, public financing does appear to increase competitiveness. But it is not clear whether Congress or most Americans would support public funding. Critics of public financing have noted that it can create "false" competitiveness, since some districts really are decidedly Republican or Democratic. Subsidizing candidates of the minority party in such districts seems unnecessary and even wasteful.

A third kind of reform involves redistricting. Proposed reforms include taking the redistricting process out of the hands of state legislatures and giving it to independent commissions. There is some evidence that independent commissions create more competitive districts (see Chapter 2). States can also adopt guidelines that promote competition—for example, by requiring that competitive districts be created whenever possible. But it

---

[30] Shigeo Hirano and James M. Snyder, Jr. 2014. "Primary Elections and the Quality of Elected Officials." *Quarterly Journal of Political Science* 9, 4: 473–500.

[31] Ballotpedia. 2016. "U.S. House Primaries, 2016: Primary Competitiveness." https://ballotpedia.org/U.S._House_primaries,_2016#Primary_competitiveness (accessed 11/11/2017).

is unclear whether such guidelines are effective, and they can actually conflict with other priorities such as the imperative to create majority-minority districts under the Voting Rights Act. In 2000, Arizonans adopted a proposition that established an Independent Redistricting Commission, as well as a list of criteria for redistricting that included competitiveness. The redistricting commission found, however, that once Native American and Hispanic (heavily Democratic communities) districts had been drawn to comply with the Voting Rights Act, few Democrats were left in the state to spread around in the interest of creating competitive districts.[32] As a result, the districts created by the new commission were no more competitive than the districts that had been drawn by the state legislature in the past.[33]

Conclusion

The Congressional scholar David Mayhew has described members of Congress as being "single-minded seekers of reelection."[34] Although this statement may be somewhat unfair to public servants who are motivated by other purposes, members of Congress do want to be reelected and spend a great deal of time pursuing reelection. The two-year House election cycle means that House members are campaigning virtually all of the time, while senators have time to focus on governing before turning their attention to the next election. However, even those senators who are not up for election may campaign on behalf of other senators in their party who are running. Thus, elections are always central for members of Congress.

Because of the permanent campaign, the lines between campaigning and governing have become blurred. Members of Congress have changed the rules and procedures of Congress to aid them in pursuing reelection. For instance, prior to the institution of electronic voting in 1973, many votes taken in the House and Senate were anonymous. Since then, it has become common to demand a recorded vote, which makes all votes public. This

---

[32] Michael P. McDonald. 2006. "Redistricting and Competitive Districts," in *The Marketplace of Democracy: Electoral Competition and American Politics*, eds. Michael P. McDonald and John Samples. Washington, DC: Brookings Institution Press, pp. 222–44; Michael McDonald. 2008. "Legislative Redistricting," in *Democracy in the States: Experiments in Election Reform*, eds. Bruce E. Cain, Todd Donovan, and Caroline J. Tolbert. Washington, DC: Brookings Institution Press, pp. 147–60.

[33] McDonald, "Legislative Redistricting," p. 150.

[34] David R. Mayhew. 2004. *Congress: The Electoral Connection*, 2nd ed. New Haven, CT: Yale University Press.

has made the legislative process more transparent, while forcing members of Congress to think of every vote as a potential campaign issue.[35] This can undermine the collegiality of Congress and contribute to gridlock.

Ultimately, focusing on electoral goals can make it difficult for party members to work together. At the same time, focusing on electoral goals is what keeps representatives "running scared" and in contact with their constituents—even if they are almost certain to win their next race. This is an important trade-off inherent in the permanent campaign: it may improve the quality of representation even as it hurts the quality of governance.

KEY TERMS

incumbent (p. 289)

open seat (p. 290)

quality challengers (p. 290)

political amateurs (p. 290)

Hill committees (p. 291)

earned media (or free media) (p. 301)

coordinated expenditures (p. 302)

independent expenditures (p. 303)

incumbency advantage (p. 303)

franking privilege (p. 304)

casework (p. 304)

personal vote (p. 304)

FOR DISCUSSION

1. What kinds of people make successful congressional candidates?

2. What roles do the parties play in congressional campaigns?

3. What are some of the causes and consequences of the incumbency advantage?

4. How does the goal of being reelected affect the ability of members of Congress to govern?

---

[35] David Brady and Morris Fiorina. 2000. "Congress in the Era of the Permanent Campaign," in *The Permanent Campaign and Its Future*, eds. Norman J. Ornstein and Thomas E. Mann. Washington, DC: American Enterprise Institute, p. 141.

CHAPTER 11

State and Local Campaigns

On the evening of Election Day 2016, Americans were paying close attention to election returns from North Carolina because it was clear that Donald Trump needed a victory there to upset Hillary Clinton and win the presidency. North Carolina, however, was interesting for another reason: incumbent Republican governor Pat McCrory was fighting for his political life against challenger Roy Cooper, the state's attorney general. The race for governor would not have been so close if Governor McCrory had not signed the controversial "bathroom bill" in March, a law that prohibited people from using public bathrooms that did not accord with the sex on their birth certificate. The bill was enacted in response to a nondiscrimination ordinance passed by the City of Charlotte that allowed transgender people to use whatever bathroom fit their gender identity.

The reaction to the bathroom bill was swift. After it passed, Deutsche Bank and PayPal cancelled plans to expand in the state. The NCAA moved all of its 2016–17 tournament games out of North Carolina. Then, one by one, entertainers including Bruce Springsteen, Pearl Jam, Maroon 5, Ringo Starr, Cyndi Lauper, Selena Gomez, and Itzhak Perlman cancelled appearances. Forbes estimated the bill cost the state $630 million in lost revenue. On top of that, North Carolina soon found it had become a punch line for late-night comedians, and Governor McCrory had earned himself the dubious title of the "Orval Faubus of Public Bathrooms"—a reference to the Arkansas governor who called in the National Guard in 1957 to prevent the integration of public schools. While Trump won the state on election night, McCrory ultimately lost after a drawn-out recount process. It had been the state's most expensive governor's race ever, with the candidates and outside groups spending over $50 million.

On the other side of the country, Chloe Eudaly was celebrating a surprise victory in a Portland City Council race over incumbent Steven Novick. Eudaly, the owner of a small bookstore called Reading Frenzy, was not a traditional political candidate: she was a high-school dropout, a single mother with a disabled child, and a renter who focused mainly on the issue of Portland's housing crisis. Eudaly's shoestring budget of $80,000, compared with Novick's $500,000, forced her to get creative. In addition to using social media to get her message out, she also enlisted the help of a local cartoonist to create an 8-page comic book about Portland's rental crisis. Her canvassers had distributed 50,000 copies of the comic book by Election Day.

Our focus in this chapter is on state and local races—that is, elections other than those that occur at the federal level. Although these elections receive far less attention than federal elections, they comprise the lion's share—a whopping 96 percent—of all elections that take place in the United States. The victors of these elections have incredible power over our lives; they tell us where we can live, how we can act in public places and in our homes, and what our children will learn in school. State and local governments also spend $3.3 trillion a year, roughly one-fifth of our gross domestic product (GDP).[1] Thus, state and local governments comprise an enormous part of America's governing structure.

State and local elections involve a wide array of offices, but an easy way to think about them is in terms of the three traditional branches of government. At the state and local levels, voters select members of the executive branch (such as governors, lieutenant governors, attorneys general, mayors), members of the legislature (state senates and houses, city councils), and often members of the judiciary (judges and justices). In addition, Americans elect a variety of other,

Core of the Analysis

- State and local political offices and election laws often differ from their federal counterparts, and these differences affect campaign strategies.
- National political realities shape both candidate strategy and the outcomes of state and local races.
- State and local campaigns are increasingly adopting the techniques of national campaigns, and thereby becoming more expensive and professionalized.
- At the same time, many state and local campaigns attract scant media attention and require little fund-raising, thereby necessitating very different campaign strategies and tactics.
- Because state and local elections are largely invisible to most voters and to the media, small groups of activists may gain additional influence in these races.

---

[1] U.S. Census Bureau. 2017. "State and Local Government Finances by Level of Government and State, 2014." U.S. Census Bureau, October 19. https://factfinder.census.gov/faces /tableservices/jsf/pages/productview.xhtml?pid=SLF_2014_00A1&prodType=table (accessed 6/4/2017).

Protesters condemn House Bill 2, also known as the Bathroom Bill, which was signed into law by North Carolina's governor Pat McCrory in March 2016. It required transgender people to use the public restroom matching the sex on their birth certificate. The controversy surrounding the bill cost McCrory reelection later that year.

nongoverning officials, including auditors, road and highway commissioners, surveyors, assessors, and coroners. This entails a vast number of elections, simply because there are so many states and localities with governments—the 50 states, over 3,000 counties, over 19,000 cities or municipalities, and nearly 14,000 school districts.[2] In addition, many states and localities afford citizens the opportunity to vote on public policies (an opportunity that does not exist at the federal level) via ballot propositions, initiatives, and referenda.

The category "state and local" is very broad, as the contrast between the North Carolina governor's election and the Portland City Council race reveals. Within this category are races that vary dramatically in their resources and thus the visibility of the campaigns themselves. Expensive statewide races, such as those for governor, are essentially analogous to U.S. Senate races. They have features similar to campaigns for federal office: professional consultants, pollsters, television and radio advertising, and so on. But many other races—in fact, most state and local races—have little if any of these features.

---

[2] John P. Pelissero. 2003. "The Political Environment of Cities in the Twenty-first Century," in *Cities, Politics, and Policy: A Comparative Analysis*, ed. John P. Pelissero. Washington, DC: CQ Press, p. 10.

They are often run on shoestring budgets. Family and friends replace paid consultants. Lawn signs (or, in Chloe Eudaly's case, comic books) replace television advertisements. If one imagines a spectrum of campaigns running from those relying on lawn signs to those relying on television advertising to get out their message, most state and local races are closer to the lawn sign end of the spectrum.

At the same time, in recent years state and local campaigns have become more professionalized. The average sum spent on many types of state and local races has increased over time, and some of them now resemble more expensive campaigns in various respects. Professional campaigns have also become increasingly common for offices and issues that previously did not feature prominent campaigns, such as elections to state courts and ballot initiatives and referenda. This trend is being driven in large part by outside groups, which have found that influencing these kinds of elections is a highly effective way to shape policy, and by political consultants who are eager to sell their services. State party organizations also encourage their candidates to professionalize their campaigns to boost their chances of winning. Thus, the strategic calculations for state and local candidates are changing.

The shoestring nature of the majority of state and local campaigns both reflects and perpetuates a simple fact: relative even to congressional elections, state and local elections are often profoundly uncompetitive. Incumbents frequently run unopposed. The news media's attention is usually elsewhere. Citizens turn out to vote in lower numbers and have little information to use in making their choices. And, just as with congressional districts, local districts can be drawn so that only one party has a realistic chance of winning. Under these circumstances, highly organized parties, activists, and interest groups can influence the campaign and election outcomes in ways that may not coincide with the preferences of most citizens in the district. Thus, state and local races—the ones that most affect schools, homes, roads, and many other aspects of citizens' daily lives—are often the ones that live up to ideals of political campaigns the least. This is particularly unfortunate because state and local elections have the potential to promote citizen participation far more than national elections. Not only does the sheer number of local and state elections offer citizens a multitude of opportunities to participate, but people also seem to be more comfortable getting involved in elections closer to home.[3] When citizens do participate, such elections move closer to the ideal.

---

[3] Andrea McAtee and Jennifer Wolak. 2011. "Why People Decide to Participate in State Politics." *Political Research Quarterly* 64, 1: 45–58.

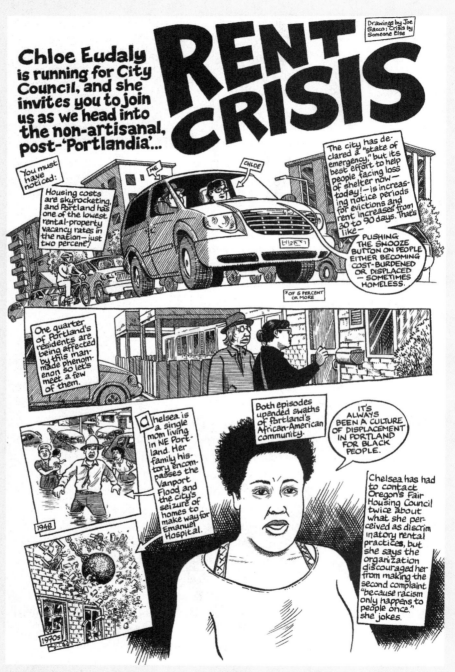

Chloe Eudaly ran for the Portland City Council on a shoestring budget in 2016 and won by using clever campaign tactics, including a comic book about the city's rent crisis.

We begin this chapter by discussing how local and state electoral rules affect these elections. We also consider how state and local elections depend on the prevailing political and economic winds—the "reality" that candidates must confront. To what degree do state and local officeholders find their fortunes bound up with broader trends—a weak economy, an unpopular party—that are beyond their control? We discuss the broader impact of rules and reality on the incumbency advantage—a feature of federal elections that is also important in state and local races and that strongly influences how competitive these races are.

We then describe how both rules and reality lead to differences among federal, state, and local campaign strategies, as well as the ways in which these strategies are becoming more similar, thanks to the creeping professionalization of state and local campaigns. We look at campaigns for state courts and ballot initiatives in particular. We also discuss how the uncompetitive features of state and local campaigns have historically advantaged, and continue to advantage, organized interests of various kinds, especially political parties. The concluding section considers the paradox of local elections and its implications for democratic ideals.

Rules and Reality in Local Elections

Local elections typically operate under a very different set of rules than state and federal elections, and they may also occur in a different context or "reality." Three important ways in which local electoral rules may differ from the electoral rules that operate at other levels of government are the use of nonpartisan ballots, at-large elections, and off-cycle elections. In addition, the reality of local elections is shaped in large part by the small scale and limited power of local governments, as well as the fact that media largely ignore local elections.

Nonpartisan Elections

The use of nonpartisan ballots reflects a particular philosophy of governance, historically associated with the Progressive movement at the turn of the last century (see Chapter 3). At that time, party machines governed many localities, especially large cities. Progressives thought that this facilitated corruption, and they promoted reforms that stripped power from parties. One of these reforms was the institution of nonpartisan elections, in which candidates are listed on the ballot without any party affiliations. This curtailed the ways in which party machines could work to choose candidates and help them get elected to office—although, as we discuss later, this has not made parties irrelevant in contemporary city politics. The reform was also intended to promote the election of city officials more concerned with the practical challenges of policy-making than with partisan politics. Today, over 75 percent of city council and mayoral elections are nonpartisan—differentiating them from the vast majority of state races and all federal races.

At-Large Elections

A second way local elections differ is in the types of constituencies that elected officeholders represent. Recall from Chapter 2 that districts for the U.S. House of Representatives elect a single representative, which makes them single-member districts. Many state legislatures also feature single-member districts. City council elections, by contrast, have a variety of methods of representation. Less than 20 percent of cities use districts, sometimes called *wards*, exclusively—although district elections are more common in the largest metropolitan areas, such as Los Angeles. Just over 20 percent use a mixed system, with some members elected from districts or wards, and other members elected at large, meaning that all voters in a city can vote for candidates for these seats. The majority of cities, however, use at-large elections exclusively; this is particularly true among small and medium-sized cities (that is, those with populations of less than 200,000).[4] Mayors, of course, are always elected in at-large elections.

Off-Cycle Elections

Local elections are often held off-cycle, meaning that they are not held concurrently with state or federal elections—another change instituted as part of Progressives' broader attempts to reform city governments. For example, more than half of city council elections across the country are held at different times than state and national elections.[5] A major consequence of this is that off-cycle local elections have significantly lower turnout. Turnout in mayoral elections held off-cycle is 27 percentage points lower than in mayoral elections held at the same time as a presidential election and 15 percentage points lower than in elections that coincide with midterm elections.[6] Nevertheless, many cities hold off-cycle elections to insulate local candidates from the events and issues that may be prominent in elections for higher levels of office.

---

[4] Timothy B. Krebs and John P. Pelissero. 2003. "City Councils," in *Cities, Politics, and Policy: A Comparative Analysis*, ed. John P. Pelissero. Washington, DC: CQ Press, p. 172.

[5] Krebs and Pelissero, "City Councils," p. 170.

[6] Thomas M. Holbrook and Aaron C. Weinschenk. 2014. "Campaigns, Mobilization, and Turnout in Mayoral Elections." *Political Research Quarterly* 67, 1: 42–55.

As a result, local elections typically center on issues unique to a community, with voters holding local officeholders accountable for their handling of those issues. For example, voters hold incumbent politicians accountable for the way they deal with natural disasters that strike their local communities. One study found that a governor who responds to an extreme weather event by asking for federal assistance boosts his or her vote share in the county where the natural disaster occurred by four percentage points on average.[7] Another study of how voters in Houston, Texas, responded to deaths and damage caused by Tropical Storm Allison in 2001 found that those who disapproved of how Houston's mayor handled the crisis were less likely to vote for him in the next election.[8]

The Reality of Small-Scale Democracy

Because local jurisdictions are small, their elected officials have limited power, and the services they provide are available to everyone in the community rather than certain groups of constituents; therefore, local elections operate under different realities than state and federal elections.[9] In small jurisdictions, elected officials can win with relatively few votes, which means their campaigns will revolve around personal connections and require less money. Smaller jurisdictions also have lower revenues and can offer fewer services than larger jurisdictions. For example, cities with less than 100,000 people rarely offer services beyond water, sewage, police, fire, parks, and street repair.[10] When elected officials' powers are so limited, voters tend to evaluate them on the basis of their ability to handle the few powers that they do have rather than their larger vision for society. Thus, voters tend to judge small-town mayors based on their ability to manage their towns' limited services rather than on their ideological leanings.[11] Moreover, the services just described are typically offered to everyone living in a city. In larger jurisdictions, government services are distributed more unevenly—much like the federal government's social security program or its tax subsidies for

---

[7] John T. Gasper and Andrew Reeves. 2011. "Make It Rain? Retrospection and the Attentive Electorate in the Context of Natural Disasters." *American Journal of Political Science* 55, 2: 340–55.

[8] Kevin Arceneaux and Robert M. Stein. 2006. "Who Is Held Responsible When Disaster Strikes? The Attribution of Responsibility for a Natural Disaster in an Urban Election." *Journal of Urban Affairs* 28, 1: 43–53.

[9] J. Eric Oliver, with Shang E. Ha and Zachary Callen. 2012. *Local Elections and the Politics of Small-Scale Democracy*. Princeton, NJ: Princeton University Press.

[10] Oliver, Ha, and Callen, *Local Elections and the Politics of Small-Scale Democracy*, p. 25.

[11] Oliver, Ha, and Callen, *Local Elections and the Politics of Small-Scale Democracy*, pp. 30–31.

farmers. Such particularistic government benefits give groups an incentive to organize and advocate for certain candidates in elections. In contrast, when a city or town offers universalistic services, groups have less of an incentive to mobilize, which makes their elections sleepier affairs.

Another reality of local elections is that they get very little television news coverage, especially if the contest is taking place in a large media market.[12] Because media markets often span large geographic areas encompassing multiple municipal, county, congressional, and even state boundaries, the media in larger markets tend to focus on higher-level races that interest a broader segment of their viewers. In fact, research has found that local elections typically account for less than five percent of campaign-related television news stories, even in midterm election years when there is no presidential contest to steal the spotlight.[13] Newspapers can make up for this to a certain extent, but they have many of the same incentives the television media have.

If local elections are different from state and federal elections in these respects, they are quite similar in another: the advantages that accrue to incumbents. Indeed, with the nonpartisan ballot in place, voters depend on information other than party affiliation, especially their basic familiarity with the candidates. Small wonder, then, that incumbents typically do well in local elections. They are better positioned to have personal contact with voters. They are more likely to get endorsements from prominent leaders and media outlets. They are better able to raise money. Research on city council races has found that incumbents get a far larger share of the vote than non-incumbents and tend to win elections at rates only slightly below those of incumbent members of Congress.[14] Despite the very different rules under which local elections are conducted, incumbency remains "the 800-pound gorilla."[15] As a consequence, many local elections—much like many congressional elections—are not very competitive.

---

[12] Scott L. Althaus and Todd C. Trautman. 2008. "The Impact of Television Market Size on Voter Turnout in American Elections." *American Politics Research* 36, 6: 824–56.

[13] Erika Franklin Fowler, Kenneth M. Goldstein, Matthew Hale, and Martin Kaplan. 2007. "Does Local News Measure Up?" *Stanford Law & Policy Review* 18, 2: 411; Martin Kaplan, Kenneth Goldstein, and Matthew Hale. "Local TV News Coverage of the 2002 General Election." Norman Lear Center. https://learcenter.org/wp-content/uploads/2014/10/LCLNAReport2.pdf (accessed 6/13/2017).

[14] Timothy B. Krebs. 1998. "The Determinants of Candidates' Vote Share and the Advantages of Incumbency in City Council Elections." *American Journal of Political Science* 42, 3: 921–35; Jessica Trounstine. 2011. "Evidence of a Local Incumbency Advantage." *Legislative Studies Quarterly* 36, 2: 255–80; Jens Hainmueller, Andrew B. Hall, and James M. Snyder, Jr. 2015. "Assessing the External Validity of Election RD Estimates: An Investigation of the Incumbency Advantage." *Journal of Politics* 77, 3: 707–20.

[15] Krebs and Pelissero, "City Councils," p. 178.

Rules and Reality in State Elections

Certain rules distinguish state elections from both local and federal elections. Many states use term limits, which have implications for both aspiring office-holders and incumbents. Variations in state laws concerning how long state legislatures are in session and how much state legislators get paid have consequences for how professionalized state legislatures are, which in turn affects state legislative elections. State elected officials also confront distinct political realities that arise from variations in the strength of state party organizations and the kinds of people who live in different states. They must also deal with the reality that national forces beyond their control may affect their chances of winning. Despite all of these particularities, however, incumbents still reign supreme in state-level contests just as they do in local and federal elections.

Term Limits

Many state elections are affected by a rule that members of Congress never confront: term limits. As noted in Chapter 2, most states limit the number of terms a governor can serve, and a substantial minority limit the terms of state legislators as well. The most common limit for governor, following the restrictions on presidents, is two consecutive terms. Statewide offices therefore see more turnover than either the U.S. House or Senate, where incumbents can accrue a considerable advantage from their years of service, as we discussed in Chapter 10. Term limits can change the calculus of both aspiring and current officeholders. Aspiring officeholders know they will be able to run for an open seat on a regular basis. Current officeholders know that their tenure is short-lived, and they may therefore be even more inclined to position themselves to run for higher levels of office once, or even before, their term has expired.

The natural conclusion, then, would be that term limits make elections more competitive, by weakening the advantages of incumbents and increasing the number of open-seat races. However, the real story is more complicated. Term limits have been instrumental in reducing the number of incumbents running in elections, but this does not necessarily make elections as a whole more competitive.[16] Instead, what often happens is that when

---

[16] Seth E. Masket and Jeffrey B. Lewis. 2007. "A Return to Normalcy? Revisiting the Effects of Term Limits on Competitiveness and Spending in California Assembly Elections." *State Politics and Policy Quarterly* 7, 1: 20–38; Scot Schraufnagel and Karen Halperin. 2006. "Term Limits, Electoral Competition, and Representational Diversity: The Case of Florida." *State Politics and Policy Quarterly* 6, 4: 448–62.

first-term officeholders run for reelection, they do so without a serious challenger. This is because serious challengers would rather wait until the incumbent leaves office at the end of the term limit than mount a long-shot challenge. Moreover, several factors often combine to make it difficult for more than one serious challenger to compete for a newly open seat. The district itself may be dominated by one party due to its underlying demography or a prior redistricting. Leaders in this dominant party may work to promote one favored candidate and thereby avoid a hotly contested primary. As a consequence, term limits do not consistently result in closer races.

Legislative Professionalism

Another category of rules concerns the **professionalism** of the legislature. The U.S. Congress is perhaps the most salient model of a professional legislature: seats in Congress are full-time jobs that come with a substantial salary and staff support. Being a legislator in the national legislature is essentially a profession, like being a doctor or lawyer. But this model is hardly universal. State legislatures are often far less professional. Depending on state law, they may meet for only a few months every other year, as in North Dakota and Texas. Legislators in some states receive only small salaries. In fact, New Mexico state legislators receive no salary, only reimbursement for expenses. State legislatures also vary widely in the number of staff employed to assist legislatures. California's professionalized state legislature has several thousand staff, but New Mexico's has fewer than 100.[17] Legislatures that are not as professionalized are sometimes called **citizen legislatures**.[18] Approximately four state legislatures might be characterized in this way. On the other end, about 25 percent of the state legislatures in the United States are highly professionalized, with the rest falling somewhere in between.[19]

The professionalism of the legislature has a two-edged effect on the incumbency advantage. On the one hand, the more professionalized the legislature, the more its incumbents are likely to attract challengers. This is not surprising: jobs in a professionalized legislature are particularly attractive. But even though they more often face challengers, incumbents in professional

---

[17] These examples come from Keith E. Hamm and Gary F. Moncrief. 2012. "Legislative Politics in the States," in *Politics in the American States: A Comparative Analysis*, eds. Virginia Gray and Russell L. Hanson. 10th ed. Washington, DC: CQ Press: 163–207.

[18] City councils also vary in their level of professionalization, although there have been fewer studies of how professionalization affects campaign strategies in local elections.

[19] National Conference of State Legislators. 2017. "Full- and Part-Time Legislatures." www.ncsl.org/research/about-state-legislatures/full-and-part-time-legislatures.aspx#average (accessed 6/14/2017).

legislatures are actually *less* vulnerable because they have more resources at their disposal. Like members of Congress, they can claim credit for significant legislative accomplishments and serve their constituents' needs via casework. They can use the perquisites of their office to raise more money than incumbents in citizen legislatures. This helps explain why incumbents in professionalized legislatures are reelected at higher rates.[20]

Characteristics of the Electorate

One reason why state (and local) elections are so interesting is that state electorates can differ dramatically from one another. Consider the differences between a state like California, with its population of 38 million that is 39 percent white, and Iowa, a state of 3 million that is 88 percent white. State legislative districts can vary just as dramatically. These demographic differences affect election outcomes. For example, candidates running in state legislative districts with electorates that are older, whiter, and more educated, or districts with more farmers and government employees, will find it easier to get voters to the polls because these groups vote at a higher rate than other groups.[21] Perhaps unsurprisingly, candidates who reside in districts with more independent voters will find there are more voters that can be persuaded.[22]

State and Local Party Organizational Strength

State and local party organizations across the country vary dramatically in terms of their strength, with Republicans generally being stronger organizationally than Democrats.[23] Party organizations have adapted themselves to the current era of candidate-centered campaigning by reinventing themselves as service organizations that supplement candidates' campaign organizations with important resources, such as financial support, polling services, media consulting, and voter mobilization programs. They also provide candidates with connections to interest groups allied with the party.

---

[20] John M. Carey, Richard G. Niemi, and Lynda W. Powell. 2000. "Incumbency and the Probability of Reelection in State Legislative Elections." *Journal of Politics* 62, 3: 671–700; Robert E. Hogan. 2004. "Challenger Emergence, Incumbent Success, and Electoral Accountability in State Legislative Elections." *Journal of Politics* 66, 4: 1283–303.

[21] Robert E. Hogan. 1999. "Campaign and Contextual Influences on Voter Participation in State Legislative Elections." *American Politics Research* 27, 4: 403–33.

[22] Nicholas R. Seabrook. 2010. "Money and State Legislative Elections: The Conditional Impact of Political Context." *American Politics Research* 38, 3: 399–424.

[23] Thomas M. Holbrook and Raymond J. La Raja. 2013. "Parties and Elections," in *Politics in the American States: A Comparative Analysis*, eds. Virginia Gray, Russell L. Hanson, and Thad Kousser. 10th ed. Washington, DC: CQ Press, p. 73.

Candidates running where their party organization is strong will have considerably more help than those running where their party organization is weak.

What determines a state or local party's organizational strength? First, urban, educated communities tend to foster better-developed party organizations.[24] Such areas tend to be dense in local organizations that create social capital, which parties can tap. There is also evidence that parties are stronger in more competitive jurisdictions because that is where they are needed most.[25] Finally, most state parties consist of an alliance of official party organizations, unofficial party organizations led by individual party leaders, and various interest groups—all of which must coordinate on candidates to support for office.[26] To the extent that there is fighting within a party or between a party and its interest group allies, a party will be weaker.

National Factors

Elections for state offices, like those for president or Congress, are strongly affected by fundamental factors such as the state of the economy. What is particularly striking about state elections is how they can be affected by conditions *outside* the state or locality. To be sure, we do not mean to suggest that individual states have no unique circumstances. One can often see clear differences between the dynamics of federal and state elections. For example, in the American South, the gradual shift from one-party rule by the Democratic Party to a strong tendency to support Republican candidates occurred much more quickly at the federal level than at the state level.[27] That said, the diverse characteristics of individual states do not make each governor's or state legislator's race immune to the effects of events in Washington or the country as a whole.

Incumbent governors and their parties can be judged not only on state economic performance but also on national economic performance, even though

---

[24] Douglas D. Roscoe and Shannon Jenkins. 2015. *Local Party Organizations in the 21st Century.* Albany, NY: SUNY Press, p. 69.

[25] Roscoe and Jenkins, *Local Party Organizations,* p. 69; James L. Gibson, Cornelius P. Cotter, John F. Bibby, and Robert J. Huckshorn. 1983. "Assessing Party Organizational Strength." *American Journal of Political Science* 27, 2: 216.

[26] Seth E. Masket. 2009. *No Middle Ground: How Informal Party Organizations Control Nominations and Polarize Legislatures.* Ann Arbor, MI: University of Michigan Press.

[27] Charles S. Bullock III. 2010. "Introduction: Southern Politics in the Twenty-first Century," in *The New Politics of the Old South: An Introduction to Southern Politics,* eds. Charles S. Bullock III and Mark J. Rozell. 4th ed. Lanham, MD: Rowman & Littlefield, pp. 1–26.

there is almost nothing they can do to affect the national economy.[28] The effects of the national economy are stronger in citizen legislatures, as professionalized legislatures provide advantages to incumbents that make them less likely to be defeated when the economy is weak.[29]

Similarly, candidates for state and local offices are often judged on the basis of the performance of someone who may be thousands of miles away: the president. State and local candidates in the president's party often do better when the president is more popular. In fact, this is true regardless of whether a presidential election is occurring at the same time that local candidates are on the ballot. Thus, just as the president's party loses seats in Congress when the economy is weak and the president unpopular, it loses seats in, and sometimes control of, state legislatures. The 2010 midterm, when Americans took out their frustration with the country's economic conditions on President Obama and the Democrats, best illustrates this point: the Democrats not only lost seats in Congress, but they also lost control of six governorships and nearly 700 state legislative seats (including the control of 21 different legislative chambers).

Coattail Effects

Candidates for state and local office can be helped by the presence of higher-profile candidates on the ballot, such as candidates for president. Rules governing the timing of federal, state, and local elections mean that, in some years, state and local elections may occur alongside more visible federal elections. However, in some states, gubernatorial elections never occur in the same year as presidential elections. New Jersey and Virginia hold their gubernatorial elections off-cycle—just as many municipalities across the nation do—so that they do not compete with any federal elections.

What happens when more-visible candidates are on the ballot? They may create a **coattail effect**: less-visible candidates will "ride the coattails" of a more visible popular candidate of the same party who is on the ballot, and thereby do better at the polls. The presence of presidential and senatorial candidates on the ballot may help candidates for governor and state legislator.

---

[28] John E. Chubb. 1988. "Institutions, the Economy, and the Dynamics of State Elections." *American Political Science Review* 82, 1: 133–54; Dennis M. Simon. 1989. "Presidents, Governors, and Electoral Accountability." *Journal of Politics* 51, 2: 286–304; Dennis M. Simon, Charles W. Ostrom, Jr., and Robin F. Marra. 1991. "The President, Referendum Voting, and Subnational Elections in the United States." *American Political Science Review* 85, 4: 1177–92.

[29] William D. Berry, Michael B. Berkman, and Stuart Schneiderman. 2000. "Legislative Professionalism and Incumbent Reelection: The Development of Institutional Boundaries." *American Political Science Review* 94, 4: 859–74.

For example, many observers attributed the Republican takeover of the Kentucky House of Representatives in 2016 (for the first time in 95 years) to Trump's strong showing in the state, where he won with 63 percent of the vote compared with Hillary Clinton's 33 percent. To put this in perspective, in 2012 Mitt Romney beat Obama in Kentucky by just 23 percentage points. As the chairwoman of the Kentucky Democratic Party said, "It was extremely difficult for any Kentucky Democrat to overcome the Trump tide."[30] It should be noted, however, that Trump's coattail effects in 2016 were concentrated in just a handful of states, such as Indiana and Missouri, and more muted elsewhere.[31]

Coattails may matter most for challengers and open-seat candidates, who do not have the advantages of incumbency. Coattails also matter more in states where voters can cast a "straight-ticket" vote by pulling a single lever or punching a single button for all the Democrats or all the Republicans on the ballot. (Currently, just nine states allow straight-ticket voting.[32])

Incumbency Advantage

The advantages that accrue to incumbent presidents, members of Congress, and even city council members are equally visible when we consider incumbents in state elections. In fact, state elections are on average less competitive than federal races. This is less true in statewide races, such as those for governor, than in races for state legislatures, where candidates run in smaller districts. Indeed, in state legislative elections, including both primary and general elections, substantial fractions of races are not even contested—meaning one candidate runs unopposed. There has been a striking decline in contested primaries for state legislative elections: from 1910 to 1938, 50 percent of primaries were contested, but from 1960 to 2000, only 25 percent were.[33] In general-election state legislative races in 2016, 42 percent of major-party

[30] Tom Loftus. 2016. "GOP Takes Kentucky House in Historic Shift." *Courier Journal,* November 8. www.courier-journal.com/story/news/politics/elections/kentucky/2016/11/08 /control-kentucky-house-up-grabs/93344114/ (accessed 6/13/2017).

[31] Eric Bradner. 2016. "5 Surprising Lessons from Trump's Astonishing Win." *CNN Politics,* November 9. www.cnn.com/2016/11/09/politics/donald-trump-wins-biggest-surprises /index.html (accessed on 6/13/2017).

[32] National Conference of State Legislatures. 2017. "Straight-Ticket Voting." www.ncsl.org /research/elections-and-campaigns/straight-ticket-voting.aspx (accessed 6/13/2017).

[33] Stephen Ansolabehere, John Mark Hansen, Shigeo Hirano, and James M. Snyder, Jr. 2006. "The Decline of Competition in U.S. Primary Elections," in *The Marketplace of Democracy: Electoral Competition and American Politics,* eds. Michael P. McDonald and John Samples. Washington, DC: Brookings Institution Press. Calculated from Table 4.1, p. 87.

FIGURE 11.1 Percentage of General Election Candidates in 2016 State Legislative Races with No Major Party Opposition

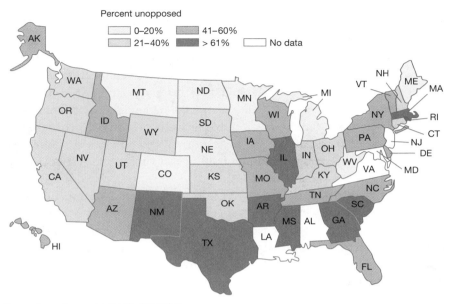

Source: Percentages calculated by the author.

candidates faced no major-party opposition (see Figure 11.1).[34] By contrast, in the 2016 U.S. House general election, this was true of only 15 percent of seats. Naturally, this lack of competitiveness tends to advantage incumbents. It is especially rare for incumbents to face challengers who have raised as much money as they have, or even anything close to it. This is one reason that a few states have adopted "clean elections" laws—full public funding for statewide and legislative elections (see Chapter 4): they wish to provide funding to lesser-known challengers.

Campaign Strategies Big and Small

As the stories at the beginning of this chapter make clear, it is not easy to generalize about the strategies of state and local campaigns. At a minimum,

---

[34] Ballotpedia. 2016. "Major Party Candidates with Major Party Competition in the 2016 State Legislative Elections." https://ballotpedia.org/Major_party_candidates_with_major_party _competition_in_the_November_2016_state_legislative_elections (accessed 6/13/2017).

of course, almost every candidate for any level of office wants the same thing: to win enough votes to win the election. Certain features of state and local governments, however, can shape candidate strategies for achieving that goal. In particular, the size of a jurisdiction, the powers of the office, and the rules that govern election to that office all interact to shape a candidate's strategy.

Perhaps the most important feature is the size of a jurisdiction. In smaller cities and districts, candidates rely mainly on personal connections for campaigning. This is why many local and state campaigns are nearly invisible. Candidates raise little money. Their campaign organizations are composed of a few friends and family, not a stable of well-compensated consultants. They take no polls and air no ads. Instead, they rely on more cost-effective forms of communication, including mailings to voters, social media, billboards and the occasional radio ad.

As the size of the jurisdiction grows, however, candidates must develop strategies for reaching larger groups of voters. One of the most effective ways to do this is to reach out to local organizations, such as churches, local clubs, and civic organizations, for help. Candidates hope these groups will mobilize their members on the candidate's behalf and provide volunteers for the campaign. Yet campaigns in even medium-sized jurisdictions still lack resources. This is particularly true for less professionalized political offices. For example, the average candidate for the Wyoming House of Representatives, a citizen legislature, spent only $7,153 in 2016.[35] That is significantly less than the $44,053 that Ralph Northam spent on office supplies in his bid for governor of Virginia in 2017.[36]

In large cities and statewide races, personal connections and groups still matter, but candidates must use mass advertising on television and radio to reach more voters. They also raise large sums of money to hire campaign consultants and take polls. Just recall the combined $50 million that Pat McCrory, Roy Cooper, and outside groups spent in North Carolina's 2016 gubernatorial contest. All this makes these campaigns resemble campaigns for federal office. A statewide campaign for governor, especially in a large state like North Carolina, is essentially a presidential campaign run on a somewhat smaller scale.

The size of a jurisdiction is related to the power its elected officials hold, which in turn affects the issues on which candidates campaign. For example,

[35] National Institute on Money in State Politics. "Election Overview: Wyoming, 2016." https://followthemoney.org/tools/election-overview/?s=WY&y=2016 (accessed 6/13/2017).

[36] The Virginia Public Access Project. "Ralph Northam: Candidate." www.vpap.org /candidates/67038/expenditures (accessed 12/20/2017).

Travis County Clerk Elections Division
November 8, 2016 Joint General and Special Elections
División Electoral de la Secretaria del Condado de Travis
el 8 de noviembre de 2016 Elecciones Generales y Especiales Conjuntas

If you do not know your election precinct, call Voter Registration at 854-9473. For candidate information call the
Travis County Clerk's Election Division at 238-VOTE (8683). www.traviscountyelections.org
Si usted no sabe su precinto de elección, llame al Registrador de Votantes 854-9473. Para candidato información sobre la elección, llame la
División de Elecciones de la Oficina del Secretario del Condado de Travis 238-VOTE (8683). www.traviscountyelections.org

Straight Party (Partido completo)

All precincts / Precintos enteros:

☐ Republican / Republicano
☐ Democratic / Democrático
☐ Libertarian / Libertariano
☐ Green / Verde

President (Presidente)

All precincts / Precintos enteros:

☐ Donald J. Trump / Mike Pence - REP
☐ Hillary Clinton / Tim Kaine - DEM
☐ Gary Johnson / William Weld - LIB
☐ Jill Stein / Ajamu Baraka - GRN
☐ Write-in (Voto Escrito)

District 10, United States Representative
(Distrito 10, Representante de los
Estados Unidos)

Precincts / Precintos: 103, 104, 105, 106, 108, 114, 118,
123, 125, 127, 131, 136, 138, 140, 141, 142, 146, 149,
150, 153, 154, 156, 200, 203, 211, 212, 217, 218, 222,
227, 235, 236, 237, 239, 240, 241, 242, 243, 245,
246, 248, 249, 252, 253, 258, 260, 262, 266, 268, 273,
321, 323, 326, 327, 331, 333, 334, 335, 336, 337, 343,
374, 375

☐ Michael T. McCaul - REP
☐ Tawana W. Cadien - DEM
☐ Bill Kelsey - LIB

District 17, United States Representative
(Distrito 17, Representante de los
Estados Unidos)

Precincts / Precintos: 102, 107, 109, 110, 111, 112, 113,
137, 145, 148, 160, 161, 163, 205, 207, 215, 216, 219,
225, 226, 229, 254, 259, 263, 267, 305, 328, 345

☐ Bill Flores - REP
☐ William Matta - DEM
☐ Clark Patterson - LIB

District 21, United States Representative
(Distrito 21, Representante de los
Estados Unidos)

Precincts / Precintos: 250, 277, 301, 309, 310, 311, 314,
315, 329, 330, 332, 339, 340, 341, 342, 344, 349, 350,
351, 352, 354, 356, 357, 363, 365, 368, 408, 408, 409,
412, 416, 418, 419, 420, 421, 422, 424, 428, 430, 431,
433, 435, 437, 446, 454, 458, 460, 461

☐ Lamar Smith - REP
☐ Tom Wakely - DEM
☐ Mark Loewe - LIB
☐ Antonio "Tony" Diaz - GRN

District 25, United States Representative
(Distrito 25, Representante de los
Estados Unidos)

Precincts / Precintos: 122, 124, 126, 129, 130, 132, 133,
135, 151, 152, 202, 206, 208, 210, 213, 214, 220, 221,
231, 232, 233, 234, 238, 244, 247, 251, 256, 274, 275,
302, 303, 304, 306, 307, 308, 312, 313, 316, 317, 318,
319, 320, 324, 325, 338, 346, 347, 358, 359, 360, 361,
362, 364, 366, 367, 369, 370, 371, 372, 373, 432, 434

☐ Roger Williams - REP
☐ Kathi Thomas - DEM
☐ Loren Marc Schneiderman - LIB

District 35, United States Representative
(Distrito 35, Representante de los
Estados Unidos)

Precincts / Precintos: 101, 115, 116, 117, 119, 120, 121,
128, 134, 139, 164, 209, 223, 224, 401, 402, 403, 404,
405, 407, 410, 411, 413, 414, 415, 417, 423, 425, 426,
427, 429, 436, 438, 439, 440, 441, 442, 443, 444, 447,
448, 450, 451, 452, 463

☐ Susan Narvaiz - REP
☐ Lloyd Doggett - DEM
☐ Rhett Rosenquest Smith - LIB
☐ Scott Trimble - GRN

Railroad Commissioner
(Comisionado de Ferrocarriles)

All precincts / Precintos enteros:

☐ Wayne Christian - REP
☐ Grady Yarbrough - DEM
☐ Mark Miller - LIB
☐ Martina Salinas - GRN

Place 3, Justice, Supreme Court
(Lugar 3, Juez, Corte Suprema)

All precincts / Precintos enteros:

☐ Debra Lehrmann - REP
☐ Mike Westergren - DEM
☐ Kathie Glass - LIB
☐ Rodolfo Rivera Munoz - GRN

Place 5, Justice, Supreme Court
(Lugar Núm. 5, Juez, Corte Suprema)

All precincts / Precintos enteros:

☐ Paul Green - REP
☐ Dori Contreras Garza - DEM
☐ Tom Oxford - LIB
☐ Charles E. Waterbury - GRN

Place 9, Justice, Supreme Court
(Lugar Núm. 9, Juez, Corte Suprema)

All precincts / Precintos enteros:

☐ Eva Guzman - REP
☐ Savannah Robinson - DEM
☐ Don Fulton - LIB
☐ Jim Chisolm - GRN

Place 2, Judge, Court of Criminal Appeals
(Lugar Núm. 2, Juez, Corte de Apelaciones
Criminales)

All precincts / Precintos enteros:

☐ Mary Lou Keel - REP
☐ Lawrence "Larry" Meyers - DEM
☐ Mark Ash - LIB
☐ Adam King Blackwell Reposa - GRN

Place 5, Judge, Court of Criminal Appeals
(Lugar Núm. 5, Juez, Corte de Apelaciones
Criminales)

All precincts / Precintos enteros:

☐ Scott Walker - REP
☐ Betsy Johnson - DEM
☐ William Bryan Strange, III - LIB
☐ Judith Sanders-Castro - GRN

Place 6, Judge, Court of Criminal Appeals
(Lugar Núm. 6, Juez, Corte de Apelaciones
Criminales)

All precincts / Precintos enteros:

☐ Michael E. Keasler - REP
☐ Robert Burns - DEM
☐ Mark W. Bennett - LIB

**District 5, Member, State Board of
Education**
(Distrito 5, Miembro de la Junta Estatal de
Educación Pública)

Precincts / Precintos: 101, 114, 115, 116, 117, 118, 119,
121, 122, 124, 126, 127, 129, 130, 132, 133, 135, 138,
142, 151, 152, 200, 202, 206, 208, 210, 212, 213, 214,
221, 235, 236, 250, 251, 256, 266, 273, 274, 275, 277,
301, 302, 303, 304, 307, 309, 310, 311, 313, 314, 315,
317, 318, 325, 329, 330, 332, 338, 339, 340, 341, 342,
344, 347, 349, 350, 351, 352, 354, 356, 357, 358, 360,
361, 362, 363, 364, 365, 366, 367, 401, 402, 403, 404,
405, 406, 407, 408, 409, 410, 411, 412, 413, 414, 415,
416, 417, 418, 419, 420, 421, 422, 423, 424, 425, 426,
427, 428, 429, 430, 431, 432, 433, 434, 435, 436, 437,
438, 439, 440, 441, 442, 443, 444, 446, 447, 448, 450,
451, 452, 454, 458, 460, 461, 463

☐ Ken Mercer - REP
☐ Rebecca Bell-Metereau - DEM
☐ Ricardo Perkins - LIB

**District 10, Member, State Board of
Education**
(Distrito 10, Miembro de la Junta Estatal de
Educación Pública)

Precincts / Precintos: 102, 103, 104, 105, 106, 107, 108,
109, 110, 111, 112, 113, 120, 123, 125, 128, 131, 134,
136, 137, 139, 140, 141, 145, 146, 148, 149, 150, 153,
154, 156, 160, 161, 163, 164, 203, 205, 207, 209, 211,
215, 216, 217, 218, 219, 220, 222, 223, 224, 225, 226,
227, 228, 229, 231, 232, 233, 234, 237, 238, 239, 240,
241, 242, 243, 244, 245, 246, 247, 248, 249, 252, 253,
254, 258, 259, 260, 262, 263, 267, 268, 305, 306, 308,
312, 316, 319, 320, 321, 323, 324, 326, 327, 328, 331,
333, 334, 335, 336, 337, 343, 345, 346, 359, 368, 369,
370, 371, 372, 373, 374, 375

☐ Tom Maynard - REP
☐ Judy Jennings - DEM

District 21, State Senator
(Distrito 21, Senador Estatal)

Precincts / Precintos: 138, 401, 402, 403, 404, 405, 410,
413, 418, 419, 420, 423, 425, 429, 431, 440, 441, 443,
446, 447, 448, 450, 451, 452, 463

☐ Judith Zaffirini - DEM

District 24, State Senator
(Distrito 24, Senador Estatal)

Precincts / Precintos: 306, 308, 312, 314, 316, 319, 320,
324, 346, 359, 361, 365, 368

☐ Dawn Buckingham - REP
☐ Virginia "Jennie Lou" Leeder - DEM

District 46, State Representative
(Distrito 46, Representante Estatal)

Precincts / Precintos: 105, 113, 116, 117, 118, 120, 121,
122, 124, 125, 126, 127, 129, 130, 131, 132, 133, 134,
135, 136, 139, 141, 142, 145, 146, 148, 151, 152, 156,
160, 203, 217, 223, 224, 436, 444

☐ Gabriel Nila - REP
☐ Dawnna Dukes - DEM
☐ Kevin Ludlow - LIB
☐ Adam Michael Greeley - GRN

District 47, State Representative
(Distrito 47, Representante Estatal)

Precincts / Precintos: 232, 233, 234, 244, 245, 302, 303,
304, 306, 308, 310, 312, 314, 315, 316, 318, 319, 320,
324, 330, 333, 334, 338, 346, 349, 359, 360, 361,
365, 367, 368, 369, 370, 371, 372, 373, 374, 375, 406,
417

☐ Paul Workman - REP
☐ Ana Jordan - DEM
☐ Scott G. McKinlay - LIB

District 48, State Representative
(Distrito 48, Representante Estatal)

Precincts / Precintos: 210, 212, 213, 220, 221, 231, 237,
238, 246, 247, 249, 251, 253, 256, 262, 266, 301, 307,
309, 317, 337, 339, 343, 344, 347, 350, 351, 352, 354,
356, 357, 358, 362, 363, 364, 366, 408, 411, 412, 413,
414, 415, 416, 418, 419, 435, 447, 451, 458, 463

☐ Donna Howard - DEM
☐ Ben Easton - LIB

District 49, State Representative
(Distrito 49, Representante Estatal)

Precincts / Precintos: 149, 200, 202, 206, 208, 209, 214,
218, 222, 228, 235, 236, 239, 240, 241, 242, 243, 248,
250, 252, 258, 260, 267, 268, 273, 274, 275, 277, 305,
311, 313, 323, 325, 329, 332, 340, 342, 345, 409, 425,
430, 446, 454, 460, 461

☐ Gina Hinojosa - DEM
☐ Rick Perkins - LIB

Many state and local races are less visible to voters, who may know little about the
candidates in down-ticket races (those below president and Congress). For example,
voters in this Texas county were called on to elect a railroad commissioner, numerous
judges, and members of the state board of education.

mayors of small towns focus almost exclusively on providing services such as fire and police protection, water, and sewage. A U.S. senator, however, may focus on foreign affairs, monetary policy, and other federal issues. As a result, a candidate for mayor in a small town is likely to emphasize his or her managerial skills, while the candidate for the Senate may express a larger vision for society that often involves taking liberal or conservative positions.[37] Candidates in larger jurisdictions also need to appeal to different groups in order to build a winning coalition. They may emphasize issues important to key constituent groups—for example, by defending the Second Amendment to appeal to gun owners. A small-town mayor will find such targeted group appeals less necessary.

We might also expect campaign strategies for state and local races to vary depending on the rules that govern them. City council races, which may involve single-member district seats, at-large seats, or both, provide good examples of these different strategies. In cities with single-member districts, prevailing patterns of housing may mean that many districts are characterized by a large majority of one ethnic group. In turn, this means that candidates must appeal to voters from the dominant ethnic group in their district. Washington, D.C., for instance. It has eight members elected from wards and five members, including the chair, elected at large. City council wards tend to be majority white or black and elect white or black city council members, respectively. Candidates for at-large seats may not need to appeal to smaller ethnic groups, however: a winning coalition can be built from the dominant or majority ethnic group within the city. One implication of at-large systems, then, is that candidates do less to appeal to ethnic groups that are minorities within the city, which then find it harder to gain representation on the city council.

Despite these differences in candidate strategy among federal, state, and local campaigns, all candidates at any level of office make similar kinds of strategic decisions about their message and the kinds of voters they will target. State and local candidates seek to articulate a message that defines and promotes their candidacy. They analyze past election results, precinct by precinct, and pore over registered voter lists to identify likely supporters who can then be targeted with media and get-out-the-vote efforts. They work to contact those supporters and ensure their participation on Election Day. But in many state and local races, these efforts are difficult to see, aside from lawn signs and perhaps a volunteer knocking at your door.

---

[37] Oliver, Ha, and Callen, *Local Elections and the Politics of Small-Scale Democracy*, p. 33.

The Push toward Professionalization

Even as state and local campaigns are, on average, less professionalized than federal campaigns, they have increasingly come to resemble them—with more spending, television advertising, and use of consultants than in the past. State parties are also driving professionalization. They conduct polls and hire consultants to help formulate strategy that can then be implemented by the party's candidates. Many political consultants focus their practice within a given state and advertise their detailed knowledge of the local terrain. To some extent, the push toward professionalization is simply an arms race: once one side raises enough money to hire consultants and air television advertising, the other side will try to do likewise. The push to professionalization is perhaps most evident in two types of campaigns: for ballot initiatives and referenda and for state judicial offices.

Ballot Initiatives

Ballot initiatives and **referenda** are proposals placed on the ballot that allow citizens to change law and public policy. Their forms vary, but in most cases, initiatives involve citizens or interest groups drafting legislation and getting it put on the ballot. These are called *direct initiatives*. In the case of referenda, the legislature refers a piece of legislation to the people to approve or reject it. The most common form of referendum is a proposed amendment to the state constitution.[38] Ballot initiatives and referenda are a form of "direct democracy" because they are voted on directly by citizens rather than by elected representatives. Twenty-four states and the District of Columbia allow ballot initiatives while 26 states allow referenda.[39] The number of initiatives or referenda varies by year. In 2016, there were 162 ballot measures across the country. Their topics ranged from one in California that would require the use of condoms during the filming of pornographic films (it passed) to an initiative in Maine that would establish a new method of voting in which voters would rank their candidate preferences on the ballot, thereby avoiding situations where a candidate wins without support from a majority (it passed, but was declared unconstitutional by the state's supreme court). Of course, 2016 also saw its share of initiatives related to marijuana legalization, raising the minimum wage, and gun control.

---

[38] Ballotpedia. "2016 Ballot Measures." https://ballotpedia.org/2016_ballot_measures (accessed 6/13/2017).

[39] Ballotpedia. "States with Initiative or Referendum." https://ballotpedia.org/States_with _initiative_or_referendum (accessed 6/13/2017).

Although direct democracy does empower citizens in some respects, many ballot initiatives are hardly the results of grassroots organizing. Instead, interest groups and wealthy individuals work to place their proposals on the ballot and then spend money to promote them. A highly controversial ballot measure in a large state will ultimately cost supporters and opponents many millions of dollars. For example, in 2016, the campaigns for and against adopting a higher tobacco tax in California spent $107 million. There is little that can be done to limit the amounts spent in ballot initiative campaigns. Supreme Court precedent forbids limits on donations to committees formed to support or oppose initiatives; it also forbids bans on corporate spending in ballot initiative campaigns. The logic is that initiatives, unlike candidates, cannot be corrupted by money, and thus there is no compelling interest that would allow restrictions on speech.[40]

With so much money involved, the task of getting a measure on the ballot and promoting it now involves a wide array of campaign professionals. There are law firms who craft the wording of the initiative, consulting firms who specialize in gathering the signatures needed to get the initiative on the ballot, media firms who produce radio and television ads promoting or denouncing the initiative, pollsters who monitor public opinion about the initiative, and direct-mail firms who design and send letters to citizens about the initiative. Consultants often relish the opportunity to work on these campaigns, which offer them greater latitude to shape the campaign message than they might have working with an actual candidate. As one consultant said, "With ballot issues you build your own candidate."[41]

Judicial Elections

Thirty-eight states have judicial elections, of which there are three types.[42] Partisan elections pit opposing candidates identified with political parties against each other. Nonpartisan elections also feature opposing candidates,

---

[40] Richard L. Hasen. 2005. "Rethinking the Unconstitutionality of Contribution and Expenditure Limits in Ballot Measure Campaigns." *Southern California Law Review* 78, 4: 885–926.

[41] Quoted in Dennis W. Johnson. 2007. *No Place for Amateurs: How Political Consultants Are Reshaping American Democracy*, 2nd ed. New York: Routledge, p. 201.

[42] American Bar Association. "Fact Sheet on Judicial Selection Methods in the States." www.americanbar.org/content/dam/aba/migrated/leadership/fact_sheet.authcheckdam.pdf (accessed 7/31/2017).

The Instrumental Uses of Ballot Initiatives

In 2004, 11 states passed ballot initiatives that banned same-sex marriages by defining marriage as a union between a man and a woman. After George W. Bush's victory in the presidential election that year, the *New York Times* wrote that these initiatives "acted like magnets for thousands of socially conservative voters in rural and suburban communities who might not have otherwise voted, even in this heated campaign."[1] Although Karl Rove, Bush's chief campaign strategist, denied he helped engineer the anti-gay marriage amendments to aid Bush's reelection, Ken Mehlman, who was Bush's campaign manager in 2004 and chairman of the Republican National Committee shortly thereafter, said he knew Rove "had been working with Republicans to make sure that anti-gay initiatives and referenda would appear on November ballots in 2004 and 2006 to help Republicans."[2]

In 2016, voters across the country had the opportunity to vote on a wide range of left-leaning initiatives, including measures that would legalize medical or recreational marijuana, raise the minimum wage, or expand gun control. Did Democrats hope these initiatives would act like a "magnet" for liberal voters in the same way that anti-gay measures did for Republicans in 2004? It's unlikely. First, political scientists are not so convinced that the same-sex marriage initiatives tipped the balance toward Bush in 2004, political scientists are not so convinced. After all, much of the debate in the 2004 election concerned the War on Terror and the Iraq War. There is some evidence that the same-sex ballot initiatives marginally helped Bush by priming voters to evaluate Bush in light of his position on the issue.[3] The 2004 initiatives may have also changed the composition of the electorate by increasing turnout among evangelicals.[4] Both of these effects were small, however. Thus, political scientists believe the spillover effects of ballot initiatives and referenda are often overblown.

Second, ballot initiatives and referenda might have served a different strategic purpose for liberal groups in 2016: they enabled these groups to pass laws by bypassing Republican-dominated state legislatures.[5] After the 2014 midterm election, Republicans had total control over 24 state governments. If liberal groups wanted to accomplish anything, ballot measures were their only hope. The results of the 2016 election suggest that their strategy was a success: eight of the nine marijuana-related ballot measures, four of the five minimum wage measures, and three of the four gun control measures passed. This success, combined with the Republicans' continuing dominance of state legislatures, suggests that we will continue to see a steady flow of liberal ballot initiatives for years to come.

[1] James Dao. 2004. "Same-Sex Marriage Issue Key to Some G.O.P. Races." *New York Times*, November 4.

[2] Marc Ambinder. 2010. "Bush Campaign Chief and Former RNC Chair Ken Mehlman: I'm Gay." *The Atlantic*, August 25.

[3] Stephen P. Nicholson. 2005. *Voting the Agenda: Candidates, Elections, and Ballot Propositions*. Princeton, NJ: Princeton University Press; Todd Donovan, Caroline J. Tolbert, and Daniel A. Smith. 2008. "Priming Presidential Votes by Direct Democracy." *Journal of Politics* 70, 4: 1217–31; but see D. Sunshine Hillygus and Todd G. Shields. 2005. "Moral Issues and Voter Decision Making in the 2004 Presidential Election." *Political Science and Politics* 38, 2: 201–9.

[4] David E. Campbell and J. Quin Monson. 2008. "The Religion Card: Gay Marriage and the 2004 Presidential Election." *Public Opinion Quarterly* 72, 3: 399–419.

[5] Liz Essley Whyte. 2016. "How Democratic Are Ballot Initiatives?" *The Atlantic*, January 6.

but they run without party labels (although political parties may endorse them). **Retention elections** are referenda on sitting judges in which voters decide whether they should remain on the bench. Normally, judges are retained but occasionally they are removed if they have made an unpopular ruling. For example, in 2010, three justices from the Iowa Supreme Court lost their retention elections after the court ruled in favor of gay marriage. Only three other judges had suffered this fate in the 48-year history of judicial elections in Iowa. The campaigns for judicial offices were once staid affairs that featured little electioneering, but they have come to resemble campaigns for executive and legislative offices.

Judicial campaigns have become increasingly costly: the total amount of money raised by state supreme court candidates across the country jumped from $6.3 million in 1989–90 to almost $61.2 million in 2003–04 (see Figure 11.2).[43] Since then, state supreme court candidates have continued to raise similar amounts in cycles including a presidential election ($57.1 million in 2007–08 and $56.4 million in 2011–12) but less in those including a midterm election ($42.8 million in 2005–06, $38.7 million in 2009–10, and $34.5 million in 2013–14). Judicial campaigns often attract the efforts of various party organizations as well as interest groups such as chambers of commerce, trial lawyer groups, and the Small Business Council of America, which donate to judicial candidates or spend independently on their behalf. In fact, in 2013–14, party and interest group funding accounted for 40 percent of the total spending in state supreme court campaigns.[44] Finally, these campaigns have featured an increasing number of television advertisements. State supreme court campaigns produced only about 23,000 ads in 2000, but voters typically see more than twice that number these days. In 2014, more than 39,000 ads aired, but that number was 51,000 in

[43] James J. Sample, Adam Skaggs, Jonathan Blitzer, and Linda Casey. 2010. "The New Politics of Judicial Elections 2000–2009: Decade of Change." New York: Brennan Center for Justice; Adam Skaggs, Maria da Silva, Linda Casey, and Charles Hall. 2011. "The New Politics of Judicial Elections 2009–2010: How Special Interest "Super Spenders" Threatened Impartial Justice and Emboldened Unprecedented Legislative Attacks on America's Courts." New York: Brennan Center for Justice. Both sources may be accessed at www.brennancenter.org/analysis/new-politics-judicial-elections-all-reports (accessed 11/12/2017).

[44] Scott Greytak, Alicia Bannon, Allyse Falce, and Linda Casey. 2015. "Bankrolling the Bench: The New Politics of Judicial Elections 2013–2014." New York: Brennan Center for Justice. www.brennancenter.org/sites/default/files/publications/The_New_Politics_of _Judicial_Election_2013_2014.pdf (accessed 11/12/2017).

FIGURE 11.2 Contributions to State Supreme Court Candidates, 1991–2014 Election Cycles

Millions (2014 Dollars)

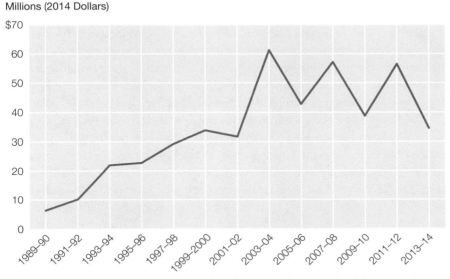

Note: 2014 dollar figures based on conversion rates from the even-numbered year of each two-year period.
Source: All sources may be found at www.brennancenter.org/analysis/new-politics-judicial-elections-all
-reports (accessed 11/12/2017).

2012.[45] The ads are frequently hard-hitting, accusing judges of sleeping during trials, "putting criminals on the street," and the like.

One reason for the increased expense of state judicial elections is that, starting in the 1990s, business groups increasingly came into conflict with trial lawyers, consumer groups, and labor unions over tort reform. Tort reform typically entails limits to the awards that plaintiffs can win from corporations and businesses for, say, an allegedly faulty product. Business groups favored these reforms, but trial lawyers and consumer groups did not. This conflict then began to spill over into the judicial arena, since appellate and state court justices would often hear tort cases on appeal and could adjust

---

[45] Brennan Center for Justice. 2012. "New Data Shows Judicial Election Ad Spending Breaks Record at $29.7 Million." www.brennancenter.org/press-release/new-data-shows-judicial -election-ad-spending-breaks-record-297-million (accessed 6/14/2017); Scott Greytak, Alicia Bannon, Allyse Falce, and Linda Casey. 2015. "Bankrolling the Bench: The New Politics of Judicial Elections 2013–2014." New York: Brennan Center for Justice. www.brennancenter .org/sites/default/files/publications/The_New_Politics_of_Judicial_Election_2013_2014.pdf (accessed 11/12/2017).

the amount of money awarded to plaintiffs. Thus, it made strategic sense for interest groups to insert themselves into state judicial campaigns. Judicial races had previously been so sleepy that these groups believed a sudden influx of spending could make a difference in electing their favored candidates.

Whether the issue is tort reform, redistricting, or collective bargaining for state workers, in general it is cheaper to influence judicial elections than to help elect a favorable majority in the state legislature or a sympathetic governor. As one Ohio union official put it, "We figured out a long time ago that it's easier to elect seven judges than to elect 132 legislators."[46]

Needless to say, such sentiments do nothing to allay the fear that expensive campaigns compromise the integrity of judges. A case in point involved a West Virginia supreme court justice, Brent Benjamin. In 2004, Benjamin defeated incumbent justice Warren McGraw with the help of Don Blankenship, the CEO of a West Virginia mining company, Massey Energy. Before the campaign, Massey Energy had been sued by Harman Mining Company for breach of contract, and a jury ruled that Massey owed $50 million. Blankenship then spent $3 million in an attempt to defeat McGraw, establishing a group called "And for the Sake of the Kids," which aired ads accusing McGraw of "voting to let a child rapist out of prison." Three years after Benjamin won the judgeship, the West Virginia supreme court heard Massey Energy's appeal of this $50 million verdict. Benjamin provided the swing vote in a 3–2 decision that overturned the verdict. Later, the U.S. Supreme Court threw out the West Virginia court's decision, arguing that Benjamin faced a conflict of interest so extreme that Harman Mining's due process rights may have been violated.[47] Such a scenario, however unusual, suggests that expensive judicial campaigns may bring with them unintended consequences.

Activists in State and Local Campaigns

The entry of interest groups into state judicial elections hints at a broader feature of many state and local campaigns: without much voter or media interest, dedicated activists, whether from party organizations or interest groups, can powerfully affect these races. Activists can often work to influence the outcome without attracting much attention or even competition.

---

[46] Quoted in Sample, Skaggs, Blitzer, and Casey, "The New Politics of Judicial Elections 2000–2009," p. 9.

[47] *Caperton v. A. T. Massey Coal Co.*, 129 S. Ct. 2252 (2009).

For them, it takes fewer resources to get a larger benefit: greater influence over state and local races than might be possible in more visible federal races.

Rules that dictate off-cycle elections can have a strong effect on the influence of interest groups, because they result in lower voter turnout. Elections with low turnout help to empower interest groups whose members are likely to vote and thus produce policy outcomes closer to their preferences.[48] For example, in school districts with off-cycle elections, teachers are typically paid more than in districts with on-cycle elections—that is, teachers' unions are more likely to get their desired outcome: larger paychecks. Small wonder, then, that parties and activists have sought to manipulate the timing of elections to maximize their electoral or policy goals.[49]

State legislative elections provide another opportunity for interest groups and party activists to assert their influence.[50] In many state legislative districts, the outcome is largely a foregone conclusion because the districts are so politically homogeneous: the majority party can essentially monopolize the district. This makes the primary election the most important election, since the majority party's nominee will almost always win the general election. If term limits are also in effect, primary elections to choose a new nominee occur more frequently, and term-limited officials often compete in primaries for higher levels of office. Few, if any, state legislative primaries attract much attention from local news organizations or from voters, most of whom could not name their state representatives if asked.[51]

The result is that local party activists have considerable leeway to shape the outcome. As they do in city elections, local party organizations work to recruit candidates, influence the primary election, and ensure that the winner remains loyal to the activists' agenda while in the state legislature. They are not machines but rather networks of like-minded officials and activists who coordinate to influence the election. The power of this network will almost always trump that of potential candidates. Most candidates are not well known or personally wealthy, and thus they need the support of the local party to get on the ballot and to win. Because they must conform to

[48] Sarah F. Anzia. 2011. "Election Timing and the Electoral Influence of Interest Groups." *Journal of Politics* 73, 2: 412–27.

[49] Sarah F. Anzia. 2012. "Partisan Power Play: The Origins of Local Election Timing as an American Political Institution." *Studies in American Political Development* 26, 1: 24–49.

[50] Masket, *No Middle Ground*.

[51] Samuel C. Patterson, Randall B. Ripley, and Stephen V. Quinlan. 1992. "Citizens' Orientations toward Legislatures: Congress and the State Legislature." *Western Political Quarterly* 45, 2: 315–38.

the views of activists, these candidates will tend to be more ideologically extreme than the voters who elect them, and the parties in the state legislature will be more polarized along ideological lines.

An example of how such a network matters comes from the rural Central Valley of California, where Bill Thomas, a Republican member of the House of Representatives, held sway for nearly 20 years.[52] Thomas's support for a local candidate was considered crucial. His endorsement signaled to others in the network, such as prominent donors, business leaders, and conservative groups, to support the chosen candidate. This network was directly responsible for punishing a Republican state legislator, Mike Briggs, who disappointed conservatives by voting for a Democratic budget plan in 2001. Briggs, who had been the frontrunner for a congressional seat, found himself with a previously unknown primary challenger, Devin Nunes, who was 28 years old, reliably conservative, and, perhaps most important, a former campaign staffer for Thomas. Nunes beat Briggs in the primary and went on to win the general election.

The Paradox of State and Local Elections

The invisibility of many state and local campaigns gives rise to a paradox. State and local leaders are in some sense "closest" to citizens: they are intimately involved with the community they represent, and their decisions affect virtually every aspect of life there—from whether schools get new textbooks to whether potholes get filled. Despite their potential significance, state and local elections engage many fewer voters than federal and especially presidential elections. With little spending by the candidates and little attention from the media, voters are unfamiliar with the candidates and do not learn much during the campaigns. The weakening of party machines, whatever its benefits, has been associated with a decline in turnout. As a consequence, state and local elections see some of the lowest turnout rates among all American elections. One study of California municipal elections found that the average turnout in mayoral races was 28 percent, and in city council races 32 percent.[53] These rates are much lower than in federal elections: turnout even in midterm elections has been higher than 32 percent in every

---

[52] Masket, *No Middle Ground*, pp. 125–28.

[53] Zoltan L. Hajnal and Paul G. Lewis. 2003. "Municipal Institutions and Voter Turnout in Local Elections." *Urban Affairs Review* 38, 5: 645–68; Neal Caren. 2007. "Big City, Big Turnout? Electoral Participation in American Cities." *Journal of Urban Affairs* 29, 1: 31–46.

election since 1792. Moreover, even when state and local elections coincide with a presidential election, voters sometimes fail to mark a choice for state and local offices (a phenomenon called "roll-off").

Some of this lack of voter involvement is because many state and local races are not competitive. Many localities are not politically diverse, and so cannot sustain competitive elections. Republicans simply do not have much hope in Berkeley, California, while Democrats stand little chance in College Station, Texas. Incumbents also have a considerable advantage, especially those who hold full-time, professionalized offices. The inequalities among candidates so frequently noted in congressional races are similarly prevalent in many state and local races.

The lack of competitiveness also stems from actions taken by leaders, parties, and interest groups. Gerrymandering is part of this story: majority parties work, to the extent possible, to draw state legislative boundaries that will maximize the number of seats they hold. In addition, political monopolies within cities promote one party's reign in part via strategies that render elections less competitive and reduce turnout.[54] Activist networks seek to control the nomination process and primary elections, often limiting the choices available to voters by "clearing the field" of opposing candidates.

None of this is necessarily problematic in terms of the goals of democratic political systems. Low voter turnout could at times reflect a degree of satisfaction with state and local representatives and governments. The enhanced role of activists may be entirely appropriate, given that they feel much more strongly than the average voter about the issues that confront state and local governments. And representatives elected in uncompetitive races still may work to represent the interests of their constituents.

At the same time, a lack of competitiveness in state and local elections may create biases that have important effects on the process of governing. The power of activists, most of whom have strong ideological views, tends to produce leaders who are more ideologically extreme than voters. This bias toward ideologues creates polarization in government—whereby the two parties strongly disagree on policy and cannot reach effective compromises. The result of such polarization is that governments struggle to develop policy solutions to important problems. In California, which has one of the most polarized state legislatures, state budgets are routinely passed months after the ostensible deadline because Democrats and Republicans cannot agree on the appropriate levels of taxation and spending.

---

[54] Jessica Trounstine. 2008. *Political Monopolies in American Cities: The Rise and Fall of Bosses and Reformers.* Chicago: University of Chicago Press, Chapter 5.

Low levels of turnout in local elections also create biases in terms of which groups are represented in government. In particular, racial and ethnic minorities are often affected—a situation exacerbated when local elections are conducted at large instead of in single-member districts. In low-turnout elections, minority candidates are more likely to lose mayoral elections and elections for city council; consequently, the spending policies of local governments are often out of step with the views of minorities.[55] Thus, the lack of competitiveness and the invisibility of many local races create another sort of political inequality: conditions that seem unfavorable to minority groups.

Unsurprisingly, then, many reformers seek to make state and local elections more competitive. As noted earlier, this is one goal of clean elections laws. Competitiveness produces more vigorous campaigns, which, on average, make voters more interested and willing to participate. Proponents of campaign finance reform and term limits often intend just that, although, as we have discussed, these reforms may have little impact. But there are important trade-offs in making campaigns more intense, ones highlighted by the trends in ballot initiative campaigns and judicial elections. Contested campaigns tend to be more professionalized and more expensive, despite the efforts of campaign finance advocates. Competitive races also attract the energies of parties and interest groups, who may spend even more money independent of the candidates. All of this can make for mean and rowdy campaigns, while the money flowing into them raises additional concerns about the possibility of corruption. This gets at the essence of the trade-off. Competitive elections provide more choices and more information for voters, increasing the chances that they will participate. Yet, absent a transformation in campaign finance, these races are more expensive and often more negative. It is hard to have one without the other. This means that many people may find the solution to the paradox of state and local elections unpalatable.

Conclusion

State and local elections may often seem like small potatoes. The candidates are typically anything but celebrities, and the campaigns are often unsophisticated. But they have considerable strategic importance. For ambitious people, state and local offices can be important for incubating political careers. Barack Obama and Jimmy Carter began their careers as state

---

[55] Zoltan Hajnal. 2010. *America's Uneven Democracy: Race, Turnout, and Representation in City Politics*. New York: Cambridge University Press.

legislators. Other presidents began their careers in elected office as governors, including Ronald Reagan, Bill Clinton, and George W. Bush.

State and local politics are especially important for candidates from groups that have traditionally been underrepresented in political office, such as women and ethnic minorities. Potential candidates from these groups face significant barriers if they want to start their political careers at higher levels of office, such as Congress. Success is more likely within state and local politics, where the barriers are lower and where they can gain the experience, visibility, and viability needed to seek higher office.

State and local politics are also important to political parties and interest groups. Decision making at these levels affects a variety of policies that parties and groups care about, including taxation, schools, prisons, roads, and health care. Moreover, state and local elections offer parties and interest groups more opportunities for influence than do federal elections. Because most state and local elections are rarely covered by the news media and thus largely invisible to voters, party and interest group activists can work behind the scenes to choose and support candidates, knowing that the local candidates depend on this support.

KEY TERMS

professionalism (p. 322)	ballot initiatives (p. 331)
citizen legislatures (p. 322)	referenda (p. 331)
coattail effect (p. 325)	retention elections (p. 334)

FOR DISCUSSION

1. What is legislative professionalism and how does it affect the advantages of incumbents in state legislatures?

2. How do the strategies employed in state and local campaigns typically differ from those in federal campaigns?

3. Why do many state and local races give political party organizations and interest groups a particular opportunity to influence elections?

4. What are the possible advantages and disadvantages of having state and local elections become more competitive?

CHAPTER 12

Voter Participation

Who votes matters in elections. This is especially true of close elections like the 2016 presidential election. Scholars and journalists will be dissecting the 2016 election for years to come to understand how Donald Trump proved most of them wrong, but one thing is clear: Trump did a better job of getting his supporters to the polls in crucial swing states than Clinton did. This is especially clear when the election is viewed through the lens of race. As we discussed in Chapter 6, certain ethnic groups tend to align more with one party than the other. Whites typically lean toward the Republican Party, while African Americans, Latinos, and other minorities tend to lean Democratic. There is evidence that Trump was able to convince some working class white voters to defect from the Democratic Party, but it is also true that he simply did a better job of getting whites to the polls, especially in battleground states.[1] Compared with 2012, white turnout across the country increased by 2.4 percent in 2016, but it increased by 3.5 percent in Florida and a hefty 5.2 percent in Pennsylvania, helping Trump clinch his surprise win in the Electoral College.[2]

In contrast, Hillary Clinton appears to have done a dismal job of turning out African Americans—an essential part of the Democratic Party coalition because they so reliably vote blue. On the eve of the election, political observers stood agape as Clinton's "firewall" states—battleground states that she needed to hold for victory—of Wisconsin and Michigan fell to Trump. The fact

---

[1] Nate Cohn. 2017. "A 2016 Review: Turnout Wasn't the Driver of Clinton's Defeat." *New York Times*, March 28. www.nytimes.com/2017/03/28/upshot/a-2016-review-turnout-wasnt-the-driver-of-clintons-defeat.html (accessed 7/10/2017).

[2] Bernard L. Fraga, Sean McElwee, Jesse Rhodes, and Brian Schaffner. 2017. "Why Did Trump Win? More Whites—and Fewer Blacks—Actually Voted." *Washington Post*, May 8. www.washingtonpost.com/news/monkey-cage/wp/2017/05/08/why-did-trump-win-more-whites-and-fewer-blacks-than-normal-actually-voted/?utm_term=.afe361813052 (accessed 7/10/2017).

that African American turnout fell by 12.3 percent in Wisconsin and 12.4 percent in Michigan from 2012 to 2016 may explain this surprising turn of events. In fact, a study that modeled the 2016 election with the same levels of white and black turnout as 2012 shows Clinton winning those states.[3] To be sure, many factors besides white and black turnout played a role in President Trump's surprise victory, but the key to winning any election is getting one's supporters to the polls.

Why do some people vote or volunteer for a campaign, while others do their best to tune out an election? Many factors explain why a person chooses to participate in politics. Some of the factors are characteristics of the individual. Does the person typically follow politics? How many years of schooling does she have? Is she enthusiastic about the candidate? Other factors, however, pertain to an individual's environment. Has her pastor or minister encouraged her congregation to vote? Has a volunteer from a campaign knocked on her door? Has her union contacted her about participating in a canvassing drive? If we want to understand why whites were more likely to turn out in 2016 than 2012 and African Americans were not, these are the factors we need to consider. During the campaign, many political observers said there was an "enthusiasm gap" between Clinton and Trump supporters: Trump supporters seemed to be fired up, while Clinton supporters were more tepid. There is also evidence that Clinton had a weak ground game, particularly in Wisconsin and Michigan, which means her supporters in those states were not getting the encouragement they

Core of the Analysis

- The rules that govern elections determine who is eligible to vote and how easy it is for an individual to participate.
- Because of its rules, the United States has lower voter turnout than other developed democracies.
- Citizens' participation depends on three factors: ability, motivation, and opportunity.
- These factors create participatory distortions when they encourage some groups of people to participate more than others.
- Mobilization by political campaigns encourages people to participate and may be responsible for recent increases in voter turnout.

---

[3] Fraga, McElwee, Rhodes, and Schaffner, "Why Did Trump Win?"

needed to ensure they voted.[4] As we discuss later in this chapter, the most effective way to get people to vote is to ask them to do so. If that request never comes, a potential voter is more likely to decide she has better things to do on Election Day.

What Is Electoral Participation?

Political participation during the electoral season can take many forms. The most common form of participation is voting, but participation encompasses other activities as well, such as trying to persuade a friend or coworker to vote for a particular candidate or writing a check to a candidate's campaign committee. **Electoral participation** refers to the range of activities through which individuals attempt to affect the outcome of an election, including not only partisan activities, which favor a particular candidate, but also non-partisan activities, such as participation in voter registration drives.

Forms of electoral participation vary along four dimensions: how often they can be performed, the personal resources required to engage in them, whether they are performed alone or with others, and how much information they convey about citizens' preferences, needs, and desires. For example, citizens have only one vote, but they can volunteer and donate as frequently as they like, especially if they have resources such as free time and money. This means that certain individuals can have an impact on the electoral process far beyond a single vote, which can create a **participatory distortion**. A participatory distortion occurs when one group of citizens has a greater impact on the political process than another group of citizens.[5] For example, senior citizens, who vote at higher rates than young people, are more concerned about issues such as Social Security and Medicare, while younger people care more about issues such as college tuition rates and environmental degradation. Because senior citizens vote more, however, elected officials pay more attention to their political agenda.

---

[4] Edward-Isaac Dovere. 2016. "How Clinton Lost Michigan—and Blew the Election." Politico.com, December 14. www.politico.com/story/2016/12/michigan-hillary-clinton -trump-232547 (accessed 7/12/2017). For a different take, see Nate Silver. 2017. "Clinton's Ground Game Didn't Cost Her the Election." *FiveThirtyEight*, February 13. https:// fivethirtyeight.com/features/clintons-ground-game-didnt-cost-her-the-election/ (accessed 7/12/2017).

[5] Sidney Verba, Kay Lehman Schlozman, and Henry E. Brady. 1995. *Voice and Equality: Civic Voluntarism in American Politics*. Cambridge, MA: Harvard University Press, p. 15.

Donald Trump's supporters give him an enthusiastic welcome at a rally in Iowa. The Trump campaign's ability to mobilize white voters played a part in Trump's 2016 victory.

In addition, some types of electoral participation can be performed alone, such as voting or making a donation to a candidate, but others involve interacting with people. While some people may find the solidarity that comes from working with other people to promote a candidate empowering, others might view such activity with trepidation because it requires speaking one's mind and carries the potential for conflict.

Finally, some forms of participation contain more information for elected representatives than other forms. Consider voting for a candidate versus writing to a newspaper to say why you support that candidate. Both actions are forms of electoral participation, but writing to a newspaper conveys more information than voting does. When citizens vote, their votes communicate their preference for one candidate over another, but not why they voted for that candidate. Winning candidates often claim a "mandate," suggesting that their victory means citizens support all of the policies they advocate. In fact, voters may disagree with many of the policy positions embraced by candidates but vote for them anyway because they seem more likeable or trustworthy than their opponent. When citizens engage in information-rich forms of electoral participation, such as letter writing, they provide candidates and elected officials with more specific guidance.

Trends in Participation in the United States

After the 2000 election, books with titles such as *The Vanishing Voter* and *Democracy at Risk* sought to explain declining levels of political participation in the United States.[6] A chief motivation for this was the trend in turnout in presidential elections between 1960 and 1996 (see Figure 12.1). With the exception of 1992, when the three-way race featuring George H. W. Bush, Bill Clinton, and Ross Perot piqued voters' interest, the turnout rate declined during this period along with other forms of participation, such as attending a meeting or rally for a candidate or volunteering for a political campaign. The only form of electoral participation that defied the trend was advocating for a candidate to family, friends, or coworkers. Yet almost as soon as these books hit the shelves, the decline in electoral participation ended. From its low level of 53 percent in 1996, turnout in presidential

FIGURE 12.1 Electoral Participation in Presidential Elections, 1952–2016

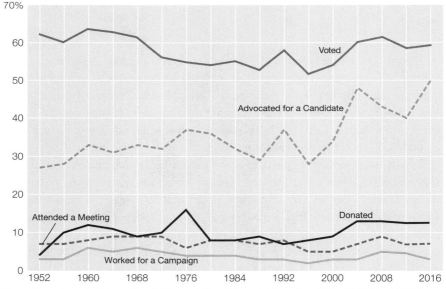

Source: Turnout rates based on voting eligible population. All turnout data are from Michael P. McDonald. 2017. United States Elections Project. www.electproject.org/home/voter-turnout (accessed 7/11/2017). The nonvoting activities data are from the American National Election Study Cumulative File and the 2016 Times Series Study.

---

[6] Thomas E. Patterson. 2002. *The Vanishing Voter: Public Involvement in an Age of Uncertainty*. New York: Knopf; Stephen Macedo, et al., 2005. *Democracy at Risk: How Political Choices Undermine Citizen Participation*. Washington, DC: Brookings Institution Press.

FIGURE 12.2 Voter Participation in Midterm Elections, 1958–2014

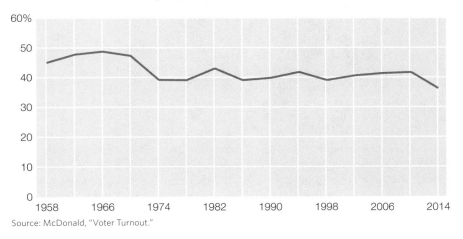

Source: McDonald, "Voter Turnout."

elections increased to 62 percent in 2008, returning to the levels of the 1960s. In the last two presidential elections, it has decreased slightly to 59 percent, but it remains elevated. For a discussion of how political scientists calculate turnout, see Box 12.1.

Figure 12.1 shows that voting remains by far the most prevalent form of electoral participation. Typically, less than 10 percent of the population attends a campaign-related event or donates, and less than five percent works for a campaign. The clearest trend in the data suggests that since 2000 more voters have tried to persuade others to vote a particular way.

Levels of electoral participation in the United States decrease sharply in midterm years, when turnout hovers around 40 percent, or 10 to 20 points lower than in presidential election years (see Figure 12.2).[7] At 36 percent, the 2014 midterm election had the lowest turnout of any midterm since 1942. All other forms of participation are less prevalent in midterm election years as well. It should be noted that there is an especially significant drop-off in the participation of young people in midterms, making the midterm electorate significantly older than the presidential electorate.[8]

---

[7] Other forms of participation are also much lower in midterm elections as well. The American National Election Studies stopped asking questions about nonvoting participation in midterms in 2002. This is why they are not included in this chart.

[8] Raymond E. Wolfinger, Steven J. Rosenstone, and Richard A. McIntosh. 1981. "Presidential and Congressional Voters Compared." *American Politics Research* 9, 2: 245–56; Robert A. Jackson. 2000. "Differential Influences on Participation in Midterm versus Presidential Elections." *Social Science Journal* 37, 3: 385–402.

VAP versus VEP: How to Calculate Voter Turnout

Calculating voter turnout seems simple: just divide the total number of ballots cast in an election by the number of people in a country or jurisdiction. The question is, what kinds of people should be included in the denominator? Typically, those calculating turnout rates divide the ballots cast by the voting age population (VAP), that is, the number of people in the United States who are over the age of 18. But not everyone over the age of 18 in the United States is actually eligible to vote. Many over the age of 18 are not citizens. In addition, over 6 million people in the United States cannot vote because they live in a state that does not allow prisoners or people who have committed a felony to vote. To take these factors into account, political scientists use the voting-eligible population (VEP)

to calculate turnout. Because the VEP is smaller than the VAP, turnout calculated using the former is usually several percentage points higher. Figure 12.3 illustrates this by showing how turnout in presidential elections differs when it is calculated with VAP and with VEP. Because the number of noncitizens and incarcerated individuals in the United States has been increasing, the gap between the two has been getting larger. This gap can be even larger when calculating state-level turnout. For example, in 2016, in California the difference in turnout rates calculated with VAP and VEP was almost 10 percentage points.[1]

---

[1] Michael P. McDonald. 2017. "2016 November General Election Rates." United States Elections Project. www .electproject.org/2016g (accessed 7/13/2017).

FIGURE 12.3 Calculating Turnout in Presidential Elections from 1980 to 2016, Using VAP and VEP

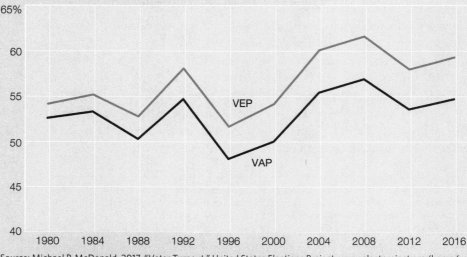

Source: Michael P. McDonald. 2017. "Voter Turnout." United States Elections Project. www.electproject.org/home/voter -turnout/voter-turnout-data (accessed 7/13/2017).

Turnout in midterm elections did not exhibit the same dip between 1960 and 1996 that we saw in presidential election years. One reason is that people who vote in midterm elections are typically "habitual voters"—people who vote in most elections. People who vote in presidential elections include habitual voters as well as those who become motivated by the excitement and media coverage generated by the election and who are mobilized by the campaigns. In fact, the decline in voter turnout in presidential elections between 1960 and 1996 may simply derive from unexciting elections: they were uncompetitive and candidates and parties invested less in **get-out-the-vote (GOTV) efforts**.[9] Both factors have changed in recent presidential elections. Not only have voters been more interested in the elections, but candidates and parties have also invested more in GOTV efforts. This investment appears to have produced results, as we will see later in this chapter.

Comparing Participation in the United States and Other Countries

Despite these recent increases in electoral participation, participation rates in the United States still lag behind those of many other countries, including many that are less developed, such as Ghana, Ecuador, and Sri Lanka. In terms of voter turnout rates, the United States ranks 27th out of the 71 countries that held presidential elections between 2004 and 2016 (see Figure 12.4).[10] Turnout rates in American midterm elections are even lower relative to those in other countries' parliamentary elections. If we compare the turnout in the most recent parliamentary elections of the 114 countries that held such elections between 2004 and 2014, the United States' 2014 turnout ranked 113th, just above Nigeria.[11]

This difference between the United States and many other democracies does not mean that Americans are less politically engaged. Americans actually report a stronger attachment to their party than do citizens of other

---

[9] Donald P. Green and Jennifer K. Smith. 2003. "Professionalization of Campaigns and the Secret History of Collective Action Problems." *Journal of Theoretical Politics* 15, 3: 321–39.

[10] The analysis was based on data obtained from the International Institute for Democracy and Electoral Assistance. Only the most recent presidential election since 2004 was used for each country. Countries with populations smaller than 1 million, or that were considered to be "not free" in the year of the election by Freedom House, were excluded from the analysis.

[11] Only the most recent parliamentary election from 2004 to 2014, which was not held at the same time as a presidential election, was used for each country.

FIGURE 12.4 Comparing Turnout in Presidential Elections, 2004–16

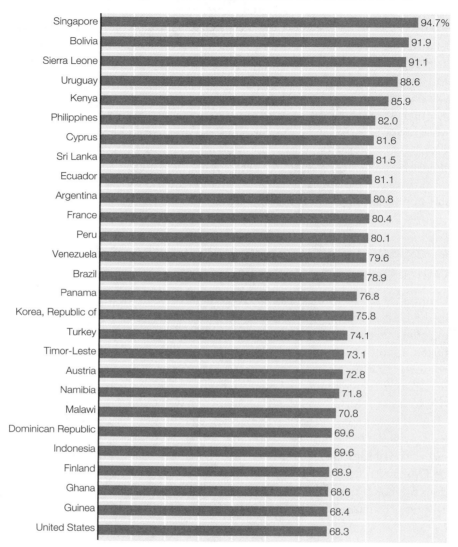

Country	Turnout
Singapore	94.7%
Bolivia	91.9
Sierra Leone	91.1
Uruguay	88.6
Kenya	85.9
Philippines	82.0
Cyprus	81.6
Sri Lanka	81.5
Ecuador	81.1
Argentina	80.8
France	80.4
Peru	80.1
Venezuela	79.6
Brazil	78.9
Panama	76.8
Korea, Republic of	75.8
Turkey	74.1
Timor-Leste	73.1
Austria	72.8
Namibia	71.8
Malawi	70.8
Dominican Republic	69.6
Indonesia	69.6
Finland	68.9
Ghana	68.6
Guinea	68.4
United States	68.3

Source: Institute for Democracy and Electoral Assistance, Voter Turnout Database. Turnout calculated based on VAP to make comparison across countries possible.

countries. Americans are also more likely to believe that voting matters.[12] Instead, many of the rules that govern elections in America depress citizen participation. For one, the United States does not make voting compulsory, as do 26 other countries, including Argentina, Australia, Brazil, Singapore, and Turkey.[13] Compulsory voting is estimated to increase turnout by 10 to 15 percentage points.[14] Second, Election Day in the United States occurs on a workday, while in many other countries it occurs on the weekend or a public holiday. Even though American employers are required by law to allow their employees to vote during work hours without docking their pay, employees may be hesitant to ask for the time off. It is important to note, however, that holding elections on "rest days" instead of workdays appears to have only a small effect on turnout.[15] Another factor that depresses turn-out is that voting is a two-step process in the United States; in every state except North Dakota, a voter must register before she is allowed to vote. If she moves, she must re-register in order to vote or apply for an absentee ballot to vote at her former address. In most Western democracies, citizens are automatically registered to vote. For example, in Canada, when a person turns 18 or becomes a citizen, he is automatically added to the voter rolls and remains on the voter rolls regardless of how many times he moves. The fact that U.S. citizens are responsible for registering adds a significant cost to voting.

Why Do People Participate in Campaigns and Elections?

People who regularly participate in campaigns and elections possess a greater *ability*, *motivation*, and *opportunity* to participate than those who do not. The following section discusses factors that affect electoral participation in terms of these three characteristics, paying close attention to the forms of participation affected. As mentioned earlier, forms of electoral participation

---

[12] Jeffrey A. Karp. 2012. "Electoral Systems, Party Mobilisation and Political Engagement." *Australian Journal of Political Science* 47, 1: 71–89.

[13] International Institute for Democracy and Electoral Assistance. "Voter Turnout Database." www.idea.int/data-tools/data/voter-turnout (accessed 7/17/2017).

[14] André Blais. 2007. "Turnout in Elections," in *Oxford Handbook of Political Behavior*, eds. Russell J. Dalton and Hans-Dieter Klingemann. Oxford: Oxford University Press, pp. 621–35.

[15] Blais, "Turnout in Elections," p. 627.

vary along a number of different dimensions, including how often they can be performed and whether they are performed with others. As a result, we cannot expect any given factor to affect every form of participation in the same way. Research has confirmed, however, that each of the following individual and contextual factors has an effect on participation *ceteris paribus*, meaning all other things being held equal. Within each subsection, the factors are discussed in order of the size of their impact on electoral participation.

Ability

The ability of an individual to participate in campaigns and elections depends a great deal on her education and income. Although it might seem obvious why this is the case, researchers have struggled to pin down what exactly accounts for the relationships between these factors and rates of participation.

Education Besides political interest, which is discussed later, a person's level of formal education is the strongest predictor of how likely she is to participate in politics overall. It seems to be especially important for forms of participation that are more time intensive and that require interacting with others.[16] The importance of education for participation has been well documented, but it is difficult to determine why it matters so much. The traditional view is that education provides citizens with the skills and resources necessary to participate in politics.[17] For example, primary and secondary education helps students understand how their democratic system functions, teaches them the importance of participating in that system by voting, and encourages students to discuss current events. These are, for example, the functions of high school civics classes. Primary and secondary education also increases students' aptitude as readers, writers, and speakers, skills that we associate with electoral participation.[18] However, a spate of recent studies shows that attending college, by contrast, has only muted effects on participation, because people who attend college are often already politically engaged.[19]

---

[16] Verba, Schlozman, and Brady, *Voice and Equality*, p. 358.

[17] Verba, Schlozman, and Brady, *Voice and Equality*.

[18] D. Sunshine Hillygus. 2005. "The Missing Link: Exploring the Relationship between Higher Education and Political Engagement." *Political Behavior* 27, 1: 25–47.

[19] Cindy D. Kam and Carl L. Palmer. 2008. "Reconsidering the Effects of Education on Political Participation." *Journal of Politics* 70, 3: 612–31; Steven Tenn. 2007. "The Effect of Education on Voter Turnout." *Political Analysis* 15, 4: 446–64; Adam J. Berinsky and Gabriel S. Lenz. 2011. "Education and Political Participation: Exploring the Causal Link." *Political Behavior* 33, 3: 357–73.

Thus, even college coursework that focuses on political science or other social sciences has only a small impact on one's likelihood of voting.[20]

Does this mean that a formal education is the only way to learn the skills necessary for electoral participation? Absolutely not. Workplaces, churches, and other institutions provide opportunities to organize events, put together presentations, and develop other skills that are useful in politics. For example, churches have long fostered political activism in the black community by mobilizing and teaching civic skills. This is one reason black churches provided the organizational backbone of the civil rights movement. At the same time, educational attainment increases the chances that an individual will be able to get the kind of job that teaches civic skills. For example, teachers and lawyers are more likely than blue-collar workers to acquire civic skills on the job.[21]

Income Income is another resource that enables individuals to participate in politics, although it matters much less than education as a predictor of most forms of electoral participation. The one exception, unsurprisingly, is contributing to a political cause. For that form of participation, income is the strongest predictor of whether and how much individuals contribute. What is surprising, however, is that those with higher incomes are more likely to engage in every form of participation—even in protests, which are sometimes considered a "weapon of the weak." What is it about having a higher income that enables wealthier people to participate more than poor people? This answer is obvious for making a political contribution, but less so for other forms of participation. It is not that people with higher incomes have more free time. Careers that provide higher incomes, like those in medicine or law, typically provide very little free time. Instead, it appears that people who have low incomes must put more of their time and energy into simply trying to get by, an effort that squeezes out room for political participation of any kind. Participation increases as income increases for those on the lowest end of the income spectrum, but once people achieve a comfortable standard of living, research has found that increases in their income no longer increase their participation rates. When people feel they no longer must live from hand to mouth, they are more able to focus on other things, including politics.[22]

---

[20] Hillygus, "The Missing Link."

[21] Verba, Schlozman, and Brady, *Voice and Equality*, pp. 314–16.

[22] Raymond E. Wolfinger and Steven J. Rosenstone. 1980. *Who Votes?* New Haven, CT: Yale University Press, pp. 23–26.

Motivation: Individual-Level Factors

People who participate in an election not only possess the resources to do so but also are motivated to get involved. Motivations can be loosely grouped into two categories: those that are individual—such as a general interest in politics—and those that are generated by the environment in which individuals live—such as a phone call from a campaign. The main individual-level factors that push people to venture into politics are their general interest in the topic, how much they know about politics, their level of commitment to a party, and a sense that they stand to gain from getting involved.

Political Interest The single most important individual-level factor affecting whether a person participates in campaigns and elections is **political interest**, which is simply a person's reported level of interest in government and public affairs. Interest matters the most in determining the willingness of a person to discuss the election with others, but it is also a strong predictor of whether one decides to cast a ballot or engages in forms of participation that require a time commitment such as attending a rally. It matters much less for donating to a candidate.

Although certain events can increase a person's political interest temporarily, it is a relatively stable characteristic that one either has or does not have.[23] Because it is stable over a person's lifetime, one must look to pre-adult factors to explain its origins. Parents can certainly pass their passion for politics on to their children, and formal education plays a role. Another source of political interest may be personality. Our basic personality traits can have an impact on how we think and act politically. For example, people who are open to new experiences—that is, those who are naturally curious and interested in learning—are significantly more likely to be interested in politics than people who are more conservative in their approach to life.[24] Recent research also suggests that genes may play a role in developing one's political interest.[25]

Political Knowledge Citizens vary substantially in how much they know about politics. This knowledge can take a variety of forms, including facts

---

[23] Markus Prior. 2010. "You've Either Got It or You Don't? The Stability of Political Interest over the Life Cycle." *Journal of Politics* 72, 3: 747–66.

[24] Jeffery J. Mondak and Karen D. Halperin. 2008. "A Framework for the Study of Personality and Political Behaviour." *British Journal of Political Science* 38, 2: 335–62.

[25] Robert Klemmensen, Peter K. Hatemi, Sara B. Hobolt, Axel Skytthe, and Asbjørn S. Nørgaard. 2012. "Heritability in Political Interest and Efficacy across Cultures: Denmark and the United States." *Twin Research and Human Genetics* 15, 1: 15–20.

about how the political process works, familiarity with elected officials, and awareness of the current issues of the day. As a predictor of political participation, its effects are on par with formal education. It is a powerful predictor of voting and whether or not a person discusses politics, but it also matters for engaging in more time-intensive campaign activities. Interestingly, it has no effect on donating. Although political knowledge might appear to be a resource that increases one's ability to engage in politics, scholars usually treat it as an objective measure of how motivated a person is to participate in politics. It is an *objective* measure because a person must be able to answer a series of questions about politics correctly to demonstrate a high level of knowledge. In contrast, people need only claim to have a high level of political interest, which makes it a *subjective* measure of engagement. In general, people who are politically interested, better educated, wealthy, and white tend to have higher levels of political knowledge than those who are not. In addition, men are usually more politically knowledgeable than women.[26]

Partisan Strength As discussed in Chapter 6, Americans typically identify with one of the two major parties or remain unaffiliated, referring to themselves as "independent." Partisan strength captures how strongly people identify with a party, with independents considered to be the weakest in partisan strength. It affects electoral participation because the more strongly people identify with a party, the more invested they are in its success. Overall, the size of partisan strength's effect on participation is less than that of education, political interest, and political knowledge, but roughly similar to that of income. It matters the most for voting, but also affects whether a person donates and discusses the campaign. Unlike political interest, partisan strength does not vary according to education, income, and gender, but age and personality seem to drive it. Partisan strength typically increases as people get older. Personality affects partisan strength because some people have a stronger need to belong, as well as a stronger need for a structure to help them interpret their political world. Specifically, people who score high on extroversion (sociability), agreeableness (cooperative), and conscientiousness (high need for structure) are more likely to be partisans.[27]

---

[26] Michael X. Delli Carpini and Scott Keeter. 1996. *What Americans Know about Politics and Why It Matters.* New Haven, CT: Yale University Press.

[27] Alan S. Gerber, Gregory A. Huber, David Doherty, and Conor M. Dowling. 2012. "Personality and the Strength and Direction of Partisan Identification." *Political Behavior* 34, 4: 653–88.

Participating in campaigns can bring people together, creating solidary benefits. Here, volunteers for Bernie Sanders's primary campaign gather after canvassing neighborhoods in early 2016.

Self-Interest People participate in politics because they derive some benefit from doing so. They may receive **material benefits**, that is, something tangible in exchange for participating. For instance, individuals may be paid to collect petition signatures to help get a candidate's name on the ballot. Individuals also participate in order to receive **solidary benefits**, which are the intangible rewards that come from being part of a collective effort, such as friendship with fellow volunteers or status in the community. In addition, individuals may participate in order to receive **purposive benefits**, which consist of satisfaction for having advanced an issue or ideological position, or for having fulfilled a duty. Ultimately, participating in a political campaign or election could bring all of these benefits, as participants benefit tangibly from getting paid for their work, enjoy the camaraderie among those working for the campaign, and feel good for having helped a worthy candidate.

Motivation: Contextual Factors

Although our own particular qualities or characteristics affect our willingness to participate in politics, the broader environment in which we live has an enormous effect on our choice to participate. We consider two types of contextual effects: those related to campaign activities and those related to an individual's social context. Political campaigns have an especially large effect on the decision to participate,[28] but the social pressure that people feel to get involved when their peers are doing so is another important contextual factor. There is very little research on how environmental factors affect different forms of participation, so here we discuss their effect on participation in general.

Mobilization The most important contextual factor promoting electoral participation is mobilization. **Mobilization** refers to the range of activities that candidates, parties, activists, and interest groups engage in to encourage people to participate. These activities usually occur during a campaign, but groups can mobilize citizens at other times and for reasons besides electing a candidate. They can encourage citizens to support certain legislation by writing letters to their members of Congress, or to show up at a town hall meeting to oppose an action of their city council. To be sure, the goal of those who mobilize is not simply to increase civic participation; it is to use that participation to achieve certain ends, such as the election of a candidate. Thus, groups target their mobilization efforts at those who share their goals.

Individuals and groups seeking to mobilize citizens do so directly and indirectly. They mobilize directly when they contact citizens and encourage them to act. They mobilize indirectly by using the social networks in which citizens are embedded to reach them, including workplaces, churches, schools, labor unions, neighborhood associations, and large national organizations such as the National Rifle Association (NRA) or the American Association of Retired Persons (AARP). During a campaign, for example, candidates seek the endorsement of community groups and national organizations in the hope that an endorsement will encourage group members to vote for them. This saves the candidate some effort, not only because the groups assume some of the costs of communicating with their members but also because group members are more likely to trust recommendations from group leaders than direct appeals from candidates themselves.

---

[28] Steven J. Rosenstone and John Mark Hansen. 1993. *Mobilization, Participation, and Democracy in America*. New York: Macmillan.

Mobilization efforts work because people respond when someone asks them to get involved. This may be because people are flattered by the request, like the idea of being involved in a collective effort, or find it difficult to say no and then feel they must follow through once they have committed. Groups seeking to mobilize members of a community are likely to focus their attention on individuals who are already active in their community. Active people have two qualities that mobilizers appreciate. First, they are easy to reach because they belong to a variety of organizations. Second, they are more likely to be influential when they do participate because they have a large social network and greater status in their community. Similarly, mobilization efforts are likely to target those with more education and higher incomes because they are more likely to participate in the first place.

As we noted earlier, much of the decline in turnout in presidential elections between 1960 and 1996 occurred because campaigns abandoned traditional mobilization activities, such as neighborhood canvassing. Instead, they turned to television advertising to communicate with voters.[29] Television advertisements, however, are not particularly effective at mobilizing voters. For example, eligible voters in media markets that witness a slew of presidential advertisements are no more likely to vote than those who live in markets that see no such advertisements. It does not make much difference whether the ads are predominantly positive (promoting a candidate) or negative (attacking a candidate). Although some commentators worry that negative advertising drives down turnout as citizens' distaste for attacks makes them feel alienated from politics, the sum of the evidence suggests that negative advertising does not affect turnout in any consistent fashion.[30]

What are the most effective mobilization strategies? Research to date has found that the specific message used in mobilization activities does not matter a great deal. For example, reminding citizens that voting is their civic duty seems to be no more or less effective than reminding them that the election will be close and so "every vote counts." In general, how voters are contacted is much more important than message content. One of the most effective strategies is in-person contact, as we noted in Chapter 5. Contacting eligible voters by having someone knock on their door and remind them to vote increases turnout by about 8 percentage points, according to one study.

---

[29] Rosenstone and Hansen, *Mobilization, Participation, and Democracy in America.*

[30] Richard R. Lau, Lee Sigelman, and Ivy Brown Rovner. 2007. "The Effects of Negative Political Campaigns: A Meta-Analytic Reassessment." *Journal of Politics* 69, 4: 1176–209.

Telephone calls, which are somewhat less personal, have a smaller effect, and then only when the phone call seems "authentic"—a quality better provided by enthusiastic volunteers or trained professionals. A phone call that seems scripted or, worst of all, is merely a recorded message has little effect on turnout. More impersonal forms of communication, such as mail and e-mail, also have little effect.[31]

The effects of campaign mobilization on citizens depend on the underlying capacity and motivation of citizens to participate. Citizens who are already very interested in politics are typically unaffected by mobilization because they are already likely to vote. Citizens who have little interest in politics are also unaffected because no mobilization effort is likely to convince them to participate. Instead, mobilization most affects citizens in the middle: those with some interest in politics who are often on the verge of voting but do not always end up making the effort. These citizens may need a reminder to vote, and campaigns can provide that.[32]

Starting in the 1998 midterm elections, the Democratic Party and its affiliated interest groups began to shift resources from advertising to voter outreach. The success enjoyed by the Democrats in the 1998 and 2000 elections led the Republican Party to focus more of their resources on voter outreach as well. As a result, 2004 saw unprecedented mobilization efforts by both parties—efforts that actually built on some of the mobilization research results we have described. This heightened focus on mobilization has continued in recent elections, including 2016. Thus, it is no accident that electoral participation has surged in recent presidential election years.

Social Contexts Family, friends, classmates, coworkers, and neighbors constitute a person's **social context**, and they can all affect one's decision to participate. In fact, a growing body of literature suggests that voting is a social behavior and even contagious.[33] For example, researchers have found that people living with a person who is contacted by a get-out-the-vote campaign are significantly more likely themselves to vote, particularly if

---

[31] Donald P. Green and Alan S. Gerber. 2008. *Get Out the Vote: How to Increase Voter Turnout*, 2nd ed. Washington, DC: Brookings Institution Press.

[32] Kevin Arceneaux and David W. Nickerson. 2009. "Who Is Mobilized to Vote? A Re-Analysis of Eleven Randomized Field Experiments." *American Journal of Political Science* 53, 1: 1–16.

[33] Meredith Rolfe. 2012. *Voter Turnout: A Social Theory of Political Participation*. Cambridge, UK; Cambridge University Press.

they are young.[34] In a massive experiment involving 61 million Facebook users, another study found that being told that close friends have voted increases the chances that individuals will seek out polling place information and vote themselves.[35] And even though there is not much difference in the effect of various mobilization messages, threatening to reveal a person's voting history to neighbors or to publish a list of voters in the local paper can be effective.[36] All of these studies demonstrate that a person's social context and the social pressure it generates is a major factor in political participation.

One of the most important social contexts is the family.[37] Parents can help to inculcate political interest and efficacy in their children. Some of this happens through mimicry. When children come of age politically, they may vote in part because they watched their parents vote. But besides acting as models for their children, parents may also deliberately try to instill political interest in their children. One important way they do this is simply by talking about politics. Conversations at the dinner table help to communicate parents' interest in politics to their children, who will then be more likely to become interested in politics themselves. Parents who adhere to the convention of not discussing politics at the dinner table might be decreasing the chances that their children will be interested in politics.[38]

---

[34] David W. Nickerson. 2008. "Is Voting Contagious? Evidence from Two Field Experiments." *American Political Science Review* 102, 1: 49–57; Edward Fieldhouse and David Cutts. 2012. "The Companion Effect: Household and Local Context and the Turnout of Young People." *Journal of Politics* 74, 3: 856–69.

[35] Robert M. Bond, Christopher J. Fariss, Jason J. Jones, Adam D. I. Kramer, Cameron Marlow, Jaime E. Settle, and James H. Fowler. 2012. "A 61-Million-Person Experiment in Social Influence and Political Mobilization." *Nature* 489, 7415: 295–98.

[36] Alan S. Gerber, Donald P. Green, and Christopher W. Larimer. 2008. "Social Pressure and Voter Turnout: Evidence from a Large-Scale Field Experiment." *American Political Science Review* 102, 1: 33–48; Costas Panagopoulos. 2010. "Affect, Social Pressure and Prosocial Motivation: Field Experimental Evidence of the Mobilizing Effects of Pride, Shame and Publicizing Voting Behavior." *Political Behavior* 32, 3: 369–86.

[37] M. Kent Jennings, Laura Stoker, and Jake Bowers. 2009. "Politics across Generations: Family Transmission Reexamined." *Journal of Politics* 71, 3: 782–99.

[38] Verba, Schlozman, and Brady, *Voice and Equality*; Molly W. Andolina, Krista Jenkins, Cliff Zukin, and Scott Keeter. 2003. "Habits from Home, Lessons from School: Influences on Youth Civic Development." *PS: Political Science and Politics* 36, 2: 275–80; Hugh McIntosh, Daniel Hart, and James Youniss. 2007. "The Influence of Family Political Discussion on Youth Civic Development: Which Parent Qualities Matter?" *PS: Political Science and Politics* 40, 3: 495–99.

Conducting Voter Mobilization Experiments during Campaigns

One challenge for political scientists studying the effects of campaign mobilization efforts has been in gaining access to real campaigns where they can run experiments. In the 1998 midterm elections, Alan Gerber and Donald Green decided to test the effectiveness of campaign tools, such as mailing postcards, phone calls, and in-person visits, in getting voters to the polls. Partnering with the League of Women Voters, Gerber and Green split the residents of New Haven, Connecticut, into three groups that each received one of the following treatments: a postcard encouraging them to vote, a phone call with the same message, or an in-person visit. For comparison purposes, a fourth group received no contact. After the election, Gerber and Green examined voting records to see who had actually voted. They found that turnout among people who had received an in-person visit was 9.8 percent higher than it was among those who received no contact. Postcards yielded less than a 1 percent boost in turnout, while telephone calls had no effect whatsoever.[1]

When Gerber and Green's study was published in 2000, it attracted the attention of campaign practitioners and ultimately led to the creation of an unofficial group called the Analyst Institute (AI). In 2007, AI became an official consulting firm, describing itself as "a clearinghouse for evidence-based best practices in progressive voter contact."[2]

AI began to conduct research challenging some of the conventional wisdom among political practitioners. For example, they found that simply asking people about their voting plans significantly boosts turnout, especially among people living alone: their turnout jumps by 10 percent. This may be because adults living together talk through their plans to vote with each other, which helps them envision casting a ballot. A campaign worker can play the same role for people living alone, encouraging them to think through how they will get to the polls.[3]

In 2016, AI ran a massive experiment for the House Majority PAC, a Democratic super PAC committed to taking back the House, which involved sending mailings to 108,000 independents and Republicans in five different states. The experiment was designed to test whether it was effective to attack a local Republican House candidate by tying him or her to Donald Trump. Not only did AI find it was better for a local Democratic candidate not to mention him, but it found that it was better for Hillary Clinton, too. It appears that trying to tie a local Republican candidate to Trump made the presidential candidate look more legitimate because it suggested he was supported by a local politician.[4] This is further evidence that experiments can help us understand the complex psychology of voters.

---

[1] Sasha Issenberg. 2010. "Nudge the Vote." *New York Times Magazine*, October 29.

[2] Analyst Institute. www.analystinstitute.org (accessed 7/11/2017).

[3] Issenberg, "Nudge the Vote."

[4] Dana Milbank. 2016. "Trump Is Too Much of a Wacko Bird to Be an Albatross." *Washington Post*, September 27.

Another important social context is schools, as we have already noted when discussing the role of formal education. Taking part in certain types of high school activities, particularly those that emphasize student government and community service, make young people more interested in politics and likely to participate as adults. Although participating in sports teams does not have the same effect, high school activities that emphasize public performance, such as debate and drama, also appear to promote political participation.[39] We can see the effects of nonathletic high school activities irrespective of a student's family income or the education level of their parents.[40] This suggests that cutting them from high school curriculums, as many school districts across the nation are doing, may have troublesome consequences for the future political participation of younger generations. Families and schools are particularly important because they open up avenues for children to think about politics at a time when there is no formal way for them to participate. They cannot vote until they are 18, for example, and generally lack other opportunities to participate meaningfully in political life.[41] It is no wonder that a recent survey of ninth graders found that they did not believe politics would affect them until they were older.[42]

Social context also matters at the level of communities. In particular, people who feel as if they belong to a community are also likely to feel empowered and to participate. By contrast, those who feel alienated or marginalized may withdraw politically. For example, studies have found that poor individuals living in wealthy communities are less likely to vote than those living in poor communities.[43] A number of studies have also shown that Democrats and Republicans living in "enemy territory"—communities dominated by the opposing party—are less likely to participate and discuss

---

[39] Daniel A. McFarland and Reuben J. Thomas. 2006. "Bowling Young: How Youth Voluntary Associations Influence Adult Political Participation." *American Sociological Review* 71, 3: 401–25; Jacquelynne S. Eccles and Bonnie L. Barber. 1999. "Student Council, Volunteering, Basketball, or Marching Band: What Kind of Extracurricular Involvement Matters?" *Journal of Adolescent Research* 14, 1: 10–43; Paul Allen Beck and M. Kent Jennings. 1982. "Pathways to Participation." *American Political Science Review* 76, 1: 94–108.

[40] McFarland and Thomas, "Bowling Young."

[41] Virginia Sapiro. 2004. "Not Your Parents' Political Socialization: Introduction for a New Generation." *Annual Review of Political Science* 7: 1–23.

[42] James G. Gimpel, J. Celeste Lay, and Jason E. Shuknecht. 2003. *Cultivating Democracy: Civic Environments and Political Socialization in America.* Washington, DC: Brookings Institution Press.

[43] R. Robert Huckfeldt. 1979. "Political Participation and Neighborhood Social Context." *American Journal of Political Science* 23, 3: 579–92.

The family is an important influence on whether individuals participate in elections and politics in general. Children often follow the models provided by their parents' political participation.

politics than their counterparts living in friendlier areas.[44] Even young people living in areas that have a significantly older population are less likely to vote than young people living among a younger population.

Finally, different **generational cohorts**—people who came of age politically at about the same time—can have distinctive patterns of electoral participation, which arise from the norms of behavior and the levels of civic and political engagement that were pervasive when that generation came of age. For example, people who grew up during the Great Depression and World War II were part of what has been called the Greatest Generation, the most civically and politically active generation of the twentieth century—one that stayed politically involved throughout their lives, even long after the Great Depression and World War II had ended. In contrast, Baby Boomers—those born between 1946 and 1964—have been less engaged in civic life and politics, even though many of them came of age in the 1960s and witnessed the civil rights movement and the Vietnam War

[44] James G. Gimpel, Joshua J. Dyck, and Daron R. Shaw. 2004. "Registrants, Voters and Turnout Variability across Neighborhoods." *Political Behavior* 26, 4: 343–75; Robert Huckfeldt and John Sprague. 1995. *Citizens, Politics, and Social Communication: Information and Influence in an Election Campaign.* New York: Cambridge University Press.

protests up close. Subsequent generations—those sometimes referred to as "Generation X," "Generation Y," and "Millennials"—have continued the trend and are even less interested in politics than are Baby Boomers.[45]

Why have later generations been less politically engaged than the "long civic generation" of the 1930s and '40s? One factor is technological change, beginning with the rapid arrival of television. Television offers citizens alternative ways to spend their leisure time that often compete with other activities, such as volunteering for a local organization or participating in politics. One study estimates that every additional hour of television viewing per day is associated with a 10 percent reduction in civic activism.[46] The arrival and penetration of the Internet, mobile phones, video games, and social media may be having a similar effect. Today, young people spend as much time with these new forms of media as they do watching television: more than 30 hours per week.[47]

Opportunity

People may have the ability and motivation to participate but still not do so because they lack the opportunity. They might not be eligible to participate, or the costs of participating—how difficult and time-consuming it is—may be too steep. As we discussed in Chapter 2, one must be an American citizen of at least 18 years of age to vote. These requirements for voting are far less stringent than in earlier periods of history, when women, African Americans, and other groups were barred from voting. The primary groups excluded today include the country's 74 million children and its 13 million permanent residents who work, live, and pay taxes here but are not citizens. As discussed earlier, 6 million felons and ex-felons cannot vote either. These groups can engage in nonvoting forms of participation, but research suggests they are much less likely to do so than those who are eligible to vote.[48] For

---

[45] Robert D. Putnam. 2000. *Bowling Alone: The Collapse and Revival of American Community.* New York: Simon & Schuster, pp. 250–51.

[46] Putnam, *Bowling Alone*, p. 228.

[47] Victoria J. Rideout, Ulla G. Foehr, and Donald F. Roberts. 2010. *Generation M²: Media in the Lives of 8- to 18-Year-Olds.* Menlo Park, CA: Kaiser Family Foundation, p. 2. www.kff .org/entmedia/upload/8010.pdf (accessed 7/17/2017).

[48] For a discussion of felon and ex-felon participation, see Jeff Manza and Christopher Uggen. 2008. *Locked Out: Felon Disenfranchisement and American Democracy.* New York: Oxford University Press, Chapters 5 and 7. For a discussion of youth political participation, see Cliff Zukin, Scott Keeter, Molly Andolina, Krista Jenkins, and Michael X. Delli Carpini. 2006. *A New Engagement? Political Participation, Civic Life, and the Changing American Citizen.* New York: Oxford University Press.

eligible Americans, the costs of voting depend on the costs entailed in each step: registering to vote and casting a ballot.

Voter Registration In most states, people who are not registered cannot vote. As discussed earlier in this chapter, it is unusual for a developed democracy to make citizens responsible for registering, which adds an additional cost to voting. This extra burden, however, is no accident. Voter registration was enacted by Progressive-era reformers in the early twentieth century (see Chapter 3) as part of a broader effort to challenge the political machines, whose power derived from their ability to mobilize immigrants and the urban working poor. The Progressives believed—often with good reason—that these machines were corrupt and that the methods by which they achieved high rates of turnout among immigrants and the poor were corrupt as well. They also believed that the vote choices of uneducated and illiterate people were manipulated by party bosses. Requirements for voter registration were intended to help prevent fraud by requiring citizens to appear periodically before local officials to verify their eligibility.

Both the timing of registration and the magnitude of registration requirements affect the cost of voting. The earlier a person must register before an election, the more difficult the process becomes because it is easier to remember to register when Election Day is near. At present, no state has a registration closing date more than 31 days before an election. Furthermore, if a person must travel to a distant location to register, that also imposes a cost.

The National Voting Rights Act of 1993, also known as the **Motor Voter Act**, requires states to allow voters to register when they are applying for a driver's license and public assistance programs, such as food stamps, or to allow Election Day registration. As a result, the costs of registering are now lower than they have been at any time since registration laws were first enacted. However, the Motor Voter Act did not significantly increase turnout in presidential or midterm elections. This raises the question of whether further weakening registration laws would actually increase turnout.[49] One registration reform that has been shown to lower the costs of voting is allowing voters to register at the same time that they vote. Same-day or Election Day registration, as it is called, increases state-level turnout by approximately 5 percentage points.[50]

---

[49] Benjamin Highton. 2004. "Voter Registration and Turnout in the United States." *Perspectives on Politics* 2, 3: 507–15.

[50] Highton, "Voter Registration and Turnout in the United States," p. 509.

Voting There are other costs associated with actually casting a ballot. About 85 percent of the people who are registered typically vote. What prevents the remaining 15 percent from getting to the polls? One possibility is that they do not know where their polling place is. Some states mail citizens polling place information or sample ballots, which are especially helpful in boosting the turnout rates for the less educated and the young.[51]

Many states have tried to boost turnout by experimenting with ways of making the act of voting itself easier. **Convenience voting** refers to methods by which registrants can vote without actually casting a ballot at a polling place on Election Day. One way to make voting easier is to allow citizens to mail in their ballots. Every state now offers some form of **absentee voting**, which enables citizens to vote by mail-in paper ballot prior to Election Day. Twenty states require individuals to state a reason for why they cannot vote in person, though the remaining states and the District of Columbia allow voters to apply for an absentee ballot without justifying their request. Eight of these states, as well as the District of Columbia, make it even easier to cast an absentee ballot by allowing any citizen to request to receive one for every future election.[52] Oregon, Washington, and Colorado have gone a step further by requiring all citizens to **vote by mail**. In these states, county administrators automatically mail out ballots to registered voters approximately three weeks before an election. Voters can either return the ballot by mail or drop it off at a designated location. Aside from absentee ballots and voting by mail, some states allow citizens to vote a week or two early at county elections offices or designated voting centers. A handful of other states allow voters to vote over the phone or to submit their ballot by fax. Currently, no state allows people to vote over the Internet.

Convenience voting is designed to make voting less costly and to increase turnout, but whether it actually does has been debated. There is some evidence that forcing state residents to vote by mail, as Oregon, Washington, and Colorado have, increases turnout, but the benefits appear to be restricted to presidential years and to wear off over time.[53] Recent research has found that allowing people to register on the same day they vote boosts turnout, but

---

[51] Raymond E. Wolfinger, Benjamin Highton, and Megan Mullin. 2005. "How Postregistration Laws Affect the Turnout of Citizens Registered to Vote." *State Politics & Policy Quarterly* 5, 1: 1–23.

[52] National Conference of State Legislatures. 2017. "Absentee and Early Voting." www.ncsl .org/research/elections-and-campaigns/absentee-and-early-voting.aspx (accessed 7/11/2017).

[53] Paul Gronke, Eva Galanes-Rosenbaum, and Peter A. Miller. 2007. "Early Voting and Turnout." *PS: Political Science and Politics* 40, 4: 639–45.

allowing people to vote early actually *depresses* turnout unless it is combined with same-day registration. This surprising finding may be explained by the fact that early voting makes it harder for campaigns to mobilize voters in a systematic fashion.[54]

Recently, many states have instituted voter identification laws, typically implemented in the interest of reducing voter fraud, that make voting somewhat less convenient. These laws require voters to show certain forms of identification at polling stations in order to vote. As we have learned, people who vote are educated and politically engaged, so they are likely to learn about voter identification laws and to figure out how to comply with them. This is borne out by numerous studies that have found the implementation of voter identification laws to have a minimal impact on turnout.[55] Yet, even if such laws are relatively harmless, those who oppose them argue that they are unnecessary since there is very little evidence of voter fraud in the United States.[56] Moreover, research has found that voter ID laws are typically adopted in states that are controlled by the Republican Party and are electorally competitive, as opposed to states where the Republican Party clearly dominates.[57] If voter ID laws were motivated by principle—for example, to ensure the integrity of American elections—then one would expect Republicans to enact them everywhere, rather than just in states where they stand to make election gains.

Electoral Competitiveness Thus far, our discussion of opportunity has focused on voting, but there are many other ways to participate politically, especially in campaigns. One factor that affects the opportunity to engage in these other forms of participation is the competitiveness of the election. When elections are close, candidates, parties, and interest groups have an incentive not only to encourage voters to participate but also to create more opportunities for participation. For example, a person who lives in a battleground

---

[54] Barry C. Burden, David T. Canon, Kenneth R. Mayer, and Donald P. Moynihan. 2014. "Election Laws, Mobilization, and Turnout: The Unanticipated Consequences of Election Reform." *American Journal of Political Science* 58, 1: 95–109.

[55] Jason D. Mycoff, Michael W. Wagner, and David C. Wilson. 2009. "The Empirical Effects of Voter-ID Laws: Present or Absent?" *PS: Political Science & Politics* 42, 1: 121–26; R. Michael Alvarez, Delia Bailey, and Jonathan Katz. 2008. "The Effect of Voter Identification Laws on Turnout." Social Science Working Paper 1267R. Pasadena, CA: California Institute of Technology, pp. 1–27.

[56] Lorraine C. Minnite. 2010. *The Myth of Voter Fraud*. Ithaca, NY: Cornell University Press.

[57] William D. Hicks, Seth C. McKee, Mitchell D. Sellers, and Daniel A. Smith. 2015. "A Principle or a Strategy? Voter Identification Laws and Partisan Competition in the American States." *Political Research Quarterly* 68, 1: 18–33.

state during a presidential election has ample opportunity to attend candidate events, help canvass neighborhoods, and call friends, because presidential candidates set up campaign organizations in these states specifically to create such opportunities.

Participating Online Campaigns use the Internet to increase opportunities for people to participate. Candidates for major offices use their websites to provide supporters a means to donate money, pledge their time and effort, and sign up for alerts about further opportunities to get involved. Candidate websites usually ask supporters to provide their ZIP codes so they will receive news about opportunities within their communities.

The Internet also allows citizens to connect and create participatory events on their own. An early example is Howard Dean's use of Meetup.com to keep supporters connected during his campaign for the presidency in 2004. Meetup.com made it possible for supporters to organize events at places, such as coffee shops and bars, where they could get together with friends and talk to them about Dean and his candidacy. During the 2016 Democratic primaries, supporters of Bernie Sanders could use his "BernKit," an online toolkit, to advertise a Sanders event or find a ride to one. Volunteers could also use the "Bernie Friend Finder" to identify friends supporting Sanders on Facebook and make sure they voted in their state's primaries. They could also download an app that made it easy to create memes to post on social media and send to friends.

Group Differences in Electoral Participation

The factors that encourage electoral participation reinforce one another. For example, people with more education are likely to have higher incomes and jobs where they can develop the confidence and skills that facilitate electoral participation. Their education and jobs also ensure that they are embedded in social networks through which they are likely to be mobilized. In addition, their education and income make it more likely that they will access the Internet and learn about opportunities to participate in a campaign. Understanding how these factors reinforce one another illuminates why certain groups in America are more likely to participate and why others are not, creating participatory distortions. Here we discuss such distortions in presidential elections, but they are typically even more extreme in midterm elections.

Figure 12.5 illustrates group differences in electoral participation. It is important to note, however, that this figure is based on self-reported

FIGURE 12.5 Self-Reported Voting in the 2016 Presidential Election

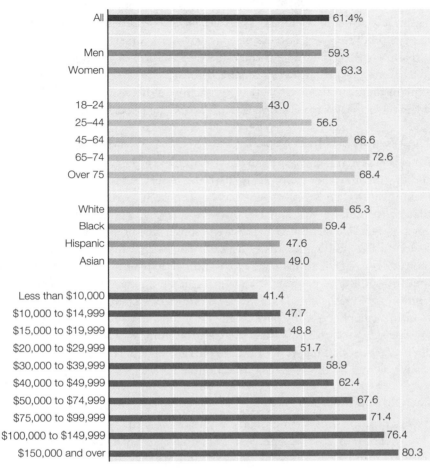

Source: Current Population Survey Voting and Registration Supplement, 2016.

behavior in elections. Although researchers have long observed that reported political participation in surveys is higher than actual participation, recent research has demonstrated that older, educated, wealthy, and politically engaged people are the most likely to misrepresent their behavior because they feel the most pressure to vote in the first place.[58] As a result, the differences in reported voting across income in particular, and to a lesser extent

---

[58] Stephen Ansolabehere and Eitan Hersh. 2012. "Validation: What Big Data Reveal about Survey Misreporting and the Real Electorate." *Political Analysis* 20, 4: 437–59.

age, are very likely exaggerated. Race is unrelated to overreporting, but men are significantly more likely than women to lie about not voting. Unfortunately, it is difficult to validate a person's reported voting behavior, so political scientists working with surveys often must take a person's word at face value.

Here we describe some of the more important group differences in electoral participation, drawing on the discussion in the previous section to explain them. In the final section, we turn to a discussion of whether these differences matter for election outcomes and government policies.

The Wealthy and the Poor

An especially large disparity in voter turnout exists between those with high and low incomes. For example, in 2016 the reported turnout among citizens making more than $75,000 per year was almost 30 percentage points higher than those making less than $20,000 (76 versus 47 percent). From a certain perspective, this inequality makes little sense. The poor should be less satisfied with the political institutions and policies that make it so difficult for them to get ahead, and thus they should participate more. Meanwhile, the wealthy should be content with the status quo, since they have benefited from it. Yet this is clearly not the case for the reasons we have discussed: wealthier people typically have more education and a professional career that provides them with skills that are useful in politics. They are also embedded in large social networks that encourage their participation and can be easily reached by those seeking to mobilize them.[59]

The Old and the Young

As discussed earlier, young people are much less likely to participate than older people. In 2016, 43 percent of people ages 18 to 24 reported voting compared with 71 percent of those 65 and over. What explains this lower rate of participation among the young? First, young people move around a lot. With each move, they must re-register, which increases the cost of voting.[60] Their mobility also makes them more difficult to mobilize, because they are harder to track. Young people are also undergoing many other transitions—leaving school, getting married, starting new jobs, having children—that in the short term may depress participation because of the

---

[59] Verba, Schlozman, and Brady, *Voice and Equality*.

[60] Benjamin Highton. 2000. "Residential Mobility, Community Mobility, and Electoral Participation." *Political Behavior* 22, 2: 109–20; M. Margaret Conway. 2000. *Political Participation in the United States*, 3rd ed. Washington, DC: CQ Press.

Young people are much less likely than older Americans to vote. In recent years, there has been a push to mobilize young voters. Here, California secretary of state Alex Padilla appears with students to publicize a new program to preregister high schoolers for voting.

physical and psychological commitments they entail.[61] Of these, the first two—leaving school[62] and getting married[63]—appear to depress turnout the most. As people settle into their jobs and marriages over time, and as their children become less dependent on them, the costs associated with political participation decrease. Independent of such life transition effects, however, aging has a strong positive effect on political participation. Although scholars are still debating why this is the case, many believe it can be explained by pure learning—that is, as one ages, one becomes more knowledgeable

[61] John M. Strate, Charles J. Parrish, Charles D. Elder, and Coit Ford III. 1989. "Life Span Civic Development and Voting Participation." *American Political Science Review* 83, 2: 443–64; Philip E. Converse and Richard Niemi. 1971. "Non-Voting among Young Adults in the United States," in *Political Parties and Political Behavior*, eds. William J. Crotty, Donald M. Freeman, and Douglas S. Gatlin. 2nd ed. Boston: Allyn & Bacon.

[62] Benjamin Highton and Raymond E. Wolfinger. 2001. "The First Seven Years of the Political Life Cycle." *American Journal of Political Science* 45, 1: 202–9.

[63] Laura Stoker and M. Kent Jennings. 1995. "Life-Cycle Transitions and Political Participation: The Case of Marriage." *American Political Science Review* 89, 2: 421–433.

about the political system and how to engage with it. An accumulation of life experience also seems to spur engagement.[64]

Whites and Nonwhites

Over time, certain groups in the United States have become more likely to participate, demonstrating that participatory inequalities are not immutable. Before the adoption of the 1965 Voting Rights Act, African American turnout was understandably poor due to discriminatory laws that effectively disenfranchised black Americans, especially in the South. The Voting Rights Act empowered the federal government to take over voter registration in southern states to ensure that African Americans could vote. This legislation quickly yielded results. Within 20 years, the gaps in registration rates between blacks and whites in the South—which had been 50 percentage points or higher in Mississippi, North Carolina, and Alabama—dropped to less than 10 points.

Today, African Americans and whites report voting at virtually the same rate in presidential elections. Their reported voting rates were identical in 2008, and the African American voting rate actually surpassed that of whites in 2012 (66 versus 62 percent). In 2016, however, only 59 percent of blacks reported voting as opposed to 63 percent of whites. There is evidence that Obama's candidacy in 2008 and 2012 created social pressure for some blacks to say they had voted when they had not.[65] If this is true, their six percent decrease in reported voting from 2012 to 2016 is less cause for concern. That said, as we discussed at the beginning of the chapter, African Americans were decidedly less enthusiastic for Hillary Clinton in 2016 than they were for Barack Obama in 2008 or 2012, so some of this decline is bound to be real.

Putting aside the debate about African American overreporting in 2008 and 2012, it should be noted that the electoral participation rates of blacks are especially remarkable because of their generally lower income and education levels. Part of the explanation for black electoral activism is mobilization that occurs in black churches. Another part may be the Democratic Party's heavy mobilization efforts in black communities. The party has

---

[64] M. Kent Jennings and Laura Stoker. 1999. "The Persistence of the Past: The Class of 1965 Turns Fifty." Presented at the annual meeting of the Midwest Political Science Association; Rosenstone and Hansen, *Mobilization, Participation, and Democracy in America.*

[65] Seth C. McKee, M. V. Hood III, and David Hill. 2012. "Achieving Validation: Barack Obama and Black Turnout in 2008." *State Politics & Policy Quarterly* 12, 1: 3–22; Bernard L. Fraga. 2016. "Candidates or Districts? Reevaluating the Role of Race in Voter Turnout." *American Journal of Political Science* 60, 1: 97–122; for an opposing view, see Ansolabehere and Hersh, "Validation: What Big Data Reveal about Survey Misreporting and the Real Electorate."

learned that it cannot assume blacks will turn out to vote even though they might be a "natural" constituency; they need to be heavily courted.[66]

Latinos and Asian Americans participate at lower rates than blacks and whites, despite being the fastest growing minority groups in the country. Between 2012 and 2016, the percentage of voting-eligible Latinos increased by 17 percent and the percentage of voting-eligible Asians increased by 16 percent. This is compared with just a two percent increase for whites and a six percent increase for blacks.[67] However, ethnicity per se does not explain the lower participation rates of Latinos and Asian Americans. Lower levels of education and income are more significant, as are the struggles with mastering the English language that immigrants often face.[68]

Men and Women

Women were excluded from voting in most American states until ratification of the Nineteenth Amendment in 1920. Today, women vote at a slightly higher rate than men, again demonstrating that participatory inequalities can be erased. In 2016, 63 percent of women reported voting, compared with 59 percent of men. The gap is especially large between unmarried men and women: in 2016, only 45 percent of unmarried men reported voting, compared with 53 percent of unmarried women.[69] There are few disparities between men and women in whether they attend political meetings or work for campaigns. The traditional gender gap emerges in other areas: men are more likely than women to report donating and discussing politics, and to actually run for elected office. Men typically have higher salaries than women, which explains why they would donate more. The difference in engagement in political discussions may arise because men also report more interest in politics, demonstrate higher levels of political knowledge, and appear to be more comfortable engaging in the

---

[66] Tasha S. Philpot, Daron R. Shaw, and Ernest B. McGowen. 2009. "Winning the Race: Black Voter Turnout in the 2008 Presidential Election." *Public Opinion Quarterly* 73, 5: 995–1022.

[67] Jens Manuel Krogstad. 2016. "2016 Electorate Will Be the Most Diverse in U.S. History." Pew Research Center, February 3. www.pewresearch.org/fact-tank/2016/02/03/2016 -electorate-will-be-the-most-diverse-in-u-s-history/ (accessed 7/16/2017).

[68] Wendy K. Tam Cho. 1999. "Naturalization, Socialization, Participation: Immigrants and (Non-)Voting." *Journal of Politics* 61, 4: 1140–55.

[69] U.S. Census Bureau. 2012. "Table 9. Reported Voting and Registration, by Marital Status, Age, and Sex: November 2012." www.census.gov/data/tables/time-series/demo/voting-and -registration/p20-580.html (accessed 7/19/2017).

kinds of heated exchanges that political discussions often entail.[70] Another factor may be the perception that politics is a "man's world." When women do hold high-profile offices, girls become more interested in politics.[71] Thus, having few women in office may create a vicious cycle whereby young girls do not develop as great an interest in politics and then do not run for office themselves, perpetuating the underrepresentation of women in political office. See Chapters 5 and 10 for a more detailed discussion of some of the factors that lead women not to run for office.

Are Voters Representative of Nonvoters?

Would politics in America be dramatically different if everyone voted? The first question to consider is whether the same candidates would be elected. The second question is whether, once elected, those candidates would advance the same kinds of policies that elected officials pursue now. If the answer to one or both of these questions is "no," then it is evidence of a participatory distortion.

The conventional wisdom regarding the relationship between turnout and electoral outcomes is that higher turnout benefits Democratic candidates because traditional nonvoters are more Democratic. Although the latter is true, research has demonstrated that increases in turnout do not consistently favor one party over the other,[72] because few elections are close enough for high turnout to make a difference.

The relationship between turnout and policy (as opposed to candidate) outcomes, however, appears to be much stronger. Although an early seminal study on the topic concluded that in terms of issue preferences, "voters are virtually a carbon copy of the citizen population," evidence has been mounting that this is not always the case.[73] The relationship between

---

[70] Sidney Verba, Nancy Burns, and Kay Lehman Schlozman. 1997. "Knowing and Caring about Politics: Gender and Political Engagement." *Journal of Politics* 59, 4: 1051–72; Stacy G. Ulbig and Carolyn L. Funk. 1999. "Conflict Avoidance and Political Participation." *Political Behavior* 21, 3: 265–82.

[71] David E. Campbell and Christina Wolbrecht. 2006. "See Jane Run: Women Politicians as Role Models for Adolescents." *Journal of Politics* 68, 2: 233–47. See also Lonna Rae Atkeson. 2003. "Not All Cues Are Created Equal: The Conditional Impact of Female Candidates on Political Engagement." *Journal of Politics* 65, 4: 1040–61.

[72] Jack Citrin, Eric Schickler, and John Sides. 2003. "What If Everyone Voted? Simulating the Impact of Increased Turnout in Senate Elections." *American Journal of Political Science* 47, 1: 75–90.

[73] Wolfinger and Rosenstone, *Who Votes?* p. 109.

turnout and policy preferences depends on the nature of the policy. It also depends on the election year. Table 12.1 shows that in 2012 the differences between voters and nonvoters were relatively small on values issues such as gun control, the death penalty, legalizing marijuana, affirmative action, and abortion, but they were often quite large with respect to economic issues, especially spending priorities.[74] The differences between voters and nonvoters were much smaller in 2016, however, and the gap between voters and nonvoters on economic issues did not appear to be especially large compared with the gap on social issues. The smaller differences in 2016 may reflect the fact that many people who do not typically vote turned out in 2016, perhaps because they were energized by Trump's candidacy, while other, more habitual voters stayed home because they were turned off by one or both candidates.

In general, nonvoters tend to favor government spending more than voters, except in the case of spending on science and technology, which voters are more likely to favor. This was true in both 2012 and 2016. There were some notable differences on social issues in 2012 and 2016. In 2016, voters were more likely to favor gun control (56 percent in 2016 versus 45 percent in 2012) while nonvoters were much more likely to think marijuana should be legal (50 percent in 2016 versus 39 percent in 2012).

The different policy preferences of voters and nonvoters affect policy outcomes, however, only if elected officials ignore the preferences of nonvoters or discount them heavily. The evidence largely suggests that they do. Members of Congress are much more likely to vote in line with the preferences of voters than nonvoters in their district,[75] because voters tend to vote for people who share their values and views. Voters are also better at communicating their preferences to elected officials than are nonvoters. Finally and unsurprisingly, elected officials pay more attention to voters than nonvoters simply because they want to get reelected.

As we've discussed, nonvoters also tend to have lower incomes than voters, and research shows that proposed government policies are much more likely to become law when they are supported by the economically advantaged.[76]

---

[74] This analysis is modeled on Jan E. Leighley and Jonathan Nagler. 2014. *Who Votes Now? Demographics, Issues, Inequality, and Turnout in the United States.* Princeton, NJ: Princeton University Press, Chapter 6. They reach similar conclusions using earlier data from the American National Election Study and Annenberg National Election Study.

[75] John D. Griffin and Brian Newman. 2005. "Are Voters Better Represented?" *Journal of Politics* 67, 4: 1206–27.

[76] Larry M. Bartels. 2008. *Unequal Democracy: The Political Economy of the New Gilded Age.* New York/Princeton, NJ: Russell Sage Foundation/Princeton University Press.

TABLE 12.1 Policy Preferences of Voters and Nonvoters in 2012 and 2016

	2012			2016		
	Nonvoters	Voters	Difference	Nonvoters	Voters	Difference
Economic Issues						
Favor reducing budget deficit	62%	82%	−20 points	73%	77%	−4 points
Increase spending for poor	49	38	11	47	41	6
Increase spending on social security	59	49	10	62	58	4
Increase spending on science and technology	39	49	−10	54	61	−7
Increase spending on child care	40	32	8	52	47	5
Increase spending on crime	57	50	7	52	47	5
Increase spending on schools	67	61	6	72	69	3
Increase spending on welfare	18	12	6	21	17	4
Increase spending on environment	45	40	5	57	53	4
Favor a millionaire's tax	75	77	−2	66	68	−2
Values Issues						
Ban all abortions	16	11	5	14	12	2
Favor more gun control	49	45	4	48	56	−8
Favor affirmative action in universities	12	14	−2	18	19	−1
Oppose death penalty	73	73	0	72	67	5
Favor marijuana legalization	39	39	0	50	44	6

Source: American National Election Study 2012 and 2016 Time Series Study. Both face-to-face and Internet samples were used with appropriate weights to calculate these percentages.

In fact, when low-income and middle-income Americans have different policy preferences than those with high incomes, research shows their preferences are largely ignored.[77] The influence of the wealthy may result from the greater frequency with which they contact their representatives and the frequency and size of their donations to the representatives' campaigns. The fact that wealthy individuals are better organized than poor and middle class Americans is very likely a factor as well.

Conclusion

Political participation comes in a wide array of forms. Turnout in elections—as the most obvious and, in some ways, least demanding form of participation—captures the most attention. Turnout in the United States is low compared with other countries and actually declined from 1960 to 1996. In recent elections, however, turnout has increased, due in part to the mobilization efforts of presidential campaigns.

Of course, one might ask why anyone participates in politics at all. Some would argue that the costs of electoral participation outweigh its benefits.[78] After all, the likelihood that a citizen's vote will decide the outcome of an election is infinitesimal. Part of the story is that citizens may value participation in politics for other reasons. Citizens receive a variety of nontangible benefits from participation that make it enjoyable—such as a sense of satisfaction from fulfilling their civic duty or from helping a cause or candidate they believe in.

What affects the participation of those citizens who do involve themselves in campaigns and elections? We have suggested that ability, motivation, and opportunity are important factors. Ability is related to formal education, financial resources, free time, and the civic skills acquired at work and through involvement in community groups. The motivation to participate stems from an interest in politics and the encouragement that

[77] Martin Gilens. 2005. "Inequality and Democratic Responsiveness." *Public Opinion Quarterly* 69, 5: 778–96.

[78] Andrew Gelman, Gary King, and W. John Boscardin. 1998. "Estimating the Probability of Events That Have Never Occurred: When Is Your Vote Decisive?" *Journal of the American Statistical Association* 93, 441: 1–9; Donald P. Green and Ian Shapiro. 1994. *Pathologies of Rational Choice Theory: A Critique of Applications in Political Science.* New Haven, CT: Yale University Press, Chapter 4; John A. Ferejohn and Morris P. Fiorina. 1974. "The Paradox of Not Voting: A Decision Theoretic Analysis." *American Political Science Review* 68, 2: 525–36; William H. Riker and Peter C. Ordeshook. 1968. "A Theory of the Calculus of Voting." *American Political Science Review* 62, 1: 25–42; Anthony Downs. 1957. *An Economic Theory of Democracy.* New York: Harper & Row.

one receives from the prevailing social context and from candidates, parties, and groups who engage in mobilization. The role of social context suggests that participation is, in a sense, contagious. Parents who care about politics and vote are more likely to have children who are politically engaged than are parents who do not care or vote. People who are politically active encourage other people in their social networks to participate. The role of mobilization also demonstrates that campaigns themselves can affect the decision to vote and the decision to participate in an election in other ways. In fact, even mobilization efforts are contagious: when campaigners knock on a door and remind the person who answers the door to vote, it makes other eligible voters in that household more likely to vote.[79] As we noted at the outset of this chapter, campaigns can matter not simply by persuading people *how* to vote, but by persuading them to vote at all.

Finally, having the ability and motivation to participate is not enough if one does not have the opportunity. In the case of voting, one has the opportunity to participate if one is eligible to vote and has registered. For other forms of participation, opportunities to participate are more likely to arise when elections are closer. Thus, citizens living in competitive jurisdictions will find themselves with ample opportunity to participate, while those living in noncompetitive jurisdictions will find they have fewer opportunities to flex their democratic muscles.

As we first noted in Chapter 2, political participation is intrinsic to many conceptions of what "good" elections look like. One such conception promotes the ideal of political equality. Egalitarians lament participatory distortions because they can produce electoral outcomes and policies that are not representative of what the general population wants. Yet, studies that have examined such questions argue that if all nonvoters participated, only some electoral outcomes and policies would change. The reason why only "some" would change is that an election must be close for the participation of nonvoters to make a difference, and close elections are becoming rarer in the United States. Beyond election outcomes, there is growing evidence that government is more responsive to those who participate than to those who do not. Thus, the way that members of Congress vote appears to reflect the preferences of voters more than the preferences of nonvoters and the preferences of the wealthy more than the preferences of the poor.[80]

---

[79] David W. Nickerson. 2008. "Is Voting Contagious? Evidence from Two Field Experiments." *American Political Science Review* 102, 1: 49–57.

[80] Griffin and Newman, "Are Voters Better Represented?"; Bartels, *Unequal Democracy*, Chapter 9.

Such findings do raise important concerns about the quality of American democracy. At the same time, however, we must think critically about whether participatory equality is the most important ideal for elections and how it should be balanced with other ideals. Those who support imposing restrictions on voter registration claim that they prevent voter fraud and corruption and mitigate how much political parties can manipulate the electoral process. Moreover, some argue that it is more important for citizens to vote in an informed manner than for all citizens to vote. In this view, it is actually worse if more people participate but do not know a lot about the candidates or the issues facing the country. Needless to say, these debates cannot be resolved easily, but as we try to understand them, it is useful to recognize that increasing electoral participation entails trade-offs between competing values.

KEY TERMS

electoral participation (p. 344)

participatory distortion (p. 344)

get-out-the-vote (GOTV) efforts (p. 349)

political interest (p. 354)

material benefits (p. 356)

solidary benefits (p. 356)

purposive benefits (p. 356)

mobilization (p. 357)

social context (p. 359)

generational cohorts (p. 363)

Motor Voter Act (p. 365)

convenience voting (p. 366)

absentee voting (p. 366)

vote by mail (p. 366)

FOR DISCUSSION

1. How much does it matter for the quality of democracy if certain groups of citizens participate more in the political process than others?

2. How can voting be made more convenient for young people?

3. Are you interested in politics? If so, who or what encouraged your interest?

4. Do you benefit from participating in politics? How?

5. Looking ahead to 2020, what new techniques do you think candidates will use to mobilize citizens?

CHAPTER 13

Voter Choice

In their postelection evaluations of the 2016 presidential race, many analysts blamed Hillary Clinton's loss on the fact that her campaign never made a compelling economic argument. Her message, critics claimed, focused too much on social issues and the importance of diversity and not enough on economic security and opportunity. And when she did talk about the economy, Clinton talked not about creating jobs but about the corrosive tendencies of Wall Street and big business. Many reporters pointed out that this was not only not what most voters wanted to hear, but also seemed disingenuous given that her campaign raised enormous amounts of money from people affiliated with the very corporations she attacked in her stump speeches.

Donald Trump, meanwhile, pounded on the theme of economic decline, citing intrusive government taxes and regulations, along with bad trade deals, as the source of voters' economic woes. He touted his skills as a businessman, capable of making good deals ("the best deals!") to turn the economy around. Journalists and pundits alike praised Trump's ability to tap into the mood of the electorate on the economy with his fiery populist rhetoric. In short, many analyses argued that Trump won the election by framing the economic debate in a way that resonated more powerfully with voters, especially the working class white voters who had tended to support Democratic candidates for the last 70 years of the twentieth century. Exit polls back this perspective: just under 60 percent of voters in 2016 said that the economy was either the same or worse than it was in 2012, and a majority of those people cast their ballots for Trump.

However, most people who cited the economy as their number one issue in exit polls actually voted for Clinton, shedding doubt on the notion that Trump's campaign was propelled to victory because it convinced voters that the economy was in bad shape—or that Clinton's campaign failed because it could not convince voters that it was in good shape. In fact, statistical measures of the national economy were ambivalent throughout 2016. There was some good news about unemployment and job growth, and there was some concerning news about production, debt, and "under-employment." As we discussed in Chapter 9, these factors are largely outside either candidate's control but still powerfully affect presidential election outcomes. Voters appeared to be anxious about the economy, but not angry or disconsolate.

Election forecasts from August 2016—before the fall campaign got underway—support the idea that the Clinton and Trump campaigns had only a limited role in reshaping voters' fundamental perceptions of the state of the economy. Political scientists offered predictive models based on an understanding of how voters incorporate factors such as the state of the economy and presidential approval into their choices, and these models estimated that Clinton would receive 50.8 percent of the two-party national vote, on average. This average forecast, as well as the individual forecasts, was fairly close: Clinton ultimately received 51.1 percent of the popular vote. To be sure, election forecasting models are not always this accurate. In 2000, for example, the models predicted that Democratic candidate Al Gore would receive about 56 percent of the two-party vote, when in fact he received just over 50 percent. And in 2016, statistical analyses relying on polling data alone predicted that Clinton's chances of winning the election (and not just the popular vote) were between 70 percent and 99 percent.[1] Still, the ambivalent mood of voters about the economy drove a close national vote in 2016, and political science models relying on economic measures were very predictive of this final vote—even though they did not take account of the general election campaign.

That vote totals in presidential elections are predictable, even months before Election Day, flies in the face of many media accounts of presidential campaigns.

Core of the Analysis

- Many Americans are not especially attentive to election campaigns and tend to rely on simple strategies for deciding among candidates.
- Individuals tend to develop a psychological attachment to a political party, and this attachment colors opinions about political issues and candidates.
- Appraisals of national conditions (especially the state of the economy) are important factors for presidential vote choice.
- Campaigns can affect voters' decisions, but mainly when voters do not have preexisting views and when one candidate outspends another by a wide margin.
- Thus, campaigns are more likely to activate the partisan predispositions of voters than they are to persuade voters.

---

[1] FiveThirtyEight.com pegged Clinton's probability of election at about 0.70 right before the election, while The Upshot had it at about 0.99.

In 2016, models created by political scientists predicted that Hillary Clinton would collect around 51 percent of the popular vote. She received just over 51 percent of the popular vote but lost in the Electoral College. What factors influence voters' decisions, and how can we understand them?

These accounts often portray the election's outcome as uncertain, creating a dramatic narrative in which crucial voters are on the fence and every twist and turn of the campaign—even a single misstatement in a debate—could make the difference between winning and losing. More to the point, the predictability of presidential elections calls into question the importance of the campaign itself. If the campaign matters, how can presidential elections be forecast with such accuracy so far in advance? Do Americans cast their votes based largely on broader economic and political realities, and not on campaign messages and events?

In this chapter, we focus on voters and their decisions about which candidates to support. We begin by exploring the reasons behind voting decisions. Our starting point is a fact we have highlighted through this book: many Americans do not follow politics very closely. Consequently, their voting decisions are not based on a wealth of information about the candidates. Instead, American voters are more likely to rely on shortcuts and rules of thumb when deciding. They tend to vote for parties that are aligned with the social groups to which they belong. They develop an attachment to the party itself that guides their decisions in elections for all levels of office. Most voters, particularly those who don't pay attention to politics and do not have strong partisan attachments, take stock of the performance of the incumbent party, especially with respect to the economy, and reward or punish it accordingly. Thus, voting decisions often depend on long-standing social and political identities or evaluations of conditions that the candidates themselves cannot change.

Does this mean, then, that political campaigns are irrelevant? Not at all. Campaigns remind people of their underlying attachments, thereby leading them to vote for the party or candidate they are naturally predisposed to support. But, as we discussed in Chapter 5, actual persuasion—changing someone's mind—is less common. Even so, under the right conditions, campaigns can move enough voters to shift the outcome of an election. We discuss several of those conditions in this chapter, such as how familiar the candidates are to citizens, and the balance of resources among the competing candidates. We conclude by considering whether the voting decisions of Americans are in line with the democratic ideals set out in Chapter 1.

What Influences Vote Choice

By and large, Americans do not spend a great deal of time following politics. This is true even in presidential elections, when politics seems extraordinarily salient. In surveys conducted in every presidential election from 1952 to 2016, fewer than half of Americans said that they were "very interested in the current campaign" (Figure 13.1). This has two implications. First, as we have discussed, campaigns may have difficulty attracting the attention of potential voters, some of whom might prefer watching football or reality television, for example. This is one reason why many scholars are skeptical about the ability of campaigns to persuade voters and shape election outcomes. Second, Americans may not have a detailed understanding of the party platforms or the positions of the candidates running for office. Their choices in elections may therefore depend on more limited information, especially on factors that enable them to make choices relatively quickly and easily. In the following sections, we consider five such factors that influence vote choice: social groups, party identification, the performance of incumbents, policy issues, and candidate traits.

Social Groups

In the aftermath of the wave of fascism that took hold in parts of Europe in the 1930s and 1940s, social scientists became fascinated with the potentially persuasive power of political communication. Some wondered, for example,

FIGURE 13.1 How Interested Are Americans in Political Campaigns?

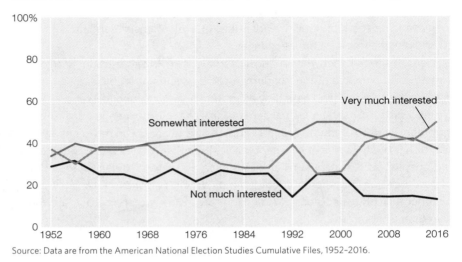

Source: Data are from the American National Election Studies Cumulative Files, 1952-2016.

whether people were easily swayed by propaganda disseminated in speeches or radio broadcasts, and whether propaganda might have allowed leaders like Adolf Hitler to gain and maintain power. Scholars at Columbia University embarked on an innovative project, identifying a random sample of citizens in the small communities of Elmira, New York, and Erie County, Ohio, and interviewing them multiple times during a presidential campaign.[2] These **panel studies** allowed researchers to understand how individuals changed their opinions in response to campaign activity.

In fact, the studies found that the campaign itself had a negligible impact on citizens. Many citizens did not appear terribly knowledgeable about or interested in politics. They were not very responsive to the campaign or its mass media outreach. Instead, they maintained attitudes about the candidates that did not change much over time. Those whose attitudes did change—most often, from being undecided about the candidates to making a choice—tended to move in a predictable direction: toward the candidate that the individual was already predisposed to support.[3]

---

[2] Bernard R. Berelson, Paul F. Lazarsfeld, and William N. McPhee. 1954. *Voting: A Study of Opinion Formation in a Presidential Campaign.* Chicago: University of Chicago Press; Paul F. Lazarsfeld, Bernard Berelson, and Hazel Gaudet. 1948. *The People's Choice.* New York: Columbia University Press.

[3] The same finding emerged in a later study of the 1980 presidential campaign. See Steven E. Finkel. 1993. "Reexamining the 'Minimal Effects' Model in Recent Presidential Campaigns." *Journal of Politics* 55, 1: 1–21.

Why were voters predisposed to support a candidate in the first place? These studies revealed a crucial fact about voters' political attitudes: they depended on the **social groups** to which voters belonged. For example, Catholic voters tended to have similar political views, as did Latino voters, union voters, African American voters, white-collar voters, and so on. In other words, voters were aligned with political parties because of class background, ethnicity, religion, or some other group affiliation. In part, this reflects the attention parties pay to group interests: the party that best serves the interests of a group may attract the enduring loyalty of its members. For example, in every election since the passage of the Voting Rights Act of 1965, about 90 percent of blacks have voted for Democrats. In 2016, 89 percent of black voters voted for the Democratic candidate Hillary Clinton. Similarly, the Republican Party's promotion of socially conservative policies, such as those limiting abortion, have garnered the support of most evangelical Christians. In 2016, 80 percent of white born-again or evangelical Christians voted for Donald Trump. Figure 13.2 shows how various social groups voted in 2016. These numbers shift from election to election, but many of the basic demographic contours of the vote have been in place since the 1960s.

Of course, voters who identify with a social group will not always automatically vote for the political party most aligned with that group. They may need some sort of "reminder"—one that essentially says: "People like you should vote for this candidate." The Columbia scholars argued that the degree to which those surveyed voted according to their social group identities often depended on their having contact and conversation with other members of their social group. Communication with other members of their church, workplace, school, and community often exposes potential voters to more politically interested and engaged voters—so-called **opinion leaders**. As the election nears, these individuals talk about the election in ways that rekindle long-standing allegiances. In the 1948 presidential election, for example, some wavering Democrats came to support the Democratic nominee, Harry Truman, when opinion leaders within Catholic churches and labor unions explained how Truman was for the "little guy," while Thomas Dewey was just another business-friendly fat cat.[4]

For voters who do not always pay much attention to politics, social group identities serve as a relatively effortless way to reach a decision. It does not take much information to align one's vote with that of one's social group. Moreover, any information necessary to do so may come without any effort

---

[4] David McCullough. 1993. *Truman*. New York: Simon & Schuster.

FIGURE 13.2 2016 Presidential Vote by Social Groups

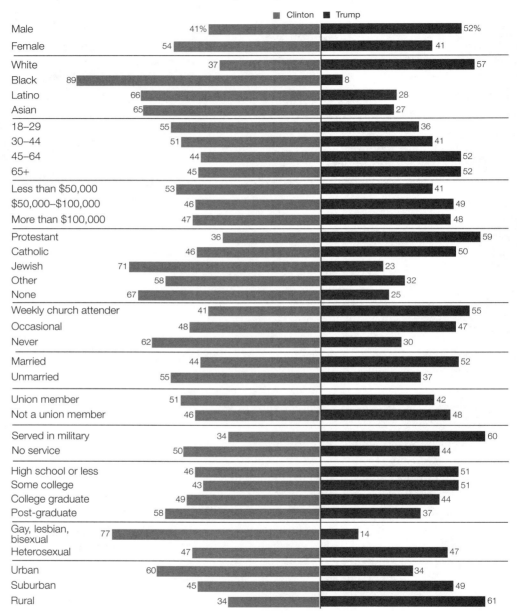

Source: 2016 National Election Pool exit poll, conducted by Edison Research (N=24,558 respondents).

on the part of the voter, perhaps just a brief conversation with a coworker or friend. And because we often trust coworkers and friends more than, say, political candidates, we will view their opinions as particularly credible. Explanations of voting that emphasize the importance of social groups implicitly suggest that campaigns have minimal effects on how voters vote, except insofar as they supply information that helps voters connect their social group identities to their choices in an election.

Party Identification

Of course, social groups are not the only factor that influences Americans when it comes to voting; another factor is the identification that voters have with political parties themselves. This idea of a psychological attachment to a political party is called **party identification**. The concept was developed by scholars at the University of Michigan drawing on nationally representative surveys conducted during the 1952 and 1956 elections.[5]

Party identification does not mean identification with particular political ideologies or opinions. For example, to identify as a Democrat is not the same as identifying as a liberal. Nor can party identification be equated with how you are registered to vote or even how you vote at the ballot box, although it is highly correlated with each. Instead, party identification is like other social identities. We feel that we are a member of a group ("I am a Democrat" or "I am a Republican"), and we tend to feel positively about that group. So we cheer when our "team" wins and the other loses.

Where does party identification come from? It is learned relatively early in life, primarily from those who are closest to us for the most extended periods of time. Thus, our parents have traditionally been the dominant influence on our party identification, although this tendency may be weakening somewhat in recent years.[6] Besides parents, other people and institutions—such as friends, schools, and churches—can also shape party identification.

The prevailing political context at the time that one comes of age also matters: people who enter young adulthood when a president is popular will be more likely to identify with the president's party than people who come of age when the president is unpopular. For example, young people who came of age when Republican Ronald Reagan was president are still more

---

[5] Angus Campbell, Philip E. Converse, Warren E. Miller, and Donald E. Stokes. 1960. *The American Voter.* Chicago: University of Chicago Press.

[6] Christopher Ojeda and Peter K. Hatemi. 2015. "Accounting for the Child in the Transmission of Party Identification." *American Sociological Review* 80, 6: 1150–74.

likely to be Republicans than those who came of age under the unpopular and scandal-ridden Republican Richard Nixon.[7] Regardless of its sources, party identification is typically formed by young adulthood. Because it is learned so early, it is a durable attitude. People tend not to change much, even as they grow up, learn more, and see their circumstances evolve. In short, with party identification, where you end up depends in large part on where you start.

Of course, this discussion raises an important question: Does everyone develop a party identification? What about those people who identify as "independent"? To assess the true number of political independents, it is important to consider how party identification is typically measured. In a survey, respondents will be asked a question such as "Generally speaking, do you consider yourself a Republican, a Democrat, or an independent?" If respondents identify as Republican or Democrat, they are then asked, "Would you call yourself a strong or a not very strong Republican/Democrat?" Respondents who say they are "independent" or express no preference are then asked, "Do you think of yourself as closer to the Republican or Democratic Party?" These questions measure the direction and intensity of party identification and are used to create a seven-point scale, charted in Figure 13.3: 1. Strong Democrat; 2. Weak Democrat; 3. Leans Democrat; 4. Independent; 5. Leans Republican; 6. Weak Republican; 7. Strong Republican.

As measured by responses to the first in this series of questions, the percentage of independents (those who do not call themselves Republicans or Democrats) is rising: from 23 percent of Americans in 1952 to 37 percent in 2016. But nearly all political independents think of themselves as closer to one party. Only 15 percent do not "lean" toward a party and could be considered "pure" independents—and, as Figure 13.3 shows, this percentage has been relatively stable since the mid-1980s. Moreover, independents who lean toward a party are almost as likely to support that party's candidates as those voters who call themselves Republicans or Democrats.

For those studying elections, party identification matters for three reasons. First, it functions as a filter or screen through which information must pass. In other words, we tend to accept information that comes from the party we identify with, or from sources closely identified with that party, and to

---

[7] Scott Keeter, Juliana Menasce Horowitz, and Alec Tyson. 2008. *Gen Dems: The Party's Advantage among Young Voters Widens.* Washington, DC: Pew Research Center for the People and the Press. www.pewresearch.org/2008/04/28/gen-dems-the-partys-advantage-among-young-voters-widens/ (accessed 11/30/2017).

FIGURE 13.3 Trends in Party Identification, 1952–2016

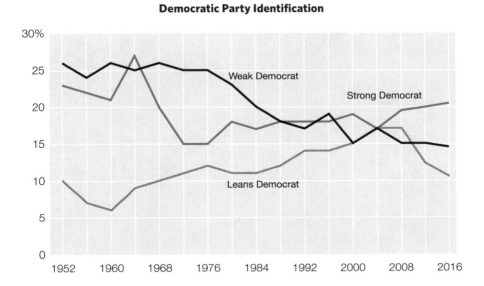

Democratic Party Identification

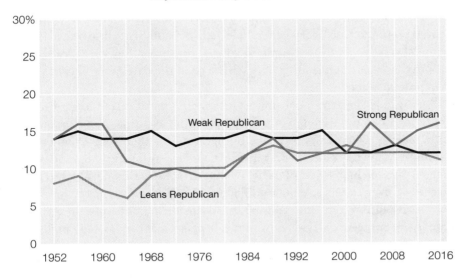

Republican Party Identification

FIGURE 13.3 Trends in Party Identification, 1952–2016 (continued)

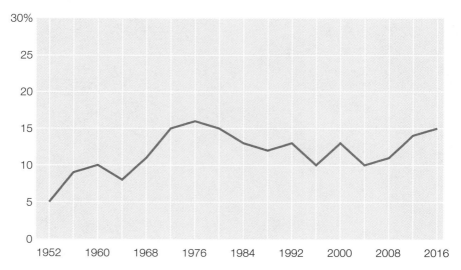

Source: Data are from the American National Election Studies Cumulative Files, 1952–2016.

discount information coming from sources on the other side.[8] This is why, as we noted in Chapter 9, partisans routinely think that their party's presidential nominee won every general election debate. Second, party identification also helps motivate people to vote; stronger partisans are more likely to vote than weak and leaning partisans, who in turn are more likely to vote than independents.

Finally, and perhaps most important, party identification is a powerful predictor of how citizens vote. In presidential elections, approximately 90 percent of Democrats and Republicans vote for their respective party's nominee. Many races at other levels of office, such as for the U.S. House and Senate, also see high levels of party loyalty. In fact, partisan loyalty has been increasing over time,[9] as shown in Figure 13.4. To be sure, party loyalty is not an absolute. From time to time, partisans defect and vote for a candidate of the opposite party—for example, because that candidate is a talented

---

[8] Philip E. Converse. 1962. "Information Flow and the Stability of Partisan Attitudes." *Public Opinion Quarterly* 26, 4: 578–99. Diana C. Mutz. 2004. "Cross-Cutting Social Networks: Testing Democratic Theory in Practice." *American Political Science Review* 96, 1: 111–26.

[9] Larry M. Bartels. 2000. "Partisanship and Voting Behavior, 1952–1996." *American Journal of Political Science* 44, 1: 35–50.

FIGURE 13.4 Percentages of Self-Identified Partisans Voting for Their Party's Candidate in Presidential Elections, 1980–2016

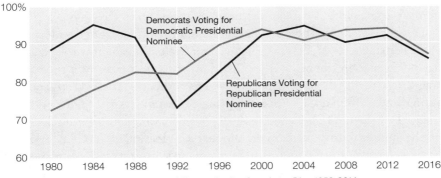

Source: Data are from the American National Election Studies Cumulative Files, 1952–2016.

incumbent who has no credible challenger. But defections are the exception rather than the rule. Because of this, campaigns typically try to reinforce partisan loyalties among their followers and to persuade independents to vote for their candidate.

Like social group identities,[10] party identification provides a useful shortcut for political decision making, especially when voters are not particularly well informed about the candidates. Thus, party identification is particularly useful in races where voters know little about the candidates except for their party affiliation.

Incumbent Performance

A third factor in many voters' decisions is the performance of the incumbent party or officeholder. The most important criterion in evaluating performance is the state of the economy. When the economy is growing, voters tend to reward the incumbent party.[11] For example, an incumbent president is more likely to be reelected when the country is prosperous. But when the economy is growing slowly or not at all, voters tend to punish the incumbent president or, if that person is not running, the nominee of the incumbent party.

---

[10] Some scholars see party identification as a social identity. For example, see Donald Green, Bradley Palmquist, and Eric Schickler. 2002. *Partisan Hearts and Minds: Political Parties and the Social Identities of Voters.* New Haven, CT: Yale University Press.

[11] See, for example, Ray C. Fair. 1978. "The Effect of Economic Events on Votes for President." *Review of Economics and Statistics* 60, 2: 159–72; Michael S. Lewis-Beck and Tom W. Rice. 1992. *Forecasting Elections.* Washington, DC: CQ Press; Edward R. Tufte. 1978. *Political Control of the Economy.* Princeton, NJ: Princeton University Press.

As we discussed in Chapters 9 and 10, macroeconomic variables, such as changes in the average income of Americans, predict presidential and even congressional election outcomes. This lends credence to the idea that economic performance is a major factor when voters go to the polls.

How do voters use their perceptions about the economy to decide how to vote? For starters, voters rely more on their evaluations of how the economy has performed in the past rather than how it might perform in the future. Using past performance to decide between candidates is called **retrospective voting**, and is often encapsulated by a single question: "Are we better off now than when the incumbent took office?" While basing one's voting decisions on the answer to this question may appear simpleminded, it is plausible that past performance predicts future performance.[12] In this way, retrospective voting provides an efficient shortcut for citizens looking to make choices about future leadership.

Previous research also indicates that voters rely more on their assessments of the national economy (**sociotropic voting**) than on assessments of their own financial situation (**pocketbook voting**).[13] Moreover, when voters assess the economy, they focus most on recent changes and, especially, changes in the election year itself.[14] Even if a president has presided over three years of a weak economy, if the economy shows strong growth in his fourth year, he is likely to be rewarded by the electorate. In this sense, voters are somewhat nearsighted: they see nearby, or more recent, economic events more clearly than events that occurred further in the past.

We should also note that voters' evaluations of the economy are biased by their party identification. When a Democrat is president, Democrats evaluate the economy more positively than do Republicans. Republicans exhibit this same tendency when a Republican is president. And even if partisans do pick up on more objective information about the economy, this does not mean that negative economic assessments will cause them to defect from their party's candidates. In 2016, for instance, nearly 57 percent of Democrats said that the economy was either "bad" or "very bad" under the incumbent Democratic administration, but 72 percent of them still voted for Hillary Clinton. Ultimately, because partisans tend to judge the performance of their own officeholders more generously, it is independent voters

---

[12] Morris P. Fiorina. 1981. *Retrospective Voting in American National Elections*. New Haven, CT: Yale University Press.

[13] Donald R. Kinder and D. Roderick Kiewiet. 1981. "Sociotropic Politics: The American Case." *British Journal of Political Science* 11, 2: 129–61.

[14] Larry M. Bartels. 2008. *Unequal Democracy: The Political Economy of the New Gilded Age*. Princeton, NJ: Princeton University Press.

whose vote choice is most influenced by the incumbent party's handling of the economy.

Finally, incumbent performance often becomes more important to voters as Election Day nears, as the campaigns tend to focus heavily on it.

Policy Issues

In a typical campaign, candidates spend a great deal of time talking about issues relating to government policy, such as the regulation of environmental pollution or the future solvency of Social Security and Medicare. When voters make choices, do they factor these sorts of issue positions into their decision?

In Chapter 5, we introduced the median voter theorem, which posits that candidates take issue positions that are close to the hypothetical median voter, whose support is necessary to win the election. The median voter theorem assumes that voters make choices in a particular way: they evaluate the candidates' ideologies or their positions on issues and then choose the candidate who, on average, has positions most similar to their own. This strategy is called **proximity voting**—voters choose the candidates whose views are closest or most proximate to theirs.

Does proximity voting actually happen? Is voting really about "the issues"? In general, it is not. The strategy of proximity voting takes more time and effort, which voters do not often invest, than the other simple decision-making shortcuts that we have described. To vote based on policy issues, voters first need to have opinions about those issues. But they often do not pay enough attention to politics to form opinions in the first place, especially about complex public policies. Even if they do have opinions, they may not pay enough attention to the campaign to discern where the candidates stand and which candidate is most proximate to them. Moreover, candidates do not always make their views clear. As we discussed in Chapter 5, candidates may have an incentive to be ambiguous.

One recent study estimated that less than half of the electorate has the requisite opinions on issues along with sufficient knowledge of candidates' views to engage in issue voting.[15] When issue voting does occur, it is usually limited to a particular group of voters within the broader electorate. These groups are called *issue publics*, and consist of voters who are more likely to have strong opinions about a particular issue, to learn where the candidates stand on this issue, and to vote for a candidate only if that candidate agrees with them. Senior citizens, who are especially attentive to

---

[15] Michael S. Lewis-Beck, William G. Jacoby, Helmut Norpoth, and Herbert F. Weisberg. 2008. *The American Voter Revisited*. Ann Arbor: University of Michigan Press, Chapter 8.

protecting their current Medicare benefits, are a good example of an issue public. However, attention to policy seems to be the exception and not the rule. Furthermore, there is some evidence that rather than voting based on their own opinions on policy, voters are more likely simply to adopt the policy positions of the candidates they already support based on party identification.[16]

Candidate Traits

Candidates spend a great deal of time promoting not only their views but also their biographies and personal qualities. Do voters draw on their perceptions of candidates' personal qualities, such as appearance or personality, when making decisions in an election? This would seem to be a simple strategy that would not demand much time or effort on the part of voters. They could merely get an impression of the candidates as people, perhaps from television advertising or candidate debates, and then use this impression to select the candidate that seems the stronger leader, more honest, better looking, and so on. Indeed, conventional accounts of political campaigns often draw attention to personal qualities. In 1960, Democrat John F. Kennedy was considered youthful, energetic, but perhaps a bit inexperienced. His Republican opponent, Richard Nixon, was considered experienced and knowledgeable, but not especially trustworthy. In 2008, Barack Obama was considered youthful, intelligent, and inexperienced (like his fellow Democrat Kennedy), while John McCain's image as a maverick unafraid to buck the system was undermined by voter concerns about his age and temperament. In 2016, Hillary Clinton was considered experienced and knowledgeable, but not very honest. Donald Trump, on the other hand, was viewed as eager to shake things up, but not very knowledgeable.

But do such qualities matter? There is some evidence that they do. For example, better-looking candidates appear to get more votes than less attractive opponents do. Similarly, the more positively people assess a candidate's personality—attributing traits to them such as honesty or capacity for leadership—the more likely they are to vote for the candidate,[17] although

---

[16] Gabriel S. Lenz. 2009. "Learning and Opinion Change, Not Priming: Reconsidering the Priming Hypothesis." *American Journal of Political Science* 53, 4: 821–37.

[17] Chappell Lawson, Gabriel S. Lenz, Andy Baker, and Michael Myers. 2010. "Looking Like a Winner: Candidate Appearance and Electoral Success in New Democracies." *World Politics* 62, 4: 561–93; Donald R. Kinder, Mark D. Peters, Robert P. Abelson, and Susan T. Fiske. 1980. "Presidential Prototypes." *Political Behavior* 2, 4: 315–37.

Like political scientists, campaign consultants recognize party identification as a strong influence on vote choice. Campaign strategists look at the partisan composition of the district as a starting point in determining whose votes they can count on and whose they can hope to win through persuasion.

partisanship (once again) affects these judgments.[18] Candidates also suffer when scandals, especially those involving allegations of official corruption, cast doubt on their character.[19] The investigation of Hillary Clinton's use of a private e-mail server while serving as secretary of state—and especially news media coverage of Clinton's response to the investigation—caused her favorability ratings to plummet in late 2015 and early 2016. Other specific negative trait perceptions—for example, Sarah Palin's incompetence in 2008—have been damaging to particular candidates in presidential elections.[20] In addition to individual personalities, perceptions of the parties also seem to influence how voters see candidates' characteristics; certain

---

[18] Danny Hayes. 2005. "Candidate Qualities through a Partisan Lens: A Theory of Trait Ownership." *American Journal of Political Science* 49, 4: 908–23.

[19] Tim Fackler and Tse-min Lin. 1995. "Political Corruption and Presidential Elections, 1929–1992." *Journal of Politics* 57, 4: 971–93; Daron R. Shaw. 1999. "A Study of Presidential Campaign Event Effects from 1952 to 1992." *Journal of Politics* 61, 2: 387–422.

[20] Gabriel S. Lenz. 2012. *Follow the Leader? How Voters Respond to Politicians' Policies and Performance.* Chicago, IL: University of Chicago Press.

traits are more likely to be "owned" by Democratic candidates (empathy) and others are more likely to be owned by Republican candidates (leadership).[21] Democrats who are able to establish themselves as strong leaders and Republicans who project caring appear to do relatively better at attracting independents and even some partisans from the other side.

At the same time, other evidence suggests that a candidate's appearance and personality may matter much less, and may be dependent on the nature of the race. For instance, one recent study demonstrates that attractive candidates tend to run in races where they have a better chance of winning.[22] Thus, if attractive candidates get more votes than less attractive candidates, it is unclear whether it was because of attractiveness or because the race was simply easier to win. The same logic may extend to other attributes of candidates, such as their personalities. A candidate's appearance or personality will typically matter most when there is little other information to draw on, such as in smaller races that feature unfamiliar candidates and attract little media coverage. In races where there is much more information—such as a presidential race—it is less clear that people's evaluations of the candidates' personalities actually decide their vote. In such races, people may have a preferred candidate for other reasons—especially because of party identification—and thus evaluate their party's candidate more favorably. Such biases are not absolute, however. In 2016, many Republicans rated Hillary Clinton as more knowledgeable. And many Democrats rated Trump as more likely to "say what he means." Nevertheless, close to 90 percent of both Democrats and Republicans voted for their party's nominee, despite any misgivings.

How Do Campaign Consultants Think about Vote Choice?

Consultants and academics have similar views about how voters decide between candidates. As we explained in Chapter 5, consultants share the belief that voters are not particularly interested in or knowledgeable about politics. This is why they advise candidates to repeat a basic message over and over—often via a barrage of television ads. Similarly, consultants often prefer emotional appeals over intellectual appeals, and negative appeals over positive appeals. Emotional appeals and negative appeals seem to be more likely to garner attention and more likely to be remembered.

---

[21] Hayes, "Candidate Qualities through a Partisan Lens: A Theory of Trait Ownership."

[22] Matthew D. Atkinson, Ryan D. Enos, and Seth J. Hill. 2009. "Candidate Faces and Election Outcomes: Is the Face–Vote Correlation Caused by Candidate Selection?" *Quarterly Journal of Political Science* 4, 3: 229–49.

Consultants, like academics, also believe that voters are strongly con-strained by their partisanship and other predispositions. Recognizing these predispositions and acting accordingly is the hallmark of smart campaigns, which often have limited resources and thus need to focus their efforts on those voters most likely to help the campaign win. This is why consultants recommend not wasting time campaigning for the votes of opposing parti-sans, but instead focusing on delivering mobilizing messages to fellow partisans and persuasive messages to independents and weak partisans.

When Campaigns Matter

Although campaign consultants and political scientists share many beliefs about vote choice, they disagree over a key question: how much the cam-paign can affect voters' attitudes toward the candidates. Campaign con-sultants believe that their activities—television and radio advertisements, phone calls, direct mail, the Internet, social media, and person-to-person contact—help persuade voters and thus win elections. Political scientists are more skeptical but nevertheless acknowledge that campaigns can sometimes change voters' minds and even affect election outcomes. The crucial task is to identify *when* campaigns are likely to matter. In this sec-tion we are particularly concerned with **persuasion**—a concept we intro-duced in Chapter 5 that means, in this context, convincing undecided voters to support a particular candidate or convincing the other party's supporters to defect.

Campaigns have their largest persuasive effects when two conditions are met. First, campaigns matter more when the candidates are relatively unfa-miliar to voters. When candidates are not well known, voters are less likely to have opinions about them. Although party identification is likely to affect their initial assessments, they will still be more susceptible to persuasive appeals by the candidates because they will not already have strongly held opinions about them.

Second, campaigns matter more when one side is able to dominate by virtue of more or better resources. That is to say, voters are more likely to be persuaded when one side can campaign more heavily than the other side, typically when it has more money and thus a more extensive cam-paign organization, a larger presence on television and other media, and a better developed infrastructure for contacting and mobilizing voters. This is often the case in local races, when a better-funded candidate can totally eclipse a relatively impoverished opponent. When opposing campaigns are more equally balanced in terms of resources, it is difficult for either campaign to get an edge. Television advertisements by one side can be matched by competing advertisements from the other side. The respective efforts of the two sides thus tend to cancel each other out. In light of these two conditions, we can evaluate how much of an impact campaigns at different levels of office will likely have.

Presidential Elections

Campaign effects tend to be most obvious and influential in the nomination phase of the presidential election. At this stage, candidates for the presidential nomination vary greatly in their resources. Some are heavyweights: politicians with national visibility and the campaign war chests, media attention, and party endorsements to show for it. In the 2016 Democratic presidential primaries, Hillary Clinton fit this description. Other candidates, however, struggle for visibility and can rarely raise as much money or attract the same level of attention as heavyweight candidates. In the run-up to the 2016 Democratic primaries, this describes candidates such as Maryland governor Martin O'Malley and Virginia senator James Webb. Disparities in campaign resources help the heavyweights dominate the field, pulling voters to their side.

The candidates in presidential primaries are also much less well known than the eventual nominees will be. Although some may be national figures, as were Hillary Clinton and Donald Trump in 2016, many others are familiar only to the voters of the state or district that they represent as members of Congress or as governor. Thus, voters do not have well-formed opinions about many primary candidates, leaving more potential for the campaign to influence these opinions. Furthermore, voters cannot rely on their party identification to make decisions: all of the candidates in a party primary obviously share the same party identification. As we discussed in Chapter 9, the primary campaign often matters in this fashion: a candidate's victories in the early caucuses and primaries signal to voters that the candidate is viable. This creates a bandwagon effect, as voters gravitate toward successful candidates, believing them to be able to compete effectively in the general election. In 2008, Obama's standing in the polls increased by about 20 points between the first caucus in Iowa on January 3 and the Super Tuesday primaries on February 5. This is a much larger swing than presidential general election campaigns create. Bernie Sanders's 2016 campaign received a smaller but still significant boost after his narrow loss to Hillary Clinton in the Iowa caucuses, while Ted Cruz shot to the forefront of the Republican race after his victory in the Hawkeye State. Thus, primary candidates know that by campaigning effectively in these early primaries and caucuses, they build the momentum necessary to contest the nomination.

But while campaign effects are common in the nomination contests, they are less noticeable as presidential campaigns move to the fall. In fact, despite the vast amounts of money that presidential candidates spend, presidential general election campaigns are less likely to decide election outcomes than campaigns at other levels of office. By the time the party conventions are over and the general election campaign has begun, the Democratic and Republican nominees are already relatively well known. They have been campaigning for months if not years, depending on when they began campaigning for the nomination. At the national party conventions, the parties spend several days promoting their nominees for a large television audience. Moreover, when incumbent presidents run for reelection, voters have had five or six years to get to know them, at least from the time their first campaign for president began.

Competing major-party presidential campaigns also tend to be roughly equal in terms of resources—including not only money but also motivation, information, and expertise. The equality of funding is a tendency in presidential races, but should not be overstated. For example, in recent years presidential campaigns have not always been on level ground in terms of money—Barack Obama had a massive spending advantage over John McCain in 2008, while Hillary Clinton significantly outspent Donald Trump in 2016. Still, highly motivated, ideological outside groups tend to help less well-heeled candidates make up the dollar gap, and (as we saw in Chapter 4) federal election campaign laws make it more difficult for one side to completely blow the other away.

Beyond money, it is obvious that the campaigns of the two major parties have equal motivation. The presidential election is, in the words of the Republican media consultant Stuart Stevens, "the big enchilada." Both parties try hard to win.

It is only slightly less obvious that the campaigns are working with equal information. Both the Democratic and Republican presidential campaigns have ready access to information about the preferences of voters via polling and focus groups. Opposition research arms both campaigns with data on the relevant issue positions and backgrounds of the candidates. And experts work with the candidates and their teams on issue positions and policy papers.

The assumption of equal expertise is based on the observation that both sides bring very talented people to the presidential election contest.

Consider the main consultants in recent presidential elections. In 2008, Obama turned to the Chicago-based media communications consultant David Axelrod, while John McCain ultimately settled on a longtime GOP message consultant, Steve Schmidt. In 2012, Obama continued to rely on Axelrod, along with organizational guru Jim Messina, whereas Mitt Romney turned to longtime GOP consultant and television ad expert Stuart Stevens. In 2016, Donald Trump leaned heavily on veteran political consultant and pollster Kellyanne Conway, along with digital and analytics expert Brad Parscale; Hillary Clinton entrusted much of her campaign to turnout and analytics whiz Robby Mook. It is, in fact, difficult to find a presidential race in which one side seemed overwhelmed by the expertise of the other side—even though commentators are always willing to claim that the winners' team was *that much* smarter after the election.

Taken in combination, these equalities lead to the possibility that presidential general election campaigns will fight to a draw. The winner will be determined not by the campaign but by the broader conditions in the country, especially the economy. Of course, even if this is true as a general rule, there are moments when the campaign itself appears crucial. It is possible, even in presidential campaigns, for one side to get a financial advantage over the other. In the 2016 presidential race, Donald Trump outspent Hillary Clinton on television and digital advertising in Michigan, Pennsylvania, and Wisconsin during the last 10 days of the campaign, which may have reversed Clinton's small edge in those key states. In 2000, George W. Bush outspent Al Gore in the battleground states late in the campaign, and the resulting advantage in advertising may have cost Gore four points off the final vote margin—a large number in states such as Florida, where the race was close.[23] In 2008, when Obama bypassed public funding and outspent John McCain by an enormous margin, Obama did better in most areas of the country than John Kerry did in 2004. More importantly, Obama did particularly well the more he outspent McCain. Obama's largest campaign spending advantages were in Florida ($28 million), Virginia ($16.3 million), Indiana ($11.4 million), and North Carolina ($7.2 million), each of which went for the Democratic challenger; these states had gone for Bush in 2004 by 5, 8, 21, and 12 points, respectively. In general, however, a presidential candidate needs a fairly substantial advantage over an opponent to shift voters in his direction, and, even

---

[23] Richard Johnston, Michael G. Hagen, and Kathleen Hall Jamieson. 2004. *The 2000 Presidential Election and the Foundations of Party Politics.* Cambridge: Cambridge University Press.

then, this shift will likely be small.[24] This is why presidential election outcomes are not usually decided by the campaign. One study of presidential campaigns from 1948 to 2000 found that in only five of the 14 presidential elections did the campaign appear to have decided the outcome.[25]

Nonpresidential Elections

Campaigns for offices below the presidential level—for U.S. House and Senate, and for state and local offices—are more likely to influence voters relative to presidential general election campaigns. Again, familiarity with the candidates and resource disparities are reasons why. As we discussed in Chapters 10 and 11, citizens know much less about their representatives at lower levels of office. They often do not know the name of their congressional representative, to say nothing of their representatives in the state legislature, the state attorney general, and so on. Thus, their views about these people can be changed by a vigorous campaign. Oftentimes, this is what we see in the campaigns of challengers to incumbents in U.S. House elections. Campaign activity matters more for challengers because so few voters know them. Challengers with more money to spend become better known than poorer challengers over the course of the campaign.[26]

This makes campaign resource disparities all the more important. And, indeed, resource disparities are common in congressional, state, and local elections. One reason that incumbents often dominate these elections is because challengers cannot raise enough money to compete with them. In congressional elections from 1972 to 2016, no challenger who raised less than $100,000 won. By contrast, almost 30 percent of those who raised at least $1 million won.[27] Campaign spending is arguably even more vital for challengers in elections for state legislature, state supreme court, and city

---

[24] Daron R. Shaw. 2006. *The Race to 270: The Electoral College and the Campaign Strategies of 2000 and 2004.* Chicago: University of Chicago Press.

[25] James E. Campbell. 2001. "When Have Presidential Campaigns Decided Election Outcomes?" *American Politics Research* 29, 5: 437–60.

[26] Gary C. Jacobson. 2006. "Measuring Campaign Spending Effects in U.S. House Elections," and Laurel Elms and Paul M. Sniderman, "Informational Rhythms of Incumbent Dominated Congressional Elections," both in *Capturing Campaign Effects*, eds. Henry E. Brady and Richard Johnston. Ann Arbor: University of Michigan Press: 199–220, 221–41.

[27] Gary Jacobson. 2008. *The Politics of Congressional Elections.* 7th ed. New York: Pearson Longman, p. 46. Amounts are in 2006 dollars and thus adjusted for inflation. Updated through 2016 by reference to spending data from www.fec.gov.

council.[28] In these elections, which attract relatively little media coverage, voters are not likely to see, hear, or read anything about challengers unless it comes from their campaigns. Thus, campaigns can be crucial to the outcomes of such elections, even if the dollar amounts spent on them are minuscule compared with what is spent in higher-profile races. That said, other factors—including party identification, the economy, and national tides—are still extremely important for understanding vote choice.

How Campaigns Matter

The preceding discussion focused on the conditions under which campaigns can persuade voters. But it has said much less about *how* campaigns persuade voters, as well as other possible effects of campaigns. In Chapter 12, we described how campaigns can mobilize citizens. Now we continue to examine how campaigns affect voters' attitudes toward the candidates. Three types of effects are important: persuasion, reinforcement, and priming.

Persuasion

As we have discussed, campaigns are more likely to persuade voters when voters are unfamiliar with the candidates and when one side can outspend the other. But this observation only scratches the surface when it comes to analyzing how campaigns persuade. Although resource disparities are important, much of campaigning is not simply about spending more than the opponent, it is about crafting specific messages that are intended to persuade voters. This is what campaign consultants focus on, using polling data, focus groups, and their own experiences to design advertisements, write speeches, and produce other kinds of media. It is also about choosing the appropriate time to air those messages so that they will have the maximum impact on voters. Unfortunately, we do not know very much about what kinds of persuasion strategies consistently work. Campaign consultants sometimes have polls or focus groups, but often they rely on guesswork and interpretations of past elections. Free from the daunting prospect of an election looming,

---

[28] Anthony Gierzynski and David Breaux. 1996. "Legislative Elections and the Importance of Money." *Legislative Studies Quarterly* 21, 3: 337–57; Chris W. Bonneau. 2007. "The Effects of Campaign Spending in State Supreme Court Elections." *Political Research Quarterly* 60, 3: 489–99; Timothy B. Krebs. 1998. "The Determinants of Candidates' Vote Share and the Advantages of Incumbency in City Council Elections." *American Journal of Political Science* 42, 3: 921–35.

social scientists tend to put little stock in such evidence, but more rigorous data are usually difficult to come by.

One aspect of persuasive messages that has been studied extensively is tone—that is, whether the messages promote a candidate (positive campaigning), attack that candidate's opponent (negative campaigning), or offer some combination of the two (contrast campaigning). Campaign consultants tend to place great faith in the power of negativity. One Democratic consultant put it this way: "The big question in most campaigns . . . is whose negative campaign is better. If it's negative, it works. If it's positive, save it for your tombstone."[29] But is negativity really that powerful?

There is some evidence that negative advertising is more memorable than positive advertising. This is because negative information typically stands out in our daily lives, which generally consist of positive interactions.[30] For example, we are much more likely to remember the couple next to us in a restaurant if they are arguing than if they are conversing pleasantly. But there is much less evidence that negative campaigning actually helps the candidate who goes on the attack. On the whole, negative campaigning makes voters feel less favorable toward the candidate being attacked, which is the goal. However, it also makes voters feel less favorable toward the attacker, and this backlash may be stronger than the effect on views of the attacked candidate.[31] Negative advertising is thus a risky strategy at best.

Besides tone, another aspect of messaging is issue content. In fact, a strategy that campaigns often employ to attempt to persuade voters is to focus on **wedge issues**. Campaigns use strategies centered around these issues to try to convince voters in the opposite party to defect from that party and vote for the other side. Legalizing marijuana is one such wedge issue. An overwhelming percentage of Democrats support decriminalizing marijuana possession; many Republicans also support this policy, often on grounds of personal freedom. In the 2016 elections, Democrats attempted to get so-called "pot initiatives" on the ballot in many states, and several Democratic congressional candidates in states where marijuana ended up on the ballot even directed digital, phone, and mail communications at "libertarian" Republican voters on the pot issue. These candidates were hoping to draw a

---

[29] Quoted in Richard R. Lau, Lee Sigelman, Caroline Heldman, and Paul Babbitt. 1999. "The Effects of Negative Political Advertisements: A Meta-Analytic Assessment." *American Political Science Review* 93, 4: 852.

[30] Susan Fiske and Shelley Taylor. 2017. *Social Cognition: From Brains to Culture.* 3rd ed. New York: Sage.

[31] Richard R. Lau, Lee Sigelman, and Ivy Brown Rovner. 2007. "The Effects of Negative Political Campaigns: A Meta-Analytic Reassessment." *Journal of Politics* 69, 4: 1176–1209.

favorable contrast with their Republican opponents, who supported government regulation of marijuana and criminal sentencing for small-time users, and ultimately to attract support from some Republican voters. Wedge issues are intended to take advantage of **cross pressures** within voters—that is, the fact that voters sometimes hold ideologically conflicting issue opinions (as in the case of a Republican who supports decriminalizing marijuana). Voters who experience such cross pressures are more susceptible than other (non-cross-pressured) voters to persuasion during a presidential campaign.[32] At the same time, given that most partisans vote loyally for their party's candidates, wedge issue strategies may not be as effective as the strategies that parties pursue to solidify their ranks.

Another aspect of persuasion is timing: When can persuasive campaigning most effectively be deployed? Typically, campaigns increase their volume of advertising and other activities as the election draws closer, believing that this is when most voters begin to focus on the choice ahead of them. If so, the most important information is that which voters encounter immediately prior to casting their ballots. For example, in 2016 Trump's campaign sent out last-minute e-mails and text messages that focused on FBI Director James Comey's October 28 announcement that he was re-opening his investigation into Clinton's use of a private e-mail server. They believed this message reinforced the argument that Clinton was not honest, and have suggested (off the record) that it might have helped put Trump over the top. More to the point, the message was effective because it went out just as voters were tuning into the campaign so they could make their final vote choice.

Other practitioners and consultants believe that campaigns should move early, before the race and its candidates are defined and the cacophony of competing messages reaches a crescendo. Available evidence suggests that early campaigning can move voters, but effects may not be lasting. A political science study of Rick Perry's 2006 Texas gubernatorial campaign found that early television ads significantly improved Perry's poll standing. The study, however, also found that this effect was temporary, fading within a week of the ads' airing.[33] A comparable analysis of other 2006 campaigns found a similarly rapid rate of "decay," suggesting again that campaign

---

[32] D. Sunshine Hillygus and Todd G. Shields. 2007. *The Persuadable Voter: Strategic Candidates and Wedge Issues in Political Campaigns*. Princeton, NJ: Princeton University Press.

[33] Alan S. Gerber, James G. Gimpel, Donald P. Green, and Daron R. Shaw. 2011. "How Large and Long-Lasting Are the Persuasive Effects of Televised Campaign Ads? Results from a Randomized Field Experiment." *American Political Science Review* 105, 1: 135–50.

Campaign Strategy and the Persuasion Model

Despite a couple of unconventional choices for president in 2016—a Republican candidate with almost no history as a Republican, and a Democratic candidate who almost lost the nomination fight to a Democratic-Socialist close to 90 percent of partisan identifiers stuck with their party's nominee on Election Day. In fact, polling for both sides showed little variance in the predicted vote across the entirety of the election cycle. The 2016 election thus continued a trend in which the number of swing voters—those who have voted for both Democrats and Republicans for a given office—has dwindled over time. Political scientist Corwin Smidt estimates that the share of true swing voters has decreased from 15 percent in the 1950s to 5 percent today.

In the past, many voters made up their minds over the course of the election campaign. Gerald Ford trailed Jimmy Carter by close to 20 points during the summer of 1976, but lost by only a point and a half on Election Day. In 1988, George H. W. Bush erased Michael Dukakis's 16-point post–Democratic National Convention lead and won the election by eight points. Since the 1990s, however, presidential elections have been marked by stasis rather than volatility. In 2016, levels of support for Clinton and Trump hardly moved despite an array of gaffes and scandals.

Political parties and candidates have adapted to this shift by changing how they campaign: The goal in many modern campaigns is to mobilize the most loyal voters rather than to persuade supporters from the other party to change sides. For the Trump campaign, a mobilization strategy meant identifying lower socioeconomic status whites and white evangelicals in heavily Republican areas. For Democrats, it meant targeting African Americans, Latinos, and young educated whites. What didn't happen was a sustained effort to win over voters who might be in the middle of the political divide.

Think of this distinction from a campaign manager's point of view. The campaign can engage in a persuasive campaign, in which you attempt to make convincing arguments to all voters and hope that a sufficient number of voters find your argument compelling enough to get you elected. Or, the campaign can engage in a mobilization campaign, in which you focus almost all of your effort on getting your core voters to the polls, running on emotional (and often polarizing) appeals.

Why have swing voters become so scarce? One reason is that partisans in the electorate have become much more negative toward the other side these days, something scholars call "affective polarization." Republicans do not give Democratic candidates the benefit of the doubt, and Democrats are not interested in what Republican candidates have to say. It is hard to persuade people when they refuse to give you a fair hearing.

Another reason stems from the way technology has changed campaigns. Since 2004, campaigns have used sophisticated data and analytics to "slice-and-dice" the electorate. While the number of truly "persuadable" voters has diminished, analysts have gotten much better at finding partisans who may not vote, and targeting them with finely tuned appeals. In short, it is easier to find and turn out a supporter than it is to convince someone who is on the fence to vote your way.

activities tend to have an immediate but short-lived impact.[34] Does this mean that early campaigning is always fruitless? Not necessarily. Candidate images and issue priorities are often established well before the last month of the campaign. Moreover, given the substantial and increasing fraction of voters who cast their ballots before Election Day, unleashing one's campaign in the waning days of October may be too late.

Reinforcement

Because we have emphasized the challenges that campaigns face in persuading voters, it may seem as if campaigns matter only if they change people's attitudes. But campaigns can also be important by reinforcing attitudes. **Reinforcement** occurs when a campaign solidifies voters' preferences. Reinforcement is particularly likely to occur when most voters are already predisposed to support one party because of social group identities or identification with that party. For example, a voter may have a natural tendency to vote Republican but not know much about or feel strongly committed to a particular Republican candidate. Campaign activity can increase this voter's level of commitment. Sometimes this is referred to as "rallying the base."

Although reinforcement is an important effect of campaigns, it is difficult to measure and thus somewhat underappreciated. Pre-election polls that simply ask voters whether they plan to vote Democratic or Republican will not capture how strongly voters feel or how certain they are of their choice. With further questioning, it might become clear that, early on in a campaign, many voters express a degree of uncertainty—one that disappears by late in the campaign, when voters have become devotees of their party's candidate and opponents of the other side's candidate. Of course, there is nothing automatic about reinforcement. A campaign might fail to rally its base. Such campaigns will naturally face long odds.

Priming

Not only can campaigns influence how people vote, they can also influence *why* they vote the way they do. That is, they affect the criteria that voters use in choosing a candidate, a process known as **priming** (Chapter 8). Why would campaigns be interested in priming? In any given election year,

---

[34] Seth J. Hill, James Lo, Lynn Vavreck, and John Zaller. 2007. "The Duration of Advertising Effects in Political Campaigns." Paper presented at the Annual Meeting of the American Political Science Association, Chicago.

candidates know that they have some biographical details, personal experiences, and issue positions that give them an advantage, and some that do not. Campaigns will work to focus attention on issues that benefit them as well as issues that disadvantage their opponents. If the campaign ultimately focuses on issues beneficial to the candidate, this may help them win. Thus, campaigns are not simply about persuasion but about controlling the agenda and defining what the election is about.

Understanding priming helps answer an interesting question about elections, and presidential elections in particular: How can elections be so predictable and yet the polls fluctuate so much? We discussed in Chapter 9 (and alluded to at the outset of this chapter) how presidential elections can be forecast with considerable accuracy based on factors such as the state of the economy. And yet, during presidential campaigns, there can be notable swings in the polls—for example, in 2008, John McCain took the lead after the Republican National Convention, only to lose it two weeks later, never recovering it for the rest of the campaign. One explanation for why poll numbers eventually converge on the forecast is priming. As the election goes on, campaign activities tend to focus voters' attention on fundamental factors like the economy.[35] As these factors become more important criteria in voters' decisions, the polls move in the direction of the candidate favored by these fundamental factors—as, for example, an incumbent president would be favored if the economy were growing robustly. Of course, if the challenger to that incumbent president successfully changes the subject so that voters focus on some other issue, the incumbent may lose. A systematic study of presidential elections since 1952 shows the importance of priming: when candidates who benefit from the state of the economy and other conditions emphasize these factors in their campaigns, they are more likely to win than similarly situated candidates who focus on some other issue.[36]

The 2016 election illustrates the importance of priming. As noted earlier, one consistent question after this election was why Hillary Clinton did not win more of the popular vote, given robust job growth in the year before the election and given her former position as a member of Barack Obama's cabinet. One possible answer is that Clinton's campaign agenda did not focus on jobs and employment, and thus did not "prime" the economy in voters'

---

[35] Andrew Gelman and Gary King. 1993. "Why Are American Presidential Election Polls So Variable When Votes Are So Predictable?" *British Journal of Political Science* 23, 4: 409–51; Thomas M. Holbrook. 1996. *Do Campaigns Matter?* Thousand Oaks, CA: Sage.

[36] Lynn Vavreck. 2009. *The Message Matters: The Economy and Presidential Campaigns.* Princeton, NJ: Princeton University Press.

minds. Clinton was somewhat leery of associating herself with positive aspects of the Obama administration's record for fear that she would also be punished for the negative aspects of the incumbent's record. Thus, some voters may not have rewarded her for job growth. Clinton's strategy contrasts sharply with Trump's, which emphasized weak economic growth and blamed the Democratic administration.

Conclusion

The decisions Americans make about political candidates—and the campaign's role in influencing those decisions—are frequently the subject of concern. Commentators speculate about whether Americans make decisions that are well informed, based on specific knowledge of the candidates and especially the voters' own views about issues. This concern speaks to the standard of *deliberation* that we introduced in the first chapter. Typically, that standard is applied to how candidates are campaigning or how the media covers campaigns. But the same standard could be applied to citizens. For one, healthy deliberation implies that citizens are themselves paying attention, willing to learn, and willing to contribute to the national conversation that happens in and around elections. Moreover, if the news media and candidates are expected to provide detailed information to voters but voters simply are not paying attention, then perhaps the voters bear as much or more responsibility as the quality of media coverage or campaign messages.

This perspective may give voters far less credit than they deserve. We have emphasized throughout this chapter that voters often rely on simple decision rules that do not require detailed information. For example, Americans often rely on long-standing psychological attachments to one of the two major political parties. They also draw on appraisals of the economy to evaluate incumbent performance. These strategies may be simple, even simplistic, but they may also be good shortcuts. What does it mean to say that something is a good shortcut? The question is whether voters who choose a Democratic or Republican candidate based on party identification would be likely to choose that same candidate if they had received and digested reams of information about the candidates. In other words, did the shortcut get voters to the same place that they would have reached had they devoted considerable time and energy to researching the alternatives? In many cases, the answer is probably yes. Some research has demonstrated that voting based on issue proximity calculations often gets citizens to the same vote choice they would have made had they relied solely on their partisanship. This is why social identities and party identification in particular may be reliable shortcuts. If so, then we might be slightly less concerned if voters do not follow the campaign closely.

A second concern raised about voters' behavior in elections concerns the impact of the campaign itself. Commentators sometimes worry that voters—particularly those who are not paying close attention to the campaign—could be unduly affected by clever television advertisements or other kinds of campaign appeals. This speaks to the standard of *free choice* that we have discussed previously. If campaigns can influence voters by airing ads that play on voters' fears with exaggerated attacks of the opponent, or ads that contain misleading information or even outright falsehoods, then perhaps voters' choices are not quite free but are instead being manipulated by the candidates.

By and large, such fears seem unfounded. Campaigns can be important for the voting process. They reinforce the views of partisans and occasionally persuade some voters who are on the fence. But their effects appear to stop well short of manipulation. Indeed, political reality—objective factors and conditions—significantly constrains how much campaigns can influence voters. Campaigns are hard-pressed to overcome political reality and voters' partisan habits, particularly when the efforts of one candidate are countered and offset by the efforts of the opponent. This is especially true for presidential election campaigns. The result is that presidents presiding over prosperous times typically win (for example, Reagan in 1984 and Clinton in 1996), and those presiding over recessions almost always lose (for example, Carter in 1980 and Bush in 1992). Only when voters know little about the candidates or when they cannot rely on shortcuts like party identification do campaigns appear more influential—and even then only when one candidate can outspend the other.

We are not suggesting that campaigns do not matter at all. For one, they might be important even if they do not persuade many voters. They provide information, mobilize voters, and force candidates to articulate policy positions that become the basis for subsequent accountability. Furthermore, in some cases, they do persuade enough voters to affect the outcome. The 2016 presidential election might be such a case, given that Trump's victory rested on only 80,000 votes in three states (Wisconsin, Pennsylvania, and Michigan). Thus, the campaign can be the difference between winning and losing—certainly at lower levels of office and perhaps even in presidential elections from time to time.

This basic understanding of voters and vote choice is shared by political scientists and campaign professionals. Understandably, the people inside the campaigns, more so than academics viewing proceedings from afar, tend to think their actions are important to voters. But consultants and campaign workers comprehend, perhaps better than anyone else, how difficult it is to capture the attention of voters and score points. Ironically, it is precisely because it is so difficult to move voters that campaigns often develop a strong belief in how important it is to allocate resources effectively, message coherently, and win the daily battle with the news media.

KEY TERMS

panel studies (p. 384)

social groups (p. 385)

opinion leaders (p. 385)

party identification (p. 387)

retrospective voting (p. 392)

sociotropic voting (p. 392)

pocketbook voting (p. 392)

proximity voting (p. 393)

persuasion (p. 397)

wedge issues (p. 403)

cross pressures (p. 404)

reinforcement (p. 406)

priming (p. 406)

FOR DISCUSSION

1. What is party identification and how does it influence the behavior of voters?

2. Why do scholars believe that most voters do not engage in issue voting?

3. Identify and briefly describe three ways in which campaigns might "matter" for voters.

4. Why is it that political scientists are particularly skeptical about the ability of presidential campaigns to determine election outcomes?

5. Do you think the 2016 presidential election confirms the findings in this chapter, or contradicts them?

CHAPTER 14

Democracy in Action or a Broken System?

It is easy to imagine political campaigns as wars in which the candidates are generals and the people they direct—staff and volunteers—are the loyal troops that engage in combat. This conception of political campaigns is evident among practitioners and scholars. For example, Mary Matalin and James Carville called their book about the 1992 presidential election *All's Fair: Love, War and Running for President*, while the Republican consultant Ed Rollins called his autobiography *Bare Knuckles and Back Rooms*.[1] Lee Atwater, a consultant for presidents Ronald Reagan and George H. W. Bush, claimed that his favorite book was Sun Tzu's *Art of War* because "Everything in it you can relate to my profession, you can relate to the campaign."[2] Consultants for more recent campaigns have been no different in their belief that campaigns are wars. Roger Stone, a longtime Republican consultant known as the "dirty trickster" who advised President Trump's 2016 campaign, lives by the rule, "Admit nothing, deny everything, launch counterattack."[3] Scholars are no less likely to use the war metaphor, as evidenced by book titles such as *The Battle for Congress*, *Campaign Warriors*, and *Air Wars*.[4]

To a certain extent, it is understandable why campaigns are depicted as wars. The word *campaign* itself derives from the Latin word *campus* ("field"), which originally referred to the period of time when an army was in the field. There are

---

[1] Ed Rollins, with Tom DeFrank. 1997. *Bare Knuckles and Back Rooms: My Life in American Politics*. New York: Broadway Books.

[2] As quoted in John J. Pitney, Jr. 2001. *The Art of Political Warfare*. Norman: University of Oklahoma Press, p. 13.

[3] Jeffrey Toobin. 2008. "The Dirty Trickster: Campaign Tips from the Man Who Has Done It All." *New Yorker*, June 8. www.newyorker.com/magazine/2008/06/02/the-dirty-trickster (accessed 12/10/2017).

[4] James A. Thurber, ed. 2001. *The Battle for Congress: Consultants, Candidates, and Voters*. Washington, DC: Brookings Institution Press; James A. Thurber and Candice J. Nelson, eds. 2000. *Campaign Warriors: Political Consultants in Elections*. Washington, DC: Brookings Institution Press; Darrell M. West. 2005. *Air Wars: Television Advertising in Election Campaigns, 1952–2004*, 4th ed. Washington, DC: CQ Press.

two problems with conceiving of political campaigns as battles, however. First, doing so makes it seem like there are no limits to the actions that political actors can take in pursuit of victory. Many political observers felt this was precisely the view embraced by President Trump during his 2016 "anything goes" campaign, which they noted featured "routine falsehoods, unfounded claims, and inflammatory language." Vin Weber, a former Republican member of Congress, lamented, "It's frightening. Our politics, because of him, is descending to the level of a third-world country. There's just nothing beneath him."[5] Second, while the metaphor might be helpful for imagining the roles of political candidates and campaign workers, it is not very helpful for imagining the role of citizens. Are they soldiers? Civilians? Most citizens do not get involved in political campaigns beyond voting, so the soldier metaphor seems inapt. Civilians, on the other hand, can be viewed either as the people who stay behind to tend the home front and support the troops or as those who dodge sniper fire as they scrounge for food and water. Needless to say, these are poor ways to conceive of citizens in a democratic society. Understanding campaigns means moving beyond martial metaphors and examining the role that campaigns play in a democracy.

Throughout this book, we have emphasized that campaigns in the United States reflect the country's laws and institutions, the strategic motivations of candidates, the choices that voters make, and the broader economic and historical context in which elections take place. In other words, campaigns make sense when one understands the incentives and constraints political actors face. The fact that there is an intelligible logic to how campaigns and elections function,

Core of the Analysis

- American campaigns and elections can be evaluated in terms of key democratic values, especially free choice, political equality, and deliberation.
- The American tradition of free speech makes it difficult to reform political campaigns and further these three values.
- American campaigns generally uphold the free choices and equality of citizens.
- Some proposed campaign reforms have promise, but it is not always clear whether those reforms would work and whether citizens and politicians would agree to them.

---

[5] Jonathan Martin. 2016. "Donald Trump's Anything-Goes Campaign Sets an Alarming Precedent." *New York Times*, September 17. www.nytimes.com/2016/09/18/us/politics/donald-trump-presidential-race.html (accessed 12/10/2017).

however, does not mean that they are serving our democracy well in their current form. The challenge of evaluating campaigns animates this chapter. Our discussion starts with the assumption that the most important role political campaigns play in a democracy is to provide citizens with information to help them make a choice on Election Day. We then ask how campaigns might promote the democratic values of free choice, political equality, and deliberation that we discussed at the beginning of this book. The discussion concludes that, although campaigns in the United States are not perfect, they do facilitate important democratic processes. How they might be improved is a complicated matter, both in theory and in practice.

Campaigns and Democratic Values

To help visualize the role that political campaigns play in democratic elections, imagine an election without them—that is, one with no television and radio advertisements, no phone calls from campaign volunteers, no glossy mailers, no debates, and no tweets. Because the candidates would not be making appearances and speeches, news outlets would rarely cover the election. On Election Day, only the most politically engaged citizens would be aware that there was even an election going on, let alone know where they needed to go to cast their ballot. Only the most motivated of those citizens would actually vote. And those who did would know very little about the candidates.

This mental exercise demonstrates that one of the most important democratic functions of political campaigns is to provide voters with information. Yet it is plainly clear to any observer that the quality of campaign information can range wildly. The goal of the following discussion is to use democratic theory to create a set of standards by which citizens can evaluate political campaigns. These standards are summarized in Table 14.1.

Free Choice

In a representative democracy, such as the United States, elections allow citizens to choose who will represent them in government. By definition, a choice involves selecting one of a number of alternatives. This means voters must be allowed to choose between at least two parties or candidates. If an election is uncontested, voters have no real choice. Yet, even when this minimal requirement has been met, free choice is not guaranteed. First, political scientists have long recognized the power of agenda-setting—that is, the

---

TABLE 14.1 What Free Choice, Political Equality, and Deliberation
Require of Campaigns and Elections

Free choice	• Citizens must have a choice between at least two candidates. • Citizens must play a role in determining the final set of candidate choices. • Citizens must not be intimidated, manipulated, or coerced into making certain vote choices.
Political equality	• Each citizen's vote should have an equal impact on election outcomes. • All candidates should be able to disseminate similar amounts of information. • The rules governing campaigns and elections must apply equally to all candidates.
Deliberation	• Candidates and citizens must have opportunities to deliberate before an election. • Citizens must have a high volume of campaign information from a diverse range of sources. • Candidates must offer reasons for the positions they take. • Candidates should not be required to refrain from criticizing one another.

---

ability to manipulate outcomes by constraining political choices.[6] As discussed in Chapter 3, party elites exercised this power prior to the fourth campaign era, when they chose which candidates would compete in the general election. The adoption of primaries by both parties following the dramatic protests of the 1968 Democratic National Convention signaled recognition that citizens must be involved in the nomination process. Free choice is also undermined when voters are coerced or manipulated into voting a particular way. Such coercion can take the form, as it does in some countries, of armed soldiers monitoring ballot boxes, or it can involve more subtle methods such as lying to voters or withholding information crucial to their vote. When this happens, voters are no longer free or autonomous.

Political Equality

Political equality has always been a central value in the American political system. The principle of "one person, one vote" is a natural extension of the

---

[6] Robert A. Dahl. 1956. *A Preface to Democratic Theory.* Chicago, IL: University of Chicago Press.

After fanning "birther" conspiracies for years, President Trump finally admitted in September 2016 that President Obama was born in the United States. In almost the same breath, however, he claimed that Hillary Clinton had started the rumor, a patently false accusation.

belief that "all men are created equal." Equal access to the ballot box, however, is not sufficient to ensure equality. Inequalities can also arise during the campaign.

In *A Preface to Democratic Theory*, the political scientist Robert Dahl argues that preserving equal political influence requires that voters possess identical information about the choices confronting them on Election Day.[7] Here, *identical* means that candidates should be able to disseminate similar amounts of information to voters so that no one candidate or party can monopolize the avenues of communication in a campaign. The constitutional scholar Ronald Dworkin arrives at the same conclusion by arguing that citizens are equals not only as voters but as candidates for office as well.[8] In fact, Dworkin contends that we should be just as concerned about the equality of candidates for office as we are about the equality of voters. He argues that

---

[7] Dahl, *A Preface to Democratic Theory*.

[8] Ronald Dworkin. 2002. *Sovereign Virtue: The Theory and Practice of Equality*. Cambridge, MA: Harvard University Press.

all citizens—including elected officials, candidates for office, and organized groups—should have a fair and equal opportunity to publish, broadcast, or otherwise command attention for their views. A candidate who controls the flow of political communication has a disproportionate influence over citizen opinion.

Political equality also requires that election rules and regulations apply equally to all candidates. In his book *Just Elections*, Dennis Thompson argues that in a truly fair election, candidates would have "comparable opportunities to raise resources, unbiased rules for conducting primaries and elections, and impartial procedures for resolving disputes."[9] Some would argue that this standard is too demanding, because candidates may not be able to raise resources for good reasons—for example, because their views are unpalatable to potential donors.

Deliberation

Like political equality, deliberation has long been associated with democracy. In his eulogy of democratic Athens, Pericles called the period of discussion preceding a political decision "an indispensable preliminary to any wise action at all." But political decisions, and even elections, are not inherently deliberative. The side with the most votes wins, whether or not there has been discussion. The possibility that political decisions are made without such discussion is particularly bothersome to those in the minority. They would prefer a more deliberative campaign process to give them an opportunity to persuade the majority. And even if they lose, such a process would leave them with the sense that they had a fair hearing.

How can we evaluate the deliberative quality of a campaign? First, there must be a large volume of information available to ensure that citizens receive at least a portion of it. Second, voters must be exposed to information from diverse sources, including candidates, parties, and interest groups, so that their views are not biased because they received information from only one side. Third, campaigns should provide reasons for supporting or opposing a particular candidate. If a candidate for office says "I oppose abortion," citizens may know where the candidate stands but not know the candidate's reasoning. When candidates offer reasons for their beliefs—for example, "I oppose abortion because I believe life begins at conception and that it is immoral to end a life"—it helps citizens understand their views and

---

[9] Dennis F. Thompson. 2002. *Just Elections: Creating a Fair Electoral Process in the United States.* Chicago: University of Chicago Press.

encourages more discussion. Finally, deliberation demands accountability. Earnest and honest discussion requires that candidates identify themselves and take responsibility for their words.

It is important to understand that deliberation does not require that candidates refrain from criticizing one another. Because deliberation requires candidates to be honest and substantive, attacks are a concern when they are misleading or irrelevant. In particular, "pants-on-fire" lies—such as Donald Trump's contention during the 2016 campaign that when Hillary Clinton ran the State Department, "$6 billion was missing" or Clinton's claim that Trump's response to rescuing the auto industry was, "Let it go"—undermine deliberation because they discourage citizens from paying attention to politics at all.[10] Who can blame people for tuning out when candidates are so disrespectful to one another? However, attacks must be distinguished from valid criticisms. Politics inevitably involves disagreement, and it is important to clarify the disagreements among opposing candidates. A useful distinction, for instance, came during the second presidential debate when Clinton claimed that she would preserve marriage equality while Trump asserted that he would appoint Supreme Court justices who would reverse it. This is a meaningful difference that voters could weigh in their voting decision.

What role do citizens play in a deliberative campaign? Ideally, they would reflect on their own values and interests, spend time learning about the candidates and their issue positions, and vote for the candidate who best represents their views. A key part of a deliberative campaign for citizens is exposure to disagreeable viewpoints: they must inform themselves about *all* of the candidates and discuss the election with people who are supporting different candidates. Of course, as we learned in Chapters 12 and 13, citizens rarely behave this way in elections, but it is important to recognize that, for a campaign to truly fulfill deliberative ideals, citizens must take advantage of the opportunities presented to engage with different perspectives.

Freedom of Speech

The First Amendment of the Constitution of the United States says that "Congress shall make no law . . . abridging the freedom of speech." The First Amendment is normally interpreted as giving American citizens the legal

---

[10] Examples taken from PolitiFact.com. www.politifact.com/truth-o-meter/lists/people /comparing-hillary-clinton-donald-trump-truth-o-met/ (accessed 8/2/2017).

right to speak freely and openly, without government regulation. Because free speech is a fundamental right in our country, it is difficult to regulate campaigns in ways that might promote some of the values just discussed, because such reforms would entail limits on speech and expression. For example, if political equality requires that candidates provide equivalent amounts of information to citizens, Congress could create a law that established spending limits in campaigns to prevent one candidate from spending more and thus providing more information than the other candidates. It could also create a law that prevented political candidates from supporting their campaigns with their own money to ensure that a wealthy candidate would not have an advantage over a less wealthy competitor. In fact, as we discussed in Chapter 4, Congress passed a law that did both things: the Federal Election Campaign Act of 1971. However, in *Buckley v. Valeo* (424 U.S. 1, 1976), the Supreme Court ruled that these provisions were unconstitutional because they violated the free speech protections of the First Amendment.

As a result of this commitment to free speech, the United States has one of the least regulated campaign systems in the world.[11] In fact, many of the laws and regulations that other countries have adopted to improve campaign discourse would very likely be overturned by the U.S. Supreme Court. For instance, political parties in Japan can use television advertising only to discuss policy positions and must refrain from mentioning the name or record of any individual candidate. Some other countries limit the duration of the campaign, or prohibit the publication of public opinion polls for a certain period of time before an election so that their results do not discourage people from voting. Even if Americans wanted to adopt such restrictions—and it is by no means clear that they do—these limits would likely violate the principle of free speech, at least as it is interpreted by contemporary U.S. courts.

In sum, the political values of free choice, equality, and deliberation require political campaigns and elections to meet certain criteria. First, free choice requires contestation, meaning that an election must feature at least two candidates, and that citizens control the nomination process. It also requires that a citizen's vote choice not be coerced or manipulated and that citizens have information about all of their vote choices. Political equality requires that citizens receive equivalent amounts of information about

---

[11] Bruce I. Buchanan. 2001. "Mediated Electoral Democracy: Campaigns, Incentives, and Reform," in *Mediated Politics: Communication in the Future of Democracy*, eds. W. Lance Bennett and Robert M. Entman. New York: Cambridge University Press, p. 366.

candidates and that the rules and regulations governing campaigns apply equally to all candidates. The value of deliberation concerns both the quantity and quality of information. Citizens must have access to a large amount of campaign information from a variety of sources. Deliberation also demands that candidates offer clear reasons for their positions and engage the arguments of their opponents. At the same time, deliberation requires citizen engagement. Even if Americans' commitment to free speech conflicts with some of these values, they are important values to keep in mind when evaluating campaigns.

The Reality of Political Campaigns

Is it realistic to expect campaigns to live up to all of the ideals discussed in the previous section? As we have emphasized, even if we agree that certain democratic values are important, there might be trade-offs among values, or limits on what we can reasonably expect from candidates and citizens. Thus, it is important to consider the "reality" of American campaigns.

What Do Citizens Want from Campaigns?

Do citizens want the kind of campaign that these values imply—one that focuses on substantive comparisons of the candidates and asks citizens to deliberate and participate in the electoral process? If not, then there arises a dilemma: Should campaigns be modeled on abstract values, even if citizens do not necessarily endorse these values, or should campaigns simply give citizens what they want?

What exactly do citizens say they want from political campaigns? It depends on how interested in politics they are.[12] Those who are interested in and informed about politics tend to favor more substantive and interactive campaigns—including candidate debates, town hall meetings where candidates interact with citizens, and, in general, more discussion of policy issues. Those who are less interested in politics, however, tend to favor campaigns that demand less of them by providing them with simple cues that enable them to make choices with minimal time and effort. For example, citizens who are not very interested in politics may be more interested in getting a sense of who the candidates are as people by evaluating each

---

[12] Keena Lipsitz, Christine Trost, Matthew Grossmann, and John Sides. 2005. "What Voters Want from Political Campaign Communication." *Journal of Political Communication* 22, 3: 337–54.

candidate's résumé, including information about the candidate's political career, such as voting records, and personal life, such as credit scores and Department of Motor Vehicles records. They do not necessarily want detailed analyses about where the candidates stand on the issues. Nor are they necessarily interested in investing time and energy in campaign events, such as town hall meetings, that provide venues for deeper discussion of the issues and the choices before voters in the election.

The fact that citizens do not necessarily agree about what constitutes an "ideal" campaign makes it complicated to reform campaigns. That some citizens prefer less substantive campaigns does not necessarily mean that reforms aimed at making campaigns more policy-oriented or deliberative should be abandoned. Instead, it may suggest that reformers should also look for ways to make campaigns more appealing to those who are not politically sophisticated—for instance, by finding ways to provide voters with simple, digestible information, such as a short description of the candidates' issue positions next to their names on a ballot. One must also consider the possibility that people who say they do not want to participate in more deliberative events might change their mind once they have experienced them. Research shows that jurors who are reluctant to report for jury duty—a highly deliberative exercise—leave the experience convinced of its value and enthusiastic about participating again.[13]

How Do American Campaigns Measure Up?

Americans love to hate political campaigns. They complain about negative ads but rarely tune them out. They bemoan the tactics of candidates but seldom seem to punish candidates who push the envelope of campaigning. For example, voters "graded" Trump's behavior during the 2016 campaign lower than any other candidate since 1988, but they still elected him.[14] As a result, Americans may actually create incentives for candidates to do the things that Americans claim to dislike. James Madison referred to the "vicious arts"[15] by which candidates win elections; but a phrase like "vicious arts" is too

---

[13] John Gastil, E. Pierre Deess, Philip J. Weiser, and Cindy Simmons. 2010. *The Jury and Democracy: How Jury Deliberation Promotes Civic Engagement and Political Participation.* New York: Oxford University Press.

[14] Carroll Doherty, Jocelyn Kiley, and Bridget Johnson. 2016. "Low Marks for Major Players in 2016 Election—Including the Winner." Pew Research Center, November 21. http://assets .pewresearch.org/wp-content/uploads/sites/5/2016/11/18174655/11-21-16-Post-Election -Release.pdf (accessed 12/10/2017).

[15] Alexander Hamilton, James Madison, and John Jay. 1961. *The Federalist Papers*, ed. Clinton Rossiter. New York: Penguin, p. 82.

strong. Evaluating campaigns by the standards of free choice, political equality, and deliberation reveals a more mixed portrait.[16]

Free Choice Most campaigns and elections in the United States promote free choice. Since the early 1970s, citizens have been able to vote in primary elections for general election candidates. They usually have two or more candidates from which to choose, as well as access to information about their choices. Overt coercion or intimidation of voters in America is now quite rare.

Certain aspects of American elections, however, do undermine individual free choice. Although citizens can now vote in primaries for all partisan offices, individuals who want to run in a primary must demonstrate their ability to raise money and earn endorsements from party elites, especially to participate in primaries for higher offices. For example, long before presidential primaries begin, individuals who want to contest them must perform well in the "invisible primary"—that is, the race for cash and endorsements that proves one is a viable candidate. Although public opinion polls do matter in this process, recent research shows that party elites have been largely successful in regaining control (the 2016 Republican presidential primary being an obvious exception).[17]

Free choice in the United States is also undermined by the fact that many elections are not competitive. Indeed, as we noted in Chapters 10 and 11, a surprising number of elections in this country are not even contested—that is, there is only one candidate, or at least only one major-party candidate, running for office. Uncontested elections occur more often in local races and state legislative races, but some U.S. House and Senate elections are also uncontested. For example, 24 House races were uncontested in the 2016 election.[18] Many other races are contested but feature only one major-party candidate. In recent years, there have often been 50 or more U.S. House races with only one major-party candidate. Most primaries for House, Senate, and statewide offices are uncontested. In fact, on average, just 30 percent of primaries featuring an incumbent are contested. Although one might argue that it is more important for a general election to be contested than a primary, keep in mind that many jurisdictions in the United States are

---

[16] This approach is advocated by and elaborated on in Keena Lipsitz. 2011. *Competitive Elections and the American Voter.* Philadelphia: University of Pennsylvania Press, Chapter 2.

[17] Marty Cohen, David Karol, Hans Noel, and John Zaller. 2008. *The Party Decides: Presidential Nominations before and after Reform.* Chicago, IL: University of Chicago Press.

[18] Richard E. Berg-Andersson and Tony Roza. 2017. TheGreenPapers.com. www .thegreenpapers.com/G16/uncontested.phtml (accessed 8/2/2017).

dominated by one of the two major parties. In such jurisdictions, where the outcome of the general election is a foregone conclusion, one can argue that the choice voters make in the primary election is as important as their choice in the general election, if not more so.

Even when races are contested by two major-party candidates, they are often not competitive. Although presidential elections remain consistently competitive, electoral competitiveness is declining in House and Senate races, in state legislative elections, and in most primary elections.[19] The level of electoral competition in local races is stable, but that is only because it is and has long been quite low. A study of mayoral races in 38 large cities from 1979 to 2003 found that the average margin of victory was 22 percentage points.[20] Most scholars consider a margin of less than 10 percent to be competitive. In short, a skeptic might argue that while citizens technically have a choice of candidates even when an election is uncompetitive, they do not really have much of a choice if one of the candidates is certain to win.

Political Equality Competitive elections are more likely to enhance political equality than those that aren't. When a race is closely contested, the Republican and Democratic Parties, along with their allies, funnel resources to it, ensuring that both major party candidates will be able to get their message out to voters. As discussed in Chapter 9, presidential elections exhibit the equalizing effects of true competition. These races are always well funded, so that major party presidential candidates invariably compete with one another on roughly equal footing. Yet, in virtually every other type of election in the United States, the lack of competitiveness means that opposing candidates compete on very unequal terms.

But is this a reason to condemn the American system? Not necessarily. First, it is important to consider whether equality of resources is always required. The standard of strict equality makes sense when applied to voters. In a democracy, there is no legitimate basis for claiming that one person's vote

---

[19] Gary C. Jacobson. 2009. *The Politics of Congressional Elections*, 7th ed. New York: Pearson/Longman; Richard G. Niemi, Lynda W. Powell, William D. Berry, Thomas M. Carsey, and James M. Snyder, Jr. 2006. "Competition in State Legislative Elections, 1992–2002," in *The Marketplace of Democracy: Electoral Competition and American Politics*, eds. Michael P. McDonald and John Samples. Washington, DC: Brookings Institution Press, pp. 53–73; Stephen Ansolabehere, John Mark Hansen, Shigeo Hirano, and James M. Snyder, Jr. 2006. "The Decline of Competition in U.S. Primary Elections, 1908–2004," in *The Marketplace of Democracy*, pp. 74–101.

[20] Neal Caren. 2007. "Big City, Big Turnout? Electoral Participation in American Cities." *Journal of Urban Affairs* 29, 1: 31–46.

should count more than another's. Political candidates, however, might not deserve equal resources. The amount of money that candidates are able to raise reflects, in part, the confidence that citizens have in them, and the belief that one of the candidates might actually be better for the job. If citizens believe certain candidates to be untrustworthy or out of step with the district, they will not contribute to their campaigns. Likewise, PACs contribute to candidates who they believe will best represent their interests in Congress. As a result, some inequality in campaign resources may be natural.

But citizens and PACs give to candidates for other reasons that are less legitimate from the standpoint of political equality. For instance, PACs contribute to incumbents because they know they are likely to win, and the PACs want to ensure access and perhaps influence the way a politician will vote on a particular piece of legislation. Citizens may decide not to donate to candidates who they like simply because they do not think the candidates will win, thereby giving an advantage to the likely victor—who, in many cases, is also an incumbent. When campaign resource inequalities result from these kinds of calculations, they are more of a concern. It is impossible to say how much of the resource inequality we see in campaigns today is due to legitimate or illegitimate reasons. Later we discuss some campaign finance reforms that might discourage giving to candidates for the illegitimate reasons we've described.

Another requirement of political equality is that the rules and regulations governing our electoral processes apply to all candidates equally. In one sense, our system reflects and promotes the goal of political equality: major-party candidates who run for any office in this country must abide by the same rules and regulations. But minor parties are uniquely burdened by a host of laws and regulations.[21] Consider the situation of minor-party presidential candidates. Whereas the names of the Democratic and Republican candidates automatically appear on the ballot in every state, minor-party candidates must petition state election officials to get their names on the ballot. As we noted in Chapter 2, this usually requires collecting a certain number of signatures from citizens, which can range from as few as 275 in Tennessee to as many as 3 percent of the state's registered voters (approximately 117,000) in Oklahoma.[22] In addition, as detailed in Chapter 4, presidential

---

[21] Steven J. Rosenstone, Roy L. Behr, and Edward H. Lazarus. 1996. *Third Parties in America*, 2nd ed. Princeton, NJ: Princeton University Press; Samuel Issacharoff and Richard H. Pildes. 1998. "Politics as Markets: Partisan Lockups of the Democratic Process." *Stanford Law Review* 50, 3: 643–717; Ian Shapiro. 2003. *The Moral Foundations of Politics*. New Haven, CT: Yale University Press.

[22] Rosenstone, Behr, and Lazarus, *Third Parties in America*, p. 21.

candidates from the two major parties are automatically eligible for public funds to finance their general election campaigns (even though they no longer take them). Minor parties, on the other hand, receive public funding *after* the general election, and then only if they receive at least five percent of the national popular vote and appear on the ballot in at least 10 states. Minor-party candidates are also not invited to participate in televised presidential debates unless polls show that at least 15 percent of the population supports their candidacy. Of course, an election system with no barriers to ballot access or public financing would be inordinately expensive and potentially confusing for voters. Still, the current system does not treat all candidates equally.

True political equality also requires that electoral disputes be settled by a neutral arbiter. In this country, elections are administered by individuals who are affiliated with political parties. In 42 states, the secretary of state or chief election official is chosen through a partisan election. In the remaining states, the position is usually filled by gubernatorial appointment. No state uses a nonpartisan election process. The most obvious consequence of having party loyalists occupying such positions is the potential for political bias. Most rules governing elections have consequences that benefit one party more than the other. For example, making it harder to vote by limiting voting hours or requiring voters to present a photo identification typically helps Republican candidates. Conversely, removing barriers to voting usually helps Democrats. Since most people do not want to wait in long lines to vote, reducing the number of polling places in an area dominated by a member of the opposing party can lower turnout among her supporters.[23]

In addition, when there are election disputes, such as in Florida after the 2000 presidential election, partisan bias has the potential to affect the outcome of an election by swaying the decisions of election officials. This is often referred to as a problem of "foxes guarding henhouses": even though election officials are supposed to protect the integrity of the electoral process, partisan self-interest may interfere with their ability to do so. An example came after the 2016 election, when President Trump repeatedly claimed that 3 to 5 million illegal votes had cost him the popular vote. He then created a 12-member Presidential Advisory Commission on Election Integrity to investigate voter fraud. The commission was heralded as being "bipartisan," but only five Democrats were appointed to it and it was co-chaired by two Republicans: Vice President Mike Pence and Kansas's Republican secretary of state Kris Kobach, whom the American Civil Liberties Union has called "the king

---

[23] Heather K. Gerken. 2009. *The Democracy Index: Why Our Election System Is Failing and How to Fix It*. Princeton, NJ: Princeton University Press, p. 16.

of voter suppression." Many political observers became concerned when the first action of the commission was to ask all secretaries of state to provide voter roll data, including sensitive information such as partial social security numbers and addresses of voters. Many states refused to comply because of concerns about the ability to store the data securely, as well as concerns that the commission's true motivation was to suppress votes. The reason is simple: a 2014 bipartisan presidential commission, as well as numerous studies by academics, journalists, and nonpartisan think tanks, had found no evidence of widespread voter fraud. Although the commission was created to "study the registration and voting processes used in Federal elections," as the executive order creating the commission contended, the fact that President Trump disbanded the commission in January 2018 after finding no evidence of voter fraud suggests that there were other motivations behind its creation.

Deliberation American campaigns do offer opportunities for deliberation, but critics argue that they could offer more. Deliberation depends on both the quantity and quality of information provided to citizens as well as the level of citizen engagement. As we have discussed, the quantity of information depends on the competitiveness of the election. Because the majority of races in the United States are not competitive, citizens are arguably receiving less information than the standard of deliberation demands.

The quality of available information depends on whether candidates address similar issues, offer specific positions on those issues, and provide the reasoning for their positions over the course of the campaign. Deliberative events such as debates offer an opportunity for candidates to communicate this kind of information. Debates require candidates to address the same topics—typically, those posed by a moderator—and give them time to explain and defend their thinking. But debates are not necessarily the best forums for deliberation. For one, their occurrence usually depends on the whims of candidates. Candidates who believe that their interests are not served by participating in a debate can avoid them. Moreover, the format of debates may reflect the strategic goals of the candidate more than what is "good" for the electorate. For example, candidates participating in presidential debates usually sign a binding contract that lays out the debate rules. In the past, these rules have stipulated that candidates have no more than 30 seconds to respond to a question and that the candidates cannot ask each other direct questions. These rules reduce uncertainty for the candidates and limit the possibility that they will make mistakes, both of which are desirable from the perspective of campaign consultants. Such restrictions could, however, undermine the "give and take" between the candidates and limit the deliberative value of the debate.

Outside of debates, candidates have much more flexibility and freedom in how they communicate with voters. Here again, competition is crucial in whether campaigns will live up to deliberative values. In competitive elections, candidates are much more likely to talk about the same issues—and thus engage in a true dialogue—during the campaign.[24] They are also more likely to offer specific statements of their issue positions.[25] For example, competition might make the difference between a candidate saying "I want to improve education" and "I want to improve education by giving students and their parents education vouchers so they can leave a failing public school." Obviously, the latter statement provides voters with a better sense of the policies a candidate will pursue if elected. Increased competition leads to greater issue specificity because candidates in tight races must be clear about their issue positions to attract money and to differentiate themselves from their opponents. When races are not competitive, however, candidates are more likely to offer bland statements that convey little information to voters.

There have been efforts to increase the quality of information provided by American campaigns. The Bipartisan Campaign Reform Act of 2002 included a "stand by your ad" provision that requires candidates to state their approval of their advertisements—for example, "I am John Smith and I approve this message." In radio advertisements, this requires an audio statement by the candidate that offers identification and approval. In television advertisements, candidates must personally approve of the ad through either a visual appearance or an audio voice-over. In addition, the candidate's name must appear at the end of the advertisement in "a clearly readable manner" for at least four seconds. Failure to comply with these provisions can result in a fine by the Federal Election Commission (FEC). More important, candidates who fail to comply with this requirement can lose their "lowest unit rate" status— political candidates are typically charged the lowest advertising rate possible for a time slot—for the duration of their campaign. This provision in the law is intended to reduce negativity, but it also forces candidates to take visible responsibility for their advertising, which contributes to deliberation.

Yet, even if campaigns provide a high volume of balanced, diverse, and truthful information about all the candidates, an election cannot be truly

---

[24] Noah Kaplan, David K. Park, and Travis N. Ridout. 2006. "Dialogue in American Political Campaigns? An Examination of Issue Convergence in Candidate Television Advertising." *American Journal of Political Science* 50, 3: 724–36.

[25] Kim Fridkin Kahn and Patrick J. Kenney. 1999. *The Spectacle of U.S. Senate Campaigns.* Princeton, NJ: Princeton University Press.

deliberative unless citizens are engaged and making use of that information. But as we learned in Chapter 13, very few Americans are interested in elections, even when the presidency is at stake, and most rely on shortcuts, such as social group identity and party identification, to make their vote choice rather than give serious thought to the candidates' positions on the issues. Thus, they share at least part of the responsibility for the fact that American campaigns are less deliberative than they could be.

Reforming Campaigns

The preceding discussion highlighted some strengths and weaknesses of American campaigns. For the most part, American campaigns protect the free choice and political equality of citizens, but they do not create equal opportunities for candidates. The resulting inequalities can undermine the deliberative quality of elections. Are there reforms that might make political campaigns better? As we have discussed throughout this book, identifying effective reforms is not easy. A reform may further one value while undermining another. For example, limiting candidate spending to help ensure that citizens have more balanced information from competing candidates would restrict freedom of speech. A reform may also simply not work. Consider televised **ad watches**, in which news programs evaluate the truthfulness of campaign advertisements. Ad watches have been shown to have the perverse effect of reinforcing the advertisement's content rather than countering it because viewers can only remember the ads, not the critiques of them.[26] Or consider the idea that candidates and campaign consultants should pledge publicly not to campaign negatively. Such a pledge may fail because few candidates and consultants are willing to adopt or respect it and because citizens actually learn as much or more from negative campaigning as they learn from positive campaigning.[27]

In this section, we examine eight reforms that advocates believe would improve the content and conduct of campaigns in the United States (see

---

[26] Lori Melton McKinnon and Lynda Lee Kaid. 1999. "Exposing Negative Campaigning or Enhancing Advertising Effects: An Experimental Study of Adwatch Effects on Voters' Evaluations of Candidates and Their Ads." *Journal of Applied Communication Research* 27, 3: 217–36.

[27] L. Sandy Maisel, Darrell M. West, and Brett M. Clifton. 2007. *Evaluating Campaign Quality: Can the Electoral Process Be Improved?* New York: Cambridge University Press; Richard R. Lau, Lee Sigelman, and Ivy Brown Rovner. 2007. "The Effects of Negative Political Campaigns: A Meta-Analytic Reassessment." *Journal of Politics* 69, 4: 1176–209.

Table 14.2). We discuss their effectiveness as measured by current research, as well as whether the public is likely to support the reforms. If citizens are not enthusiastic about a reform and do not understand its importance, then its chances of being adopted are slim.

Making All Elections Publicly Financed

Although presidential candidates have access to public financing, most other candidates for political office in the United States do not. Providing candidates with public financing would enhance political equality because it would

TABLE 14.2 Reforming American Campaigns and Elections

Reform	Free Choice	Equality	Deliberation	Support among Public?
Publicly finance campaigns	✓	✓		Medium*
Make campaign donations anonymous		✓		None
Adopt the national popular vote		✓		Medium[†]
Reform the redistricting process		✓		Medium[‡]
Create neutral election administration positions		✓		None
Use deliberative polls			✓	None
Create a national day of deliberation			✓	None
Use citizen juries to make recommendations			✓	Low**

* David Primo. 2002. "Public Opinion and Campaign Finance: Reformers versus Reality." *Independent Review* 7, 2: 207–19.

[†] Level of support based on number of newspapers endorsing the National Popular Vote, including the *New York Times*, *Chicago Sun-Times*, and *Los Angeles Times*, among others. Polls conducted for the National Popular Vote also indicate a high level of support, although it is unclear how much of a priority the reform is.

[‡] Joshua Fourgere, Stephen Ansolabehere, and Nathaniel Persily. 2010. "Partisanship, Public Opinion, and Redistricting." *Election Law Journal* 9, 4: 325–47.

** Based on the adoption of the Citizens' Initiative Review (CIR) panel in Oregon.

Note: Support among the public is categorized as "low" support or "medium" support, but could theoretically range higher. In the cases where we have indicated "None" we mean that most people have never heard of the reform, which is why there is no support for it.

help underfunded challengers compete with well-heeled incumbents. It would also improve electoral competitiveness, which encourages candidates to provide voters with the kinds of information that facilitate deliberation.[28] Public financing may also improve individual free choice by encouraging more people to run for office and ensuring that more elections are contested. But the effects have been shown to depend on the amount of public funding provided. For example, Hawaii and Wisconsin provide only a small amount of public money to state legislative candidates, rendering their programs less effective. Other states, such as Minnesota and Arizona, provide more money and appear to have had greater success with respect to enhancing competitiveness.[29]

Citizens must therefore be prepared to fund public financing programs generously to make them work. There is little evidence, however, that Americans are willing to do so. For example, fewer than 12 percent of U.S. citizens filing federal tax returns typically check the box on their tax form indicating that they would like to donate $3 to the Presidential Election Campaign Fund (the source of public funding for presidential candidates).[30] Citizens are reluctant to check this box even though the tax form assures them that doing so does not increase the amount of tax they pay. As we noted in Chapter 4, even if a majority of citizens support publicly financed campaigns in the abstract, they do not necessarily consider campaign finance reform an important priority.[31] Moreover, incumbent politicians have little incentive to pass a reform that would essentially give campaign funds to their opponents.

Making Campaign Donations Anonymous

Another way to reform campaigns would be to make all donations anonymous. This reform accepts the role of private donations; there may be nothing inherently wrong with citizens contributing to a candidate who they feel will represent them effectively. The potential problem is that some citizens

---

[28] Lipsitz, *Competitive Elections and the American Voter.*

[29] Kenneth R. Mayer, Timothy Werner, and Amanda Williams. 2006. "Do Public Financing Programs Enhance Competition?" in *The Marketplace of Democracy*, eds. Michael P. McDonald and John Samples. Washington, DC: Brookings Institution Press, pp. 245–67.

[30] Tax Foundation. 2008. "Presidential Election Campaign Fund Untapped by Obama Claims Little Support from Taxpayers." News Release. https://taxfoundation.org/press -release/presidential-election-campaign-fund-untapped-obama-claims-little-support -taxpayers/ (accessed 12/18/2017).

[31] David M. Primo. 2002. "Public Opinion and Campaign Finance: Reformers versus Reality." *Independent Review* 7, 2: 207–19.

may contribute to candidates because they want access or a favor in return. Making donations anonymous would eliminate this possibility, since candidates could never learn who had given them money. Candidates and political parties would no longer be able to accept checks directly from individuals and PACs. Instead, an individual or PAC would give to a blind trust established in the candidate's or political party's name. It is possible that individuals could tell a candidate or party that they made a large contribution, but talk is cheap, and under this system anyone could make such a claim. Supporters call this idea the **donation booth**: just as ballots are cast in secret in the voting booth, donations would be made in secret as well.[32]

A relevant question is whether anonymous donations would reduce the amount of money—and, hence, the amount of communication—in campaigns. Many contributors might not give money if they do not think candidates will acknowledge their donations. Moreover, few Americans have heard of this reform, so its advocates will have the additional burden of explaining to citizens what it is.

Limiting Campaign Spending

Although U.S. citizens are ambivalent about public financing, they do support limits on campaign spending. Even so, there is considerable debate about how spending limits would affect elections. The debate hinges on the methodologically thorny question of whether incumbents or challengers get more bang (vote share) for the buck in campaigns. If challengers do, then spending limits would hurt them because they need to spend as much as possible to successfully compete against incumbents.[33] If incumbent spending is more effective, however, then spending limits would be helpful for challengers.[34] Irrespective of their effects, the Supreme Court has ruled that spending limits are a violation of free speech and, consequently, cannot be imposed on candidates. Candidates can, however, volunteer to limit their spending in exchange for public funding (see Chapters 4 and 9). Thus, public financing

---

[32] Ian Ayres and Jeremy Bulow. 1998. "The Donation Booth: Mandating Donor Anonymity to Disrupt the Market for Political Influence." *Faculty Scholarship Series*, Paper 1259. http://digitalcommons.law.yale.edu/cgi/viewcontent.cgi?article=2258&context=fss_papers (accessed 12/10/2017).

[33] Jacobson, *The Politics of Congressional Elections*, p. 49.

[34] Alan S. Gerber. 1998. "Estimating the Effect of Campaign Spending on Senate Election Outcomes Using Instrumental Variables." *American Political Science Review* 92, 2: 401–11; Steven D. Levitt. 1994. "Using Repeat Challengers to Estimate the Effect of Challenger Spending on Election Outcomes in the U.S. House." *Journal of Political Economy* 102, 4: 777–98.

and spending limits are usually linked in our political system. This means that the fate of the latter depends on the fate of the former.

Reforming the Redistricting Process

As we discussed in Chapter 2, states typically redraw the boundaries of congressional and state legislative districts after the decennial national census. State legislatures are most often responsible for determining these boundaries, and their plans must be approved by the state's governor. This process means that any party that controls the legislature and governor's mansion can draw district lines in a manner that protects its members, as well as incumbents more generally. Thus, redistricting has been linked to two trends: the increase in the incumbency advantage and the decrease in electoral competitiveness. Both of these limit free choice and political equality. As discussed in Chapter 10, the proposals for reforming the redistricting process involve either bypassing the state legislatures and giving power to independent commissions or officially adopting redistricting guidelines that mandate enhanced competition.

There is some evidence that such redistricting reforms do, in fact, work against incumbents to enhance electoral competitiveness, but scholars continue to debate the magnitude of their effects.[35] The other question concerns who will pursue such reforms. As was the case with public financing, politicians often have little incentive to support redistricting reform, especially if they believe it would alter the boundaries of their own districts or cost their party seats in Congress or the state legislature. Surveys show that Americans who have an opinion about redistricting procedures tend to believe that district lines drawn by independent commissions are fairer than those drawn by state legislatures, but 40 percent of those surveyed had no opinion on the topic.[36] As a result, the biggest obstacle to adoption of redistricting reform is the low salience of the topic for voters. But as Californians demonstrated in 2008, when they voted to adopt such an independent redistricting commission, voter education and outreach can work.

---

[35] See Nicholas R. Seabrook. 2017. *Drawing the Lines: Constraints on Partisan Gerrymandering in U.S. Politics.* Ithaca, NY: Cornell University Press; Michael P. McDonald. 2006. "Drawing the Line on District Competition." *PS: Political Science and Politics* 39, 1: 91–94; Michael P. McDonald. 2006. "Re-Drawing the Line on District Competition." *PS: Political Science and Politics* 39, 1: 99–102; Alan I. Abramowitz, Brad Alexander, and Matthew Gunning. 2006. "Drawing the Line on District Competition: A Rejoinder." *PS: Political Science and Politics* 39, 1: 95–98.

[36] Joshua Fourgere, Stephen Ansolabehere, and Nathaniel Persily. 2010. "Partisanship, Public Opinion, and Redistricting." *Election Law Journal* 9, 4: 325–47.

An upcoming Supreme Court case, however, may make all of these efforts to reform redistricting irrelevant. In June 2017, the Supreme Court agreed to review a lower court's decision to throw out a redistricting map drawn up by Wisconsin's Republican-controlled state legislature. The lower court held that the map constituted an "unconstitutional partisan gerrymander" because it enabled Republicans to win 60 of 99 seats in the state assembly despite winning only 49 percent of the two-party vote in the state. No matter what the Supreme Court decides, its decision will have enormous consequences. One of the problems the Court had in a 2004 partisan gerrymandering case is that a majority of the Justices believed that certain forms of extreme partisan gerrymandering might be unconstitutional, but they could not find an acceptable standard for determining when a partisan gerrymander had gone too far. If the Court can find an acceptable standard, it will unleash a flood of challenges to existing maps. Conservatives on the Court, however, have argued that courts should not be able to review partisan redistricting claims. If they have their way, redistricting losers will have little recourse. The Court is likely to issue its decision in 2018, just before the midterm elections.

Reforming or Abolishing the Electoral College in Presidential Elections

The Electoral College undermines citizen equality because it makes the votes of citizens in smaller states worth more than the votes of citizens in larger states. This makes it possible for the winner of the popular vote to lose the Electoral College, just as Al Gore did in 2000 and Hillary Clinton did in 2016. We have also discussed how the Electoral College creates incentives for campaigns to allocate more time, money, and attention to citizens in battleground states, ignoring so-called "safe" states. Electoral College reformers tend to fall into one of two categories: those who would abolish or effectively bypass it; and those who would simply eliminate the "winner-take-all" rule—where the winner takes all of the state's electors—in exchange for a more representative allocation of electoral votes. As mentioned in Chapter 9, some reformers in the first category advocate requiring states to allocate their state's electoral votes to the winner of the national popular vote (this is the so-called National Popular Vote [NPV] movement). This reform is more likely to be adopted than the constitutional amendment that would be required to eliminate the Electoral College. A constitutional amendment requires the support of three-quarters (38) of the states, but the NPV could theoretically pass with the support of just 11 states. This is because it will take effect as long as the states that adopt it have a combined total of 270 electoral votes—the number needed to decide a presidential election—between them. The second class of reforms usually involves exchanging the winner-take-all rule for either a proportional allocation or an allocation of electoral votes based on electoral outcomes in individual congressional districts. Because basing electoral votes on candidate performance in congressional districts would politicize the redistricting process even more than it already is, most reformers prefer allocating electoral votes according to a system of proportional representation.

Although many Americans have a sense of what it means to live in a battleground state during a presidential election, only the most politically astute understand how the Electoral College works and why the NPV might be desirable.[37] Despite the lack of widespread popular support, NPV bills have been introduced in virtually every state. Ten states—California, Hawaii, Illinois, Maryland, Massachusetts, New Jersey, New York, Rhode Island, Vermont, and Washington—as well as the District of Columbia, have passed an NPV measure, which will take effect only when enough states have adopted the reform to provide the winner with an Electoral College majority (270). At this point, the law has been enacted by jurisdictions with a total of 165 electoral votes.

Adopting a national popular vote for president, however, would not necessarily enhance citizen equality. Candidates who currently campaign in battleground states because of the Electoral College would not allocate their resources evenly across the nation if there were a national vote. Instead, they would focus on areas of the country where large concentrations of swing voters reside. The bottom line is that candidates have finite resources and, as we have stressed throughout this book, will be strategic about how they use them.

Making Election Administration Neutral

Political equality requires that the rules and regulations governing elections be enforced in a neutral manner, but most election officials in the United States are party loyalists. One way to reform the system would be to implement nonpartisan, professional election administration, as most of the world's democracies have.[38] For example, all Canadian federal elections are

---

[37] Darshan Goux. 2006. "A New Battleground? Media Perceptions and Political Reality in Presidential Elections, 1960–2004." Paper presented at the American Political Science Association Annual Meeting, Philadelphia, PA.

[38] Electoral Knowledge Network. http://aceproject.org/epic-en (accessed 8/3/2017).

administered by an independent chief electoral officer (CEO), who is the only Canadian citizen who is not allowed to vote in federal elections. In addition to the CEO, no Canadian election official can engage in partisan activity, belong to a party, or make a contribution. Although it is unlikely the United States will nationalize election administration in the near future, rather than having elections administered by partisan secretaries of state, commissions could be formed to choose neutral election administrators. Such commissions might include representatives from major and minor parties to ensure that the enforcement of election laws does not discriminate against minor parties or the nonincumbent party. Once selected by the commission, these election administrators could serve for long terms to further insulate them from partisan politics.

In the wake of the 2000 presidential election, many hoped that Congress or the courts would address election administration reform. Their hopes have met with disappointment. As a result, election law scholars have offered alternative methods to enhance democracy. One scholar proposed a **Democracy Index** that would rank all states and localities based on election performance.[39] This has been implemented in the form of the new Pew Elections Performance Index, which ranks states on the basis of a variety of factors, including whether the state has a neutral election official, how easy it is to register, voter waiting times, and whether every vote is counted properly, among others. It is intended to influence through embarrassment; its proponents believe that states ranked at the bottom will want to improve their marks. Other scholars have recommended a more conventional approach of pushing election reform packages through Congress and the state legislatures. History shows that election reforms can be passed when there is unified party control of the executive and legislative branches.[40]

Irrespective of the path to reform, the fair and neutral administration of American elections is likely to improve political equality. But reformers face an "invisibility" problem when pushing for election reform. Citizens become concerned about election administration problems only when the election is close. Once the election is over, they quickly forget about the problems. Furthermore, the practical consequences of administering elections in a partisan manner are not always obvious. If a Democratic administrator fails to provide a sufficient number of ballots to a Republican precinct, it may or

---

[39] Gerken, *The Democracy Index*.

[40] Richard Hansen. 2010. "Election Administration Reform and the New Institutionalism." *California Law Review* 98, 3: 1075–100.

may not influence who wins the election. Improving the administration of elections would be good for democracy, but this reform may seem less important unless citizens see that it affects election outcomes.

Increasing Opportunities for Deliberation

A final set of reforms is intended to improve opportunities for voter deliberation within campaigns. Many proposals focus on increasing the frequency of candidate debates and town hall meetings, the two most obvious forums in which candidates and voters interact. There are also some more innovative ideas for enhancing deliberation. One is the **deliberative poll**.[41] Deliberative polls, which were developed in the United States and have been used around the world, begin by identifying and interviewing a random sample of citizens about some set of issues or candidates. Then respondents to the poll are asked to travel (all expenses paid) to some location for two or three days, where they listen to a range of different speakers and arguments about the same issues or candidates. They are then reinterviewed, and changes in their opinions are taken as evidence of the impact of deliberation. Ideally, these deliberative polls are aired on television so that other citizens can watch what happens when fellow citizens are given the time and space to think deeply about issues or electoral choices. A companion proposal would have the federal government sponsor a national **Deliberation Day**, in which citizens are given paid time off from work to attend meetings to discuss the upcoming election.[42]

Another proposal is to convene **citizen juries**—randomly selected panels of people who deliberate for several days about the choices in an election—to develop recommendations about which ballot measures and candidates to support.[43] Voters learn about the recommendations and endorsements of these citizen panels through voting guides or sample ballots. In 2011, the Oregon state legislature implemented this concept with the creation of a Citizens' Initiative Review (CIR) panel to provide voters with recommendations on ballot initiatives. A study of the CIR's effects shows that voters who read its recommendations find them helpful, and many report that the information provided by the CIR makes them take into account arguments and

---

[41] James S. Fishkin. 1995. *The Voice of the People: Public Opinion and Democracy.* New Haven, CT: Yale University Press.

[42] Bruce Ackerman and James S. Fishkin. 2005. *Deliberation Day.* New Haven, CT: Yale University Press.

[43] John Gastil. 2000. *By Popular Demand: Revitalizing Representative Democracy through Deliberative Elections.* Berkeley: University of California Press.

pieces of information they would not have considered otherwise.[44] These findings suggest citizen juries simultaneously increase deliberation and lessen the costs of voting for individual citizens.

Despite their potential benefits, it is unclear how eager citizens are to participate in a citizen jury or an event like Deliberation Day. Furthermore, individuals who are exposed to disagreement—a natural part of these deliberative exercises—can become ambivalent about politics and less likely to participate in elections.[45] Thus, achieving the goal of increased deliberation in campaigns and elections might come at the cost of lower participation.

There are some practical concerns as well. Deliberative forums are relatively expensive and place substantial demands on the participants. These forums also require that the candidates or their representatives take an active part in the process, something they may be reluctant to do.

Conclusion

Campaigns in the United States are heavily influenced by rules and institutions, by the broader political reality, by strategic considerations, and by the voters themselves. The larger point is that campaigns function in a logical manner given the context of the American political system. This is not to say that campaigns are perfect or should not be improved. It is simply to say that they are neither inherently bad nor somehow irrational. They can be analyzed systematically and judged on their own terms.

But campaigns also play a vital role in democracy. So while they can be judged and analyzed on their own terms, they should also be measured against the standards of democratic theory. We have evaluated American campaigns in terms of three standards: free choice, political equality, and deliberation. In some ways, American campaigns live up to these standards. When contested, campaigns force incumbent politicians to account for themselves, provide voters with information about their electoral choices, and encourage citizens to become politically involved. In other ways, American campaigns fall short. Uncompetitive campaigns, particularly, fail to meet these ideals because competition directly facilitates each of these three values. The year 2016 also saw a troubling amount of misinformation being

---

[44] John Gastil and Katie Knobloch. 2010. "Evaluation Report to the Oregon State Legislature on the 2010 Oregon Citizens' Initiative Review." http://jgastil.la.psu.edu/CIR /OregonLegislativeReportCIR.pdf (accessed 8/3/2017).

[45] Diana C. Mutz. 2006. *Hearing the Other Side: Deliberative versus Participatory Democracy.* Cambridge: Cambridge University Press.

spread to voters, which undermined the quality of the campaign when measured against these standards

There are reforms that could improve the democratic performance of election campaigns in the United States, but it is not clear whether enough citizens or politicians support these reforms or whether reforms would withstand challenges on free-speech grounds. Perhaps the most practical and effective reforms would be establishing neutral election administration and adopting citizen juries, as Oregon has. Neutral election administration would help guarantee that election rules apply to all candidates and parties equally. Creating institutions such as the CIR would provide voters with information from people like themselves who have had an opportunity to deliberate. And while parties and candidates will surely resist these reforms because of the increased uncertainty and risk that they would bring, they are likely less opposed to these reforms than many others, such as public financing and redistricting reform.

These changes would not make American campaigns perfect. In fact, even if all of the reforms considered here were to be adopted tomorrow, citizens would almost certainly still have reservations about their politicians and the election process. Some of this reflects partisan reactions to a competitive system: when your side loses, you tend to question the process. This also may reflect the long and honorable American tradition of complaining about politics and politicians. But despite Americans' avowed distaste for election campaigns, surveys show that they still believe that their democratic system is the best in the world. Furthermore, campaigns in other parts of the world are beginning to look more like those in the United States. The question, then, is how to expand the engaging and informative aspects of the American experiment in mass democracy, as well as its overall fairness. The answer is critical to the long-term health of the American system of government.

KEY TERMS

ad watches (p. 428)

donation booth (p. 431)

Democracy Index (p. 435)

deliberative poll (p. 436)

Deliberation Day (p. 436)

citizen juries (p. 436)

FOR DISCUSSION

1. Which of the values discussed in this chapter—free choice, equality, deliberation, or free speech—do you think is most important for campaigns in democratic elections? Why?

2. Given the challenges facing this country, how important do you think it is to reform our political campaigns?

3. Would you participate in a town hall meeting about local candidates? Why or why not?

4. Both Donald Trump and Hillary Clinton were accused of lying during the 2016 campaign. Assuming at least some of these accusations were true, did the lies affect how people voted? How harmful are the lies political candidates tell during campaigns to the role that elections play in a democracy?

5. The authors of this book argue that political campaigns receive a passing grade in terms of how they serve democracy. Have they convinced you?

GLOSSARY

501(c) organizations—Organizations that are exempt from federal taxation and may be able to engage in political activity, subject to certain restrictions

527 organizations—Officially designated political organizations under the tax code, and required to disclose their contributors to the Internal Revenue Service. These organizations came to the fore in 2004, the first election after BCRA's ban on soft money for parties.

absentee voting—The process by which citizens who cannot vote in person on Election Day request that ballots be mailed to their homes, and then vote by mailing those ballots to election officials

ad watches—Features in media outlets in which journalists study campaign ads and comment on their content and truthfulness

agenda setting—The news media's ability to influence the issues that the public regards as important by selecting which stories to cover

analytics—In the context of American elections, the use of sophisticated statistical models to identify politically meaningful patterns within large sets of voter data

at-large elections—Geographic units that elect multiple members as their representatives

attack ads—Advertisements in which supporters of one candidate question the character, ethics, and/or integrity of their candidate's opponent

Australian ballot—A method of voting by secret ballot, widely adopted in the United States in the early part of the 1900s, that made it impossible for casual observers or party workers to determine for whom a citizen had cast a vote

ballot initiative campaigns—Campaigns surrounding specific propositions put directly to voters for their approval. Since there are

no candidates, interest groups are the main actors in influencing voters.

ballot initiatives—Measures that affect laws or public policy and that are proposed by interested citizens and then voted on by citizens in elections

battleground (or swing) states—States that are competitive between the major party candidates and whose outcome may decide the presidential election

big data—In the context of American elections, large data sets containing extensive information on individual voters

Bipartisan Campaign Reform Act (BCRA)—2002 law that prohibited soft money spending by national, state, and local parties; limited soft money spending by outside groups; and increased individual contribution limits

blanket (or jungle) primary—Election in which all candidates for each office are listed on the ballot, and anyone registered to vote in that election may vote for any one candidate; typically, the top two vote-getters advance to a second, runoff election

blogs—Websites with regularly updated stories that often have a more personalized and conversational style; originally short for web logs

Buckley v. Valeo—1976 decision overturning the Federal Election Campaign Act's limits on spending by federal candidates as a violation of the First Amendment

campaign—An organized effort to persuade and mobilize voters to support or oppose a party or candidate

campaign agenda—The issue areas discussed during a campaign

campaign strategy—A campaign's understanding of how its candidate is going to win the election, who will vote for the candidate, and why

casework—The work performed by members of Congress or their staff to help constituents deal with government bureaucracies

caucuses—Relatively closed affairs in which registered partisans attend meetings at election precinct locations and vote to select delegates to the county or state party conventions

citizen juries—Randomly selected panels of people who deliberate about the choices in the election to develop recommendations for other citizens

citizen legislatures—Legislatures in which serving as a legislator is a part-time position that comes with relatively little salary or staff support

Citizens United v. Federal Election Commission—2010 decision holding that under the First Amendment corporate funding of independent political broadcasts in candidate elections cannot be limited

civil service—Government jobs or positions in which employment and promotions are based on professional qualifications and performance

clean elections systems—A system of campaign finance whereby candidates who raise a minimum amount of private donations qualify for public funding from the government. Once they accept public funding, they cannot spend any more money raised from private donors.

closed primary—Election for the party's nominee in which only those registered as party members can vote

coattail effect—When a popular high-profile candidate is on the ballot, lesser known candidates in that candidate's party benefit from that candidate's appeal to voters—they "ride the coattails" of the high-profile candidate

communities of interest—Redistricting principle that districts should attempt to keep together citizens in areas that share a political history or set of interests

constituencies—Subsets of the American public for which interest groups or candidates claim to speak, such as ethnic or religious groups

contrast advertisements—Advertisements in which supporters of a candidate seek to favorably compare their candidate's record and positions to their opponents' record and positions

convenience voting—Absentee, early, or mail-in voting conducted before Election Day to facilitate turnout

convention bump/convention bounce—Increased support for a candidate resulting from the party's national convention

coordinated expenditures—Money that political parties spend to help cover a candidate's campaign costs in a federal election. Such expenditures are limited by law.

cross pressures—Two or more beliefs, identities, or issue positions that pull a voter in different partisan directions

delegates—People chosen to vote for the presidential nominee of the party at the national convention

Deliberation Day—A paid day for citizens to take time off from work to attend meetings to discuss an upcoming election

deliberative poll—A type of survey in which a random sample of citizens are asked about some set of issues or candidates, then attend a meeting in which they think about or discuss these issues more, and then answer a second set of questions to see if their opinions have changed

Democracy Index—A ranking of all states and localities based on how democratic their elections are

Democratic Party—Political party from 1828–present, associated with Andrew Jackson, representing interests suspicious of entrenched commercial class; the first party to embrace mass democratic participation

Democratic-Republican Party—Political party from 1796–1824, associated with Thomas Jefferson, representing a more limited view of federal governing power, preferring state and local governing authority; support was strongest in the southern and western states

donation booth—A blind trust established in a candidate's or political party's name into which individuals or PACs can make anonymous donations

Duverger's Law—Single-member, simple plurality election systems tend to produce two major political parties

earned media (or free media)—The publicity that candidates get by engaging in promotional activities

election—The selection of persons to hold public office by means of a vote

electoral participation—The range of activities by which individuals attempt to affect the outcome of an election

era of pre-democratic campaigns—Time between the ratification of the U.S. Constitution in 1788 and the widespread expansion of elected public offices in the 1820s

express advocacy—Specifically advocating the election or defeat of a candidate

Federal Election Campaign Act (FECA)—1971 law, substantially amended in 1974, that set limits on contributions to federal campaigns, provided for public funding of presidential election campaigns, mandated contribution disclosure and finance report filings, established the Federal Election Commission to oversee finance laws, and set limits on candidate spending. The last of these provisions was overturned by the Supreme Court.

Federal Election Commission (FEC)—The regulatory agency that enforces the laws governing federal elections

Federalist Party—Political party from 1796–1828, associated with Alexander Hamilton, representing a more expansive view of federal governing power, especially with respect to regulating commercial interests; support was strongest in the northeastern states

field experiments—A form of research in which subjects (in the case of campaigns, voters) are randomly assigned into treatment and control groups, treatment groups receive a particular stimulus, and outcomes are compared between the two groups; an important new way for campaigns to test outreach and persuasion

focus groups—A form of qualitative research in which a group of people is asked about their perceptions, opinions, beliefs, and attitudes toward a product, service, concept, advertisement, idea, or packaging. Questions are asked in an interactive group setting where participants are free to talk with other group members. In campaigns, small groups of persuadable voters are interviewed in depth to gather additional data and test specific issue positions.

framing—Choosing the language to define a debate and fitting individual issues into the contexts of broader story lines. The news media's ability to influence what the public thinks is at stake in a debate by categorizing issues into one of many possible interpretations.

franking privilege—The ability of members of Congress to send mail to constituents without postage

front-loading—Moving statewide nominating contests earlier in the calendar to increase their influence

front-porch campaign—Tactic whereby the candidate stays at home and allows his campaign team to arrange for select meetings with news media outlets

front-runners—Candidates perceived to have the money, experience, and popular support to win

generational cohorts—Groups of people who came of age politically at about the same time

gerrymandering—Drawing district lines to maximize some political interest

get-out-the-vote (GOTV) efforts—The efforts of candidates, parties, and interest groups to get citizens to vote

hard money—Money raised in accord with campaign finance laws

Hill committees—A term used to refer to the four major party campaign committees involved in congressional elections

horse race journalism—News reporting that focuses on which candidates are becoming more or less likely to win an election as well as what each candidate is doing to improve their standing in the polls

incumbency advantage—The vote share earned by an incumbent compared to what a nonincumbent would have earned if he or she had run

incumbent—The candidate in an election who already occupies the office

independent candidates—Persons running for office who are not affiliated with any particular political party

independent expenditure committees—Political action committees that can raise unlimited donations from various sources and then spend money to advocate for or against candidates

independent expenditures—A piece of campaign communication by an independent group that engages in express advocacy; party expenditures made without consulting or coordinating with a candidate

infotainment—Media content that provides a combination of information and entertainment, such as comedy news programs or coverage of celebrities

interest group—A collection of people with the shared goal of influencing public policy that does not run its own candidates for office

interpretive journalism—News reporting that includes analysis of the reasons why events happen and the likely effects that the events will have

issue advocacy—Advocating a position on a political issue without explicitly advocating for the election or defeat of a candidate

issue ownership—Concept that political parties have differential credibility on certain issues, and that their candidates try to win elections by convincing voters that issues they "own" are the most important for a given election

literacy tests—Knowledge questions asked by election officials at the polls; used to prevent blacks from voting in southern states, and were suspended in states where turnout was less than 50 percent of the age-eligible population by the Civil Rights Act (1965)

magic words—Words that make an advertisement subject to campaign finance laws and regulations

majority-minority districts—Districts in which racial or ethnic minorities form a majority of the population

malapportionment—Any significant differences in the number of citizens across districts

material benefits—Rewards or payments received in exchange for political participation

median voter theorem—In a majority election, if voter policy preferences can be represented as a point along a single dimension, and if all voters vote for the candidate who commits to a policy position closest to their own preference, and if there are only two candidates, then a candidate maximizes her votes by committing to the policy position preferred by the median voter

message—Information repeated by a candidate or surrogates during a campaign that communicates who the candidate is and why voters should cast their ballots for him or her

microtargeting—Rating the voting behavior of every individual on the registered voter list based on a statistical model of the vote estimated from a large random sample

mobilization—The range of activities that candidates, parties, activists, and interest groups engage in to encourage people to participate

Motor Voter Act—A federal law requiring states to allow voters to register when they are applying for a driver's license and public assistance programs or to allow Election Day registration

narrow-casting—Targeting a message to a small audience using e-mail, direct mail, and telephone calls

negative campaigning—Campaign messages that consist of criticism leveled by one candidate against another during a campaign

news media—Regular communicators of information designed to reach large audiences

news values—The criteria reporters and editors use to determine what is newsworthy, such as how recently an event occurred and whether it was unexpected

one person, one vote—The principle that each person's vote should have equal weight in determining representation; first articulated in *Reynolds v. Sims* (1964)

open primary—Election for the parties' nominees in which registrants are allowed to vote in any primary they choose (but only in one)

open seat—An election in which no incumbent is running

opinion leaders—Individuals who follow politics and help inform other members of the group about issues and candidates

pack journalism—The tendency of reporters to read and discuss each other's stories and converge on a similar narrative about the campaign

panel studies—Surveys that interview respondents at one point in time and then reinterview at a later point in time in order to measure change in their opinions

participatory distortion—Occurs when certain groups of citizens have a greater impact on the political process than other groups

party-as-organization—The institutions, professionals, and activists that administer party affairs, including the official bodies that raise funds and create the rules for the party

party identification—A citizen's allegiance to one of the political parties, including both party preference and level of commitment

party-in-government—The members of a party who hold public office

party-in-the-electorate—The group of citizens who identify with a political party or regularly support candidates from one party

permanent campaign—The notion that candidates never stop campaigning because of the constant need to raise money for the next election cycle

personal vote—That portion of an elected official's vote share that can be attributed to their relationship with constituents

persuadable (swing) votes—The number of voters in a given election who are not committed to supporting a particular candidate. This is usually estimated by the

percentage point difference between the maximum and minimum vote for a major party's candidates across recent elections.

persuasion—Convincing undecided voters to support a particular candidate or convincing the other party's supporters to defect

plurality rule—A way of determining who wins elections in which the candidate with the most votes wins (even if they do not get a majority of the votes)

pocketbook voting—Choosing between candidates based on how one's personal finances have faired during the incumbent party's rule

political action committees (PACs)—Private groups organized to elect political candidates

political amateurs—Candidates with no political experience

political interest—Having an ongoing interest in politics

political machines—Party organizations that mobilized lower status citizens to win office, and then used government to reward party workers and bestow services and benefits to their constituents

political parties—Group of people with the shared interest of electing public officials under a common label

poll taxes—Fee requirements for voting; typically used to keep blacks from voting in southern states, and outlawed by the Voting Rights Act of 1965

positive campaigning—Campaign messages in which candidates make an affirmative case for their election based on their background, experience, record, or issue positions

primary election—Election in which voters select the candidate that will run for the party in the general election

priming—The news media's ability to influence the criteria that citizens use to make judgments about people by selecting which stories to cover

probability samples—Some number of individuals from a certain population randomly selected and asked a set of questions; the key is that every individual in the population of interest has a known probability of being selected

professionalism—A quality of legislatures that captures how much work legislators perform and status they receive. In a more professionalized legislature, serving as a legislator is a full-time job with a substantial salary and staff support.

Progressive (or "Bull Moose") Party—Political party from 1912–14, associated with Theodore Roosevelt, representing disaffected Republicans who favored greater power and democratic prerogatives for the "little man" and regulation of major industries

proportional representation—System in which seats are allocated based on the percentage of the vote won by each party

proximity voting—Choosing a candidate based on how close the candidate's views are to one's own views across a range of relevant issues

public funding—Campaign funds provided by the government

purposive benefits—The satisfaction one derives from having advanced an issue or ideological position, or from having fulfilled a duty

quality challengers—Candidates with the experience and backing necessary to run a competitive campaign

reapportionment—Process of determining the number of representatives allotted to each state after the decennial census count

Reconstruction—Era immediately after the Civil War in which policies were enacted to protect the freedoms and rights of black citizens. Reconstruction policies were particularly important in the southern states, where Union troops were stationed to enforce these policies. The Reconstruction era ended at different times for different states, but many believe that the Compromise of 1877 effectively ended Reconstruction.

redistricting—Drawing new district lines after the decennial census count

referenda—Measures that affect laws or public policy that allow citizens to vote on a statute already passed by state legislatures

reinforcement—The notion that news consumers interpret information as giving added strength or support to their existing views. The process of solidifying voters' support for a candidate.

Republican L—The pattern formed by Republican-leaning states in the mountain west and southern states

Republican Party—Political party from 1860–present, originally associated with Abraham Lincoln and representing interests opposed to slavery and favoring the continuation of the Union

retail politics—Face-to-face communication about political positions and arguments between candidates and voters

retention elections—Judicial elections in which voters decide whether a sitting judge should continue in that position; these elections do not feature a competition between the sitting judge and an opponent

retrospective voting—Choosing between candidates according to broad appraisals of whether things have improved or gotten worse under the incumbent

right to equal time—A Federal Communications Commission rule that requires most radio and television broadcasters to treat candidates equally when selling or giving away airtime

roll-call vote—At a party convention, the aggregation of state-by-state votes of delegates

same-day (or Election Day) registration—System in which eligible citizens may register to vote as late as Election Day itself

semi-closed primary—Election for the party's nominee in which party registrants and those unaffiliated with any party are allowed to vote

single-member districts—Geographic units that elect only one person to represent the entire unit

social context—The people with whom one communicates and interacts, such as family, friends, classmates, coworkers, and neighbors

social groups—Associations of people who share a class background, ethnicity, religion, or some other affiliation. Perceived social group membership may affect political attitudes.

sociotropic voting—Choosing between candidates based on how one thinks the country has faired under the incumbent party's rule

soft money—Money raised outside the limits normally established by campaign finance laws

solidary benefits—Intangible rewards for participation that come from being part of a collective effort

sorting—People's partisan preferences have become more closely aligned with their political views

sound bite—A short segment of sound or video used in a news report as an excerpt of an event or interview

strategic voting—In an election with more than two candidates, voting for a candidate other than one's first choice in order to prevent an undesirable outcome

super PACs—PACs that can collect unlimited amounts of donations as a consequence of a recent Supreme Court decision, *Citizens United v. FEC*. Super PACs are required to disclose their donors.

survey research—A research method involving the use of questionnaires and/or statistical surveys to gather data about people and their thoughts and behaviors

term limits—Legal restrictions on the maximum time a person can hold a specific office

Tillman Act—1907 law banning corporate contributions to political campaigns

viability—Ability to win the nomination

vote by mail—When jurisdictions conduct elections by ballots that are automatically mailed to voters instead of using polling stations

vote targets—Estimates of how many votes a candidate will need to win the election. These are based on calculations of how many people will vote in a particular election, what percentage of the vote will be needed to win, how many votes can be counted on, and how many votes are persuadable.

voter identification (voter ID) calls—Calls, usually via telephone, to every person on the voter list to ask about the candidates and issues in the upcoming election

Voting Rights Act of 1965 (VRA)—Congressional legislation designed to end discriminatory practices disenfranchising blacks, especially in the South

wedge issues—Political issues intended to persuade voters to abandon the party they traditionally support and support the opposite party

Whig Party—Political party from 1832–52 that rose in response to the Democratic Party in the 1830s, representing voters concerned by Jackson's expansive view of the presidency and his attacks on commercial interests

wholesale politics—Mass communication about political positions and arguments from candidates directed to voters

wire services—A news agency that collects and distributes news stories to many outlets

CREDITS

INDEX

In this index, page references in *italic type* refer to illustrative material.